A·N·N·U·A·L E·D·I·T·I·O·N·S

Race and Ethnic Relations

00/01

Tenth Edition

EDITOR

John A. Kromkowski
Catholic University of America

John A. Kromkowski is president of The National Center for Urban Ethnic Affairs in Washington, D.C., a nonprofit research and educational institute that has sponsored and published many books and articles on ethnic relations, urban affairs, and economic revitalization. He is Assistant Dean of the College of Arts and Sciences at the Catholic University of America, and he coordinates international seminars and internship programs in the United States, England, Ireland, and Belgium. He has served on national advisory boards for the Campaign for Human Development, the U.S. Department of Education Ethnic Heritage Studies Program, the White House Fellows Program, the National Neighborhood Coalition, and the American Revolution Bicentennial Administration. Dr. Kromkowski has edited a series sponsored by the Council for Research in Values and Philosophy titled *Cultural Heritage and Contemporary Change*. These volumes include scholarly findings and reflections on urbanization, cultural affairs, personhood, community, and political economy.

Dushkin/McGraw-Hill
Sluice Dock, Guilford, Connecticut 06437

Visit us on the Internet
http://www.dushkin.com/annualeditions/

Credits

1. Race and Ethnicity in the American Legal Tradition
Unit photo—Dushkin/McGraw-Hill illustration by Mike Eagle.
2. Immigration and the American Experience
Unit photo—United Nations photo by P.S. Sudhakaran.
3. Indigenous Ethnic Groups
Unit photo—© 2000 by PhotoDisc, Inc.
4. Hispanic/Latino Americans
Unit photo—© 2000 by PhotoDisc, Inc.
5. African Americans
Unit photo—© 2000 by Cleo Freelance Photography.
6. Asian Americans
Unit photo—© 2000 by PhotoDisc, Inc.
7. Mediterranean and Eastern European Americans
Unit photo—© 2000 by PhotoDisc, Inc.
8. The Ethnic Legacy
Unit photo—© 2000 by PhotoDisc, Inc.
9. The Ethnic Factor: Challenges for the New Century
Unit photo—© 2000 by Cleo Freelance Photography.
10. Understanding Cultural Pluralism
Unit photo—© 2000 by PhotoDisc, Inc.

Copyright

Cataloging in Publication Data
Main entry under title: Annual Editions: Race and Ethnic Relations. 2000/2001.
1. Race relations—Periodicals. 2. United States—Race relations—Periodicals.
3. Culture conflict—United States—Periodicals. I. Kromkowski, John A., *comp.* II. Title: Race and ethnic relations.
ISBN 0–07–236574–9   305.8'073'05   ISSN 1075–5195

Tenth Edition

Cover image © 2000 PhotoDisc, Inc.

Printed in the United States of America   1234567890BAHBAH543210   Printed on Recycled Paper

To the Reader

In publishing ANNUAL EDITIONS we recognize the enormous role played by the magazines, newspapers, and journals of the public press in providing current, first-rate educational information in a broad spectrum of interest areas. Many of these articles are appropriate for students, researchers, and professionals seeking accurate, current material to help bridge the gap between principles and theories and the real world. These articles, however, become more useful for study when those of lasting value are carefully collected, organized, indexed, and reproduced in a low-cost format, which provides easy and permanent access when the material is needed. That is the role played by ANNUAL EDITIONS.

New to ANNUAL EDITIONS is the inclusion of related World Wide Web sites. These sites have been selected by our editorial staff to represent some of the best resources found on the World Wide Web today. Through our carefully developed topic guide, we have linked these Web resources to the articles covered in this ANNUAL EDITIONS reader. We think that you will find this volume useful, and we hope that you will take a moment to visit us on the Web at *http://www.dushkin.com* to tell us what you think.

The information explosion, which has led to an expansion of knowledge about the range of diversity among and within societies, has increased awareness of ethnicity and race. During previous periods of history, society was discussed in terms of a universal sense of common humanity. Differences between societies and the arrangements of economic production were noted, but they were usually explained in terms of theories of progressive development or of class conflict. Consciousness of the enduring pluralism expressed in ethnic, racial, and cultural diversity has emerged throughout the world. The dimensions of diversity are significantly, if not essentially, shaped by social, economic, cultural, and, most important, political and communitarian processes. Creativity, imagination, and religion influence ethnic and racial relations.

This collection was designed to assist you in understanding ethnic and racial pluralism in the United States and in several other countries. Unit 1, for example, illustrates how the most basic legal principles of a society—and especially the U.S. Supreme Court's historical interpretation of them—are especially significant for the delineation of ethnic groups, for the acceptance of cultural pluralism, and for the political and moral foundations from which contemporary challenges to the promise of American liberties may be addressed. The immigration of people, the focus of unit 2, into a relatively young society such as America is of particular concern, because the fragility of social continuity is exposed by the recognition of changes in the ethnic composition of American society.

The contemporary experiences of indigenous groups, including Native Americans, are described in unit 3. Discussion of the experiences and mobility strategies of the descendants of the earliest groups and the most recently arrived ethnic populations and the legal framework for participating in America is extended in unit 4 on Hispanic/Latino Americans and unit 5 on African Americans. Unit 6 explores various dimensions of the Asian American experience. In unit 7 the ways in which the experiences of ethnics from the Mediterranean and Eastern Europe are woven into the fabric of American diversity are added to the cluster of concerns addressed in the recent ethnic studies, which focus on marginality, minority, and alienation. Unit 8, titled "The Ethnic Legacy," articulates an acute dimension of regional ethnicity derived from American rural life prior to industrial and urban development. Such Southern and Appalachian mentalities stand in contrast to a pluralistic vision of diversity derived from the cosmopolitan and catholic moral imagination of urban ethnics. Unit 9, "The Ethnic Factor: Challenges for the New Century," extends prior concerns and addresses national and international implications of ethnic exclusivity and the imperatives of new approaches to group relations. Unit 10 focuses on understanding the origins of racialism and the religious and ethical origins that shape consciousness of group affinities and, especially, the emergence of scientific claims of racialism and religious exclusion in public affairs.

For nearly eight decades, Americans have become increasingly aware of the ways that group and personal identity are interwoven, forming a dense network of culture, economy, polity, and sociality. This perspective on the American reality was fashioned from the necessity and the moral imagination of the children and grandchildren of immigrants to the United States. Their contribution was the articulation of the urban experience and its evocation of a new form of cultural pluralism—beyond the insularity, isolation, and dichotomous mentalities derived from the rural foundations of Anglo-Scot-Irish American culture. As a result, the Anglo-colonial cultural form and its language and practices of racial division and ethnic group relations has tried to refashion the dichotomous logic of social divisiveness, but has not entirely transformed their race and color consciousness and institutional legacies. A host of disciplines have been energized in this reinterpretive project in support of a more complex matrix of ethnicities and an appreciation of the various ethnic cultures that constitute the American reality and our common humanity. Readers are invited to retrace and to rethink the historical development of ethnic group relations by examining the legal frameworks that legitimated racialism and those that affirmed cultural democracy, equality, and the value of diversity. The voices of various ethnic communities within America and the issues of intergroup relations are presented to engage your own search for ethnic identity and to assess ethnicity and race for its strength and limits as an explanatory factor and as an ideology of social, economic, cultural, and political development.

In addition to the annotated *table of contents*, this edition of *Annual Editions: Race and Ethnic Relations* contains a list of *World Wide Web* sites that can be used to further explore article topics. These sites are cross-referenced by number in the *topic guide*.

Readers may have input into the next edition of *Annual Editions: Race and Ethnic Relations* by completing and returning the prepaid article rating form in the back of the book.

John A. Kromkowski
Editor

Contents

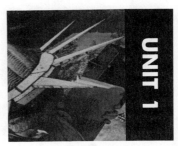

UNIT 1

Race and Ethnicity in the American Legal Tradition

Six articles in this section present the
foundational legal definitions of race
and citizenship and the historical
landmarks of equal protection and
due process found in Supreme
Court decisions regarding schools,
employment, and government
contracting, as well as the legislative
history and current legal revisions
and revisited arguments that express
the search for new directions
and challenges that define and
refine the post–civil rights era.

UNIT 2

Immigration and the American Experience

Four articles in this section review the historical record of immigration that reveals its ongoing process and refocuses current concerns regarding immigration and the legal, social, cultural, and community-based features that shape the American experience.

UNIT 3

Indigenous Ethnic Groups

Five articles in this section review the issues and problems of indigenous peoples, portray the new relationships indigenous people are forging with concurrent governments, discuss group identity, new cultural and economic forms that are emerging, and processes that protect indigenous traditions within pluralistic societies.

The concepts in bold italics are developed in the article. For further expansion please refer to the Topic Guide and the Index.

UNIT 4

Hispanic/Latino Americans

Three articles in this section reveal the demographics of Hispanic/ Latino Americans as well as the economic and political cultural dynamics of these diverse ethnicities.

UNIT 5

African Americans

Six articles in this section review historical experiences derived from slavery and segregation and then explore current contexts and persistent concerns of African Americans.

UNIT 6

Asian Americans

Three articles in this section explore dimensions of pluralism among Asian Americans and the issues related to the cultural, economic, and political dynamics of pluralism.

The concepts in bold italics are developed in the article. For further expansion please refer to the Topic Guide and the Index.

UNIT 7

Mediterranean and Eastern European Americans

Four articles in this section
examine the ethnicity of communities derived from eastern and
southern Europe whose intersection
with each other in America and
with cultures of others rooted in the
English colonial system established the
northern model of group diversity.

UNIT 8

The Ethnic Legacy

Three articles in this section
examine neglected dimensions
of ethnic communities, their
intersection with each other,
and the influence of interethnic
protocols within American society.

UNIT 9

The Ethnic Factor: Challenges for the New Century

Five articles in this section look at the intersections of ethnicities and the impact of ethnic conflict and cooperation on domestic and international affairs.

The concepts in bold italics are developed in the article. For further expansion please refer to the Topic Guide and the Index.

UNIT 10

Understanding Cultural Pluralism

Four articles in this section examine
the origins of misunderstandings
regarding human variety, indicate the
influence of race and ethnic opinions
in selected contexts, and discuss the
range of challenges that must be
addressed to forge new approaches
to understanding cultural pluralism.

The concepts in bold italics are developed in the article. For further expansion please refer to the Topic Guide and the Index.

Topic Guide

This topic guide suggests how the selections and World Wide Web sites found in the next section of this book relate to topics of traditional concern to students and professionals involved with the study of race and ethnic relations. It is useful for locating interrelated articles and Web sites for reading and research. The guide is arranged alphabetically according to topic.

The relevant Web sites, which are numbered and annotated on pages 4 and 5, are easily identified by the Web icon (◎) under the topic articles. By linking the articles and the Web sites by topic, this ANNUAL EDITIONS reader becomes a powerful learning and research tool.

TOPIC AREA	TREATED IN	TOPIC AREA	TREATED IN
Affirmative Action	24. Why Minority Recruiting Is Alive 42. End of the Rainbow ◎ **3, 5, 7, 12, 13, 14, 15, 30**		10. Newcomers and Established Residents 14. American Indians in the 1990s 19. 10 Most Dramatic Events 20. Black America 23. Race, Politics and 2000
Civil Rights	1. *Dred Scott v. Sandford* 2. Racial Restrictions in the Law 3. In Judicial 'What If,' Indians Revisit a Case 4. *Brown et al. v. Board of Education of Topeka et al.* 5. Black America 6. Black Progress 12. 12th Session of UN Working Group 14. American Indians in the 1990s 19. 10 Most Dramatic Events 21. Shock Therapy 22. Color of Justice 24. Why Minority Recruiting Is Alive 29. Italian Americans 32. Unsealing Mississippi's Past 39. Ethnicity Is No Excuse ◎ **1, 2, 3, 4, 5, 7, 20, 30**		24. Why Minority Recruiting Is Alive 25. Misperceived Minorities 29. Italian Americans 32. Unsealing Mississippi's Past 33. White Girl? 34. Unbearable Whiteness of Being ◎ **1, 3, 5, 7, 12, 13, 15, 21, 28, 30**
		Discrimination	1. *Dred Scott v. Sandford* 2. Racial Restrictions in the Law 4. *Brown et al. v. Board of Education of Topeka et al.* 5. Black America 6. Black Progress 8. New Immigrants 10. Newcomers and Established Residents 19. 10 Most Dramatic Events 21. Shock Therapy 22. Color of Justice 23. Race, Politics and 2000 24. Why Minority Recruiting Is Alive 25. Misperceived Minorities 29. Italian Americans 32. Unsealing Mississippi's Past 33. White Girl? 34. Unbearable Whiteness of Being 41. Color Blind 42. End of the Rainbow ◎ **7, 10, 11, 12, 13, 14, 15, 16, 21, 25, 26, 27, 30, 31, 32**
Courts	1. *Dred Scott v. Sandford* 2. Racial Restrictions in the Law 3. In a Judicial 'What If,' Indians Revisit a Case 4. *Brown et al. v. Board of Education of Topeka et al.* 7. Migration to the Thirteen British North American Colonies 10. Newcomers and Established Residents 11. New Answers to an Old Question: Who Got Here First? 14. American Indians in the 1990s 17. Latin USA 18. Hardliners v. "Dialogueros" 28. Who Are We? 29. Italian Americans 30. Blind Spot of Multiculturalism 31. Mr. Dybek's Neighborhood 33. White Girl? 34. Unbearable Whiteness of Being 36. Don't Expect This Conflict to End 37. Belonging in the West 38. Ethnicity: An African Predicament 41. Color Blind ◎ **5, 6, 7**		
		Education	4. *Brown et al. v. Board of Education of Topeka et al.* 10. Newcomers and Established Residents 15. Indians Hear High-Tech Drumbeat 19. 10 Most Dramatic Events 24. Why Minority Recruiting Is Alive 27. Trapped on a Pedestal 30. Blind Spot of Multiculturalism 40. Geometer of Race ◎ **2, 4, 7, 8, 12, 13, 14, 15, 16, 20, 21, 32**
Demography	2. Racial Restrictions in the Law 7. Migration to the Thirteen British North American Colonies 8. New Immigrants 9. U.S. Immigration 10. Newcomers and Established Residents 11. New Answers to an Old Question 14. American Indians in the 1990s 16. Specific Hispanics 17. Latin USA 20. Black America 25. Misperceived Minorities 26. Challenges for U.S. Asians 43. American Ethnicities ◎ **4, 9, 10, 11, 21, 27, 28, 29**	**Government**	1. *Dred Scott v. Sandford* 2. Racial Restrictions in the Law 3. In a Judicial 'What If,' Indians Revisit a Case 4. *Brown et al. v. Board of Education of Topeka et al.* 8. New Immigrants 12. 12th Session of UN Working Group 13. Deadly Mix 18. Hardliners v. "Dialogueros" 23. Race, Politics and 2000 24. Why Minority Recruiting Is Alive 35. Balancing Act 36. Don't Expect This Conflict to End 38. Ethnicity: An African Predicament 39. Ethnicity Is No Excuse 42. End of The Rainbow ◎ **1, 5, 7, 11, 28, 30**
Desegregation	4. *Brown et al. v. Board of Education of Topeka et al.* 5. Black America		

2

● AE: Race and Ethnic Relations

The following World Wide Web sites have been carefully researched and selected to support the articles found in this reader. If you are interested in learning more about specific topics found in this book, these Web sites are a good place to start. The sites are cross-referenced by number and appear in the topic guide on the previous two pages. Also, you can link to these Web sites through our DUSHKIN ONLINE support site at *http://www.dushkin.com/online/*.

The following sites were available at the time of publication. Visit our Web site—we update DUSHKIN ONLINE regularly to reflect any Changes.

General Sources

1. Library of Congress
http://www.loc.gov
Examine this extensive Web site to learn about resource tools, library services/resources, exhibitions, and databases in many different fields related to race and ethnicity.

2. Social Science Information Gateway
http://sosig.esrc.bris.ac.uk
Access an online catalog of thousands of Internet resources relevant to social science education and research at this site. Every resource is selected and described by a librarian or subject specialist.

3. Sociosite
http://www.pscw.uva.nl/sociosite/TOPICS/index.html
Open this enormous site of the University of Amsterdam's Sociology Department to gain insights into a number of social issues. It provides links in affirmative action, race and ethnic relations, and much more.

4. University of Pennsylvania/Library
http://www.library.upenn.edu/resources/subject/social/sociology/sociology.html
This site provides a number of valuable indexes of culture and ethnic studies, population and demographics, and statistical sources.

Race and Ethnicity in the American Legal Tradition

5. American Civil Liberties Union (ACLU)
http://www.aclu.org
This site contains links to the ACLU's archives of information about civil rights in the United States and around the world, now and historically. Consult the index to find discussions of such topics as racial equality and immigrants' rights.

6. Human Rights Web
http://www.hrweb.org
The history of the human-rights movement, text on seminal figures, landmark legal and political documents, and ideas on how individuals can get involved in helping to protect the rights of all peoples around the world can be found at this valuable site.

7. Supreme Court/Legal Information Institute
http://supct.law.cornell.edu/supct/index.html
Open this site for current and historical information about the Supreme Court. The archive contains many opinions issued since May 1990 as well as a collection of nearly 600 of the most historical decisions of the Court.

Immigration and the American Experience

8. Child Welfare League of America (CWLA)
http://www.cwla.org
The CWLA is the United States' oldest and largest organization devoted entirely to the well-being of vulnerable children and their families. This site provides links to information about issues related to the process of becoming multicultural.

9. National Immigrant Forum
http://www.immigrationforum.org
This pro-immigrant organization offers this page to examine the effects of immigration on the U.S. economy and society.

10. The National Network for Immigrant and Refugee Rights (NNIRR)
http://www.nnirr.org
The NNIRR serves as a forum to share information, to educate communities, and to develop and coordinate plans of action on important immigrant and refugee issues.

11. U.S. Immigration and Naturalization Service (INS)
http://www.ins.usdoj.gov
Visit the home page of the INS to learn U.S. policy vis-à-vis immigrants, laws and regulations, and statistics.

Indigenous Ethnic Groups

12. American Indian Science and Engineering Society (AISES)
http://spot.colorado.edu/~aises/aises.html
This AISES "Multicultural Educational Reform Programs" site provides a framework for learning about science, mathematics, and technology. There are useful links to programs for Native American education.

Hispanic/Latino Americans

13. Latino On-Line News Network
http://www.latnn.com
The purpose of this site is to empower Latinos. The site and its links address housing, employment, ethnicity, income, and political issues, and presents the latest world news daily.

14. National Council of La Raza (NCLR)
http://www.nclr.org
Explore NCLR's home page for links to health and education issues in the Hispanic community. Many other economic, political, and social concerns are also covered at this site.

African Americans

15. National Association for the Advancement of Colored People (NAACP)
http://www.naacp.org
Open this home page to explore the NAACP's stances regarding many topics in race and ethnic relations. Many links to other organizations and resources are provided.

Asian Americans

16. Asian Community Online Network
http://www.igc.apc.org/acon/links/index.html
Search through the links presented here for information on the political, historical, legal, and other concerns and interests of a wide variety of Asian American groups.

Mediterranean and Eastern European Americans

17. American Immigration Home Page
http://www.bergen.org/AAST/Projects/Immigration/index.html
Information on how different groups of immigrants were treated in different time periods as well as facts about why they decided to come to America are available at this site.

18. International Migration as a Dynamic Process: Kybernetes
http://www.mcb.co.uk/services/articles/liblink/k/diamanti.htm
This study of international migration contains a section on the migration of Greeks and Cypriots to the United States.

19. Italian American Web Site of New York
http://www.italian-american.com/main.htm
This site links to Italian American organizations, geneology, famous Italians, matters of affirmative action, defamation and discrimination, politics, and more.

The Ethnic Legacy

20. African American Heritage Preservation Foundation
http://www.preservenet.cornell.edu/aahpf/homepage.htm
Explore this site for information about ongoing and planned projects in preserving historical African American sites. Find here links to related archaeological digs.

21. American Indian Ritual Object Repatriation Foundation
http://www.repatriationfoundation.org
Visit this home page of the American Indian Ritual Object Repatriation Foundation, which aims to assist in the appropriate return of sacred ceremonial material.

22. American Studies Web
http://www.georgetown.edu/crossroads/asw/
This eclectic site provides links to a wealth of resources on the Internet related to race and ethnic relations.

23. The International Center for Migration, Ethnicity, and Citizenship
http://www.newschool.edu/icmec/
The Center is engaged in scholarly research and public policy analysis bearing on international migration, refugees, and the incorporation of newcomers in host countries.

The Ethnic Factor: Challenges for the New Century

24. Africa News Online
http://www.africanews.org

Open this site for Africa News on the Web. This source provides extensive, up-to-date information on all of Africa, with reports from Africa's newspapers and other news sources.

25. Cultural Survival
http://www.cs.org
This nonprofit organization works to defend and protect the human rights and cultural autonomy of indigenous peoples and oppressed ethnic minorities around the world. Learn about policies intended to avoid genocide and ethnic conflict.

26. Human Rights and Humanitarian Assistance
http://info.pitt.edu/~ian/resource/human.htm
Through this site you can conduct research into a number of human rights concerns around the world. The site provides links to many topics of interest in the study of race and ethnicity.

27. The North-South Institute
http://www.nsi-ins.ca/ensi/index.html
Searching this site of the North-South Institute—which works to strengthen international development cooperation and enhance social equity—will help you find information on a variety of issues related to international race and ethnicity issues.

28. U.S. Agency for International Development
http://www.info.usaid.gov
This Web site covers such issues as democracy, population and health, race and ethnicity, and economic growth.

Understanding Cultural Pluralism

29. Anthropology Resources Page, University of South Dakota
http://www.usd.edu/anth/
Many cultural topics can be accessed from this site. Click on the links to find information about differences and similarities in values and lifestyles among the world's peoples.

30. National Center for Policy Analysis
http://www.public-policy.org/~ncpa/pd/pdindex.html
Through this site, you can read discussions on an array of topics that are of major interest in the study of American politics and government from a sociological perspective.

31. Patterns of Variability: The Concept of Race
http://www.as.ua.edu/ant/bindon/ant101/syllabus/race/race1.htm
This site provides a handy, at-a-glance reference to the prevailing concepts of race and the causes of human variability since ancient times.

32. STANDARDS: An International Journal of Multicultural Studies
http://www.colorado.edu/journals/standards/
This site provides access to the STANDARDS archives and links to topics of interest in the study of cultural pluralism.

We highly recommend that you review our Web site for expanded information and our other product lines. We are continually updating and adding links to our Web site in order to offer you the most usable and useful information that will support and expand the value of your Annual Editions. You can reach us at:
http://www.dushkin.com/annualeditions/.

www.dushkin.com/online/

Unit 1

Unit Selections

Key Points to Consider

❖ In the late 1960s, proposals that sought to depolarize race issues argued for a policy of benign neglect, meaning that although equal protection and opportunity were essential, economic and education policy should focus on the needs of persons and groups and regions regardless of their race. What can be said in support of such criteria? Is there much public support for a redistributive national policy to address lack of opportunity? What does this political climate of public policy forecast about race and ethnic relations?

❖ Does competition for protection and specific remedies among minority groups exacerbate race and ethnic relations? Comment on the idea that the American political process has relied too extensively on the Supreme Court. What policy outcomes or initiatives in race relations do you support?

❖ Should affirmative action be based on race and ethnicity or economic standing and income? Defend your answer.

❖ The U.S. Congress is the lawmaking institution that authorized national policies of equal protection that are constitutionally guaranteed to all. What explains the disparity between the patently clear proclamation of equality and the painfully obvious practices of racial/ethnic discrimination?

❖ Why was the constitutional penalty found in U.S. Constitution Amendment 14, Section 2, which reduces the number of members in the House of Representatives from states that denied voting rights, not applied?

❖ Do aspects of race relations in America vary from region to region and state to state? What dimensions of discrimination are most onerous? Which are declining and diminishing? How does the law influence group and personal behavior?

 **Links**   # **www.dushkin.com/online/**

5. **American Civil Liberties Union (ACLU)**
   http://www.aclu.org
6. **Human Rights Web**
   http://www.hrweb.org
7. **Supreme Court/Legal Information Institute**
   http://supct.law.cornell.edu/supct/index.html

These sites are annotated on pages 4 and 5.

The legal framework established by the original U.S. Constitution illustrates the way that the American founders handled ethnic pluralism. In most respects, they ignored the cultural and linguistic variety within and between the 13 original states, adopting instead a legal system that guaranteed religious exercise free from government interference, due process of law, and freedom of speech and the press. The founders, however, conspicuously compromised their claims of unalienable rights and democratic republicanism with regard to the constitutional status of Africans in bondage and indigenous Native Americans. Even after the Civil War and the inclusion of constitutional amendments that ended slavery, provided for political inclusion of all persons, and specifically mandated the loss of representation in the House of Representatives for those states that denied equal protection of the laws to all, exclusionary practices continued. Decisions by the U.S. Supreme Court helped to establish a legal system in which inequality and ethnic discrimination—both political and private—were legally permissible. The Supreme Court's attempt to redress the complex relationship between our constitutional system and the diverse society it governs is mediated by a political leadership that has not persistently sought "equal justice under the law" for all people.

Morever, the history of American immigration legislation, from the Alien and Sedition Laws at the founding to the most recent statutes, reveals an ambiguous legacy. This legal framework mirrors political forces that influenced the definition of citizenship and the constitution of ethnic identity and ethnic groups in America.

The legacies of African slavery, racial segregation, and ethnic discrimination established by the Constitution and by subsequent Court doctrines are traced in the following abbreviated U.S. Supreme Court opinions.

In *Dred Scott v. Sandford* (1856), the Supreme Court addressed the constitutional status of an African held in bondage who had been moved to a state that prohibited slavery. U.S. Supreme Court Chief Justice Roger B. Taney attempted to resolve the increasingly divisive issue of slavery by declaring that the "Negro African race"—whether free or slave—was "not intended to be included under the word 'citizens' in the Constitution, and can therefore claim none of the rights and privileges that instrument provides for and secures to citizens of the United States." Contrary to Taney's intentions, however, *Dred Scott* further fractured the nation, ensuring that only the Civil War would resolve the slavery issue.

In *Plessy v. Ferguson* (1896), the Supreme Court upheld the constitutionality of "Jim Crow" laws that segregated public facilities on the basis of an individual's racial ancestry. The Court reasoned that this "separate but equal" segregation did not violate any rights guaranteed by the U.S. Constitution, nor did it stamp "the colored race with a badge of inferiority." Instead, the Court argued that if "this be so, it is not by reason of anything found in the act but solely because the colored race chooses to put that construction upon it." In contrast, Justice John M. Harlan's vigorous dissent from the Court's *Plessy* opinion contends that "our Constitution is color-blind, and neither knows nor tolerates classes among citizens." The history of the Court's attention to citizenship provides a view of a culturally embedded character of color consciousness and the strict textual dependence of the justices who interpreted the Constitution. Another perspective, however, emerges from the congressional debate that occurred when a civil rights law ensuring equal protection and voting rights was passed shortly after the Civil War. That legislative history is cited extensively in *Shaare Tefila/Al-khasraji* (1987). This expansive view of protection for all ethnic groups cited in these decisions and the origin of these views in congressional intention voiced by elected legislators are indications of the Court's new directions. The Court's dependence on statutes rather than on the exercise of constitutional authority as the judiciary, and thus as a policy maker and initiator, appears to be waning. Moreover, the Court, under the influence of a color-blind doctrine, seems ready to challenge policies that significantly rely on race and ethnicity, thus changing the landscape as well as the discussion of race and ethnicity, inviting all of us to reexamine both the intentions and outcomes of all legislation in this field.

In *Brown et al. v. Board of Education of Topeka et al.* (1954), the Supreme Court began the ambitious project of dismantling state-supported racial segregation. In *Brown*, a unanimous Court overturned *Plessy v. Ferguson*, arguing that "in the field of public education the doctrine of 'separate but equal' has no place," because "separate educational facilities are inherently unequal."

However, this era of civil rights consensus embodied in the landmark actions of the Supreme Court has been challenged by contemporary plaintiffs who have turned to the Court for clarification regarding specific cases related to the significance of race and ethnic criteria in public affairs. The lack of popular support for the administration and implementation of policies and the judicial leadership of those policies in California emerged in Proposition 209. This issue of popular concern was played out in the referendum that was supported by the electorate, but their decision will be played out in the court as the country braces itself for another cycle of tension and acrimony between the will of the people in a particular state and the rule and supremacy of national law. The mediation between law and popular expression, the political nexus of state and federal legitimacy, will no doubt be challenged by these contentions.

Nearly a generation after the civil rights era, our national public understanding of the thrust of that period can be regained by reviewing the congressional deliberation in support of the Civil Rights Act and its goal of equal protection and equality before the law. Contemporary legal arguments and current judicial politics pose a far more complex set of considerations. Fuller and more careful analysis of our legal foundations and expectations for the next epoch of equality with the legal tradition will emerge from these reconsiderations and from the new search for remedies.

The implementation of desegregation remedies, affirmative action, and voting rights remedies have been challenged in judicial rulings as well as in the decision to avoid court action that might compromise hard-won gains for minority populations. The politics of affirmative action include advocates and opponents who have become more strident and have exacerbated competition for rewards and benefits. Even the most popular accounts of race in the American legal tradition have been changed and revalued in the crucible of persistent racism and ongoing political and media manipulation of racial passion in pursuit of remedies and privilege.

DRED SCOTT v. SANDFORD

December Term 1856.

Mr. Chief Justice Taney delivered the opinion of the court.

This case has been twice argued. After the argument at the last term, differences of opinion were found to exist among the members of the court; and as the questions in controversy are of the highest importance, and the court was at that time much pressed by the ordinary business of the term, it was deemed advisable to continue the case, and direct a re-argument on some of the points, in order that we might have an opportunity of giving to the whole subject a more deliberate consideration. It has accordingly been again argued by counsel, and considered by the court; and I now proceed to deliver its opinion.

There are two leading questions presented by the record:

1. Had the Circuit Court of the United States jurisdiction to hear and determine the case between these parties? And

2. If it had jurisdiction, is the judgment it has given erroneous or not?

The plaintiff in error, who was also the plaintiff in the court below, was, with his wife and children, held as slaves by the defendant, in the State of Missouri; and he brought this action in the Circuit Court of the United States for that district, to assert the title of himself and his family to freedom.

The declaration is in the form usually adopted in that State to try questions of this description, and contains the averment necessary to give the court jurisdiction; that he and the defendant are citizens of different States; that is, that he is a citizen of Missouri, and the defendant a citizen of New York.

The defendant pleaded in abatement to the jurisdiction of the court, that the plaintiff was not a citizen of the State of Missouri, as alleged in his declaration, being a negro of African descent, whose ancestors were of pure African blood, and who were brought into this country and sold as slaves.

To this plea the plaintiff demurred, and the defendant joined in demurrer. The court overruled the plea, and gave judgment that the defendant should answer over. And he thereupon put in sundry pleas in bar, upon which issues were joined; and at the trial the verdict and judgment were in his favor. Whereupon the plaintiff brought this writ of error.

Before we speak of the pleas in bar, it will be proper to dispose of the questions which have arisen on the plea in abatement.

That plea denies the right of the plaintiff to sue in a court of the United States, for the reasons therein stated.

If the question raised by it is legally before us, and the court should be of opinion that the facts stated in it disqualify the plaintiff from becoming a citizen, in the sense in which that word is used in the Constitution of the United States, then the judgment of the Circuit Court is erroneous, and must be reversed.

It is suggested, however, that this plea is not before us; and that as the judgment in the court below on this plea was in favor of the plaintiff, he does not seek to reverse it, or bring it before the court for revision by his writ of error; and also that the defendant waived this defence by pleading over, and thereby admitted the jurisdiction of the court.

But, in making this objection, we think the peculiar and limited jurisdiction of courts of the United States has not been adverted to. This peculiar and limited jurisdiction has made it necessary, in these courts, to adopt different rules and principles of pleading, so far as jurisdiction is concerned, from those which regulate courts of common law in England, and in the different States of the Union which have adopted the common-law rules.

In these last-mentioned courts, where their character and rank are analogous to that of a Circuit Court of the United States; in other words, where they are what the law terms courts of general jurisdiction; they are presumed to have jurisdiction, unless the contrary appears. No averment in the pleadings of the plaintiff is necessary, in order to give jurisdiction. If the defendant objects to it, he must plead it specially, and unless the fact on which he relies is found to be true by a jury or admitted to be true by the plaintiff, the jurisdiction cannot be disputed in an appellate court.

Now, it is not necessary to inquire whether in courts of that description a party who pleads over in bar, when a plea to the jurisdiction has been ruled against him, does or does not waive his plea; nor whether upon a judgment in his favor on the pleas in bar, and a writ of error brought by the plaintiff, the question upon the plea in abatement would be open for revision in the appellate court. Cases that may have been decided in such courts, or rules that may have been laid down by common-law pleaders, can have no influence in the decision in this court. Because, under the Constitution and laws of the United States, the rules which govern the pleadings in its courts, in questions of jurisdiction, stand on different principles and are regulated by different laws.

This difference arises, as we have said, from the peculiar character of the Government of the United States. For although it is sovereign and supreme in its appropriate sphere of action, yet it does not possess all the powers which usually belong to the sovereignty of a nation. Certain specified powers, enumerated in the Constitution, have been conferred upon it; and neither the legislative, executive, nor judicial departments of the Government can lawfully exercise any authority beyond the limits marked out by the Constitution. And in regulating the judicial department, the cases in which the courts of the United States shall have jurisdiction are particularly and specifically enumerated and defined; and they are not authorized to take cognizance of any case which does not come within the description therein specified. Hence, when a plaintiff sues in a court of the United States, it is necessary that he should show, in his pleading, that the suit he brings is within the jurisdiction of the court, and that he is entitled to sue there. And if he omits to do this, and should, by any oversight of the Circuit Court, obtain a judgment in his favor, the judgment would be reversed in the appellate court for want of jurisdiction in the court below The jurisdiction would not be presumed, as in the case of a common-law English or State court, unless the contrary appeared. But the record, when it comes before the appellate court, must show, affirmatively that the inferior court had authority under the Constitution, to hear and determine the case. And if the plaintiff claims a right to sue in a Circuit Court of the United States, under that provision of the Constitution which gives jurisdiction in controversies between citizens of different States, he must distinctly aver in his pleading that they are citizens of different States; and he cannot maintain his suit without showing that fact in the pleadings.

This point was decided in the case of *Bingham v. Cabot,* (in 3 Dall., 382,) and ever since adhered to by the court. And in *Jackson v. Ashton,* (8 Pet., 148,) it was held that the objection to which it was open could not be waived by the opposite party because consent of parties could not give jurisdiction.

It is needless to accumulate cases on this subject. Those already referred to, and the cases of *Capron v. Van Noorden,* (in 2 Cr., 126) and *Montalet v. Murray,* (4 Cr., 46,) are sufficient to show the rule of which we have spoken.

The case of *Capron v. Van Noorden* strikingly illustrates the difference between a common-law court and a court of the United States. . . .

If, however, the fact of citizenship is averred in the declaration, and the defendant does not deny it, and put it in issue by plea in abatement, he cannot offer evidence at the trial to disprove it, and consequently cannot avail himself of the objection in the appellate court, unless the defect should be apparent in some other part of the record. For if there is no plea in abatement, and the want of jurisdiction does not appear in any other part of the transcript brought up by the writ of error, the undisputed averment of citizenship in the declaration must be taken in this court to be true. In this case, the citizenship is averred, but it is denied by the defendant in the manner required by the rules of pleading, and the fact upon which the denial is based is admitted by the demurrer. And, if the plea and demurrer, and judgment of the court below upon it, are before us upon this record, the question to be decided is, whether the facts stated in the plea are sufficient to show that the plaintiff is not entitled to sue as a citizen in a court of the United States. . . .

We think they are before us. The plea in abatement and the judgment of the court upon it, are a part of the judicial proceedings in the Circuit Court, and are there recorded as such; and a writ of error always brings up to the superior court the whole record of the proceedings in the court below And in the case of the *United States v. Smith,* (11 Wheat., 172) this court said, that the case being brought up by writ of error, the whole record was under the consideration of this court. And this being the case in the present instance, the plea in abatement is necessarily under consideration; and it becomes, therefore, our duty to decide whether the facts stated in the plea are or are not sufficient to show that the plaintiff is not entitled to sue as a citizen in a court of the United States.

This is certainly a very serious question, and one that now for the first time has been brought for decision before this court. But it is brought here by those who have a right to bring it, and it is our duty to meet it and decide it.

The question is simply this: Can a negro, whose ancestors were imported into this country and sold as slaves, become a member of the political community formed and brought into existence by the Constitution of the United States, and as such become entitled to all the rights, and privileges, and immunities, guaranteed by that instrument to the citizen? One of which rights is the privilege of suing in a court of the United States in the cases specified in the Constitution.

It will be observed, that the plea applies to that class of persons only whose ancestors were negroes of the African race, and imported into this country and sold and held as slaves. The only matter in issue before the court, therefore, is, whether the descendants of such slaves, when they shall be emancipated, or who are born of parents who had become free before their birth, are citizens of a State, in the sense in which the word citizen is used in the Constitution of the United States. And this being the only matter in dispute on the pleadings, the court must be understood as speaking in this opinion of that class only, that is, of those persons who are the descendants of Africans who were imported into this country, and sold as slaves.

The situation of this population was altogether unlike that of the Indian race. The latter, it is true, formed no part of the colonial communities, and never amalgamated with them in social connections or in government. But although they were uncivilized, they were yet a free and independent people, associated together in nations or tribes, and governed by their own laws. Many of these political communities were situated in territories to which the white race claimed the ultimate right of dominion. But that claim was acknowledged to be subject to the right of the Indians to occupy it as long as they thought proper, and neither the English nor colonial Governments claimed or exercised any dominion over the tribe or nation by whom it was occupied, nor claimed the right to the possession of the territory until the tribe or nation consented to cede it. These Indian Governments were regarded and treated as foreign Governments, as must so as if an ocean had separated the red man from the white; and their freedom has constantly been acknowledged, from the time of the first emigration to the English colonies to the present day by the different Governments which succeeded each other. Treaties have been negotiated with them, and their alliance sought for in war; and the people who compose these Indian political communities have always been treated as foreigners not living under our Government. It is true that the course of events has brought the Indian tribes within the limits of the United States under subjection to the white race; and it has been found necessary, for their sake as well as our own, to regard them as in a state of pupilage, and to legislate to a certain extent over them and the territory they occupy. But they may, without doubt, like the subjects of any other foreign Government, be naturalized by the authority of Congress, and become citizens of a State, and of the United States; and if an individual should leave his nation or tribe, and take up his abode among the white population, he would be entitled to all the rights and privileges which would belong to an emigrant from any other foreign people.

We proceed to examine the case as presented by the pleadings.

The words "people of the United States" and "citizens" are synonymous terms, and mean the same thing. They both describe the political body who, according to our republican institutions, form the sovereignty and who hold the power and conduct the Government through their representatives. They are what we familiarly call the "sovereign people," and every citizen is one of this people, and a constituent member of this sovereignty. The question before us is, whether the class of persons described in the plea in abatement compose a portion of this people, and are constituent members of this sovereignty? We think they are not, and that they are not included, and were not intended to be included, under the word "citizens" in the Constitution, and can therefore claim none of the rights and privileges which that instrument provides for and secures to citizens of the United States. On the contrary, they were at that time considered as a subordinate and inferior class of beings, who had been subjugated by the dominant race, and, whether emancipated or not, yet remained subject to their authority and had no rights or privileges but such as those who held the power and the Government might choose to grant them.

It is not the province of the court to decide upon the justice or injustice, the policy or impolicy of these laws. The decision of that question belonged to the political or law-making power; to those who formed the sovereignty and framed the Constitution. The duty of the court is, to interpret the instrument they have framed, with the best lights we can obtain on the subject, and to administer it as we find it, according to its true intent and meaning when it was adopted.

In discussing this question, we must not confound the rights of citizenship which a State may confer within its own limits, and the rights of citizenship as a member of the Union. It does not by any means follow, because he has all the rights and privileges of a citizen of a State, that he must be a citizen of the United States. He may have all of the rights and privileges of the citizen of a State, and yet not be entitled to the rights and privileges of a citizen in any other State. For, previous to the adoption of the Constitution of the United States, every State had the undoubted right to confer on whomsoever it pleased the character of citizen, and to endow him with all its rights. But this character of course was confined to the boundaries of the State, and gave him no rights or privileges in other States beyond those secured to him by the laws of nations and the comity of States. Nor have the several States surrendered the power of conferring these rights and privileges by adopting the Constitution of the United States. Each State may still confer them upon an alien, or any one it thinks proper, or upon any class or description of persons; yet he would not be a citizen in the sense in which that word is used in the Constitution of the United States, nor entitled to sue as such in one of its courts, nor to the privileges and immunities of a citizen in the other States. The rights which he would acquire would be restricted to the State which gave them. The Constitution has conferred on Congress the right to establish a uniform rule of naturalization, and this right is evidently exclusive, and has always been held by this court to be so. Consequently, no State, since the adoption of the Constitution, can by naturalizing an alien invest him with the rights and privileges secured to a citizen of a State under the Federal Government, although, so far as the State alone was concerned, he would undoubtedly be entitled to the rights of a citizen, and clothed with all the rights and immunities which the Constitution and laws of the State attached to that character.

It is very clear, therefore, that no State can, by any act or law of its own, passed since the adoption of the Constitution, introduce a new member into the political community created by the Constitution of the United States. It cannot make him a member of this community by making him a member of its own. And for the same reason it cannot introduce any person, or description of persons, who were not intended to be embraced in this new political family which the Constitution brought into existence, but were intended to be excluded from it.

The question then arises, whether the provisions of the Constitution, in relation to the personal rights and privileges to which the citizen of a State should be entitled, embraced the negro African race, at that time in this country or who might afterwards be imported, who had then or should afterwards be made free in any State; and to put it in the power of a single State to make him a citizen of the United States, and endue him with the full rights of citizenship in every other State without their consent? Does the Constitution of the United States act upon him whenever he shall be made free under the laws of a State, and raised there to the rank of a citizen, and immediately clothe him with all the privileges of a citizen in every other State, and in its own courts?

The courts think the affirmative of these propositions cannot be maintained. And if it cannot, the plaintiff in error could not be a citizen of the State of Missouri, within the meaning of the Constitution of the United States, and, consequently, was not entitled to sue in its courts.

It is true, every person, and every class and description of persons, who were at the time of the adoption of the Constitution recognised as citizens in the several States, became also citizens of this new political body; but none other; it was formed by them, and for them and their posterity but for no one else. And the personal rights and privileges guarantied to citizens of this new sovereignty were intended to embrace those only who were then members of the several State communities, or who should afterwards by birthright or otherwise become members, according to the provisions of the Constitution and the principles on which it was founded. It was the union of those who were at that time members of distinct and separate political communities into one political family, whose power, for certain specified purposes, was to extend over the whole territory of the United States. And it gave to each citizen rights and privileges outside of his State which he did not before possess, and placed him in every other State upon a perfect equality with its own citizens as to rights of person and rights of property; it made him a citizen of the United States.

It becomes necessary, therefore, to determine who were citizens of the several States when the Constitution was adopted. And in order to do this, we must recur to the Governments and institutions of the thirteen colonies, when they separated from Great Britain and formed new sovereignties, and took their places in the family of independent nations. We must inquire who, at that time, were recognised as the people or citizens of a State, whose rights and liberties had been outraged by the English Government; and who declared their independence, and assumed the powers of Government to defend their rights by force of arms.

In the opinion of the court, the legislation and histories of the times, and the language used in the Declaration of Independence, show, that neither the class of persons who had been imported as slaves, nor their descendants, whether they had become free or not, were then acknowledged as a part of the people, nor intended to be included in the general words used in that memorable instrument. . . .

Racial Restrictions in the Law of Citizenship

Ian F. Haney Lopez

The racial composition of the U.S. citizenry reflects in part the accident of world migration patterns. More than this, however, it reflects the conscious design of U.S. immigration and naturalization laws.

Federal law restricted immigration to this country on the basis of race for nearly one hundred years, roughly from the Chinese exclusion laws of the 1880s until the end of the national origin quotas in 1965.[1] The history of this discrimination can briefly be traced. Nativist sentiment against Irish and German Catholics on the East Coast and against Chinese and Mexicans on the West Coast, which had been doused by the Civil War, reignited during the economic slump of the 1870s. Though most of the nativist efforts failed to gain congressional sanction, Congress in 1882 passed the Chinese Exclusion Act, which suspended the immigration of Chinese laborers for ten years.[2] The Act was expanded to exclude all Chinese in 1884, and was eventually implemented indefinitely.[3] In 1917, Congress created "an Asiatic barred zone," excluding all persons from Asia.[4] During this same period, the Senate passed a bill to exclude "all members of the African or black race." This effort was defeated in the House only after intensive lobbying by the NAACP.[5] Efforts to exclude the supposedly racially undesirable southern and eastern Europeans were more successful. In 1921, Congress established a temporary quota system designed "to confine immigration as much as possible to western and northern European stock," making this bar permanent three years later in the National Origin Act of 1924.[6] With the onset of the Depression, attention shifted to Mexican immigrants. Although no law explicitly targeted this group, federal immigration officials began a series of round-ups and mass deportations of people of Mexican descent under the general rubric of a "repatriation campaign." Approximately 500,000 people were forcibly returned to Mexico during the Depression, more than half of them U.S. citizens.[7] This pattern was repeated in the 1950s, when Attorney General Herbert Brownwell launched a program to expel Mexicans. This effort, dubbed "Operation Wet-back," indiscriminately deported more than one million citizens and noncitizens in 1954 alone.[8]

Racial restrictions on immigration were not significantly dismantled until 1965, when Congress in a major overhaul of immigration law abolished both the national origin system and the Asiatic Barred Zone.[9] Even so, purposeful racial discrimination in immigration law by Congress remains constitutionally permissible, since the case that upheld the Chinese Exclusion Act to this day remains good law.[10] Moreover, arguably racial discrimination in immigration law continues. For example, Congress has enacted special provisions to encourage Irish immigration, while refusing to ameliorate the backlog of would-be immigrants from the Philippines, India, South Korea, China, and Hong Kong, backlogs created in part through a century of racial exclusion.[11] The history of racial discrimination in U.S. immigration law is a long and continuing one.

As discriminatory as the laws of immigration have been, the laws of citizenship betray an even more dismal record of racial exclusion. From this country's inception, the laws regulating who was or could become a citizen were tainted by racial prejudice. Birthright citizenship, the automatic acquisition of citizenship by virtue of birth, was tied to race until 1940. Naturalized citizenship, the acquisition of citizenship by any means other than through birth, was conditioned on race until 1952. Like immigration laws, the laws of birthright citizenship and naturalization shaped the racial character of the United States.

Birthright Citizenship

Most persons acquire citizenship by birth rather than through naturalization. During the 1990s, for example, naturalization will account for only 7.5 percent of the increase in the U.S. citizen population.[12] At the time of the prerequisite cases, the proportion of persons gaining citizenship through naturalization was probably somewhat higher, given the higher ratio of immigrants to total population, but still far smaller than the number of people gaining citizenship by birth. In order to situate the prerequisite laws, therefore, it is useful first to review the history of racial discrimination in the laws of birthright citizenship.

The U.S. Constitution as ratified did not define the citizenry, probably because it was assumed that the English common law rule of *jus soli* would continue.[13] Under *jus soli*, citizenship accrues to "all" born within a nation's jurisdiction. Despite the seeming breadth of this doctrine, the word "all" is qualified because for the first one hundred years and more of this country's history it did not fully encompass racial minorities. This is the import of the *Dred Scott* decision.[14] Scott, an enslaved man, sought to use the federal courts to sue for his freedom. However, access to the courts was predicated on citizenship. Dismissing his claim, the United States Supreme Court in the person of Chief Justice Roger Taney declared in 1857 that Scott and all other Blacks, free and enslaved, were not and could never be citizens because they were "a subordinate and inferior class of beings." The decision protected the slave-holding South and infuriated much of the North, further dividing a country already fractured around the issues of slavery and the power of the national government. *Dred Scott* was invalidated after the Civil War by the Civil Rights Act of 1866, which declared that "All persons born . . . in the United States and not subject to any foreign power, excluding Indians not taxed, are declared to be citizens of the United States."[15] *Jus soli* subsequently became part of the organic law of the land in the form of the Fourteenth Amendment: "All persons born or naturalized in the United States, and subject to the jurisdiction thereof, are citizens of the United States and of the state wherein they reside."[16]

Despite the broad language of the Fourteenth Amendment—though in keeping with the words of the 1866 act—some racial minorities remained outside the bounds of *jus soli* even after its constitutional enactment. In particular, questions persisted about the citizenship status of children born in the United States to noncitizen parents, and about the status of Native Americans. The Supreme Court did not decide the status of the former until 1898, when it ruled in *U.S. v. Wong Kim Ark* that native-born children of aliens, even those permanently barred by race from acquiring citizenship, were birthright citizens of the United States.[17] On the citizenship of the latter, the Supreme Court answered negatively in 1884, holding in *Elk v. Wilkins* that Native Americans owed allegiance to their tribe and so did not acquire citizenship upon birth.[18] Congress responded by granting Native Americans citizenship in piecemeal fashion, often tribe by tribe. Not until 1924 did Congress pass an act conferring citizenship on all Native Americans in the United States.[19] Even then, however, questions arose regarding the citizenship of those born in the United States after the effective date of the 1924 act. These questions were finally resolved, and *jus soli* fully applied, under the Nationality Act of 1940, which specifically bestowed citizenship on all those born in the United States "to a member of an Indian, Eskimo, Aleutian, or other aboriginal tribe."[20] Thus, the basic law of citizenship, that a person born here is a citizen here, did not include all racial minorities until 1940.

Unfortunately, the impulse to restrict birthright citizenship by race is far from dead in this country. Apparently, California Governor Pete Wilson and many others seek a return to the times when citizenship depended on racial proxies such as immigrant status. Wilson has called for a federal constitutional amendment that would prevent the American-born children of undocumented persons from receiving birthright citizenship.[21] His call has not been ignored: thirteen members of Congress recently sponsored a constitutional amendment that would repeal the existing Citizenship Clause of the Fourteenth Amendment and replace it with a provision that "All persons born in the United States . . . of mothers who are citizens or legal residents of the United States . . . are citizens of the United States."[22] Apparently, such a change is supported by 49 percent of Americans.[23] In addition to explicitly discriminating against fathers by eliminating their right to confer citizenship through parentage, this proposal implicitly discriminates along racial lines. The effort to deny citizenship to children born here to undocumented immigrants seems to be motivated not by an abstract concern over the political status of the parents, but by racial animosity against Asians and Latinos, those commonly seen as comprising the vast bulk of undocumented migrants. Bill Ong Hing writes, "The discussion of who is and who is not American, who can and cannot become American, goes beyond the technicalities of citizenship and residency requirements; it strikes at the very heart of our nation's long and troubled legacy of race relations.[24] As this troubled legacy reveals, the triumph over racial discrimination in the laws of citizenship and alienage came slowly and only recently. In the campaign for the "control of our borders," we are once again debating the citizenship of the native-born and the merits of *Dred Scott*.[25]

Naturalization

Although the Constitution did not originally define the citizenry, it explicitly gave Congress the authority to establish the criteria for granting citizenship after birth. Article I grants Congress the power "To establish a uniform Rule of Naturalization."[26] From the start, Congress exercised this power in a manner that burdened naturalization laws with racial restrictions that tracked those in the law of birthright citizenship. In 1790, only a few months after ratification of the Constitution, Congress limited naturalization to "any alien, being a free white person who shall have resided within the limits and under the jurisdiction of the United States for a term of two years."[27] This clause mirrored not only the de facto laws of birthright citizenship, but also the racially restrictive naturalization laws of several states. At least three states had previously limited citizenship to "white persons": Virginia in 1779, South Carolina in 1784, and Georgia in 1785.[28] Though there would be many subsequent changes in the requirements for federal naturalization, racial identity endured as a bedrock requirement for the next 162 years. In every naturalization act from 1790 until 1952, Congress included the "white person" prerequisite.[29]

The history of racial prerequisites to naturalization can be divided into two periods of approximately eighty years each. The first period extended from 1790 to 1870, when only Whites were able to naturalize. In the wake of the Civil War, the "white person" restriction on naturalization came under serious attack as part of the effort to expunge *Dred Scott*. Some congressmen, Charles Sumner chief among them, argued that racial barriers to naturalization should be struck altogether. However, racial prejudice against Native Americans and Asians forestalled the complete elimination of the racial prerequisites. During congressional debates, one senator argued against conferring "the rank, privileges, and immunities of citizenship upon the cruel savages who destroyed [Minnesota's] peaceful settlements and massacred the people with circumstances of atrocity too horrible to relate."[30] Another senator wondered "whether this door [of citizenship] shall now be thrown open to the Asiatic population," warning that to do so would spell for the Pacific coast "an end to republican government there, because it is very well ascertained that those people have no appreciation of that form of government; it seems to be obnoxious to their very nature; they seem to be incapable either of understanding or carrying it out."[31] Sentiments such as these ensured that even after the Civil War, bars against Native American and Asian naturalization would continue.[32] Congress opted to maintain the "white person" prerequisite, but to extend the right to naturalize to "persons of African nativity, or African descent."[33] After 1870, Blacks as well as Whites could naturalize, but not others.

During the second period, from 1870 until the last of the prerequisite laws were abolished in 1952, the White-Black dichotomy in American race relations dominated naturalization law. During this period, Whites and Blacks were eligible for citizenship, but others, particularly those from Asia, were not. Indeed, increasing antipathy toward Asians on the West Coast resulted in an explicit disqualification of Chinese persons from naturalization in 1882.[34] The prohibition of Chinese naturalization, the only U.S. law ever to exclude by name a particular nationality from citizenship, was coupled with the ban on Chinese immigration discussed previously. The Supreme Court readily upheld the bar, writing that "Chinese persons not born in this country have never been recognized as citizens of the United States, nor authorized to become

such under the naturalization laws."[35] While Blacks were permitted to naturalize beginning in 1870, the Chinese and most "other non-Whites" would have to wait until the 1940s for the right to naturalize.[36]

World War II forced a domestic reconsideration of the racism integral to U.S. naturalization law. In 1935, Hitler's Germany limited citizenship to members of the Aryan race, making Germany the only country other than the United States with a racial restriction on naturalization.[37] The fact of this bad company was not lost on those administering our naturalization laws. "When Earl G. Harrison in 1944 resigned as United States Commissioner of Immigration and Naturalization, he said that the only country in the world, outside the United States, that observes racial discrimination in matters relating to naturalization was Nazi Germany, 'and we all agree that this is not very desirable company.' "[38] Furthermore, the United States was open to charges of hypocrisy for banning from naturalization the nationals of many of its Asian allies. During the war, the United States seemed through some of its laws and social practices to embrace the same racism it was fighting. Both fronts of the war exposed profound inconsistencies between U.S. naturalization law and broader social ideals. These considerations, among others, led Congress to begin a process of piecemeal reform in the laws governing citizenship.

In 1940, Congress opened naturalization to "descendants of races indigenous to the Western Hemisphere."[39] Apparently, this "additional limitation was designed 'to more fully cement' the ties of Pan-Americanism" at a time of impending crisis.[40] In 1943, Congress replaced the prohibition on the naturalization of Chinese persons with a provision explicitly granting them this boon.[41] In 1946, it opened up naturalization to persons from the Philippines and India as well.[42] Thus, at the end of the war, our naturalization law looked like this:

The right to become a naturalized citizen under the provisions of this Act shall extend only to—

(1) white persons, persons of African nativity or descent, and persons of races indigenous to the continents of North or South America or adjacent islands and Filipino persons or persons of Filipino descent;
(2) persons who possess, either singly or in combination, a preponderance of blood of one or more of the classes specified in clause (1);
(3) Chinese persons or persons of Chinese descent; and persons of races indigenous to India; and
(4) persons who possess, either singly or in combination, a preponderance of blood of one or more of the classes specified in clause (3) or, either singly or in combination, as much as one-half blood of those classes and some additional blood of one of the classes specified in clause (1).[43]

This incremental retreat from a "Whites only" conception of citizenship made the arbitrariness of U.S. naturalization law increasingly obvious. For example, under the above statute, the right to acquire citizenship depended for some on blood-quantum distinctions based on descent from peoples indigenous to islands adjacent to the Americas. In 1952, Congress moved towards wholesale reform, overhauling the naturalization statute to read simply that "[t]he right of a person to become a naturalized citizen of the United States shall not be denied or abridged because of race or sex or because such person is married."[44] Thus, in 1952, racial bars on naturalization came to an official end.[45]

Notice the mention of gender in the statutory language ending racial restrictions in naturalization. The issue of women and citizenship can only be touched on here, but deserves significant study in its own right.[46] As the language of the 1952 Act implies, eligibility for naturalization once depended on a woman's marital status. Congress in 1855 declared that a foreign woman automatically acquired citizenship upon marriage to a U.S. citizen, or upon the naturalization of her alien husband.[47] This provision built upon the supposition that a woman's social and political status flowed from her husband. As an 1895 treatise on naturalization put it, "A woman partakes of her husband's nationality; her nationality is merged in that of her husband; her political status follows that of her husband."[48] A wife's acquisition of citizenship, however, remained subject to her individual qualification for naturalization—that is, on whether she was a "white person."[49] Thus, the Supreme Court held in 1868 that only "white women" could gain citizenship by marrying a citizen.[50] Racial restrictions further complicated matters for noncitizen women in that naturalization was denied to those married to a man racially ineligible for citizenship, irrespective of the woman's own qualifications, racial or otherwise.[51] The automatic naturalization of a woman upon her marriage to a citizen or upon the naturalization of her husband ended in 1922.[52]

The citizenship of American-born women was also affected by the interplay of gender and racial restrictions. Even though under English common law a woman's nationality was unaffected by marriage, many courts in this country stripped women who married noncitizens of their U.S. citizenship.[53] Congress recognized and mandated this practice in 1907, legislating that an American woman's marriage to an alien terminated her citizenship.[54] Under considerable pressure, Congress partially repealed this act in 1922.[55] However, the 1922 act continued to require the expatriation of any woman who married a foreigner racially barred from citizenship, flatly declaring that "any woman citizen who marries an alien ineligible to citizenship shall cease to be a citizen."[56] Until Congress repealed this provision in 1931,[57] marriage to a non-White alien by an American woman was akin to treason against this country: either of these acts justified the stripping of citizenship from someone American by birth. Indeed, a woman's marriage to a non-White foreigner was perhaps a worse crime, for while a traitor

lost his citizenship only after trial, the woman lost hers automatically.[58] The laws governing the racial composition of this country's citizenry came inseverably bound up with and exacerbated by sexism. It is in this context of combined racial and gender prejudice that we should understand the absence of any women among the petitioners named in the prerequisite cases: it is not that women were unaffected by the racial bars, but that they were doubly bound by them, restricted both as individuals, and as less than individuals (that is, as wives).

Notes

1. U.S. COMMISSION ON CIVIL RIGHTS, THE TARNISHED GOLDEN DOOR: CIVIL RIGHTS ISSUES IN IMMIGRATION 1–12 (1990).
2. Chinese Exclusion Act, ch. 126, 22 Stat. 58 (1882). *See generally* Harold Hongju Koh, *Bitter Fruit of the Asian Immigration Cases*, 6 CONSTITUTION 69 (1994). For a sobering account of the many lynchings of Chinese in the western United States during this period, *see* John R. Wunder, *Anti-Chinese Violence in the American West, 1850–1910*, LAW FOR THE ELEPHANT, LAW FOR THE BEAVER: ESSAYS IN THE LEGAL HISTORY OF THE NORTH AMERICAN WEST 212 (John McLaren, Hamar Foster, and Chet Orloff eds., 1992). Charles McClain, Jr., discusses the historical origins of anti-Chinese prejudice and the legal responses undertaken by that community on the West Coast. Charles McClain, Jr., *The Chinese Struggle for Civil Rights in Nineteenth Century America: The First Phase, 1850–1870*, 72 CAL. L. REV. 529 (1984). For a discussion of contemporary racial violence against Asian Americans, *see* Note, *Racial Violence against Asian Americans*, 106 HARV. L. REV. 1926 (1993); Robert Chang, *Toward an Asian American Legal Scholarship: Critical Race Theory, Post-Structuralism, and Narrative Space*, 81 CAL. L. REV. 1241, 1251–58(1993).
3. Act of July 9, 1884, ch. 220, 23 Stat. 115; Act of May 5, 1892, ch. 60, 27 Stat. 25; Act of April 29, 1902, ch. 641, 32 Stat. 176; Act of April 27, 1904, ch. 1630, 33 Stat. 428.
4. Act of Feb. 5, 1917, ch. 29, 39 Stat. 874.
5. U.S. COMMISSION ON CIVIL RIGHTS, *supra*, at 9.
6. *Id. See* Act of May 19, 1921, ch. 8, 42 Stat. 5; Act of May 26, 1924, ch. 190, 43 Stat. 153.
7. U.S. COMMISSION ON CIVIL RIGHTS, *supra*, at 10.
8. *Id.* at 11. *See generally* JUAN RAMON GARCIA, OPERATION WETBACK: THE MASS DEPORTATION OF MEXICAN UNDOCUMENTED WORKERS IN 1954 (1980).
9. Act of Oct. 2, 1965, 79 Stat. 911.
10. Chae Chan Ping v. United States, 130 U.S. 581 (1889). The Court reasoned in part that if "the government of the United States, through its legislative department, considers the presence of foreigners of a different race in this country, who will not assimilate with us, to be dangerous to its peace and security, their exclusion is not to be stayed." For a critique of this deplorable result, *see* Louis Henkin, *The Constitution and United States Sovereignty: A Century of Chinese Exclusion and Its Progeny*, 100 HARV. L. REV. 853 (1987).
11. For efforts to encourage Irish immigration, *see, e.g., Immigration Act of 1990*, § 131, 104 Stat. 4978 (codified as amended at 8 U.S.C. § 1153 (c) [1994]). Bill Ong Hing argues that Congress continues to discriminate against Asians. "*Through an examination of past exclusion laws, previous legislation, and the specific provisions of the Immigration Act of 1990, the conclusion can be drawn that Congress never intended to make up for nearly 80 years of Asian exclusion, and that a conscious hostility towards persons of Asian descent continues to pervade Congressional circles.*" Bill Ong Hing, Asian Americans and Present U.S. Immigration Policies: A Legacy of Asian Exclusion, ASIAN AMERICANS AND THE SUPREME COURT: A DOCUMENTARY HISTORY 1106, 1107 (Hyung-Chan Kim ed., 1992).
12. Louis DeSipio and Harry Pachon, Making Americans: Administrative Discretion and Americanization, 12 CHICANO-LATINO L. REV. 52, 53 (1992).

13. CHARLES GORDON AND STANLEY MAILMAN, IMMIGRATION LAW AND PROCEDURE § 92.03[1][b] (rev. ed. 1992).

14. Dred Scott v. Sandford, 60 U.S. (19 How.) 393 (1857). For an insightful discussion of the role of Dred Scott *in the development of American citizenship,* see JAMES KETTNER, THE DEVELOPMENT OF AMERICAN CITIZENSHIP, 1608–1870, at 300–333 (1978); see also KENNETH L. KARST, BELONGING TO AMERICA: EQUAL CITIZENSHIP AND THE CONSTITUTION 43–61 (1989).

15. Civil Rights Act of 1866, ch. 31, 14 Stat. 27.

16. U.S. Const. amend. XIV.

17. 169 U.S. 649 (1898).

18. 112 U.S. 94 (1884).

19. Act of June 2, 1924, ch. 233, 43 Stat. 253.

20. Nationality Act of 1940, § 201(b), 54 Stat. 1138. See generally *GORDON AND MAILMAN,* supra, *at § 92.03[3][e].*

21. Pete Wilson, Crack Down on Illegals, *USA TODAY,* Aug. 20, 1993, at 12A.

22. H. R. J. Res. 129, 103d Cong., 1st Sess. (1993). An earlier, scholarly call to revamp the Fourteenth Amendment can be found in PETER SCHUCK and ROGER SMITH, CITIZENSHIP WITHOUT CONSENT: ILLEGAL ALIENS IN THE AMERICAN POLITY (1985).

23. Koh, supra, *at 69–70.*

24. Bill Ong Hing, Beyond the Rhetoric of Assimilation and Cultural Pluralism: Addressing the Tension of Separatism and Conflict in an Immigration-Driven Multiracial Society, *81 CAL. L. REV. 863, 866 (1993).*

25. Gerald Neuman warns against amending the Citizenship Clause. Gerald Neuman, Back to *Dred Scott? 24 SAN DIEGO L. REV. 485, 500 (1987).* See also *Note,* The Birthright Citizenship Amendment: A Threat to Equality, *107 HARV. L. REV. 1026 (1994).*

26. U.S. Const. art. I, sec. 8, cl. 4.

27. Act of March 26, 1790, ch. 3, 1 Stat. 103.

28. KETTNER, supra, *at 215–16.*

29. One exception exists. In revisions undertaken in 1870, the "white person" limitation was omitted. However, this omission is regarded as accidental, and the prerequisite was reinserted in 1875 by "an act to correct errors and to supply omissions in the Revised Statutes of the United States." Act of Feb. 18, 1875, ch. 80, 18 Stat. 318. See *In re Ah Yup,* 1 F.Cas. 223 (C.C.D.Cal. 1878) ("*Upon revision of the statutes, the revisors, probably inadvertently, as Congress did not contemplate a change of the laws in force, omitted the words 'white persons.'* ").

30. Statement of Senator Hendricks, 59 CONG. GLOBE, 42nd Cong., 1st Sess. 2939 (1866). See also *John Guendelsberger,* Access to Citizenship for Children Born Within the State to Foreign Parents, *40 AM. J. COMP. L. 379, 407–9 (1992).*

31. Statement of Senator Cowan, 57 CONG. GLOBE, 42nd Cong., 1st Sess. 499 (1866). For a discussion of the role of anti-Asian prejudice in the laws governing naturalization, see generally *Elizabeth Hull,* Naturalization and Denaturalization, *ASIAN AMERICANS AND THE SUPREME COURT: A DOCUMENTARY HISTORY 403 (Hyung-Chan Kim ed., 1992)*

32. The Senate rejected an amendment that would have allowed Chinese persons to naturalize. The proposed amendment read: "That the naturalization laws are hereby extended to aliens of African nativity, and to persons of African descent, and to persons born in the Chinese empire." BILL ONG HING, MAKING AND REMAKING ASIAN AMERICA THROUGH IMMIGRATION POLICY, 1850–1990, at 239 n.34 (1993).

33. Act of July 14, 1870, ch. 255, § 7, 16 Stat. 254.

34. Chinese Exclusion Act, ch. 126, § 14, 22 Stat. 58 (1882).

35. Fong Yue Ting v. United States, 149 U.S. 698, 716 (1893).

36. Neil Gotanda contends that separate racial ideologies function with respect to "other non-Whites," meaning non-Black racial minorities such as Asians, Native Americans, and Latinos. Neil Gotanda, "Other Non-Whites" in American Legal History: A Review of *Justice at War,* 85 COLUM. L. REV. 1186 (1985). *Gotanda explicitly identifies the operation of this separate ideology in the Supreme Court's jurisprudence regarding Asians and citizenship. Neil Gotanda,* Asian American Rights and the "Miss Saigon Syndrome," *ASIAN AMERICANS AND THE SUPREME COURT: A DOCUMENTARY HISTORY 1087, 1096–97 (Hyung-Chan Kim ed., 1992).*

37. Charles Gordon, The Racial Barrier to American Citizenship, *93 U. PA. L. REV. 237, 252 (1945).*

38. . MILTON KONVITZ, THE ALIEN AND THE ASIATIC IN AMERICAN LAW 80–81 (1946) (citation omitted).

39. Act of Oct. 14, 1940, ch. 876, § 303, 54 Stat. 1140.

40. Note, The Nationality Act of 1940, *54 HARV. L. REV. 860, 865 n.40 (1941).*

41. Act of Dec. 17, 1943, ch. 344, § 3, 57 Stat. 600.

42. Act of July 2, 1946, ch. 534, 60 Stat. 416.

43. Id.

44. Immigration and Nationality Act of 1952, ch. 2, § 311, 66 Stat. 239 (codified as amended at 8 U.S.C. 1422 [1988]).

45. Arguably, the continued substantial exclusion of Asians from immigration not remedied until 1965, rendered their eligibility for naturalization relatively meaningless. "[T]he national quota system for admitting immigrants which was built into the 1952 Act gave the grant of eligibility a hollow ring." Chin Kim and Bok Lim Kim, Asian Immigrants in American Law: A Look at the Past and the Challenge Which Remains, *26 AM. U. L. REV. 373, 390 (1977).*

46. See generally *Ursula Vogel,* Is Citizenship Gender-Specific? *THE FRONTIERS OF CITIZENSHIP 58 (Ursula Vogel and Michael Moran eds., 1991).*

47. Act of Feb. 10, 1855, ch. 71, § 2, 10 Stat. 604. Because gender-based laws in the area of citizenship were motivated by the idea that a woman's citizenship should follow that of her husband, no naturalization law has explicitly targeted unmarried women. GORDON AND MAILMAN, supra, *at § 95.03[6] ("An unmarried woman has never been (statutorily* barred from naturalization.").

48. PRENTISS WEBSTER, LAW OF NATURALIZATION IN THE UNITED STATES OF AMERICA AND OTHER COUNTRIES 80 (1895).

49. Act of Feb. 10, 1855, ch. 71, § 2, 10 Stat. 604.

50. Kelly v. Owen, 74 U.S. 496, 498 (1868).

51. GORDON AND MAILMAN, *supra* at § 95.03[6].

52. Act of Sept. 22, 1922, ch. 411, §2, 42 Stat. 1021.

53. GORDON AND MAILMAN, *supra* at § 100.03[4][m].

54. Act of March 2, 1907, ch. 2534, § 3, 34 Stat. 1228. This act was upheld in MacKenzie v. Hare, 239 U.S. 299 (1915) (expatriating a U.S.-born woman upon her marriage to a British citizen).

55. Act of Sept. 22, 1922, ch. 411, §3, 42 Stat. 1021.

56. *Id.* The Act also stated that "[n]o woman whose husband is not eligible to citizenship shall be naturalized during the continuance of the marriage."

57. Act of March 3, 1931, ch. 442, §4(a), 46 Stat. 1511.

58. The loss of birthright citizenship was particularly harsh for those women whose race made them unable to regain citizenship through naturalization, especially after 1924, when the immigration laws of this country barred entry to any alien ineligible to citizenship. Immigration Act of 1924, ch. 190, § 13(c), 43 Stat. 162. *See, e.g.,* Ex parte (Ng) Fung Sing, 6 F.2d 670 (W. D. Wash. 1925). In that case, a U.S. birthright citizen of Chinese descent was expatriated because of her marriage to a Chinese citizen, and was subsequently refused admittance to the United States as an alien ineligible to citizenship.

Legal Journal

In a Judicial 'What If,' Indians Revisit a Case

By WILLIAM GLABERSON

LAWRENCE, Kan., Oct. 21—It was all white men on the Supreme Court who handed down the milestone rulings that helped decide the fate of American Indians more than a century ago.

Now, here at the University of Kansas School of Law, Indian lawyers are acting out a legal "what if" experiment: What if Indians had been on the Supreme Court of the 1800's?

Eight American Indian lawyers gathered here on Oct. 10 and played the roles of Justices in an elaborate moot court. The panel heard a full "reargument" of one of the most important of the early Supreme Court cases, Cherokee Nation v. Georgia. In the 1831 decision, Chief Justice John Marshall ruled that tribes were not foreign nations entitled to be dealt with equally but more "domestic dependent nations." The ruling in Georgia's favor laid the legal foundation for much that was to come in America's relations with the Indians.

Although fictitious, the reconsideration of the case is not a carefree task. Years ago in law school at the University of Wisconsin, said Laura Soap, one of the moot-court Justices,

she felt no emotion as she studied the famous Supreme Court rulings dealing with Indians. But as the arguments have been replayed in the moot court, she said, "I find myself getting a little angry, the more I think about it. I find myself thinking: How am I going to explain this to my kids?" Ms. Soap is a Kickapoo Indian; her husband is a Cherokee.

A milestone ruling that set course for American relations with the Indians.

The moot-court judges surprised no one by announcing after the arguments that, this time, the Cherokee Nation had won. But, just like real Justices, the eight Indian lawyers are deliberating over a written opinion to justify their decision. It is to be published in a law review.

At the invitation of a reporter, Ms. Soap and another of the moot-court Justices, Russell A. Brien, a member of the Iowa tribe, met at the law

school to hash out their views in the drafting of an opinion the way real judges might. On a bright Kansas afternoon, they struggled with the history of the legal system's treatment of their people.

Justice Marshall concluded 167 years ago that, no matter how real their grievances might be, tribes could not appeal to the Supreme Court. The ruling left the tribes with no redress for acts like the breaking of treaties and the forced removal of native people from their homelands.

Ms. Soap, 38, is an associate justice of the real Supreme Court of the Sac and Fox Nation of Kansas and Missouri. If she had the chance to hear the Cherokee case, she said, she would try to be practical in contending with Justice Marshall's view that the Supreme Court lacked jurisdiction to hear the Cherokees' case.

Perhaps she could concede, she said, that the Indians could not enforce their treaties. But closing the door of the country's highest court to Indians, she said, diminished the ideals of America. "I would talk to Marshall," she said, "and I would say: 'Maybe the treaties are no good. But we need to do it the way the

Americans do it: We need to have the issues heard in court.' "

In real life, Mr. Brien, 32, is a lawyer in a Kansas City firm who works on repackaging mortgage loans as securities. He tried a legalistic approach to the Cherokees' case.

"Clearly the Indians were here first," Mr. Brien said. "The Indians' title to the land has not been extinguished."

He said that one way to deal with Justice Marshall's view was to convince him that if the court did not treat the Indians' claims as legitimate in 1831, the Indians' anger could fester for a long time. "You might as well address it now, rather than wait till later," Mr. Brien said.

Before the meeting of the two justices, the professor who convened the moot court, Robert B. Porter, had explained the goal of the exercise. Mr. Porter, a Harvard-education lawyer and a member of the Seneca Nation, is the director of the Tribal Law and Government Center at the law school here.

As Indian nations across the country struggle to reassert their sovereign powers over their own people, he said, Indian lawyers must study the way America used the law to establish what he called colonial domination. The moot court and similar exercises, he said, are intended "to lay the intellectual foundation for our decolonization."

It is not an easy task. Mr. Brien and Ms. Soap said that as lawyers trained in the American system, it was nearly impossible for them to view the Cherokees' case of 1831 with anything like the eyes of their ancestors.

Mr. Brien said that his family left the reservation years ago and he had become involved in tribal matters only in recent years. As he learned his tribe's modern legal system, he said, he discovered that over the generations it had come to mirror the American system. Older ways, he said, had been forgotten.

"I don't have my tribe's dispute resolution system," he said. "That's lost to me. And I am still in the process of trying to learn my tribe's traditions."

How would an Indian Justice of the Supreme Court view the Cherokees' case? Mr. Brien said it was hard for him to know.

BROWN et al.

v.

BOARD OF EDUCATION

OF TOPEKA et al.

347 U.S. 483 (1954)

MR. CHIEF JUSTICE WARREN delivered the opinion of the Court.

These cases come to us from the States of Kansas, South Carolina, Virginia, and Delaware. They are premised on different facts and different local conditions, but a common legal question justifies their consideration together in this consolidated opinion.[1]

In each of the cases, minors of the Negro race, through their legal representatives, seek the aid of the courts in obtaining admission to the public schools of their community on a nonsegregated basis. In each instance, they had been denied admission to schools attended by white children under laws requiring or permitting segregation according to race. This segregation was alleged to deprive the plaintiffs of the equal protection of the laws under the Fourteenth Amendment. In each of the cases other than the Delaware case, a three-judge federal district court denied relief to the plaintiffs on the so-called "separate but equal" doctrine announced by this Court in *Plessy v. Ferguson,* 163 U.S. 537. Under that doctrine, equality of treatment is accorded when the races are provided substantially equal facilities, even though these facilities be separate. In the Delaware case, the Supreme Court of Delaware adhered to that doctrine, but ordered that the plaintiffs be admitted to the white schools because of their superiority to the Negro schools.

The plaintiffs contend that segregated public schools are not "equal" and cannot be made "equal," and that hence they are deprived of the equal protection of the laws. Because of the obvious importance of the question presented, the Court took jurisdiction.[2] Argument was heard in the 1952 Term, and reargument was heard this Term on certain questions propounded by the Court.[3]

Reargument was largely devoted to the circumstances surrounding the adoption of the Fourteenth Amendment in 1868. It covered exhaustively consideration of the Amendment in Congress, ratification by the states, then existing practices in racial segregation, and the views of proponents and opponents of the Amendment. This discussion and our own investigation convince us that, although these sources cast some light, it is not enough to resolve the problem with which we are faced. At best, they are inconclusive. The most avid proponents of the post–War Amendments undoubtedly intended them to remove all legal distinctions among "all persons born or naturalized in the United States." Their opponents, just as certainly, were antagonistic to both the letter and the spirit of the Amendments and wished them to have the most limited effect. What others in Congress and the state legislatures had in mind cannot be determined with an degree of certainty.

An additional reason for the inconclusive nature of the Amendment's history, with respect to segregated schools, is the status of public education at that time.[4] In the South, the movement toward free common schools, supported by general taxation, had not yet taken hold. Education of white children was largely in the hands of private groups. Education of Negroes was almost nonexistent, and practically all of the race were illiterate. In fact, any education of Negroes was forbidden by law in some states. Today in contrast, many Negroes have achieved outstanding success in the arts and sciences as well

From *U.S. Reports,* 1954. Opinion of the Supreme Court, 1954.

as in the business and professional world. It is true that public school education at the time of the Amendment had advanced further in the North, but the effect of the Amendment on northern States was generally ignored in the congressional debates. Even in the North, the conditions of public education did not approximate those existing today. The curriculum was usually rudimentary; ungraded schools were common in rural areas; the school term was but three months a year in many states; and compulsory school attendance was virtually unknown. As a consequence, it is not surprising that there should be so little in the history of the Fourteenth Amendment relating to its intended effect on public education.

In the first cases in this Court construing the Fourteenth Amendment, decided shortly after its adoption, the Court interpreted it as proscribing all state-imposed discriminations against the Negro race.[5] The doctrine of "separate but equal" did not make its appearance in this Court until 1896 in the case of *Plessy v. Ferguson, supra,* involving not education but transportation.[6] American courts have since labored with the doctrine for over half a century. In this Court, there have been six cases involving the "separate but equal" doctrine in the field of public education.[7] In *Cumming v. County Board of Education,* 175 U.S. 528, and *Gong Lum v. Rice,* 275 U.S. 78, the validity of the doctrine itself was not challenged.[8] In more recent cases, all on the graduate school level, inequality was found in that specific benefits enjoyed by white students were denied to Negro students of the same educational qualifications. *Missouri ex rel. Gaines v. Canada,* 305 U.S. 337; *Sipuel v. Oklahoma,* 332 U.S. 631; *Sweatt v. Painter,* 339 U.S. 629; *McLaurin v. Oklahoma State Regents,* 339 U.S. 637. In none of these cases was it necessary to reexamine the doctrine to grant relief to the Negro plaintiff. And in *Sweatt v. Painter, supra,* the Court expressly reserved decision on the question whether *Plessy v. Ferguson* should be held inapplicable to public education.

In the instant cases, that question is directly presented. Here, unlike *Sweatt v. Painter,* there are findings below that the Negro and white schools involved have been equalized, or are being equalized, with respect to buildings, curricula, qualifications and salaries of teachers, and other "tangible" factors.[9] Our decision, therefore, cannot turn on merely a comparison of these tangible factors in the Negro and white schools involved in each of the cases. We must look instead to the effect of segregation itself on public education.

In approaching this problem, we cannot turn the clock back to 1868 when the Amendment was adopted, or even to 1896 when *Plessy v. Ferguson* was written. We must consider public education in the light of its full development and its present place in American life throughout the Nation. Only in this way can it be determined if segregation in public schools deprives these plaintiffs of the equal protection of the laws.

Today education is perhaps the most important function of state and local governments. Compulsory school attendance laws and the great expenditures for education both demonstrate our recognition of the importance of education to our democratic society. It is required in the performance of our most basic public responsibilities, even service in the armed forces.

It is the very foundation of good citizenship. Today it is a principal instrument in awakening the child to cultural values, in preparing him for later professional training, and in helping him to adjust normally to his environment. In these days, it is doubtful that any child may reasonably be expected to succeed in life if he is denied the opportunity of an education. Such an opportunity, where the state has undertaken to provide it, is a right which must be made available to all on equal terms.

We come then to the question presented: Does segregation of children in public schools solely on the basis of race, even though the physical facilities and other "tangible" factors may be equal, deprive the children of the minority group of equal educational opportunities? We believe that it does.

In *Sweatt v. Painter, supra,* in finding that a segregated law school for Negroes could not provide them equal educational opportunities, this Court relied in large part on "those qualities which are incapable of objective measurement but which make for greatness in a law school." In *McLaurin v. Oklahoma State Regents, supra,* the Court, in requiring that a Negro admitted to a white graduate school be treated like all other students, again resorted to intangible considerations: " . . . his ability to study, to engage in discussions and exchange views with other students, and, in general, to learn his profession." Such considerations apply with added force to children in grade and high schools. To separate them from others of similar age and qualifications solely because of their race generates a feeling of inferiority as to their status in the community that may affect their hearts and minds in a way unlikely ever to be undone. The effect of this separation on their educational opportunities was well stated by a finding in the Kansas case by a court which nevertheless felt compelled to rule against the Negro plaintiffs:

> "Segregation of white and colored children in public schools has a detrimental effect upon the colored children. The impact is greater when it has the sanction of the law; for the policy of separating the races is usually interpreted as denoting the inferiority of the negro group. A sense of inferiority affects the motivation of a child to learn. Segregation with the sanction of law, therefore, has a tendency to [retard] the educational and mental development of negro children and to deprive them of some of the benefits they would receive in a racial[ly] integrated school system."[10]

Whatever may have been the extent of psychological knowledge at the time of *Plessy v. Ferguson,* this finding is amply supported by modern authority.[11] Any language in *Plessy v. Ferguson* contrary to this finding is rejected.

We conclude that in the field of public education the doctrine of "separate but equal" has no place. Separate educational facilities are inherently unequal. Therefore, we hold that the plaintiffs and others similarly situated for whom the actions have been brought are, by reason of the segregation complained of, deprived of the equal protection of the laws guaranteed by the Fourteenth Amendment. This disposition makes unnecessary any discussion whether such segregation also violates the Due Process Clause of the Fourteenth Amendment.[12]

Because these are class actions, because of the wide applicability of this decision, and because of the great variety of local conditions, the formulation of decrees in these cases presents problems of considerable complexity. On reargument, the consideration of appropriate relief was necessarily subordinated to the primary question—the constitutionality of segregation in public education. We have now announced that such segregation is a denial of the equal protection of the laws. In order that we may have the full assistance of the parties in formulating decrees, the cases will be restored to the docket, and the parties are requested to present further argument on Questions 4 and 5 previously propounded by the Court for the reargument this Term.[13] The Attorney General of the United States is again invited to participate. The Attorneys General of the states requiring or permitting segregation in public education will also be permitted to appear as *amici curiae* upon request to do so by September 15, 1954, and submission of briefs by October 1, 1954.[14]

It is so ordered.

NOTES

1. In the Kansas case, *Brown v. Board of Education,* the plaintiffs are Negro children of elementary school age residing in Topeka. They brought this action in the United States District Court for the District of Kansas to enjoin enforcement of a Kansas statute which permits, but does not require, cities of more than 15,000 population to maintain separate school facilities for Negro and white students. Kan. Gen. Stat. § 72-1724 (1949). Pursuant to that authority, the Topeka Board of Education elected to establish segregated elementary schools. Other public schools in the community, however, are operated on a nonsegregated basis. . . .

In the South Carolina case, *Briggs v. Elliott,* the plaintiffs are Negro children of both elementary and high school age residing in Clarendon County. They brought this action in the United States District Court for the Eastern District of South Carolina to enjoin enforcement of provisions in the state constitution and statutory code which require the segregation of Negroes and whites in public schools. . . .

In the Virginia case, *Davis v. County School Board,* the plaintiffs are Negro children of high school age residing in Prince Edward County. They brought this action in the United States District Court for the Eastern District of Virginia to enjoin enforcement of provisions in the state constitution and statutory code which require the segregation of Negroes and whites in public schools. . . .

In the Delaware case, *Gebhart v. Belton,* the plaintiffs are Negro children of both elementary and high school age residing in New Castle county. They brought this action in the Delaware Court of Chancery to enjoin enforcement of provisions in the state constitution and statutory code which require the segregation of Negroes and whites in public schools. . . .

2. technical footnote deleted.
3. technical footnote deleted.
4. technical footnote deleted.
5. technical footnote deleted.
6. technical footnote deleted.
7. technical footnote deleted.
8. technical footnote deleted.
9. technical footnote deleted.
10. technical footnote deleted.
11. K. B. Clark, Effect of Prejudice and Discrimination on Personality Development (Midcentury White House Conference on Children and Youth, 1950); Witmer and Kotinsky, Personality in the Making (1952), c. VI; Deutscher and Chein, The Psychological Effects of Enforced Segregation: A Survey of Social Science Opinion, 26 J. Psychol. 259 (1948); Chein, What Are the Psychological Effects of Segregation Under Conditions of Equal Facilities?, 3 Int. J. Opinion and Attitude Res. 229 (1949); Brameld, Educational Costs, in Discrimination and National Welfare (MacIver, ed., 1949), 44–48; Frazier, The Negro in the United States (1949), 674–681. And see generally Myrdal, An American Dilemma (1944).
12. technical footnote deleted.
13. technical footnote deleted.
14. technical footnote deleted.

BLACK AMERICA

The Rough Road to Racial Uplift

CHRISTOPHER H. FOREMAN, JR.

From the beginning, "civil rights" was a misleading term, perhaps an outright misnomer. The moral, legal, and rhetorical pursuit of collective rights of access was but an essential strategy in a multifront war for a much larger prize: the uplift of a people, once mostly enslaved, afterward still widely despised. "Civil rights" could never mean just individual rights, any more than NAACP denoted a National Association for the Advancement of Coherent Principles. Indeed, black leaders and organizations have always known that they must pursue the vast and varied interests of their stigmatized and marginalized constituents by any realistic mechanism available. Rights were more a means than an end. If progress appears to have stalled, it is largely because the successive strategies embraced by the champions of racial uplift have all encountered their practical and political limits. For the most part these strategies have not so much failed as fallen victim to inevitable exhaustion and diminishing returns.

Everyone now recognizes that the strategy of securing basic legal access, pursued during an era of heroic civil

Christopher H. Foreman, Jr., is a senior fellow in the Brookings Governmental Studies Program and the author of The Promise and Peril of Environmental Justice *(Brookings, 1998).*

rights advocacy, has long since run its course. As textbooks today routinely teach, that phase of the struggle began in the courts during the 1930s, shifting trajectory toward Congress a generation later as favorable public opinion, nurtured by a disciplined plea for simple justice and bouts of segregationist violence, made such a turn politically feasible. The basic access argument was simple and therefore potent. Individuals ought not to be proscribed, purely for reasons of color, from plainly quotidian activities available to other citizens: voting for mayor, viewing a movie from a seat of one's choosing, wolfing down a cheeseburger at a dimestore lunch counter. The great majority of white Americans had no particular affection for blacks, but had never felt the need for separate water fountains. Such relatively petty outrages proved hard to defend outside the Deep South. Thankfully, it has now been a long while since even most white southerners would have insisted that, say, Harvard's distinguished Afro-Americanist Henry Louis Gates, Jr., ought not teach at a "white" university.

But the high moral perch afforded by the access agenda always had stringent limits, and they became apparent early. Formal doors to advancement might stand unlocked, perhaps even wide open, but how many black Americans would or could walk through? A Skip Gates might march off to Yale, but how many others would follow, especially

From the *Brookings Review*, Spring 1998, pp. 8-11. © 1998 by The Brookings Institution. Reprinted by permission.

if all the university did was mail out a brochure to Harlem with a road map to New Haven enclosed? Legally desegregated schools and workplaces could not, by themselves, yield diverse student bodies and workforces, much less ensure equal graduation and promotion rates.

Not surprisingly, as far back as the 1960s, the access agenda was giving way to rather less lofty (and still ongoing) haggles over dollars and numbers. Congress could target funds on numerous problems, creating new legal authorities when a favorable combination of support and indifference prevailed. A less openly democratic approach to black uplift lay in the dull machinery of administration, amidst the arcana of government regulations and guidance memoranda, subject to policing by the courts. Merely offering individualized redress for particular claimants according to each specific grievance appeared dreadfully inadequate to the scale of the social challenge—rather like restoring a beach by hauling in one grain of sand at a time. More institutionally aggressive efforts, formal and informal, seemed warranted.

Thus were born goals and timetables, minority contracting set-asides, and the entire regime of both "hard" (formal, mandated, quantitatively monitored) and "soft" (informal, voluntary, improvisational, hortatory) affirmative action. (This writer is a product of that regime. Every professional appointment and educational credential I have held would likely have been unattainable absent the—mostly informal—bestowal of crucial "breaks" tied at least implicitly to my race. For what it's worth, I have felt no attendant stigma. That's because of my own sense that most success in life is a matter of breaks exploited via work—a very American intuition.)

Advocates for black uplift heard a new and disturbing thunder in the distance as far back as the mid-1960s. Early lightning struck as a government report entitled *The Negro Family: The Case for National Action.* Crafted by then-Assistant Secretary of Labor Daniel Patrick Moynihan, the report suggested serious new tears in black America's social fabric that might widen in time. But neither a leadership anchored securely in the safe harbor of its access–affirmative action agenda, nor the increasingly strident voices gathering under the Black Power rubric, were in any mood to hear some Irishman's embarrassing prattle about "Negro family structure," however plainly sympathetic and data-laden. America's social policy researchers have been making up for considerable lost time as a result.

This issue of the *Brookings Review* reflects a sense that on racial matters the American condition is overall dramatically improved, but far more complicated than it used to seem, and in important respects continually depressing. A significant black middle class has emerged (and not solely through affirmative action). White racial attitudes are astonishingly transformed from where they stood during Franklin Roosevelt's presidency, when lynching blacks was still an informally listed entree on the menu of southern civic entertainments.

Yet some devilishly tenacious ills remain, for which neither access nor affirmative action is satisfactory medicine: low skills and abysmal test scores among minority youngsters; opportunity-sapping teenage pregnancies; the vastly disproportionate involvement of black males with the criminal justice system; the lure of drug money and addiction among the black underclass. A foray into the Brookings library recently yielded a new issue of the *Journal of Human Resources,* in which Howard S. Bloom and several collaborators assess the Job Training and Partnership Act's income effects for adults and out-of-school youths. Since I had not seen the results of the National JTPA Study trumpeted across the front page of the *Washington Post,* I should have known what was coming. Still, I winced at what I read (emphasis below added):

> Findings from the National JTPA Study parallel those from the few other studies of employment and training programs that have employed experimental designs. The *modest positive impacts* on earnings experienced by adult women . . . are consistent with the impacts observed by previous randomized studies of work-welfare programs. . . . The *modest positive impacts* experienced by adult men . . . are consistent with the impacts observed for men by the several existing randomized studies of programs for displaced workers. . . .
>
> For out-of-school youths, there is a *disturbingly consistent lack of program earnings gains across several major studies.* . . .
>
> For adults, we still do not know what works best for whom. . . . For out-of-school youths, we are at a more primitive stage in our understanding of how to increase labor market success; we *have not found any* way to do so. . . .

But it will not help to seek refuge in comfortable fictions. The genuine racism that lingers in white America is not a primary cause of these difficulties, and the view that "nothing has fundamentally changed" on America s racial landscape is insupportable. In their book *America in Black and White,* Abigail and Stephan Thernstrom opine that such a "flat-Earth view of white attitudes" can only be held by those who believe that social science evidence is worthless."

Actually, as even they realize, that is too simple an explanation for overreliance on the rhetorical hammer of "racism." For many African Americans, "racism" is simply an intuitively appealing way to make sense of a complicated and disturbing social and economic milieu. Resort to "racism" (which takes its most extreme form as belief in anti-black conspiracies) is fundamentally symptomatic of a deeply frustrated popular groping for answers to questions triggered, ironically, by the vanquishing of the old racial order and by the failure of rising tides to lift all ships and wash away all problems. Indeed, the burial of Jim Crow was followed by social challenges that scarcely seemed to exist when it was alive. This may help persuade some African Americans that a malicious chicanery must be afoot.

For activists and the intelligentsia, "racism" offers obvious political leverage for claiming the moral high ground and sustaining pressure for social change. Trouble is, there is just enough real racism left to render "racism" both a plausible explanation to the black masses and a convenient advocacy fulcrum for black elites.

African-American leadership may be frustrated, but it is not stupid. Its members doubtless appreciate that the current malaise afflicting poor blacks is largely a concomitant of forces like middle-class residential and educational choices and broader economic developments. (When Jim Crow flourished, it was far more commonly possible for a man with no education beyond the primary grades to feed a family.) One also detects, especially among black clergy, a grim awareness that personal and collective values, not just skill acquisition, are essential to strong communities and enhanced life chances. But the leadership game also dictates that one play with the cards available, and the "race card" can be hard to resist, even when inappropriate. Just ask New York City's indefatigable Al Sharpton.

> **Possibly the most insidious effect of the affirmative action furor is to shift precious time in the national spotlight away from our low-income black citizens whose long-term fates merit the hardest thinking of all.**

We need hard and courageous thinking about the complex array of troubles that plague the black community and the nation, but we do not suffer for lack of chatter about race. Any careful empirical study of the attention accorded race in both the electronic and print media would surely find impressive amounts of race-related news, as well as opinion reflecting every conceivable viewpoint. We may not always be completely forthright with one another, but the subject is never very far off any sentient citizen's radar screen. As Donald Horowitz recently remarked, Americans today may be enduring a serious case of "race fatigue."

We *do* lack both crucial knowledge (about how to produce various positive policy effects) and the political consensus essential to making available dramatically increased resources for ambitious policy initiatives. It is unclear that franker interracial talk, however desirable, will spur much change on either front. If anyone can lead a probing national seminar on race, surely that person is President Clinton. But even he is all too aware that presidents are most likely to spark successful conversations when "success" has a narrow and precise meaning—such as adoption of a Civil Rights Act or a Strategic Defense Initiative.

Affirmative action certainly warrants hard thinking, though enduring disagreement on that front appears inescapable. Our collective attachment to the notion of meritocracy, of individually earned rewards, runs deep. The ideals of colorblindness and racial diversity remain hard to reconcile, at least for the present. As Harvard Law Professor Christopher Edley argues in a recent volume, the subject is far more complex than simple slogans allow. Unfortunately, that is true even of the slogan coined by Edley's former boss, President Clinton: "mend it, don't end it." As a nation we are not going to dispense with affirmative action entirely. Nor do we wish to. Aggressive outreach and job training targeted at African Americans stir controversy mainly by falling short of their announced goals. And corporate America is reasonably content with the status quo, as the Reagan administration quickly discovered.

But some varieties of affirmative action (such as race-normed tests and further breaks for the already conspicuously advantaged) have proved difficult to defend. One specific approach in need of mending is any academic admissions process that displaces deserving white candidates to make room for minorities with weaker credentials who cannot or do not complete the program to which they've been admitted. As an affront to both efficiency and justice, failures of this sort ought to concern conservatives and liberals alike. To the degree that a policy slips toward all cost and no benefit, it would appear perverse by definition. Moreover, the Clinton administration's mantra that "quotas are illegal" may be disingenuous if de facto quotas (which afford the advantage of hard targets to aim for) operate in place of legal ones.

But how common are such defects in the affirmative action universe? More common, one suspects, are efforts that regularly spawn both successes and failures, and where a quota smear won't easily stick. The obvious example of a Colin Powell, who redeems whatever jumpstart he may have enjoyed through distinguished performance, is bound to give even some affirmative action critics a moment's hesitation. That's clearly why President Clinton tried to squeeze Abigail Thernstrom with the Powell example during a televised town hall meeting on race last December.

Possibly the most insidious effect of the affirmative action furor is to shift precious time in the national spotlight away from our low-income black citizens, whose long-term fates merit the hardest thinking of all. Affirmative action, a boon to middle-class blacks like me, promises little help on that front. Nor does the continuing university-based mudwrestle over multiculturalism. The symposium in this issue of the *Brookings Review* concentrates specifically on what might be called "the black predicament." This represents another conscious editorial choice, grounded in the conviction that the great social question of the new millennium is less likely to be "can we all get along?" than "can we all get ahead?"

BLACK PROGRESS

HOW FAR WE'VE COME—

AND HOW FAR WE HAVE TO GO

**ABIGAIL THERNSTROM
AND STEPHAN THERNSTROM**

Let's start with a few contrasting numbers.

60 and 2.2. In 1940, 60 percent of employed black women worked as domestic servants; today the number is down to 2.2 percent, while 60 percent hold white-collar jobs.

44 and 1. In 1958, 44 percent of whites said they would move if a black family became their next door neighbor; today the figure is 1 percent.

18 and 86. In 1964, the year the great Civil Rights Act was passed, only 18 percent of whites claimed to have a friend who was black; today 86 percent say they do, while 87 percent of blacks assert they have white friends.

Progress is the largely suppressed story of race and race relations over the past half-century. And thus it's news that more than 40 percent of African Americans now consider themselves members of the middle class. Forty-two percent own their own homes, a figure that rises to 75 percent if we look just at black married couples. Black two-parent families earn only 13 percent less than those who are white. Almost a third of the black population lives in suburbia.

Because these are facts the media seldom report, the black underclass continues to define black America in the view of much of the public. Many assume blacks live in ghettos, often in high-rise public housing projects. Crime

Abigail Thernstrom is a senior fellow at the Manhattan Institute in New York; Stephan Thernstrom is the Winthrop Professor of History at Harvard University. They are co-authors of America in Black and White: One Nation, Indivisible *(Simon and Schuster, 1997), from which this article is adapted.*

and the welfare check are seen as their main source of income. The stereotype crosses racial lines. Blacks are even more prone than whites to exaggerate the extent to which African Americans are trapped in inner-city poverty. In a 1991 Gallup poll, about one-fifth of all whites, but almost half of black respondents, said that at least three out of four African Americans were impoverished urban residents. And yet, in reality, blacks who consider themselves to be middle class outnumber those with incomes below the poverty line by a wide margin.

A FIFTY-YEAR MARCH OUT OF POVERTY

Fifty years ago most blacks were indeed trapped in poverty, although they did not reside in inner cities. When Gunnar Myrdal published *An American Dilemma* in 1944, most blacks lived in the South and on the land as laborers and sharecroppers. (Only one in eight owned the land on which he worked.) A trivial 5 percent of black men nationally were engaged in nonmanual, white-collar work of any kind; the vast majority held ill-paid, insecure, manual jobs—jobs that few whites would take. As already noted, six out of ten African-American women were household servants who, driven by economic desperation, often worked 12-hour days for pathetically low wages. Segregation in the South and discrimination in the North did create a sheltered market for some black businesses (funeral homes, beauty parlors, and the like) that served a black community barred from patronizing "white" establishments. But the number was minuscule.

Beginning in the 1940s, however, deep demographic and economic change, accompanied by a marked shift in white racial attitudes, started blacks down the road to much greater equality. New Deal legislation, which set minimum wages and hours and eliminated the incentive of southern employers to hire low-wage black workers, put a damper on further industrial development in the region. In addition, the trend toward mechanized agriculture and a diminished demand for American cotton in the face of international competition combined to displace blacks from the land.

As a consequence, with the shortage of workers in northern manufacturing plants following the outbreak of World War II, southern blacks in search of jobs boarded trains and buses in a Great Migration that lasted through the mid-1960s. They found what they were looking for: wages so strikingly high that in 1953 the average income for a black family in the North was almost twice that of those who remained in the South. And through much of the 1950s wages rose steadily and unemployment was low.

Thus by 1960 only one out of seven black men still labored on the land, and almost a quarter were in white-collar or skilled manual occupations. Another 24 percent had semiskilled factory jobs that meant membership in the stable working class, while the proportion of black women working as servants had been cut in half. Even those who did not move up into higher-ranking jobs were doing much better.

A decade later, the gains were even more striking. From 1940 to 1970, black men cut the income gap by about a third, and by 1970 they were earning (on average) roughly 60 percent of what white men took in. The advancement of black women was even more impressive. Black life expectancy went up dramatically, as did black homeownership rates. Black college enrollment also rose—by 1970 to about 10 percent of the total, three times the prewar figure.

In subsequent years these trends continued, although at a more leisurely pace. For instance, today more than 30 percent of black men and nearly 60 percent of black women hold white-collar jobs. Whereas in 1970 only 2.2 percent of American physicians were black, the figure is now 4.5 percent. But while the fraction of black families with middle-class incomes rose almost 40 percentage points between 1940 and 1970, it has inched up only another 10 points since then.

AFFIRMATIVE ACTION DOESN'T WORK

Rapid change in the status of blacks for several decades followed by a definite slowdown that begins just when affirmative action policies get their start: that story certainly seems to suggest that racial preferences have enjoyed an inflated reputation. "There's one simple reason to support affirmative action," an op-ed writer in the New York Times argued in 1995. "It works." That is the voice of conventional wisdom.

In fact, not only did significant advances pre-date the affirmative action era, but the benefits of race-conscious politics are not clear. Important differences (a slower overall rate of economic growth, most notably) separate the pre-1970 and post-1970 periods, making comparison difficult.

We know only this: some gains are probably attributable to race-conscious educational and employment policies. The number of black college and university professors more than doubled between 1970 and 1990; the number of physicians tripled; the number of engineers almost quadrupled; and the number of attorneys increased more than sixfold. Those numbers undoubtedly do reflect the fact that the nation's professional schools changed their admissions criteria for black applicants, accepting and often providing financial aid to African-American students whose academic records were much weaker than those of many white and Asian-American applicants whom these schools were turning down. Preferences "worked" for these beneficiaries, in that they were given seats in the classroom that they would not have won in the absence of racial double standards.

On the other hand, these professionals make up a small fraction of the total black middle class. And their numbers would have grown without preferences, the historical record strongly suggests. In addition, the greatest economic gains for African Americans since the early 1960s were in the years 1965 to 1975 and occurred mainly in the South, as economists John J. Donahue III and James Heckman have found. In fact, Donahue and Heckman discovered "virtually no improvement" in the wages of black men relative to those of white men outside of the South over the entire period from 1963 to 1987, and southern gains, they concluded, were mainly due to the powerful antidiscrimination provisions in the 1964 Civil Rights Act.

With respect to federal, state, and municipal set-asides, as well, the jury is still out. In 1994 the state of Maryland decided that at least 10 percent of the contracts it awarded would go to minority- and female-owned firms. It more than met its goal. The program therefore "worked" if the goal was merely the narrow one of dispensing cash to a particular, designated group. But how well do these sheltered businesses survive long-term without extraordinary protection from free-market competition? And with almost

30 percent of black families still living in poverty, what is their trickle-down effect? On neither score is the picture reassuring. Programs are often fraudulent, with white contractors offering minority firms 15 percent of the profit with no obligation to do any of the work. Alternatively, set-asides enrich those with the right connections. In Richmond, Virginia, for instance, the main effect of the ordinance was a marriage of political convenience—a working alliance between the economically privileged of both races. The white business elite signed on to a piece-of-the-pie for blacks in order to polish its image as socially conscious and secure support for the downtown revitalization it wanted. Black politicians used the bargain to suggest their own importance to low-income constituents for whom the set-asides actually did little. Neither cared whether the policy in fact provided real economic benefits—which it didn't.

While blacks and whites now graduate at the same rate from high school today and are almost equally likely to attend college, on average they are not equally educated.

WHY HAS THE ENGINE OF PROGRESS STALLED?

In the decades since affirmative action policies were first instituted, the poverty rate has remained basically unchanged. Despite black gains by numerous other measures, close to 30 percent of black families still live below the poverty line. "There are those who say, my fellow Americans, that even good affirmative action programs are no longer needed," President Clinton said in July 1995. But "let us consider," he went on, that "the unemployment rate for African Americans remains about twice that of whites." Racial preferences are the president's answer to persistent inequality, although a quarter-century of affirmative action has done nothing whatever to close the unemployment gap.

Persistent inequality is obviously serious, and if discrimination were the primary problem, then race-conscious remedies might be appropriate. But while white racism was central to the story in 1964, today the picture is much more complicated. Thus while blacks and whites now graduate at the same rate from high school today and are almost equally likely to attend college, on average they are not equally educated. That is, looking at years of schooling in assessing the racial gap in family income tells us little about the cognitive skills whites and blacks bring to the job market. And cognitive skills obviously affect earnings.

The National Assessment of Educational Progress (NAEP) is the nation's report card on what American students attending elementary and secondary schools know. Those tests show that African-American students, on av-

erage, are alarmingly far behind whites in math, science, reading, and writing. For instance, black students at the end of their high school career are almost four years behind white students in reading; the gap is comparable in other subjects. A study of 26- to 33-year-old men who held full-time jobs in 1991 thus found that when education was measured by years of school completed, blacks earned 19 percent less than comparably educated whites. But when word knowledge, paragraph comprehension, arithmetical reasoning, and mathematical knowledge became the yardstick, the results were reversed. Black men earned 9 percent more than white men with the same education—that is, the same performance on basic tests.

Other research suggests much the same point. For instance, the work of economists Richard J. Murnane and Frank Levy has demonstrated the increasing importance of cognitive skills in our changing economy. Employers in firms like Honda now require employees who can read and do math problems at the ninth-grade level at a minimum. And yet the 1992 NAEP math tests, for example, revealed that only 22 percent of African-American high school seniors but 58 percent of their white classmates were numerate enough for such firms to consider hiring them. And in reading, 47 percent of whites in 1992 but just 18 percent of African Americans could handle the printed word well enough to be employable in a modern automobile plant. Murnane and Levy found a clear impact on income. Not years spent in school but strong skills made for high long-term earnings.

THE WIDENING SKILLS GAP

Why is there such a glaring racial gap in levels of educational attainment? It is not easy to say. The gap, in itself, is very bad news, but even more alarming is the fact that it has been widening in recent years. In 1971, the average African-American 17-year-old could read no better than the typical white child who was six years younger. The racial gap in math in 1973 was 4.3 years; in science it was 4.7 years in 1970. By the late 1980s, however, the picture was notably brighter. Black students in their final year of high school were only 2.5 years behind whites in both reading and math and 2.1 years behind on tests of writing skills.

Had the trends of those years continued, by today black pupils would be performing about as well as their white classmates. Instead, black progress came to a halt, and serious backsliding began. Between 1988 and 1994, the racial gap in reading grew from 2.5 to 3.9 years; between 1990 and 1994, the racial gap in math increased from 2.5 to 3.4 years. In both science and writing, the racial gap has widened by a full year.

There is no obvious explanation for this alarming turnaround. The early gains doubtless had much to do with the growth of the black middle class, but the black middle class did not suddenly begin to shrink in the late 1980s. The poverty rate was not dropping significantly when educational progress was occurring, nor was it on the increase when the racial gap began once again to widen. The huge rise in out-of-wedlock births and the steep and steady decline in the proportion of black children growing up with two parents do not explain the fluctuating educational performance of African-American children. It is well established that children raised in single-parent families do less well in school than others, even when all other variables, including income, are controlled. But the disintegration of the black nuclear family—presciently noted by Daniel Patrick Moynihan as early as 1965—was occurring rapidly in the period in which black scores were rising,

> If all our efforts as a nation to resolve the "American dilemma" have been in vain— if we've been spinning our wheels in the rut of ubiquitous and permanent racism, as Derrick Bell, Andrew Hacker, and others argue—then racial equality is a hopeless task, an unattainable ideal.

so it cannot be invoked as the main explanation as to why scores began to fall many years later.

Some would argue that the initial educational gains were the result of increased racial integration and the growth of such federal compensatory education programs as Head Start. But neither desegregation nor compensatory education seems to have increased the cognitive skills of the black children exposed to them. In any case, the racial mix in the typical school has not changed in recent years, and the number of students in compensatory programs and the dollars spent on them have kept going up.

What about changes in the curriculum and patterns of course selection by students? The educational reform movement that began in the late 1970s did succeed in pushing students into a "New Basics" core curriculum that included more English, science, math, and social studies courses. And there is good reason to believe that taking tougher courses contributed to the temporary rise in black test scores. But this explanation, too, nicely fits the facts for the period before the late 1980s but not the very different picture thereafter. The number of black students going through "New Basics" courses did not decline after 1988, pulling down their NAEP scores.

We are left with three tentative suggestions. First, the increased violence and disorder of inner-city lives that came with the introduction of crack cocaine and the drug-related gang wars in the mid-1980s most likely had something to do with the reversal of black educational progress. Chaos in the streets and within schools affects learning inside and outside the classroom.

In addition, an educational culture that has increasingly turned teachers into guides who help children explore whatever interests them may have affected black academic performance as well. As educational critic E. D. Hirsch, Jr., has pointed out, the "deep aversion to and contempt for factual knowledge that pervade the thinking of American educators" means that students fail to build the "intellectual capital" that is the foundation of all further learning. That will be particularly true of those students who come to school most academically disadvantaged—those whose homes are not, in effect, an additional school. The deficiencies of American education hit hardest those most in need of education.

And yet in the name of racial sensitivity, advocates for minority students too often dismiss both common academic standards and standardized tests as culturally biased and judgmental. Such advocates have plenty of company. Christopher Edley, Jr., professor of law at Harvard and President Clinton's point man on affirmative action, for instance, has allied himself with testing critics, labeling preferences the tool colleges are forced to use "to correct the problems we"ve inflicted on ourselves with our testing standards." Such tests can be abolished—or standards lowered—but once the disparity in cognitive skills becomes less evident, it is harder to correct.

Closing that skills gap is obviously the first task if black advancement is to continue at its once-fast pace. On the map of racial progress, education is the name of almost every road. Raise the level of black educational performance, and the gap in college graduation rates, in attendance at selective professional schools, and in earnings is likely to close as well. Moreover, with educational parity, the whole issue of racial preferences disappears.

THE ROAD TO TRUE EQUALITY

Black progress over the past half-century has been impressive, conventional wisdom to the contrary notwithstanding. And yet the nation has many miles to go on the road to true racial equality. "I wish I could say that racism and prejudice were only distant memories, but as I look around I see that even educated whites and African Americans . . . have lost hope in equality," Thurgood Marshall said in 1992. A year earlier *The Economist* magazine had reported the problem of race as one of "shattered dreams." In fact, all hope has not been "lost," and "shattered" was much too strong a word, but certainly in the 1960s the civil rights community failed to anticipate just how tough the voyage would be. (Thurgood Marshall had envisioned an end to all school segregation within five years of the Supreme Court s decision in *Brown v. Board of Education.*) Many blacks, particularly, are now discouraged. A 1997 Gallup poll found a sharp decline in optimism since 1980; only 33 percent of blacks (versus 58 percent of whites) thought both the quality of life for blacks and race relations had gotten better.

Thus, progress—by many measures seemingly so clear—is viewed as an illusion, the sort of fantasy to which intellectuals are particularly prone. But the ahistorical sense of nothing gained is in itself bad news. Pessimism is a self-fulfilling prophecy. If all our efforts as a nation to resolve the "American dilemma" have been in vain—if we've been spinning our wheels in the rut of ubiquitous and permanent racism, as Derrick Bell, Andrew Hacker, and others argue—then racial equality is a hopeless task, an unattainable ideal. If both blacks and whites understand and celebrate the gains of the past, however, we will move forward with the optimism, insight, and energy that further progress surely demands.

Unit Selections

7. **Migrations to the Thirteen British North American Colonies, 1770–1775: New Estimates,** Aaron Fogleman
8. **The New Immigrants,** Charles S. Clark
9. **U.S. Immigration,** Rodger Doyle
10. **Newcomers and Established Residents,** Robert L. Bach

Key Points to Consider

❖ The U.S. Census reports the number of foreign-born and American-born persons and the ethnicity and/or ancestry of persons. What differentiates these various methods and categories?

❖ In what respects are historical accounts of America's immigration tradition relevant to contemporary immigration issues and policies?

❖ On December 10, 1996, the Mexican government passed a law to allow dual citizenship to persons living in the U.S. What does this policy portend for the relationship between Mexico and the United States? Should statehood for northern Mexico become an option? At present, is this law of citizenship a threat to or an opportunity for ethnic group relations?

❖ Why do periods of economic crisis appear to exacerbate tensions and strain relations among ethnic groups?

❖ The clustering of ethnic populations in various regions of America has produced patterns that are worth pondering. Discuss the importance of locality to understanding American ethnicities. Do you think that the immigration question is really a local issue, and not a national concern? Why or why not?

❖ In what respect do immigrants influence U.S. foreign policy toward the countries from which they and/or their ancestors came?

❖ What remedies for language diversity are acceptable in a democratic society? Is English becoming the world's second language?

 **Links**   **www.dushkin.com/online/**

8. **Child Welfare League of America (CWLA)**
   http://www.cwla.org
9. **National Immigrant Forum**
   http://www.immigrationforum.org
10. **The National Network for Immigrant and Refugee Rights (NNIRR)**
    http://www.nnirr.org
11. **U.S. Immigration and Naturalization Service (INS)**
    http://www.ins.usdoj.gov

These sites are annotated on pages 4 and 5.

The history of immigration and ethnic group diversity is embedded in the history of America from earliest times. Recent archaeological discoveries have considerably extended the time and process of peopling this continent. These social historical facts have often been ignored or forgotten in contemporary debates about our tradition of being an immigrant-receiving continent.

From the 1850s to the 1870s immigrants from Britain and northern Europe settled in America. To these European and perhaps to some Asian immigrants in the American West, America represented freedom to enter the economic struggle without constraints of state- and status-bound societies whose limits could not be overcome except through emigration. Yet this historical pathway to liberty, justice, and opportunity came to be perceived as a "tarnished door" when the deep impulses of exclusion and exclusivity came to the fore. The victims were aliens who, ironically, achieved the American promise but were denied the reward of acceptance and incorporation into the very culture they helped to fashion. The following articles describe the immigrant experience and raise once again the issues that every large-scale multiethnic regime must address: How can unity and diversity be channeled into political, economic, and cultural well-being? What are the legitimate limits and strengths of ethnic groups in the expression of policy regarding countries toward which some affinity may be attributed?

The history of immigration law does not champion American ethnic groups. Immigration laws include the Chinese Exclusion Acts of the 1880s, the National Origins Quota System of the 1920s, the Mexican Repatriation Campaign of the 1950s, and the McCarran-Walter Act in 1952. A new era began with the inclusiveness of the mid–1960s. The findings of the 1990 U.S. Census point to a range of demographic, economic, and social indicators in this most recent era of immigration in the United States. Both the immediate impact of present-day newcomers and the changes in America that can be attributed to the conflicts and contributions of previous immigrants appear to be facets of nearly every contemporary social issue.

The U.S. Census documents the consequences of decades and generations of immigration. It enables us to discern the spectrum of American ethnicities and the regional patterns of ethnic settlement. The stories of new immigrants are aspects of a worldwide drama. The European and American contexts discussed in this unit provide perspectives on immigrant adjustment and their reception in various regimes and cultures. The ongoing issue of cultural formation through language and the political artifices used to heighten or diminish ethnicity as a political factor are explored. The movement of people induces change and growth that poses great potential for well-being and economic development. Nevertheless, the influx of persons and cultures requires awareness of our cultural diversity and common humanity as well as energy, mutual openness to talent, and participation of all in the experience of being and becoming Americans.

Full employment and social-economic mobility in countries from which persons are coming to the United States would decrease incentives for migration. Political and religious freedom in other countries would negate another cause for the movement of people from oppressive regimes to democratic and liberal societies.

As the unit articles make clear, immigration not only has an impact on the receiving country but also affects nations that lose the talents, skills, and loyalty of disaffected migrants. Immigration, moreover, contributes to an already complex process of intergenerational relationships and the socialization of persons whose experiences of profound cultural change are intensified by competition, patterns of settlement, options for mobility, and the consciousness of ethnic traditions that conflict with dominant cultural and educational institutions.

Michael Piore's assessment of children born to immigrant workers suggests an interesting lens through which the following articles may be read. Dr. Piore writes:

> There is nothing in the immigration process that ensures that this second generation will be able to move up to the higher level jobs toward which they aspire. Indeed, historically industrial societies appear consistently to disappoint the expectations of the second generation in this regard. That disappointment has in turn been the source of enormous social tension. The sit-down strikes in the late thirties which sparked the industrial unions movement in the United States may in large measure be attributed to the reaction of the children of pre–World War I European immigrants to their labor market conditions. Similarly, the racial disturbances in Northern urban ghettos in the middle and late 1960s may be looked upon as a revolt of the black migrants against a society bent upon confining them to their parents' jobs.

As a guide for your own study, the U.S. Commission on Civil Rights has noted that increased immigration raises the following issues for both recent arrivals and Americans by birth:

Employment: The areas of occupation selected by or imposed upon various ethnic populations trace ethnic group mobility strategies and ethnic succession in the workplace, especially in manufacturing, hospitals, restaurants, and maintenance and custodial positions. Some ethnic populations appear to have greater numbers of highly educated persons in professional or semiprofessional positions.

Institutional and societal barriers: The job preferences and discrimination against the ethnic enclaves and persons in small communities that are isolated from mainstream English-speaking society suggest the value of second-language competencies. Mutual accommodation is required to minimize the effect of inadequate language skills and training and difficulties in obtaining licenses, memberships, and certification.

Exploitation of workers: The most common form is the payment of wages below minimum standards. Alien workers have been stereotyped as a drain on public services. Such scapegoating is insupportable.

Taking jobs from Americans: Fact or fiction?: The stunning fact is that immigrants are a source of increased productivity and a significant, if not utterly necessary, addition to the workforce as well as to the consumer power that drives the American economy.

Immigration and the American Experience

Migrations to the Thirteen British North American Colonies, 1700–1775: New Estimates

Aaron Fogleman

Mainstream historians have finally begun to study the long-neglected, yet extremely important topic of eighteenth-century immigration. Bailyn and DeWolfe's study, *Voyagers to the West*, and other monographs and articles on this subject appeared with increasing frequency during the 1980s.[1] Accurate statistics for immigration during the eighteenth century as a whole are lacking, however, and this gap has forced historians to rely on approximations which are sometimes sketchy and do not reveal much about the varied and complex nature of immigration during that century.

Although it is difficult to compile immigration statistics for the eighteenth century, it is still possible to update the work of previous historians, and for many reasons it is important to do so. With better information on immigration available, historians can compare the relative effects of immigration and natural increase in causing the phenomenal population growth of the colonies in the eighteenth century and of the United States during the early national period. Also, if one simply wants to know approximately how many people of each ethnic or racial group arrived and helped to shape early American society, a single reference with this information would be valuable. In this article, I review some recent estimates of eighteenth-century immigration, showing their accomplishments and problems, and then present an alternative method which corroborates some earlier estimates and provides more information for reference purposes than was heretofore available.

It is impossible to establish definitively the volume of eighteenth-century immigration to America. The only records kept over a long period of time for any ethnic group are the ship lists maintained in Philadelphia for German-speaking passengers arriving from 1727 to 1808.[2] Still, there is enough demographic and other data available for eighteenth-century America to allow historians cautiously to estimate the levels of immigration (and other demographic measures)—not crude, "ballpark" guesses, but cautious estimates which can illuminate a great deal about life in early America. Historians will continually correct and hopefully improve these estimates as they rework old data, discover new data, and develop new methods. But what we have now is suggestive.

Whereas in the past historians relied on rough guesses of the levels of eighteenth-century immigration, they have recently begun to use sophisticated residual methods which may be more accurate. Twenty-five years ago, Potter estimated that 350,000 whites immigrated from 1700 to 1790—an estimate which was, in his own words, "little more than a shot in the dark." About ten years later, Henretta concluded that "nearly 400,000" whites arrived between 1700 and 1775. Higham suggested that about 450,000 came in the eighteenth century, over half of whom were Irish. More recently, Fogel and several of his colleagues used a simulation model of generational progression and an estimated set of mortality, net reproduction, and gross reproduction rates to measure net migration as a residual, concluding that 822,000 more whites arrived in the colony-states from 1607 to 1790 than migrated out of this region. For the period 1700 to 1790 their figure was 663,000 whites. Yet in 1981 Galenson, using a different residual method, in which he took into account the high mortality of immigrants shortly af-

Aaron Fogleman is Assistant Professor of History at the University of South Alabama.

The author thanks John Shy, Kenneth Lockridge, and Rosalind Remer for their helpful comments on this article.

1. See Bernard Bailyn, with the assistance of Barbara DeWolfe, *Voyagers to the West: A Passage in the Peopling of America on the Eve of the Revolution* (New York, 1986). This book, along with Bailyn's companion volume, *The Peopling of British North America: An Introduction* (New York, 1986), provide important bibliographic material on the subject.

2. The most comprehensive and best-edited publication of these lists is Ralph B. Strassburger and William J. Hinke (eds.), *Pennsylvania German Pioneers. A Publication of the Original Lists of Arrivals in the Port of Philadelphia from 1727–1808,* (Norristown, Pa., 1934), 3 v. They list all males sixteen years and older (and some women and children) well enough to disembark upon arrival and sign oaths of loyalty to the British king. Because the large majority of Germans landed in Philadelphia after 1726, these lists are the starting point for any estimation of German immigration into all ports during the colonial period.

From *Journal of Interdisciplinary History*, Spring 1992, pp. 691-709. © 1992 by the Massachusetts Institute of Technology and the editors of *The Journal of Interdisciplinary History*. Reprinted by permission.

than migrated out of this region. For the period 1700 to 1790 their figure was 663,000 whites. Yet in 1981 Galenson, using a different residual method, in which he took into account the high mortality of immigrants shortly after their arrival, as they adjusted to the new disease environment, concluded that a net migration of 435,694 whites and 220,839 blacks took place between 1650 and 1780, and that 346,099 whites and 196,411 blacks arrived from 1700 to 1780, a figure close to Potter's.[3]

Still more recently, Gemery has provided the best summation of all these estimates, as well as many older ones, and pointed out some problems with their sources and methodologies. Given the scarcity of appropriate statistics for the eighteenth century, it is not surprising that the range for net migration calculated by the previously mentioned historians is fairly substantial—from 350,000 to 663,000 for 1700 to 1790. Realizing that estimates of early mortality and fertility rates were tenuous at best, Gemery opted to present a set of plausible immigration estimates from 1700 to 1820, rather than making a single estimate. Using a scale of annual rates of natural increase based on various estimates by historians measuring fertility and mortality, along with his own estimates for mortality during the overseas passage and the period of adjustment by migrants thereafter, Gemery concludes that the "New England pattern" was the most favorable for demographic growth and all other regions were moving in that direction during the eighteenth century. He calculates net migration as a residual, with the results being a plausible range of 765,000 to 1,300,000 white immigrants for the period 1700 to 1820 and a more precise one of 278,400 to 485,300 for the period 1700 to 1780. Allowing for the fact that this estimate does not cover the decade 1780 to 1790, his range runs only somewhat below that established by previous estimates. Gemery understands the difficulties in measuring and generalizing from mortality and fertility rates in early America. He concludes his article with a call for more research—more precise demographic data—so that the range of migration estimates can be narrowed.[4]

This note suggests an alternative method for measuring eighteenth-century migration—one that avoids the impasse created by relying too heavily on fertility and mortality rates, which are difficult to establish for the colonial period. My method is also somewhat simpler, yet corroborates the results of residual methods, especially Gemery's, while yielding more detailed information. The method relies on three sources of information for estimating the volume and timing of eighteenth-century immigration, all of which yield strong estimates for some ethnic groups and time periods, and somewhat weaker estimates for others. The first source is the work of ethnic-group historians who have produced plausible estimates of immigration for their respective groups. The second source (most important for the British and Irish immigration) is the more qualitative aspects of the ethnic-group historians' work on the timing, flow, and general conditions of the various migrations. The last source is an improved surname analysis of the first federal census in 1790, which, when used in conjunction with the above two sources, allows one to infer what the levels of migration may have been in previous decades, producing what Gemery calls "quasi-numbers."

The first source produces the strongest estimates. Ethnic-group historians have used information on ship departures and arrivals, as well as samples of how many immigrants could be carried by different kinds of ships, to arrive at reasonable estimates of total immigration of Germans, northern and southern Irish, Scots, African slaves, and others. Grouping the best of these estimates by decade and ethnic group into an estimate of overall immigration in the eighteenth century conveys a clear sense of how immigration varied over time and between ethnic groups, something other estimates have not done.

In the past, relying heavily on the estimates of ethnic-group historians would have been a risky enterprise. However, the recent trend among historians has been to lower the estimates of their perhaps more filiopietistic predecessors. Since Dunaway's calculation of at least 250,000 Scots-Irish immigrants in the eighteenth century, Leyburn estimated 200,000 from 1717 to 1775. Still later, Dickson found approximately 109,000 to 129,000 for the years 1718 to 1775. And very recently, Wokeck has found even Dickson's estimates to be too high. For Germans, older estimates of 200,000 to North America before 1800 by both Mönckmeier, along with 225,000 to 250,000 before 1770 by Clarence Ver Steeg, have been revised downward by Fenske (125,000 for the entire century) and Wokeck (about 100,000 in the years 1683 to 1776). Butler has drastically revised the immigration estimates for French Huguenots by Higonnet from 14,000 to about 1,500 (or at most 2,000)—all before 1700. On the other hand, Bailyn and DeWolfe conclude that 100,000 to 150,000 Scots-Irish came before 1760 and over 55,000 Protestant Irish arrived from 1760 to 1775. Furthermore, they raise Graham's estimate for Scots from less than 25,000 for 1763–1775 to approximately 40,000 for 1760–1775. And Doyle has recently emphasized that there was a large southern Irish immigration into the colonies, which Dickson may have overlooked. Extreme accuracy will never be possible, given the nature of eighteenth-century statistics, but given such re-

3. See James Potter, "The Growth of Population in America, 1700–1860," in David V. Glass and D.E.C. Eversley (eds.), *Population in History: Essays in Historical Demography* (London, 1965), 645; James A. Henretta, *The Evolution of American Society, 1700–1815: An Interdisciplinary Analysis* (Lexington, Mass., 1973), 11; John Higham, *Send These to Me. Immigrants in Urban America* (Baltimore, 1984; rev. ed.), 18; Robert W. Fogel et al., "The Economics of Mortality in North America, 1650–1910: A Description of a Research Project," *Historical Methods*, XI (1978), 100; David W. Galenson, *White Servitude in Colonial America: An Economic Analysis* (Cambridge, 1981), 212–218.
4. Henry A. Gemery, "European Immigration to North America, 1700–1820: Numbers and Quasi-Numbers," *Perspectives in American History*, I (1984), 318, 320.

cent work, we can make significantly better estimates of the volume of immigration of some ethnic groups than was previously possible.[5]

The second source of information for this method, the discussions by the ethnic-group historians of the more qualitative aspects of migration, helps give one a sense of when peaks and valleys in immigration occurred, even when no actual data on volume are available. Population pressure, famine, unemployment, rack-renting (the doubling or tripling of rents after the expiration of long-term leases in order to accelerate the removal of tenants from the land), and active recruitment by colonials were major causes of the British and Irish emigration to the colonies. Extended discussions of these developments throughout the eighteenth century give a rough indication of how the total estimated immigration for each group should be distributed over the decades.

The third source of information, Purvis' recent surname analysis of the 1790 federal census, serves as a check and a supplement to estimates of immigration of each ethnic group by indicating to some extent the plausible proportions of the total immigration one could expect from various groups. Purvis calculated the percentage distribution of each white ethnic group (immigrants and their descendants) in the total population of 1790. His work contains some problems, but represents a marked improvement over Hansen and Barker, and the McDonalds, who did not include non-British ethnic groups.[6]

The method allows one to make use of the expertise of those who best understand the history of immigration. Using conservative estimates for each group tends to correct any bias toward inflation of numbers for filiopietistic or other reasons. This method essentially represents a trade-off: instead of the residual methods using decennial population figures from *Historical Statistics* and the sketchy fertility and mortality data compiled by other historians, my method relies on an improved surname analysis of the 1790 census as a check for the increasing expertise of ethnic-group historians who, in turn, rely on

actual data regarding immigrants—ship and passenger lists. The results are presented in Tables 1, 2, and 3.

The quality of the estimates varies by time and ethnic group, but the tables as a whole are useful. The "most accurate" estimates are based on solid information produced by the ethnic-group historians. The "less accurate" estimates should be used with care, but the sum totals for these ethnic groups, especially Africans, Germans, northern and southern Irish, and to some extent the Scots, and Welsh, are plausible and the distribution by decade probably reflects a small margin of error in most cases. It is only the "least accurate" estimates that are dubious, and for this reason they should be used with the greatest care, if at all.

In spite of the problem with filling in the gaps which ethnic-group historians have not yet thoroughly covered, this method as a whole produces enlightening results for most ethnic groups during most of the period in question. The sum total of 585,800 immigrants—278,400 blacks and 307,400 whites—is consistent with Gemery's findings (from 278,400 to 485,300 whites). Indeed, the two methods, one using fertility and mortality data calculating immigration as a residual, and the other relying on actual estimates of immigration by the ethnic-group historians, tend to provide a check for each other. Yet the second method provides much more reference information, listing immigration by decade and ethnic group instead of merely the sum total.

5. Wayland F. Dunaway, *The Scotch-Irish of Colonial Pennsylvania* (Chapel Hill, 1944), 41; James G. Leyburn, *The Scotch-Irish: A Social History* (Chapel Hill, 1962), 180–181; R.J. Dickson, *Ulster Emigration to Colonial America, 1718–1775* (London, 1966), 20–64; Marianne Wokeck, "Irish Immigration to the Delaware Valley before the American Revolution," forthcoming in David B. Quinn (ed.), *Ireland and America, 1500–1800*; Wilhelm Mönckmeier, *Die deutsche uberseeische Auswanderung. Ein Beitrag zur deutschen Wanderungsgeschichte* (Jena, 1912), 13; Clarence Ver Steeg, *The Formative Years, 1607–1763* (New York, 1964), 167; Hans Fenske, "International Migration: Germany in the Eighteenth Century," *Central European History*, (1980), 344; Marianne Wokeck, "German Immigration to Colonial America: Prototype of a Transatlantic Mass Migration," in Frank Trommler and Joseph McVeigh (eds.), *America and the Germans: An Assessment of a Three-Hundred-Year History* (Philadelphia, 1985), I, 12; Jon Butler, *The Huguenots in America: A Refugee People in New World Society* (Cambridge, Mass., 1983), 49; Patrice L. R. Higonnet, "French," in Stephan Thernstrom, Ann Orlov, and Oscar Handlin (eds.), *Harvard Encyclopedia of American Ethnic Groups* (Cambridge, Mass., 1980), 381; Bailyn and DeWolfe, *Voyagers to the West*, 25–26; Ian C.C. Graham, *Colonists from Scotland: Emigration to North America, 1707–1783* (Ithaca, 1956), 185–189; David N. Doyle, *Ireland, Irishmen and Revolutionary America, 1760–1820* (Dublin, 1981), 51–76.

6. The oft-quoted figures from U.S. Bureau of the Census, *Historical Statistics of the United States, Colonial Times to 1970, Bicentennial Edition, Part 2* (Washington, D.C., 1975), Series Z 20–23, 1168 originate from a study conducted primarily by Howard F. Barker and Marcus L. Hansen, "Report of the Committee on Linguistic and National Stocks in the Population of the United States," American Historical Association, *Annual Report for the Year 1931*, (Washington, D.C., 1932), I, 107–441. Forrest McDonald and Ellen Shapiro McDonald recently revised these estimates, "The Ethnic Origins of the American People, 1790," *William and Mary Quarterly*, XXXVII (1980), 179–199. See Thomas L. Purvis, "The European Ancestry of the United States Population, 1790," *William and Mary Quarterly*, XLI (1984), 98. A symposium in that volume contains an enlightening discussion between Purvis, Donald H. Akensen, and the McDonalds on the problems and merits of the various estimates available for the 1790 population.

Purvis improves upon previous work by more carefully analyzing distinctive surnames known to be borne by a certain percentage of a European group and then calculating an arithmetical coefficient sufficiently accurate to allow computation of the proportion of people belonging to that nationality within the United States in 1790. The number of individuals with the same surnames, multiplied by the appropriate numerical constant, equals the approximate size of the group in the United States. The problem with this method is that the surnames from the base population with which Purvis initially worked was not always representative of the actual immigrant population. For immigrants from the European continent he found sufficient passenger lists and other information which adequately reflect the actual population of immigrants. For British and Irish immigrants, however, the dearth of seventeenth- and eighteenth-century passenger lists and censuses forced Purvis to rely on nineteenth-century surname lists from Britain and Ireland, rather than surname lists from the actual immigrant population. Another problem with Purvis' method is that he was unable to distinguish between Scots-Irish and Scottish surnames, which forced him to assume that the number of Scots-Irish was twice the number of Scots in 1790.

Table 1

Estimated Decennial Immigration by Ethnic Group into the Thirteen Colonies, 1700–1775

DECADE	AFRICANS	GERMANS	NORTHERN IRISH	SOUTHERN IRISH	SCOTS	ENGLISH	WELSH	OTHER	TOTAL
1700–09	9,000	(100)	(600)	(800)	(200)	<400>	<300>	<100>	(11,500)
1710–19	10,800	(3,700)	(1,200)	(1,700)	(500)	<1,300>	<900>	<200>	(20,300)
1720–29	9,900	(2,300)	(2,100)	(3,000)	(800)	<2,200>	<1,500>	<200>	(22,000)
1730–39	40,500	13,000	4,400	7,400	(2,000)	<4,900>	<3,200>	<800>	(76,200)
1740–49	58,500	16,600	9,200	9,100	(3,100)	<7,500>	<4,900>	<1,100>	(110,000)
1750–59	49,600	29,100	14,200	8,100	(3,700)	<8,800>	<5,800>	<1,200>	(120,500)
1760–69	82,300	14,500	21,200	8,500	10,000	<11,900>	<7,800>	<1,600>	157,800
1770–75	17,800	5,200	13,200	3,900	15,000	7,100	<4,600>	<700>	67,500
Total	278,400	84,500	66,100	42,500	35,300	<44,100>	<29,000>	<5,900>	(585,800)

NOTE Figures were rounded to the nearest 100 immigrants. Estimates are divided into three categories: most accurate–no demarcation, less accurate–( ), and least accurate–< >.

SOURCES See Appendix.

Table 2

Estimated Proportional Distribution of Ethnic-Group Immigrants in the Thirteen Colonies by Decade, 1700–1775

DECADE	AFRICANS	GERMANS	NORTHERN IRISH	SOUTHERN IRISH	SCOTS	ENGLISH	WELSH	OTHER	TOTAL
1700–09	.03	(.00)	(.01)	(.02)	(.01)	<.01>	<.01>	<.02>	(.02)
1710–19	.04	(.04)	(.02)	(.04)	(.01)	<.03>	<.03>	<.03>	(.03)
1720–29	.04	(.03)	(.03)	(.07)	(.02)	<.05>	<.05>	<.03>	(.04)
1730–39	.14	.15	.07	.17	(.06)	<.11>	<.11>	<.14>	(.13)
1740–49	.21	.20	.14	.22	(.09)	<.17>	<.17>	<.19>	(.19)
1750–59	.18	.35	.21	.19	(.11)	<.20>	<.20>	<.20>	(.20)
1760–69	.30	.17	.32	.20	.28	(.27)	<.27>	<.27>	.27
1770–75	.06	.06	.20	.09	.42	.16	<.16>	<.12>	.12
Total	1.00	1.00	1.00	1.00	1.00	1.00	1.00	1.00	1.00

NOTE The estimates are divided into three categories: most accurate–no demarkation, less accurate–( ), and least accurate–< >. Slight adjustments were made to account for rounding errors.

SOURCE From Table 1.

Table 3

Estimated Proportional Distribution of Immigration per Decade in the Thirteen Colonies by Ethnic Group, 1700–1775

	1700–09	1710–19	1720–29	1730–39	1740–49	1750–59	1760–69	1770–75	TOTAL 1700–75
Africans	.78	.53	.45	.53	.53	.41	.52	.26	.48
Germans	(.01)	(.18)	(.10)	.17	.15	.24	.09	.08	.14
Northern Irish	(.05)	(.06)	(.09)	.06	.08	.12	.14	.20	.11
Southern Irish	(.07)	(.08)	(.14)	.10	.08	.07	.05	.06	.07
Scots	(.02)	(.03)	(.04)	(.03)	(.03)	(.03)	.06	.22	(.06)
English	<.03>	<.06>	<.10>	<.06>	<.07>	<.07>	(.08)	.10	<.08>
Welsh	<.03>	<.05>	<.07>	<.04>	<.05>	<.05>	<.05>	<.07>	<.05>
Other	<.01>	<.01>	<.01>	<.01>	<.01>	<.01>	<.01>	<.01>	<.01>
Total	1.00	1.00	1.00	1.00	1.00	1.00	1.00	1.00	1.00

NOTE The estimates are divided into three categories: most accurate–no demarcation, less accurate–( ), and least accurate–< >. Slight adjustments were made to account for rounding errors.

SOURCE From Table 1.

Further study of individual ethnic groups will surely require that adjustments be made to these tables, but they do reflect in a simpler and more usable way the approximate magnitude of colonial immigration in the eighteenth century. I do not mean to evoke the old, filiopietistic practice of inflating numbers (I have used conservative estimates for each ethnic group), but it is ironic that the work of ethnic-group historians, once looked upon with disdain by many, may have provided the beginning of a methodology which yields important and usable results that corroborate the work of more sophisticated techniques.

APPENDIX

AFRICANS   If immigrants are people who voluntarily leave their homeland to find a better life elsewhere, then African slaves are not immigrants. But in strictly demographic terms immigrants are people who came from somewhere else, as opposed to being a product of the natural increase in the indigenous population. In this sense everyone who came from elsewhere was an immigrant, including slaves, transported convicts, and so forth. I have included Africans in these tables of immigration by "ethnic" group because they contributed to early American demographic growth in the same ways as the other groups in the tables. The Africans actually came from a variety of different ethnic backgrounds, but taken together, their numbers more than triple those of the largest European group, the Germans. (On the importance of ethnicity among African slaves in the American colonies see, for example, Ira Berlin, "Time, Space, and the Evolution of Afro-American Society," *American Historical Review*, LXXXV [1980], 44–78.)

Since the appearance of Philip D. Curtin, *The Atlantic Slave Trade, A Census* (Madison, 1969), a bitter debate has arisen on the volume of the Atlantic slave trade and Curtin's figures are no longer acceptable without qualification. (For a good summary of the debate see David Henige, "Measuring the Immeasurable: The Atlantic Slave Trade, West African Population and the Pyrrhonian Critic," *Journal of African History*, XXVII [1986], 295–313.) I have used Curtin's figures for North America (137) as modified by Paul E. Lovejoy in "The Volume of the Atlantic Slave Trade: A Synthesis," *Journal of African History*, XXIII (1982), 487.

GERMANS   I have used my own method to calculate the volume and distribution of colonial German immigration. The large majority of Germans came through the port of Philadelphia, for which there are good records (passenger lists), especially for the period after 1726. The greatest difficulty occurs when one tries to measure the volume and distribution for other ports. To do this I divided the ethnic-German population of 1790 into two geographical groups—one settled overwhelmingly by immigrants through the port of Philadelphia, the other settled by immigrants through all other ports. Next, a ratio of immigrants to 1790 population was calculated for the first, or Philadelphia, group which was then extended to the second group to estimate the number of immigrants necessary to produce the known 1790 population for that group.

GROUP I

State	1790 white population	% German	Total Germans
Tennessee	31,913	6.6	2,106
Kentucky	61,913	4.9	2,996
New Jersey	169,954	6.5	11,047
Pennsylvania	424,049	38.0	161,139
Delaware	46,310	2.6	1,204
2/3 Maryland	139,099	12.7	17,666
2/3 Virginia	294,745	4.5	13,264
7/8 North Carolina	252,179	5.1	12,861
TOTAL	1,420,162	15.7	222,283

GROUP 2

State	1790 white population	% German	Total Germans
Maine	96,002	1.2	1,152
New Hampshire	141,097	0.1	141
Vermont	85,268	0.2	171
Massachusetts	373,324	0.3	1,120
Rhode Island	64,470	0.1	64
Connecticut	232,374	0.4	929
New York	314,142	9.1	28,587
1/3 Maryland	69,550	12.7	8,833
1/3 Virginia	147,372	4.5	6,632
South Carolina	140,178	5.5	7,710
1/8 North Carolina	36,025	5.1	1,837
Georgia	52,886	3.5	1,851
TOTAL	1,752,688	3.4	59,027

Using Purvis' surname analysis of the ethnic-German population in 1790 ("European Ancestry," 98), the following two geographical groups were created. The German population of some states had to be divided because its roots were in the immigration through Philadelphia and other ports:

To measure the immigration through Philadelphia I used a variety of sources. For the early period (1700–1726) these included the text from Strassburger and Hinke, *Pennsylvania German Pioneers;* Julius F. Sachse, *The German Pietists of Provincial Pennsylvania* (Philadelphia, 1895), 1–10; Martin G. Brumbaugh, *A History of the German Baptist Brethren in Europe and America* (Morris, Ill., 1899), 54–70. Also, I estimated that approximately 500 Germans, who were part of the large migration to New York beginning in 1709, eventually moved to Pennsylvania and contributed to the growth of the population in Group 1—see Walter A. Knittle, *Early Eighteenth Century Palatine Emigration* (Philadelphia, 1937); Henry Z. Jones, *The Palatine Families of New York* (Universal City, Calif., 1985).

For the period 1727–1775 I used the passenger lists in Strassburger and Hinke, which are not entirely comprehensive, but do represent the best collection of immigrant lists for any ethnic group in the eighteenth century. They include all male passengers sixteen years and older well enough to disembark at Philadelphia and sign an oath of allegiance to the king. Further, many of the more than 300 ship lists for this period also contain lists of women and children, or list a total number of passengers and/or "freights" (children were counted as half freights or not at all). This allows one to calculate the ratio of total passengers to adult males, a figure that changed over the decades. After controlling for these changes, the difference between "passengers" and "freights," and adding the Moravian immigrants, who settled in Pennsylvania but im-migrated primarily through New York (see John W. Jordan, "Moravian Immigration to Pennsylvania, 1734–1765," *Pennsylvania Magazine of History and Biography,* III [1909], 228–248; *idem,* "Moravian Immigration to America, 1734–1800," unpub. ms. [Historical Society of Pennsylvania, Philadelphia, n.d.]), a fairly complete picture of German immigration through Philadelphia for the years 1700–1775 can be compiled.

Records for other ports are incomplete, although historians and genealogists constantly make new discoveries. I have reproduced data from several sources here to give an idea of the distribution through other ports which produced the ethnic-German population for Group 2 in 1790. These sources include Knittle, *Early Eighteenth Century Palatine Emigration;* Jones, *Palatine Families in New York;* Daniel I. Rupp, *Thirty Thousand Names of German, Swiss, Dutch, French, and Other Immigrants in Pennsylvania from 1727 to 1776* (Philadelphia, 1875); newspaper and other accounts located in the research files of the Museum of Early Southern Decorative Arts in Winston-Salem, N.C.; Jane Revill, (ed.), *A Compilation of the Original Lists of Protestant Immigrants to South Carolina, 1763–1773* (Columbia, 1939).

	GROUP 1		GROUP 2	
	N	%	N	%
1700–09	0	0	50	0
1710–19	1,000	2	2,548	41
1720–29	2,161	3	0	0
1730–39	12,477	19	138	2
1740–49	14,201	21	594	9
1750–59	24,971	37	1,033	16
1760–69	7,712	12	1,690	27
1770–75	4,211	6	242	4
TOTAL:	66,733	100%	6,295	100%

The following is the estimated distribution by decade for all known immigrants by port of entry (Group 1—Philadelphia, Group 2—other ports). Group 1 is fairly complete, but Group 2 is incomplete:

	GROUP 1	GROUP 2	
1700–75 immigration:	66,700	x	x ≈ 17,700
1790 population:	222,300	59,000	

Because the data in Group 2 is so incomplete, I have extended the ratio of immigrants-to-1790 population for Group 1 to Group 2, for whom the 1790 population is known. The following results were achieved:

Total immigration through 1770–75: 66,700 + 17,700 = 84,400. (All figures were rounded to the nearest 100 persons.)

About 17,700 Germans (21 percent of the total) immigrated through ports other than Philadelphia, and 84,400 immigrated through all ports of the thirteen colonies during the period 1700–1775. (The final estimate in Table 1 was adjusted to account for rounding errors.)

The validity of this calculation rests on two assumptions (in addition to the assumption that Purvis' surname analysis is reasonably accurate). The first is that the fertility/mortality experience, or rate of natural increase, was the same for both groups. The second is that the time pattern of arrival was the same for both groups, or that the differences were such that the net effect was the same.

To deal with the first assumption, the work of Gemery must be addressed ("European Immigration to North America"). He found that the widest discrepancies in the rate of natural increase during the colonial period occurred between northern and southern colonies in the seventeenth century. By the eighteenth century the fertility/mortality experience for whites in all regions was becoming similar. This, along with the fact that both Group 1 and Group 2 contain inhabitants from northern and southern colonies, tends to make this assumption reasonable, although there is some error introduced in the final estimates because of it.

The second assumption is more difficult to make, since the above table clearly shows a discrepancy in the distribution of known immigrants in the two groups. There are many factors which could have contributed to the same number of immigrants from 1700 to 1775 producing differing numbers of inhabitants in 1790. These include when they arrived, their age, and to what degree they came as families (early or late in the reproductive period), or single individuals. Group 2 contains more earlier immigrants, which means they had time to produce more descendants by 1790 than their counterparts in Group 1. On the other hand, there were also more immigrants in Group 2 in the 1760s and 1770s (relative to the middle decades of the century) than were in Group 1, which means that more of Group 2 had relatively less time to reproduce by 1790 than was true for Group 1. These two characteristics tend to cancel one another out, at least to a degree. There is no doubt some error was introduced by assuming equal growth rates and timing of immigration for both groups, but the reasons outlined above and the fact that a large majority clearly emigrated to Philadelphia tends to indicate that the margin of error in the final estimates of Tables 1–3 is small.

Lastly, German immigration from 1775 to 1790 did have some effect on the population of 1790, but it was very slight. During the war years, 1775–1783, German immigration ceased almost completely, except for some 3,000 "Hessian" deserters (see Rodney Atwood, *The Hessians: Mercenaries from Hessen-Kassel in the American Revolution* [Cambridge, 1980], 254). Immigration into Philadelphia resumed in 1785, and by 1790 only 1,467 persons had arrived (calculated from Strassburger and Hinke, III. 3–44).

The final estimate in Table 1—84,500—is lower than Wokeck's generally accepted figure of 100,000 German-speaking persons immigrating through all ports before 1776 (see "German Immigration to Colonial America," 12). I distributed the final total, including the "unknown" immigrant figure arrived at by the above calculation, according to that of the known immigrants listed above. Some adjustments were made for the early decades, however, because there are fairly complete records for the large emigration from 1709 to 1714 to New York and North Carolina (represented in Group 2). Therefore few "unknown" immigrants in Group 2 were added to the period before 1720.

NORTHERN AND SOUTHERN IRISH Estimates of the volume of northern Irish, which includes primarily people of Scottish descent ("Scots-Irish"), but also native Irish from the northern counties, have fluctuated wildly through the years. Dunaway estimated 250,000 Scots-Irish arrived in the eighteenth century (*The Scotch-Irish of Colonial Pennsylvania*, 41) and Maldwyn A. Jones calculated the same number for the entire colonial period

("Scotch-Irish," in Thernstrom, *Harvard Encyclopedia of American Ethnic Groups*, 896). Further, Leyburn concluded that 200,000 Scots-Irish immigrants arrived from 1717 to 1775 (*The Scotch-Irish*, 180–181). Until recently, Dickson was the only historian to present some quantitative evidence justifying his calculations, and to show how the flow of immigration varied over time. He concluded that 109,000 to 129,000 Ulster Irish immigrated into the colonies from 1718 to 1775.

On the other hand, the immigration of Catholic, "southern," or non-Ulster Irish was largely ignored until the work of Audrey Lockhart, *Some Aspects of Emigration from Ireland to the North American Colonies between 1660 and 1775* (New York, 1976) and David N. Doyle, *Ireland, Irishmen and Revolutionary America, 1760–1820* (Dublin, 1981) appeared. Although Lockhart does not attempt to estimate the numbers of immigrants arriving, she does present important evidence on the volume of immigrant-carrying ships, which, when used with other evidence, allows one to make an estimate of the total number of immigrants arriving and to show how this migration varied over time. Doyle's work has helped alert historians to this large immigration. He also showed with qualitative evidence how southern Irish emigration varied over the decades, paralleling to a large degree Ulster Irish emigration.

But Doyle has overestimated the numbers of this emigrant group. He states that about 90,000 southern Catholic Irish came before 1776 (almost all in the eighteenth century), up to 30,000 native (that is, Catholic) Ulster Irish, and 10,000 southern Anglo-Irish (Protestant), even though there were only 156,000 to 166,000 inhabitants in the United States in 1790 who descended from all these groups. He attributes their slow natural growth rate to the large number of single men emigrating, who had to marry non-Irish women in America (51–76, especially 61 and 70–71). They did marry and have children, however, and even if all "Irish" found by surname analysis in the 1790 census were not really "100 percent" Irish (due to marriage migration), the number of immigrants from which they descended must have been much lower than Doyle indicates.

My estimates of 66,100 northern and 42,500 southern Irish in Table 1 are based upon Lockhart, Dickson, and the very recent work of Wokeck, who has found passenger lists for the Delaware ports which allowed her to calculate approximate passenger-per-ship ratios for both northern and southern Irish and extend them to the

DECADE	SOUTHERN	NORTHERN	TOTAL
1729	723	296	1,019
1730–39	3,328	2,510	5,838
1740–49	4,106	5,225	9,331
1750–59	3,639	8,099	11,738
1760–69	3,811	12,067	15,878
1770–74	1,689	7,202	8,891
TOTAL	17,296	35,399	52,695

number of ships arriving from 1729 to 1774. See "Irish Immigration to the Delaware Valley." Wokeck calculated 17,296 southern Irish and 35,399 northern Irish arriving in the Delaware ports from 1729 to 1774. I have grouped them by decade as follows:

According to Lockhart's tables, 45 percent of all the immigrant-carrying ships went to the Delaware ports during this same time period (calculated from Appendix C, 175–208). From Dickson's tables (Appendix E, 282–287) one can calculate that 57 percent of immigrant-carrying ships from northern Ireland went to Delaware Valley

SOUTHERN IRISH				TOTAL
1729	723	÷	.45 =	1,607
1730–39	3,328	÷	.45 =	7,396
1740–49	4,106	÷	.45 =	9,124
1750–59	3,639	÷	.45 =	8,087
1760–69	3,811	÷	.45 =	8,469
1770–74	1,689	÷	.45 =	3,753
TOTAL	17,296	÷	.45 =	38,436

NORTHERN IRISH				TOTAL
1729	296	÷	.57 =	519
1730–39	2,510	÷	.57 =	4,404
1740–49	5,225	÷	.57 =	9,167
1750–59	8,099	÷	.57 =	14,209
1760–69	12,067	÷	.57 =	21,170
1770–74	7,202	÷	.57 =	12,635
TOTAL	35,399	÷	.57 =	62,104

ports, although this data only reflects the situation in the years 1750 to 1775. If one extends Dickson's figure to the entire period 1729–1774, the following calculations can be made for total Irish immigration into all ports of the thirteen colonies in the years 1729 to 1774:

To estimate immigration for the remaining years, 1700–1728 and 1775, the following steps were taken. According to Lockhart's tables, 13 percent of all immigrant-carrying ships from southern Ireland from 1700 to 1775 arrived in the first three decades of the eighteenth century—2 percent from 1700 to 1709, 4 percent from 1710 to 1719, and 7 percent from 1720 to 1729. Thus 87 percent arrived in the years 1730 to 1775. Subtracting the 1,903 that Wokeck found for 1729, and extending her passenger-per-ship ratio for 1770–1774 to the nine ships Lockhart found arriving in the colonies in 1775, one can calculate total southern Irish immigration from 1700 to 1775 as follows:

$$38,436 - 1,903 + 180 = .87x$$
$$x = 42,199 \text{ immigrants}$$

This total number is distributed as follows for 1700–1729:

$$1700–09 \quad .02 \times 42,199 = \quad 844$$
$$1710–19 \quad .04 \times 42,199 = 1,688$$
$$1720–29 \quad .07 \times 42,199 = 2,954$$

In Table 1, I inflated the figure for the 1720s to 3,500 because of the higher passenger-per-ship ratio prevalent for that decade in the few instances in Lockhart's tables where this information was given.

Since Dickson's tables do not include the number of ships arriving before 1750, and since Wokeck has shown that Dickson's method consistently overestimated the number of immigrants per ship, the only option remaining for calculating northern Irish immigration from 1700 to 1728 is to make use of the proportion of southern Irish to total Irish for the period closest to 1700–1728. From 1729 to 1739 southern Irish immigration equaled 58 percent of the total. Thus one can calculate:

	SOUTHERN	TOTAL	NORTHERN
1700–09	844 ÷ .58 =	1,455	1,455 − 844 = 611
1710–19	1,688 ÷ .58 =	2,910	2,910 − 1,688 = 1,222
1720–29	2,954 ÷ .58 =	5,093	5,093 − 2,954 = 2,139

All these calculations can be summarized as follows:

Total Irish Immigration Through All Ports, 1700–1775

DECADE	SOUTHERN	NORTHERN	TOTAL
1700–09	844	611	1,455
1710–19	1,688	1,222	2,910
1720–29	2,954	2,139	5,093
1730–39	7,396	4,404	11,800
1740–49	9,124	9,167	18,291
1750–59	8,087	14,209	22,296
1760–69	8,469	21,170	29,639
1770–75	3,933	13,185	17,118
TOTAL	42,495	66,107	108,602

In Table 1 all figures were rounded to the nearest 100 immigrants. Purvis found 16.3 percent (c. 520,000 persons) of the white population in 1790 to be of Scots-Irish and Irish descent, or northern and southern Irish (see "European Ancestry," 98). The ratio of immigrants 1700–1775 to the total population in 1790 was thus .21 (108,600 ÷ 520,000), a factor which will be used to help calculate immigration for other ethnic groups with less quantitative evidence available than the Irish.

SCOTS   It is difficult to get a sense of the overall number of Scottish immigrants in eighteenth-century America. Graham estimates that emigration to America was "sporadic" from 1707 to 1763. From 1763 to 1775 less than 25,000 departed. Emigration was truly massive only in the years 1768 to 1775, when 20,245 left Scotland for America, see *Colonists from Scotland*, 185–189. Graham's figures, however, are probably too low. Using the same ratio of immigrants to 1790 population as existed for the northern and southern Irish (.21), combined with Purvis' finding that 5.3 percent (or c. 168,000) of the white population in 1790 was of Scottish descent ("European Ancestry," 98) allows an estimate of 35,300 Scottish immigrants from 1700 to 1775.

The lack of good data for pre-1760 immigration prohibits the labeling of these estimates as "most accurate." Nevertheless, because of the similarities between the Scottish and Irish emigration experience to America—both began in the early eighteenth century, and were caused by population pressure, rack-renting, and agricultural dislocations which occurred in both places at about the same time—I have opted to distribute the total immigration for the period 1700–60 in the same manner as the Irish (both northern and southern combined). It is only in the late 1760s and 1770s that Scottish emigration to the North American colonies noticeably differs form the Irish. The Irish emigration was larger in real numbers, but the Scottish emigration became relatively more intense (compared to the earlier Scottish migrations) as Graham has shown. For these reasons I have labeled the pre-1760 estimates as "less accurate" and the post-1760 estimates, based on Graham's work, as "most accurate."

ENGLISH   Estimates of English immigrants are even scarcer than those for Scottish. Furthermore, the English are the only ethnic group for which significant immigration occurred in both the seventeenth and eighteenth centuries, which makes it impossible to use Purvis' surname analysis of the 1790 census to assist in calculating eighteenth-century immigration. E. Anthony Wrigley and Roger S. Schofield, *Population History of England, 1541–1871: A Reconstruction* (Cambridge, Mass., 1981) found net migration in England from 1701 to 1775 to be 423,162 (calculated from Table 7.11, 219), but the only period for which there are statistics available for arrivals in the thirteen colonies is the 1770s. Here Bailyn and DeWolfe found about 4,500 English emigrants bound for America during the years 1773–1776 in the Register maintained in London, as opposed to 3,600 Scottish emigrants *(Voyagers to the West,* 92). In the absence of any other data I have made the assumption that the ratio of English to Scottish emigrants in the 1770s extended back to 1700, which would mean about 44,100 English immigrants arrived in the colonies during the period in question. This is not to say that the emigration history of Scotland and England are exactly parallel and there is little reason to accept this figure as being very accurate, but it does compare well with Richard S. Dunn's estimate of 25,000 English servants arriving in the colonies during these years, see "Servants and Slaves: The Recruitment and Employment of Labor," in Jack P. Greene and J.R. Pole (eds.), *Colonial British America: Essays in the New History of the Early Modern Era* (Baltimore, 1984), 159. Similar to the Scottish and Irish emigrants, the English, too, were plagued by population pressure and agricultural dislocations that coincided with these developments elsewhere in the realm. Thus I have distributed the total figure throughout the decades in the same manner as the southern and northern Irish. My figures for English immigrants are no doubt the weakest in Table 1 and for this reason I have labeled them "least accurate."

WELSH   There is little literature on Welsh immigration in eighteenth-century America and quantitative estimates are virtually nonexistent. Rowland Berthoff found the first "sizable" Welsh immigration to have taken place in the years 1680 to 1720, when a few hundred arrived in Pennsylvania. But he does not discuss any other Welsh immigration before the nineteenth century. See "Welsh," in Thernstrom, *Harvard Encyclopedia,* 1011–1012. Yet Arthur H. Dodd did find Welsh settlements in Maryland (1703), North Carolina (1733), South Carolina (1737 and 1780), and Virginia (1740 and 1762), although he made no estimate of their numbers. See *The Character of Early Welsh Emigration to the United States* (Cardiff, 1953), 2. In contrast to the English, most Welsh emigration to the colonies appears to have taken place in the eighteenth century, making it possible to use Purvis' work in this calculation. My estimate of 29,000 Welsh immigrants is based upon his estimate of 4.3 percent of the white population being of Welsh descent in 1790 (Purvis, 98), or about 138,000 people, and the same ratio of immigrants to 1790 population used for the Irish (.21). The 29,000 figure is distributed over the decades in the same manner as the Irish. The advantage of being able to use Purvis' work is offset, however, by the lack of discussion in the literature of the causes, conditions, and timing of the Welsh emigration in the eighteenth century, which has led me to label all these estimates "least accurate."

OTHERS   Purvis ("European Ancestry," 98) gives the following percentages for white ethnic distribution in 1790: Dutch 3.1, French 2.1, and Swedish 0.3. Most of these groups arrived before 1700, but there were occasional immigrations of these and other groups during the eighteenth century. For example, over 200 French-speaking passengers arrived in Charleston from 1763 to 1773 (calculated from Revill, *Protestant Immigrants to South Carolina,* [Columbia, 1939], 18, 112, 127). I have placed "other" immigration at a minimal 1 percent of the total per decade to cover this and other such scattered examples during this period and labeled them "least accurate."

The New Immigrants

BY CHARLES S. CLARK

THE ISSUES

The bustling mall, with a tire store at one end and a variety store at the other, seems typical of shopping centers in affluent American suburbs—save one key detail: Almost all the shops and restaurants display neon signs in Vietnamese. Restaurants advertise *pho*, a traditional Asian noodle soup; travel agents specialize in trans-Pacific flights and currency transfers; nightclubs blare the latest pop hits in Saigon; and posters in video stores promote sexy Asian film stars.

Welcome to Eden Center in Falls Church, Va., just outside Washington. The site that just a decade ago housed a quintessentially American retail arcade—complete with a paint store, greeting card shop and ice cream parlor—is now said to be the largest Vietnamese shopping center in the United States.

"I'd like to take credit, but it really just happened by itself," says owner Norman Ebonstein, of Boca Raton, Fla. "It just grew bigger, the place became a meeting center, so we sort of fell into the plan."

Today, 70 percent of the customers at the 250,000-square-foot shopping center are Asian, Ebonstein says. He credits his success to his tenants, and their "homogeneous, hard-working, family-oriented society."

Ebonstein "gets a kick" out of his involvement in Vietnamese small business. He flies the South Vietnamese and American flags in the parking lot. He and the merchants are erecting Oriental archways at the center's entrance, and they built a

replica of a landmark clock tower in Saigon. Ebonstein also contributes to Vietnamese charities, organizes checkers tournaments for Asian senior citizens and joins in celebrations of Vietnam's Armed Forces Day.

Eden Center reflects the dramatic impact of immigrants in modern America, an impact that affects both the new arrivals and long-time residents. In the 1990s, Americans who grew up in a historically white, Anglo-Saxon society are having to adjust to a Polish-born chairman of the Joint Chiefs of Staff, John Shalikashvili; to Spanish-language editions of *People* magazine on Seven-11 shelves; and to Buddhist temples and Islamic mosques rising in their communities.[1]

Today's America contains nearly 23 million foreign-born residents, or about 8.4 percent of the population,

and about 32 million residents whose primary language is not English. Los Angeles, the Census Bureau says, is now about 40 percent foreign-born, while 88 percent of its Monterey Park neighborhood is Asian and Hispanic.

The impact of immigration is not spread evenly across the country, notes George Vernez, director of the Center for Research on Immigration Policy at the RAND Corp. For example, most Cubans stream to Miami; people from the Caribbean and Central America flock to New York City; and Asians make Seattle a prime destination. California is home to fully 45 percent of the nation's Mexican immigrants, which strains California schools because Mexicans tend to have lower education levels than other immigrants.

Though earlier historical periods have seen as much or more immigration, many of today's immigrants differ from their 19th- and early 20th-century counterparts. The classic stories of American immigrants have focused on the "tired and poor," but many modern immigrants are well-educated and even wealthy—witness the 12,000 Chinese technicians working in Silicon Valley computer firms or the well-heeled Iranian expatriots so visible in Beverly Hills.

Over the past three decades, Asians, Latinos and Caribbean immigrants have outpaced the numbers of Irish, Italian and Eastern European immigrants so familiar at the turn of the century, sometimes prickling racial tensions among native-born Americans. And Hispanics and Asians, in particular, have be-

Saigon in the Suburbs

Flying the U.S. and South Vietnamese flags, sprawling Eden Center in Suburban Falls Church, Va., boasts dozens of shops and restaurants catering to Vietnamese-Americans.

Thomas J. Colin

Thomas J. Colin

come politically more influential, as evidenced by the important political races in 1996 that turned on the Latino vote and by the current concern over Asian involvement in President Clinton's campaign financing.

"Political loyalty has dropped in weight due to globalization, the end of the Cold War and the rise of the United Nations," says Harvard University sociologist Nathan Glazer, author of the forthcoming book *We Are All Multiculturalists Now.* "The world of today's immigrants has two main differences from the immigrants' world of the 1920s. One is the rise of the welfare state that offered a safety net for immigrants, having replaced the [modest] private welfare efforts of the 1920s that prompted many immigrants to give up and return home. Secondly, the whole thrust toward Americaniza-

tion in language and culture that used to be common in this country has weakened."

Perhaps because of their daily encounters in the new "melting pot," many Americans have grown weary of high immigration, viewing it as a drain on jobs and government social spending. Indeed, an NBC News/*Wall Street Journal* survey of 2,000 Americans in December found that 72 percent want the number of immigrants reduced, a huge increase from the 33 percent who wanted reductions in 1965. For several years now, states and the federal government have been planning cutbacks in welfare, health and education benefits for immigrants both legal and illegal.[2]

The new immigrants have not stood by idly. Taking advantage of newly streamlined procedures at the Immigration and Naturalization Ser-

vice (INS), thousands who have been in the country the required five years have been applying for citizenship. "Since welfare reform," says Vilay Chaleunrath, executive director of the Indochinese Community Center in Washington, D.C., "there's been a surge of applications, especially among the elderly, who used to think they would one day go back and die in the old country."

In 1996, an estimated 1.1 million people took the citizenship oath, up from an average of only 200,000 in the early 1990s. The increase in part reflects newly eligible illegal aliens who won amnesty following the 1986 Immigration Reform and Control Act. The INS predicts 1.7 million applications in fiscal 1997.

"Naturalization builds bridges between new immigrant groups and the existing society, much as labor unions, political parties and public schools have done in the past," says INS Commissioner Doris Meissner.[3] That's one reason that Hungarian-born billionaire George Soros last September set up his $50 million Emma Lazarus Fund to help immigrants become citizens.

The rush to citizenship, however, is not welcomed by all. In her recent book, *Americans No More: The Death of Citizenship,* journalist Georgie Anne Geyer blasts immigrants and government policies that encourage immigrants to view citizenship as an opportunity for economic benefits rather than civic responsibility.

Indeed, she says, immigrants take naturalization about as seriously as "joining a health club." And, she told a Senate panel, Americans seem reluctant to assert their national identity. If not countered, she warns, the trend "will destroy America as we have known it and substitute a very different country, one that is spiritually incoherent, humanly conflict-ridden and economically hobbled."[4]

John Fonte, a visiting scholar at the American Enterprise Institute, denounces immigrant demands for ethnic-group rights, such as multicultural education and bilingual ballots. "Today we face a crisis of citizenship," he told the Senate panel. "Our goal should be Americanization, stated clearly without apology and without embarrassment.... Americanization does not mean giving up our ethnic traditions, customs, cuisine, or birth languages. It means patriotic assimilation."[5]

Finally, a perception that immigrants tend to vote Democratic has led some Republicans in Congress to charge that the Clinton administration's INS was partisan and even corrupt in its efforts to streamline the naturalization process so that new citizens could vote in the last elections.

Immigration supporters—including many who belong to the Republican Party, which is split over immigration—argue that new immigrants traditionally have been among the most patriotic Americans and that all they want is help in making the transition. Some accuse immigration "restrictionists" of veiled racism and xenophobia, of scapegoating immigrants for many social ills.

John Kromkowski, president of the National Center for Urban Ethnic Affairs, challenges the notion of a fixed and superior American identity. "America itself is a history of changes, of developments, not of static categories," he says. "The nativists are out of touch with the real situation and the process. And their whole anti-immigrant hysteria has recently done what the League of Women Voters never could do: produce record voter registration and citizenship."

Today, says a 1993 Ford Foundation study, "America's story is no longer one simply of 'coming to America.' It is also an account of the places where immigrants settle and how those already there change."[6]

As policy-makers and everyday citizens consider the nation's immigration policies, these are some of the questions being asked:

Are immigrants doing enough to fit into American life?

"There is a central American culture that goes beyond our legal institutions," writes former State Department official Francis Fukuyama. "America was founded with liberal political institutions, but it is the sectarian nature of American Protestantism that set the cultural tone."[7]

How newcomers fare at picking up on this "cultural tone" is the focus of much anxiety among Americans who look askance at the immigration in flux from places such as Latin America and the Caribbean. "Successful" societies value education, says Massachusetts Institute of Technology international studies Professor Lawrence Harrison, citing Western Europe, North America, East Asia and Australia as examples. In Latin America, by contrast, "the tradition has been a focus not on the future, not on progress, but on the present, or on the past. Work has been seen as a necessary evil, importantly informed by the slavery experience. Education is something which has been made available principally to the elite.... Merit plays a relatively unimportant role in how people get ahead. Connections—family—are much more important.... the idea of fair play is not well-developed."[8]

Immigrants from such societies, the argument goes, inevitably produce the kind of tensions that arose, for example, in Mount Kisco, N.Y., recently, when citizens complained that Latino day laborers who gather every morning in parking lots were too often publicly intoxicated. "We want our town back," longtime residents wrote in the local paper.[9]

Complaints are not limited to whites. "A for-sale sign in our neighborhood causes panic," writes an African-American of the arrival of Hispanic immigrants in South-Central Los Angeles. "We know who will get that house. There will be 20 to 30 people living in it, they will keep goats, they will grow corn in their front yard, they will hang their wash on the front fence."[10]

Critics such as Geyer cite examples of immigrant crime, singling out the Middle Eastern terrorists convicted of the 1993 World Trade Center bombing, or Ethiopians who seek to import the practice of female genital mutilation. *Forbes* magazine writer Peter Brimelow, himself a U.S.-naturalized Briton, warns of the day when America is no longer majority white. "This unprecedented demographic mutation," he writes of current immigration levels, is creating an America in which people are "alien to each other."[11]

What has disappeared, says Daniel A. Stein, executive director of the Federation for American Immigration Reform (FAIR), "is the old immigrants' idea that you would never go home, that you were so proud to learn English that you would be insulted if someone spoke your old language. Immigrants are no longer grateful to be here."

It is the high level of immigration itself that prevents many immigrants from assimilating, adds Yeh Ling-Ling, founder of the Diversity Coalition for an Immigration Moratorium, in San Francisco. "In schools in places like Monterey [Calif.], many immigrants are surrounded only by other immigrants while they receive bilingual education and multiculturalism. I get calls from immigrants saying they're angry at the ethnic activists who tell them, 'You'll never be an American. Your yellow skin will never turn white.'"

According to an Urban Institute report, the number of immigrants who told 1990 census takers that they "don't speak English well" totaled about half the population of Miami, a fifth of New York and a third of Los Angeles.[12]

Polls, however, show that immigrants do not see themselves so ghettoized. Fifty-eight percent of immigrants who have been in the U.S. less than 10 years report that they spend time with "few or none of their fellow countrymen," according to a May-June 1995 *USA Today/CNN/Gallup* survey. An identical 58 percent felt it is important to blend into American culture, compared with only 27 percent who said it was important to maintain their own culture. (Surprisingly, a higher portion of

Naturalizations on the Rise

During the 1990s, the number of immigrants who became naturalized American citizens skyrocketed. Several factors caused the rise, including efforts to deny public assistance to non-citizens and the large group of illegal immigrants who became eligible for citizenship through the 1986 amnesty law.

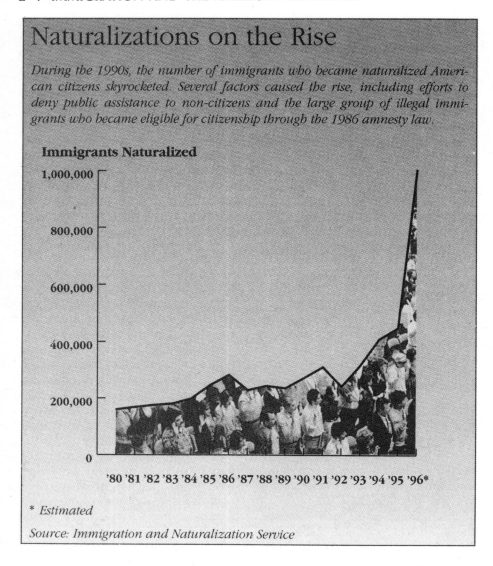

Immigrants Naturalized

'80 '81 '82 '83 '84 '85 '86 '87 '88 '89 '90 '91 '92 '93 '94 '95 '96*

* *Estimated*

Source: Immigration and Naturalization Service

native-born Americans—32 percent—said the immigrants should maintain their own culture.)

Studies show that many of the most visible immigrant enclaves are constantly turning over, with new arrivals replacing veterans who acquire education and skills that permit them a better job and housing. The 1995 annual housing survey by the Federal National Mortgage Association (Fannie Mae) found that 55 percent of immigrants who are renters are more likely to see themselves as foreigners temporarily living in America; among immigrants who own a home, the percentage with that feeling drops to 41. The Commerce Department, meanwhile, recently reported that the number of

Hispanic-owned businesses jumped 76 percent from 1987 to '92.[13]

"Walk into any Latino neighborhood and you see all the American icons, from Dallas Cowboys posters to the New York Yankees to rock and roll," says Raul Yzaguirre, president of the National Council of La Raza, the nation's largest Latino civil rights group. "Hispanics are learning English faster than previously, and there are 50,000 waiting for night classes in Los Angeles alone. Latinos are hardworking and patriotic, and in the armed forces they win more medals proportionately than their numbers."

Rather than generalizing about a whole continent and culture, Yzaguirre adds, critics should understand

that persistent Hispanic poverty has to do with job discrimination, which he says has been documented time and again in controlled studies.

Other immigrants' spokesmen stress the importance to transplants of maintaining their self-esteem by staying in touch with their cultural roots, even if that means disguising it. "Concealing one's real emotional feelings was particularly useful while dealing with the white majority," wrote a Japanese immigrant woman in 1981. "To show a 'good face' as a representative of the Japanese in general insured greater acceptance by the majority society."[14]

Critics of new immigrants, says Frank Sharry, executive director of the National Immigration Forum, a lobbying and research group, "overlook that there's a tremendous desire to belong, to participate, to embrace America, to love it and wrestle with it while maintaining one's own sense of identity. This is a good thing. Citizenship is a classic example of how dynamic and vibrant American democracy is. But in the public mind, it is largely the Latino population that seems not to have embraced America the way average Joes want them to."

But Linda Chavez, president of the Center for Equal Opportunity and a critic of ethnic lobbies that cry racism, says "the first generation that is born here is the dividing line. If they fully take part in American life, then all is fine, and it is not impossible for the country to absorb large numbers of immigrants. Unless you're too old, you must learn English to take part. The foreign-language newspapers that many immigrants read are too concentrated on news from the old country."

Speaking foreign languages creates barriers, she adds, which produce frustration among Americans that leads to the anti-immigrant backlash and the debate over English as the official language.

The language debate, though often discussed in the context of government administration and official documents, has an emotional undercurrent relating to political domination.[15] Recently retired Rep. Toby Roth, R-Wis., one of the leaders of the official-English legislation movement in Congress, told a press conference in December that new Americans were some of his biggest supporters because they see learning English as the key to economic opportunity. "One tells me that Spanish is the language of bellhops and busboys, while English is the language of doctors and lawyers," he says.

Yzaguirre finds such views "suggestive of the offensive, ugly-American attitude that has gotten us in trouble all over the world. We've got to stop having America be the world's most linguistically ignorant country."

Dennis Gallagher, executive director of the Refugee Policy Group, acknowledges that there are limits to how much new immigrants should assert their native cultures. "My [Indian-born] wife is appalled by the garish show some Hindu groups make in building temples in prominent places in the United States, some of which would be extreme even in their own countries," he says. But, Gallagher adds, having a group of 100,000 Iranians, some of whom succeed or fail only within boundaries of that community, is not a threat to our overall society. They won't get us to learn Farsi. They're a part of America now.

"Immigrants bring different attitudes and values and perceptions of who the good and bad guys are in international affairs," he adds. "That's both the benefit and cost of diversity. We're getting more frightened of that. We shouldn't be, because in the longer term, it makes us stronger."

Should immigrants be permitted to hold dual citizenship?

"American citizenship is more precious than any other status a man or woman can have," recently retired Sen. Alan K. Simpson, R-Wyo., told the Senate Judiciary hearing in October. "Not only does it guarantee membership in the society that offers the most political and civil liberty of any nation . . . and the opportunity to participate in choosing the govern-

ment and therefore in crafting the laws that will help shape its future—in addition, it provides the immense emotional satisfaction of being part of a nation with a very special and wonderful history."[16]

Given the allure of U.S. citizenship, Simpson and others question an increasingly common practice among immigrants: dual citizenship. Commonplace among Britons who emi-

Immigration and Naturalization Service/Rick Kenney

Attorney General Janet Reno administers the oath of citizenship to 3,000 new citizens at a 1995 ceremony at the U.S. Air Arena in Maryland, near Washington, D.C.

grate to the United States and American Jews who move to Israel, dual citizenship in recent years has become popular among Central American and Asian immigrants as well, in part due to advances in worldwide mass communication. In New York City, seven of the 10 largest immigrant groups come from countries that permit it, said Linda Basch, author of a 1985 book on transnationalism. "Many people live an existence that's transnational," she wrote. "They have families in both places. They invest in both places. They get involved in politics in both places."[17]

By law, the United States does not recognize dual citizenship, says an INS spokesman, though the Supreme Court has ruled that a foreigner need not renounce foreign citizenship to apply for U.S. citizenship. When a qualified immigrant

takes the oath of U.S. citizenship, the State Department notifies the government of his native country, and it is up to that government to determine whether to revoke citizenship.

Critics question the loyalty of dual citizens, warning of war-time defections and the risk of the proverbial "fifth column" of espionage agents. They point to dual citizens who have become pawns in international aggression, as in the late-1930s, when Adolf Hitler cited the presence of German nationals in Czechoslovakia as a pretext for launching an invasion.

"Dual nationality with Britons or Israelis at least involves a shared cultural legacy," says Stein of FAIR. "But now, with immigration from neighboring countries such as Mexico and Latin America, it involves huge income differentials and claims to ancestral territory" within the United States.

Efforts to discourage dual citizenship have put new pressure on immigrants who have been willing to forgo such privileges as government employment opportunities and security clearances in order to maintain links with their native land. "My wife is not quite comfortable giving up her ties [to India] because of tax advantages and the loss to her

Chronology

1800s *U.S. gains reputation as world's most welcoming immigrant society.*

1845–49

Ireland's potato famine sends more than a million Irish immigrants to the United States.

1886

President Grover Cleveland dedicates Statue of Liberty, a gift from France.

1898

Supreme Court rules in *United States v. Wong Kim Ark* that a man born in California to Chinese parents is a U.S. citizen.

1900s *The white Anglo-Saxon Protestant establishment grows concerned about open immigration by Irish, Italians, Greeks and Jews.*

1908

Opening of Israel Zangwill's play "The Melting Pot" in Washington.

1910

Census shows 13.5 million Americans out of a total population of 92 million are foreign-born.

1920s–1950s *Growing concern about immigration leads to restrictions.*

1924

Congress tightens immigration, implementing quotas that favor Northern Europeans.

1941

Japanese attack on Pearl Harbor prompts U.S. to hold Japanese-Americans in internment camps.

1952

Immigration and Nationality Act limits non-Western Hemisphere immigrants and give preference to high-skill workers.

1960s–1970s *Government "Great Society" programs lay groundwork for aid to immigrants.*

1965

Immigration and Nationality Act Amendments increase immigration, invite more non-Europeans and stress family unification.

1972

Congress passes Ethnic Heritage Studies Programs Act.

1980s *Debate over high immigration levels produces compromise legislation.*

1980

Refugee Act calls for refugees to be processed separately from immigrants and offers social services.

1986

Immigration Reform and Control Act gives amnesty to illegal aliens, who in early 1990s will become eligible for citizenship.

1988

Immigration amendments promote diversity by allowing visas for countries that have sent few immigrants to the U.S. in recent years.

1990s *Efforts to Streamline citizenship processing cause controversy.*

1990

Immigration Act (IMMACT) streamlines citizenship process for 4 million eligible citizens.

1994

Census reports that 22.3 million Americans are foreign-born. Jordan Commission on Immigration Reform recommends reducing number of immigrants. California voters pass Proposition 187 ("Save Our State") in November, denying school and health benefits to non-citizens including children; courts later block its implementation.

August 1995

Immigration and Naturalization Service (INS) launches Citizenship USA drive.

Aug. 1, 1996

House votes 259–169 to declare English the official language of the federal government.

September 1996

Financier George Soros sets up $50 million fund to help immigrants become citizens. President Clinton signs continuing resolution containing immigration bill beefing up border security. Congress holds hearings on whether INS and Vice President Al Gore sought to pressure INS to speed naturalizations to create Democratic voters.

Dec. 4, 1996

Supreme Court agrees to hear *Arizonans for Official English v. Arizona* on whether government services must be in English.

identity," Gallagher says. "Even some of our non-xenophobic but well-traveled friends tell her that after 25 years, what's so bad about having to make up your mind? And she could probably get her Indian citizenship back later if it were withdrawn when she became an American."

"But it's not a trivial thing, psychologically," he adds. "She told me when we married that she had to give up a lot when she moved here, and now has to give up that last remaining link to home. Americans don't seem to understand. Their nationalism is so strong, they don't seem to respect it in other countries."

The legal arguments against dual citizenship, says Douglas Klusmeyer, editor of the *Stanford Humanities Review,* "more often than not are red herrings. The modern trend in international law and in state practice has been to acknowledge that in today's mobile world, the phenomenon of dual citizenship is simply going to increase." Moreover, says Klusmeyer, who testified before the Senate panel, banning it in the United States will simply perpetuate a fiction, because "if their countries of origin are willing to issue new passports, there's no way you can stop it."

The country whose dual citizenship policy raises the most concern is Mexico. In December its Parliament voted to allow dual citizenship so that Mexicans who naturalize in the United States could still go back to Mexico to own property and get a Mexican passport, but not to vote. This move was alarming to some Americans, particularly those in Southern California who worked on the 1994 measure passed by California to halt public benefits to immigrants (since blocked by courts). The fear is that dual citizenship openly encourages Mexicans to move to the U.S. and try to influence U.S. policy toward Mexico. Latino college students and the occasional state legislator often talk of banning English in parts of the United States gained from Mexico under the 1848 Treaty of Guadalupe Hidalgo.

"This is not immigration, this is colonization," Stein says. "If at some point down the line Mexico were to decide to run its [boundary] across parts of the southern United States, which side of the conflict would these dual nationals fall on? The Mexican mythology that the Americans stole their land," Stein adds, "means that a time could come when Southern California will say we need a regional Hispanic council and then become as fragmented and

confused as the Weimar Republic" was in Germany.

The large number of Mexican immigrants in the Southwest gives new credence to the theory of Mexican irredentism known as the "reconquista," agrees historian David M. Kennedy. "There is no precedent in American history for these possibilities. No previous immigrant group had the size and concentration and easy access to its original culture that the Mexican immigrant group in the Southwest has today." [18]

Such theories are "crazy," says La Raza's Yzaguirre. "Even if there were too many Mexican-Americans in the Southwest, I know of no serious movement that talks about seceding. Being American is one of the most prized attributes—there has never been a Mexican-American turncoat in U.S. history."

Are Americans doing enough to ease the transition of new immigrants?

In New York City, 90 percent of the 45,000 cab drivers are foreign-born. So last year, when the city's Taxi and Limousine Commission was looking to boost the industry, it decided to provide new business opportunities for immigrants. For the first time since 1937, it increased the number of licensed cabs, adding 400 "medallions" to the 12,000 coveted plaques already in use.

"Many drivers in the past put their kids through college by owning a medallion," says Allan Fromberg, the taxi authority's assistant commissioner for public affairs. "But today it means more because it also means freedom, whether from religious persecution or an absence of economic opportunity. We're proud to have a part in it."

In the hotel industry, Marriott International Inc. has been leading a trend toward stabilizing corporate work forces by offering day care and social service referrals to the Bosnian, Chinese and Mexican immigrants who staff its cleaning and kitchen crews.[19]

The federal government aids immigrants with money provided by the 1982 Job Training Partnership Act and by State Legalization Impact Assistance Grants, as well $262 million annually for bilingual education programs for Asian and Hispanic students.

On the religious front, the Council of Jewish Organizations in Brooklyn recently launched its Business Outreach Center to help ethnic small businesses. And the Catholic Legal Immigration Network (CLINIC) has long provided legal aid, mentoring and training to indigent immigrants. "In many ways, the human condition is that of an immigrant," says John Swenson, executive director of migration and refugee services for the U.S. Catholic Conference. "Yes, some national limits on immigration are reasonable, but Catholic social policy emphasizes what is necessary for the preservation of individual dignity, even for illegal immigrants."

Public schools have an interest in being effective for immigrants, says Michael A. Resnick, senior associate executive director of the National School Boards Association. "Immigrants are an investment because the chances are they will be here the rest of their lives. Many of them come from countries with higher poverty rates and are illiterate even in their native language. And they require help not just with language transition problems but also with the larger cultural context. Some children from Mexico, for example, sometimes stay home for several weeks during the Christmas season because they're not used to having just a week off."

According to the 1995 Fannie Mae survey, 35 percent of immigrants say that native-born Americans are warm and welcoming, while 14 percent say they are cold and negative.

And just as there are extremes of anti-social immigrants, there are examples of home-grown misbehavior. South Asian newcomers settling on Staten Island, N.Y., for example, were recently greeted with graffiti reading "Indians go home. Leave or

Die."[20] And in Houston, a Vietnamese immigrant was beaten to death by skinheads.

To accuse average Americans of xenophobia, however, is unfair, says Yeh of the diversity coalition. "In Minnesota or Iowa, where immigration numbers are low, Americans will help newcomers, even if they don't speak English," she says. "But in a high-impact state like California or New York City, most people think immigration has made life worse. you don't have an obligation to adopt your neighbor's children. It's a burden. And if there are high numbers, it doesn't matter what color the people are. People in Oregon, Idaho and Montana are getting up in arms about the high numbers of white Californians coming to their states."

Immigration restriction advocates also argue that offering generous social services merely makes the United States a magnet for immigrants who are either illegal or too numerous. FAIR's Stein believes that America does not have to have a diverse society if it doesn't want to. "If we as a nation choose to believe it's better, more productive of human happiness not to be, then it's our own business.

"Most Americans don't see why we have immigration," he says. "They're told by *The Wall Street Journal* that it's a free lunch, but then they're told that immigrants are getting on welfare. How far can we stretch it without social turmoil? We could admit Moslems or Buddhists at rates that would overwhelm us, but why? Would it be the same country? I won't pass judgment on whether it would be for better or for worse, but it *would be* different. The old ties that bind are easy to ignore when the economic pie is growing, but the test is in periods of crisis."

The same arguments against racial and ethnic diversity "were made early in this century against Jews, Italians and Greeks, who were even called 'blacks' then because of their dark hair," Chavez says. "But I don't disagree that we have to have an American common culture and that the largest part of it is not merely European but in fact English. People adjust to it."

Such talk of preserving American culture is fine, "but which culture?" asks Gregory Fossedal, chairman of the Alexis de Tocqueville Institute; a pro-immigrant think tank in Arlington, Va. "When I drive along Wilson Boulevard in Arlington and see it teeming with hard-working Koreans and Vietnamese, I see the teamwork of new Americans. No one has established that difficulties are economic or culturally due to immigrants. There may be cultural limits, but we don't know where those limits are, and they would be at least three-to-five-times the current immigration levels because we handled that amount in the past with the Irish and Italians."

If immigration critics "can find an America that doesn't include these foreign influences," Fossedal says, "I'd like to see it."

NOTES

1. See "Asian Americans," *The CQ Researcher*, Dec. 13, 1991, pp. 945–968, and "Hispanic Americans," *The CQ Researcher*, Oct. 30, 1992, pp. 929–952.
2. See "Cracking Down on Immigration,", *The CQ Researcher*, Feb. 3, 1995, pp. 97–120; "Illegal Immigration," *The CQ Researcher*, April 24, 1992, pp. 361–384; and "Welfare, Work and the States," *The CQ Researcher*, Dec. 6, 1996, pp. 1057–1080.
3. National Conference of State Legislatures, *America's Newcomers: An Immigrant Policy Handbook*, September 1994, p. 57.
4. Testimony before the Senate Judiciary Subcommittee on Immigration, Oct. 22, 1996.
5. *Ibid.*
6. Ford Foundation, "Changing Relations" (1993), p. 4.
7. Manhattan Institute and Pacific Research Institute, *Strangers at Our Gate: Immigration in the 1990s* (1994), p. 76.
8. Senate Judiciary hearing, *op. cit.*
9. *The New York Times*, Dec. 1, 1996.
10. Terry Anderson, "The Culture Clash in South-Central L.A." *Los Angeles Times*, May 29, 1996.
11. Peter Brimelow, *Alien Nation*, (1995), p. xix.
12. National Conference of State Legislatures, *op. cit.*, p. 60.
13. *The Wall Street Journal*, July 11, 1996.
14. Quoted in National Endowment for the Humanities, "A National Conversation: How We Act in Private and in Public," 1994.
15. See "Debate Over Bilingualism" *The CQ Researcher*, Jan. 19, 1996, pp. 49–72.
16. Senate Judiciary hearings, *op. cit.*
17. Quoted in *The New York Times*, Dec. 30, 1996.
18. David M. Kennedy, "Can We Still Afford to be a Nation of Immigrants?" *The Atlantic Monthly*, November 1996, p. 58.
19. See "Low-Wage Lessons," *Business Week*, Nov. 11, 1996, p. 109.
20. See Juan F. Perea (ed.,) *Immigrants Out! The New Nativism and the Anti-Immigrant Impulse in the United States* (1997), p. 13.

BY THE NUMBERS

U.S. IMMIGRATION

From the founding of the republic to the mid-1920s, U.S. immigration was largely unrestricted, but shortly thereafter Congress passed legislation severely limiting entry from all regions except northwestern Europe. Beginning in 1965 and continuing thereafter, it passed a series of more liberal laws, including the Immigration and Reform Act of 1986, under which 2.7 million illegal aliens, mostly from Mexico, were given legal immigrant status. The new laws not only promoted diversity but also opened the door to the longest and largest wave of immigration ever—27 million since 1965, including illegal entries. Until now, the two largest waves had been from 1899 through 1914, which reached 13.6 million, and from 1880 through 1898, which reached 8.6 million. Not all immigrants stay: in recent years, emigration has been about 220,000 annually.

In 1996, a more or less typical year, there were 916,000 legal immigrants plus an estimated 275,000 who came illegally. Favorite immigrant destinations were California, where one third went, and the New York metropolitan area, which drew about one in six. As a group, immigrants are less skilled and younger than the average American. Of the legal immigrants, 65 percent entered under family reunification programs and 13 percent under employment-based preference programs; 14 percent were refugees or asylum seekers. From 1990 through 1998, an average of 460,000 immigrants a year became citizens.

There is sharp disagreement over immigration policy. Some, like Virginia Abernethy of Vanderbilt University, say that high immigration threatens American labor and the environment; Roy Beck, Washington editor of Social Contract, says it contributes to "demographic Balkanization." But the late Julian Simon of the University of Maryland believed that immigration is beneficial, because an increase in population raises the number of creative minds

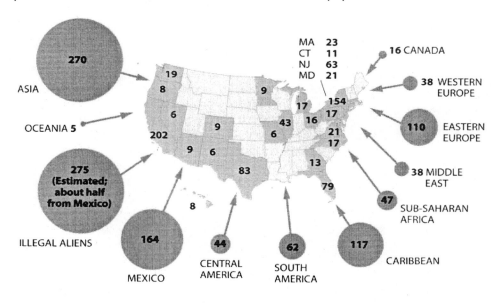

STATES WHERE MOST IMMIGRANTS SETTLE

REGIONS WHERE IMMIGRANTS ORIGINATE

SOURCE: U.S. Immigration and Naturalization Service. Numerals indicate number of immigrants in thousands. Map shows states with at least 5,000 legal immigrants in 1996. Circles show immigrants by country of birth.

Reprinted from *Scientific American*, September 1999, pp. 28–29. Reprinted by permission.

and hence the pace of innovation. And then there are those who, like historian Arthur M. Schlesinger, Jr., feel that "any curtailment of immigration offends something in the American soul."

On at least two points virtually everyone agrees. The first is that the U.S. population will grow enormously, absent a drastic reduction in immigration. A big drop in immigration does not seem imminent in view of pressures from many ethnic groups, which generally support a heterogeneous society, and from employers who depend on low-wage labor. The U.S. Census Bureau's latest projection, which assumes a continuation of recent immigration and emigration levels over the next half a century, puts the U.S. population at 394 million in 2050. Of the 122 million increase between now and then, 80 million would be added because of immigration. The prospects beyond 2050 depend on a variety of factors, among them population growth in developing countries, incomes in developing countries relative to those in the U.S., the availability of alternative host countries and the cost of transportation to the U.S. Of these, only population can be predicted with even a moderate degree of confidence.

The second point of agreement is that the U.S. will become increasingly more diverse. In 1980 the U.S. was 80 percent Anglo—that is, non-Hispanic white. It is now 72 percent Anglo, and by 2050, according to Census Bureau projections, it will be 53 percent. California and New Mexico are now slightly less than half Anglo, and by 2015 Texas will also be a minority Anglo state. There is much apprehension that continued immigration of Mexican nationals will lead to dominance of the Spanish language in the Southwest. Such fears seem to be overblown, for several studies show that most second-generation Mexican-Americans speak fluent English.

—*Rodger Doyle (rdoyle2@aol.com)*

Newcomers and Established Residents

Robert L. Bach

Ours is a time of crossing, blurring, and redefining boundaries. Not since the turn of the century have communities throughout America reflected the diversity of cultures, nationalities, languages, and religions brought by immigrants during the last two decades. According to the 1990 census, there are nearly 20 million foreign-born residents in America. As established communities receive these newcomers, diversity is recasting relations among groups, ethnic identities, community associations, and political alliances. Once again, America is changing.

In 1987 a national board of scholars launched a project to examine the interactions of new immigrants and established, long-term residents. Changes in immigration law in the 1960s shifted both the magnitude and composition of new immigrant populations. They opened the gates to immigration from Asia and the Pacific and stabilized flows from Latin America and the Caribbean. The share of European immigrants declined. This new mix of diverse newcomers became an essential ingredient in the transformation of community life. The National Board of the Changing Relations Project sought to identify the ways in which recent immigrants interacted with ethnically diverse established residents, how they organized themselves, in which social institutions they participated, and how host communities were adapting to the newcomers. The board examined, within the context of rapid economic change and frequently deep social divisions, if and how newcomers and established residents crossed social, cultural, and political boundaries to create and to maintain community.

From the outset, the board was concerned with popular reports of dramatic instances of unrest and conflict between members of immigrant and established resident groups. Spectacular incidents, such as conflict between Southeast Asian refugees and Texas shrimp farmers, had been highlighted in the national press and had even become the subject of full-length movies. Similarly dramatic accounts of Korean shopkeepers in conflict with host African-American communities implied unyielding hardship. Invidious comparisons of immigrant success stories with impoverished minorities also fueled a widespread mythology about job competition. Did these incidents suggest what was to become of the nation's increasingly diverse communities?

The Changing Relations Project was launched during a highly charged national debate over reform of U.S. immigration policy. For only the fourth time in U.S. history, the nation sought to change who could immigrate and to reform the rules governing how people could enter. Throughout the debate, undercurrents of concern about the absorptive capacity of U.S. communities remained unsettled. The answers found in this study, from the rare and exceptional nature of incidents of open conflict to infrequent but promising efforts at intergroup coalition-building, respond to those undercurrents. The answers are not only about immigrants. They demand that attention be given to community conditions both newcomers and established residents face and struggle to overcome together.

The Changing Economic Background

As a nation, we have been here before. America thrives on its immigrant heritage. Part history, part ideology, immigration embodies the theme of national renewal, rebirth, hope. Uprooted abroad, newcomers become transplants in a land that promises opportunity. Yet America has also become settled. At the turn of the century, the foreign-born accounted for roughly 14 percent of the U.S. population. Today, they make up about one-half. The context of reception, as well as the capacity of immigration to reform community life, has also changed. The story is no longer only that of the uprooted, settled on an open frontier or in industrial cauldrons; it is also the story of subsequent U.S.-born generations that have blossomed or been left behind by the march of American history.

Most Americans today were born when the nation was at its most insular and provincial. In the 1950s few could have foreseen the turnaround in immigration flows that would result from political changes in the 1960s. As America emerged from World War II, the share of the population that was foreign-born was declining. As those who entered the United States in earlier years aged and immigration restrictions excluded entire regions of the world, the proportion of foreign-born dropped from almost 9 percent to 5 percent in the 1950s. In the 1960s, before immigration policy reforms were implemented, the share fell again to historical lows, with less than 5 percent of the total population being foreign-born.

If few could foresee the changes in immigration, even fewer anticipated the transformation of the American political economy that today is popular wisdom. In the last two decades, the U.S. economy lost much of its strength and position in the world. Although it is still the largest economy in the world, it now accounts for only one-fifth of the world's output, compared with one-third during the 1950s and 1960s. The U.S. economy also became increasingly internationalized during that period. Foreign trade grew to become a much larger proportion of the nation's economic activities, but that change brought with it an imbalance that made America not only economically interdependent but financially dependent on foreign capital. In the last decade, rapid increases in foreign investment and foreign ownership of highly visible U.S. property reinforced the image that more and more essential economic decisions were being made abroad.

For many Americans these changes were personal. Manufacturing jobs disappeared and new opportunities were limited primarily to the service sector or to jobs that required higher skills or specialized education. New groups entered the labor market. The proportion of women participating in the labor force increased dramatically, and the share of ethnic minorities working in particular jobs grew rapidly.

Economic restructuring has also realigned the nation's geographical balance. Demographic, economic, and political power has shifted away from the Midwest and Northeast toward high-growth areas in the South and Southwest. The redistribution has been highly uneven, spawning patches of rapid growth alongside pockets of decline. These economic shifts were accompanied by political decentralization, characterized by fierce competition among states, counties, and cities to attract or to hold on to sectors of dynamic economic activity. The result was a redistribution of the nation's political and economic power toward regions and localities. Regional economies, each comprising specific combinations of jobs, markets, and people, became the primary focus of economic vitality. With huge budget deficits handcuffing the federal government, these regions, their political localities, and the unique combinations of people living there assumed the obligations of responding to the social consequences of large-scale political and economic challenges.

Increases in the volume and diversity of immigration were both a response and further stimulus to this restructuring, accentuating the unevenness of regional growth. Immigration has not occurred in all areas of the United States, however. Concentrating in particular areas, newcomers have become inextricable parts of the character and identity of those areas. In New York, Los Angeles, Miami, Chicago, Houston, and other large cities, long-term residents soon lived, worked, and played alongside newcomers.

In the 1950s and 1960s, few observers could have predicted the full implications of this uneven regional concentration and the ways in which it would entangle immigrants and long-established urban populations. The concerns of that earlier period were the increasing concentration and resulting ghettoization of black Americans in urban centers. Successive national commissions warned of the consequences these changes would have for relations between blacks and whites. Yet, few envisioned the emergence of a new generation of ethnically diverse Americans resulting from the increased immigration of diverse peoples to the United States.[1]

---

1. It should be noted that throughout this report, group labels such as white, black, Hispanic, and Asian have been used according to usage in the research site or for clarity of presentation and comparison. It should also be noted that the board of the Changing Relations Project and the researchers recognize the diversity of the groups that are inappropriately classified by such simple terms. In fact, much of the report's discussion points to the importance of the heterogeneity of immigrant and established minority groups.

The simultaneous concentration of established ethnic minorities and new immigrants in rapidly changing regions sharpened the differences among these groups and reshaped opportunities for interactions among them, heightening awareness and concern for their unequal economic status. In many cities, poverty and wealth grew side by side. As poverty became primarily an urban phenomenon, so did immigration. How was it that some groups were moving into dynamic sectors of the U.S. economy and society, while others were stagnating? How did this unevenness affect opportunities for group interactions and perceptions of common interests and goals as the number of nationalities and ethnic groups multiplied?

Decades of uneven political and economic change have rekindled fundamental arguments over how immigrants adapt to America. Some observers have renewed a traditional interest in assimilation and Americanization by focusing on the potential harmful effects of immigrants' linguistic, political, and social differences, turning public attention to the so-called quality of new immigrants and the different capacities of individuals to move into the dominant culture.

Others have stressed the persistence of ethnic differences and the nation's commitment to pluralism. Rather than individual qualities, this pluralist perspective emphasizes group resources and the limits to social advancement imposed by highly uneven economic and political opportunities. These contrasting views are more than disagreements about immigrant adaptation. They represent fundamentally different conceptions of the role of diversity in American society. As different as these two perspectives are, they share similar shortcomings. Both focus primarily on immigrants themselves, how well they perform economically, and how fast they settle and succeed. As a result, their focus is one-sided, concentrating only on immigrants' individual and group characteristics, or on newcomers' unique positions in U.S. society. They fail to capture the full range of interactions among newcomers and established resident groups and the potential consequences of new, multidimensional relations.

Structure of the Study

In carrying out the research project, the multidisciplinary Changing Relations Board adopted an approach that de-emphasized group charac-

teristics and differences and highlighted interactions and relations. The researchers' goal was to examine the social construction of groups, starting with day-to-day activities, including face-to-face contacts among individuals in daily encounters, group interactions, and relationships between such institutions as community and civic organizations.

The board developed three strategies for studying relations among newcomers and established residents. The first was to capture the diversity of place. Economic and political restructuring, demographic shifts, and immigration have changed the composition of activities in particular localities and have created unique combinations of individuals, groups, and social activities. People understand and act differently within the specific contexts of where they settle.

To reflect the importance of regionalism and to show different segments of the nation's reordered economy, the six sites selected for the study included areas of new growth and capital restructuring in the South and Southwest, deindustrializing rust-belt cities, as well as a range of urban, suburban, and rural areas. The selection also stressed variations in the size of the local immigrant population, and coverage of as many of the largest immigrant and established groups as possible. (For data on the percentages of the foreign-born in the six sites see Table 1.)

The sites selected were:

- *Albany Park, Chicago, Illinois.* An area northwest of downtown Chicago, Albany Park has grown with successive waves of immigrants. The contemporary social mix contains a remarkable degree of diversity, including Southeast Asians, Poles, Koreans, African Americans, Middle Easterners, and Jews, among others. In a city known for immigrant neighborhoods, Albany Park reflects a new pattern of dispersed ethnicity, where members of various groups are distributed within a wide geographical area. Still, most residents confine their relationships to their own ethnic group. Research for this study concentrated on community organizations, including ward-level political organizations and neighborhood civic associations; the use of public space, including streets, sidewalks, bus stops, public schools, libraries, and commercial establishments; and group relationships within a large apartment building.

Table 1: Percent Foreign Born in Total Population

Research Site	1950	1960	1970	1980	1990
Monterey Park, California	8.0	10.2	13.6	31.2	51.8
Miami, Florida	10.4	12.0	24.2	35.6	45.1
Chicago, Illinois	12.8	9.7	8.1	10.5	13.1
Garden City, Kansas	2.5	2.1	1.4	3.8	-
Philadelphia, Pennsylvania	9.2	7.3	5.4	5.4	5.3
Houston, Texas	2.5	2.3	2.5	7.6	13.3

Sources: United States Department of Commerce. Bureau of the Census.

- *Garden City, Kansas.* For Garden City, a small town caught up in a new round of rural industrialization, the opening of the world's largest meatpacking plant sparked a decade of rapid economic growth and profound social change. During that period, Garden City grew faster than any other town in Kansas. The work attracted immigrants and influenced the community response to them. It turned a community of long-term resident Anglos and Mexican Americans into a diverse town that included Southeast Asian refugees and new immigrants from Mexico and Central America. Faced with rapidly increasing demands on housing, social services, education, and other community services, the residents of Garden City responded with church-led alliances, electoral changes, and increased financial support.

- *Houston, Texas.* Responding to cycles of economic decline and recovery, novel patterns of settlement in Houston have emerged. These include a new settlement of Central American immigrants within an Anglo section of town and an older neighborhood of low-income African American and Latino residents. Community organizations created many of the opportunities for interaction among these groups. By examining a housing complex, an umbrella organization of 30 Hispanic community organizations whose interests were in social issues such as education and employment, and two churches, the study was able to compare efforts that brought people together and also divided people. The effects of the Immigration Reform and Control Act of 1986 were of special interest. The opportunity for undocumented immigrants to legalize and become full social participants changed their relations with established groups and local institutions.

- *Miami, Florida.* The number and concentration of newcomers have made the interplay of immigrants and established residents a central theme of Miami's identity and character. Miami is marked by the contrast of relations among resident Anglos and upper-class Cuban immigrants with relations among working-class Cubans, African Americans, and Haitians. Race plays a dominant role in the control and distribution of resources and in the organization of groups as seen at an apparel factory, a construction site, and two hotels. In the schools, the focus of attention is on relations between Haitian and African-American students.

- *Monterey Park, California.* A middle-class Los Angeles suburb that historically housed the residentially and economically mobile, Monterey Park is feeding off rapid growth throughout the region. It combines Anglos, Latinos, and Asian Americans, and is particularly a magnet for large-scale immigration from Taiwan, Hong Kong, and China. Rapid commercial and residential development, much of it owned and fueled by elite Chinese newcomers, coincided with problems of inflation and congestion. Anglos have retained political power although the city has a Chinese majority. Monterey Park provides a textbook case for the political struggle over language, wealth, community development, and political representation.

- *Philadelphia, Pennsylvania.* Against a backdrop of deeply entrenched black-white relations that have shaped Philadelphia politics and community settlement

Table 2: Selection of Research Sites and Arenas

Monterey Park	Houston	Garden City	Chicago	Miami	Philadelphia
Neighborhood	Apartment Complex	Trailer Park	Apartment Complex	Neighborhood	
Community Organizations	Community Organizations	Community Organizations	Community Organizations	Community Organizations	Community Organizations
		Workplaces		Workplaces	Workplaces
		Schools		Schools	Schools
City Council			Chamber of Commerce	Chamber of Commerce	

for decades, immigrants faced an ambivalent reception. They have not dominated any particular locality, but have been incorporated into established struggles over community stability and between neighborhoods and the city government. A city-wide network of social institutions devoted to relations among groups has influenced both coalition-building efforts and the ideology of accommodation. Arenas of interaction, like business strips and schools, bring together not only whites, blacks, and mainland- and island-born Puerto Ricans, but Koreans, recent Polish emigres, Vietnamese, Indians, Portuguese, Chinese, Cambodians, Laotians, Cubans, Guatemalans, Nicaraguans, and Colombians, as well.

The board's second research strategy involved selection of arenas within the local communities in which to observe contact and interaction among newcomers and established residents. Social distance and spatial segregation of groups within these six sites made arenas of interaction rare and special. The arenas presupposed an opportunity for interaction and a particular purpose in bringing people of diverse backgrounds together. The arenas selected included five broad groupings—community organizations, schools, workplaces, places of worship, and neighborhoods. Considerable variation exists within these broad categories. For example, the neighborhood arena includes interactions within three very different housing areas, including a mobile home park, an apartment complex, and an apartment building. (See Table 2.)

The third research strategy incorporated the specificity and uniqueness of local knowledge, history, and perceptions in the national design. The board put together teams of researchers whose members had extensive experience in the localities and arenas of interaction and who represented the groups they were to study. Board members helped craft the local research plans and, from more than 100 initial applications, selected the six that finally constituted this project.

For two years, the research teams spent considerable time in their communities. They interviewed, observed, participated, organized, and lived in the neighborhoods and among those they studied. They recorded detailed descriptions of behavior, activities, and perceptions. They often served as volunteers in organizing community festivals, neighborhood groups, and issue-oriented coalitions, and worked in election campaigns and civic organizations. They were employed in local industries and businesses, shopped in nearby stores, attended neighborhood public events, and became part of everyday interactions among friends and strangers. They complemented these ethnographic techniques with open-ended interviews, formal surveys, and collection of secondary source, statistical information. Each of the six research teams constructed answers to the following five questions that guided the national project.

- What is the nature of relations between native-born or longer-resident Americans and new immigrants? What are the primary settings for interactions among these groups? What situations bring individuals

---

2. Each research team gave the board a site report addressing the five questions of the study. At times, portions of site reports are paraphrased in this book.

from various groups together or keep them apart?

- What are cultural conceptions of American identity and American life, and how do these take shape through intergroup interactions?
- What sources of conflict, distance, tolerance, accommodation and competition exist among these groups and what factors promote or inhibit their presence?
- To what extent have large-scale, long-term changes in the economy, the population structure, and the polity influenced the way in which immigrants and established residents interact?
- What situations, actions, and strategies promote communication, understanding, accommodation, and accord when multigroup interactions occur?

Board Report and Project Themes

The purpose of this report by the National Board of the Changing Relations Project is to synthesize the findings of the six research teams in a way that addresses questions of national significance.[2]

Chapter 2 examines the influence of economic and political restructuring in the formation of social diversity. In particular, it focuses on the recomposition of the American working class and the subsequent change in opportunities for interaction, tension, separation, and accommodation.

Chapter 3 examines interactions directly. It explores how groups are brought together, organized, and divided. It examines which social institutions are involved in shaping these relations. Part of this analysis involves highlighting the remaking of community in areas deeply influenced historically by racial and class divisions. Chapter 4 focuses on interactions among groups that overcome social divisions and move toward some form of accommodation. It highlights the organizing strategies and attempts of groups and organizers to change community conditions where immigrants and established residents live. It focuses on the processes of inclusion and exclusion and, ultimately, on "membership" in and identity with American society. Finally, Chapter 5 identifies activities, goals, and policies that contribute to cohesion rather than to disintegration, and that promote interaction and accommodation between groups.

Throughout its planning, discussions, and meetings, the board found itself coming back to several consistent themes which reverberate throughout each of the following chapters.

Diversity. The America that immigrants face today is very different from the America of earlier historical periods. The increasing reality of and political commitments to pluralism create a new reference point for adaptation to U.S. society. Notions of Anglo conformity or assimilation to a single culture simply have no immediate relevance in situations in which newcomers and established resident racial and ethnic minorities interact as dominant groups. These mixed settings further legitimize diversity and provide role models that depart from any idealized notion of what America means.

Settlement. Geographical boundaries of settlement have always been important to organizing relations among newcomers and established residents. Traditional notions of community were shaped by relations formed out of the geographical concentration of work and residence. These boundaries are changing. Particularly compelling are persistent issues of segregation, along with the unanticipated consequences of the pressure on the few institutions and places where diverse groups come into contact. Tension and conflict as well as cooperation emerge from these rare contacts.

Conflict. Dramatic episodes of violent conflict are infrequent throughout the six sites of this study. More prevalent relations include competition, tension, and opposition. Although these relations often deeply divide, their consequences are controlled by social rules created and enforced by a community's own institutions and modes of accommodation. The issue is not simply the infrequency of conflict, but the strength of these rules and institutions.

Class and Gender. The importance of social class is often ignored in popular commentaries on immigration and social change in America. To some extent this reflects the historical theme of individual opportunity that permeates the nation's immigrant heritage. It also results from a pervasive discourse on race and ethnicity as the primary sources of social divisions. Yet social class, intertwined with race, ethnicity, and gender, remains a cornerstone of the structure of communities and is essential for understanding relations among newcomers and established residents. Women are an essential component of these class-based relations, often serving on the "front lines" of interactions among newcomers and established residents. Service-sector jobs put them there, and participation in community organizations reinforces their involvement. Recognition of common interests also motivates women to organize activities that cross group lines.

Language. Beyond segregation and social distance, it should come as no surprise that communication—language—stands out as the most important feature of interactions among newcomers and established residents. Language binds and separates. Patterns of language usage often express power relations. But they also reveal individual and collective perceptions of the human experience. Language serves throughout diverse communities as a source of intergroup conflict, tension, and distance. Creating institutional settings for language acquisition, however, also provides a source of shared interests, an opportunity for interaction and a purpose behind cooperation.

Racial Stratification. Immigration highlights the social and cultural dimensions of race and ethnicity. The diversity of people and places in this study highlights the blurring and remaking of racial boundaries. It challenges popular conceptions of the so-called browning of America. Immigrants do not simply reflect intermediate colors on a unidimensional scale representing more or less black or white. Rather, they engage in multidimensional relations that form complex interactions crossing several social boundaries simultaneously. Current immigration challenges the traditional correlation of race and ethnicity with class and economic status. The immigration of groups with wealth who are not classified as white is reshaping the intertwining of color, ancestry, and background with class, power, and privilege.

Community Control. A common experience of crisis in many of America's communities limits interactions and possibilities for cooperation. Yet, these same problems also create shared interests and compatible goals. Many of the most promising signs of leadership and intergroup organization focus on local issues of community standards, including the availability, cost, and value of housing, social

services, schools, education, law enforcement, and safety.

Policy

The policy questions raised in this report do not necessarily ask whether America should reduce or increase the volume of immigration or change the national origins or skills of those it admits. These are issues largely settled by recent congressional debate and passage of the Immigration Act of 1990. Rather, the immigrants in which this study is interested have already arrived and have become part of the nation. Our question is how America is absorbing these newcomers and, in turn, how these newcomers are changing America. The nation frequently forgets its responsibility for immigration; movement to America occurs primarily by invitation. What established Americans have never fully understood, but which immigrants never forget, is that America is deeply implicated in the migration flow and its destiny. American employers fuel the immigration, American foreign policy embraces it, and American family values maintain it.

The policy issues addressed in this report concern a framework for action and development. With the increasing diversity of groups becoming social and political actors, the questions for the future will be what effective responses can be developed and by whom? Reshaping community organizations should be a priority. As diversity increases, many current arrangements may not hold. The decentralization of political authority, for instance, has led to gaps between federal policies and regional and local interests. Social distances among groups within communities are reflected in the gap between local and national policy makers. To overcome difficulties encountered by local communities, including financial impasses and politics of disengagement as well as politics of apportioning blame, a new political discourse may be needed that focuses on efforts to organize diversity, to build activities that involve many groups working together.

Contrary to some popular celebrations of pluralism, however, diversity does not mean simple harmony. The challenge for America may be less in harmonizing relations among groups than in mobilizing intergroup cooperation into strategies for economic and political advancement. If the national goal is to create harmony, then the struggle must not be just for social peace but for opportunity and equality.

Unit Selections

Key Points to Consider

❖ Novel approaches toward the peaceful reconciliation of conflict should be explored more thoroughly. For example, unlike conflict among ethnic groups in the United States, conflict between the United States and Native Americans is regulated by treaties. The struggle over claims regarding the rights of nations and the interests of the U.S. government and its citizens is no longer at the margin of public affairs. Does the definition of this conflict as an issue of foreign and not domestic policy provide a meaningful distinction? Should the claims of ethnic groups in defense of culture, territory, and unique institutions be honored and protected by law and public policy? Why or why not? Is sovereignty an issue? Defend your answer.

❖ How should commitments to the self-determination of people be ensured and enforced? What levels of tolerance are assumed by the UN Working Group? What value conflicts, if any, are beyond compromise?

❖ What are the most compelling issues that face indigenous ethnic communities? Economy? Culture? What social, economic, and political conditions will affect the next indigenous ethnic generation?

❖ Because of the strides of the current Native American community, will the next generation enter the middle class mainstream of America? Should that be a goal? Does improving economically and in terms of other quality of life indicators mean the denial of traditional cultural values and practices?

❖ How much devolution of authority to Native Americans are state legislatures willing to negotiate? What role should the national government play: an advocate for Native Americans or states? An honest broker? Does the role depend on the issue? Water? Casinos? Mining? Taxation? What about cultural rights?

 **Links**   **www.dushkin.com/online/**

12. **American Indian Science and Engineering Society (AISES)**
    http://spot.colorado.edu/~aises/aises.html

These sites are annotated on pages 4 and 5.

The contemporary issues of Native Americans as well as the descendants of all conquered indigenous peoples add their weight to the claims for cultural justice, equal protection, and due process in our hemisphere, but in fact this is a worldwide phenomenon. The United Nations provided a media forum for attention to indigenous populations, and NGOs (nongovernmental organizations) committed to human rights address global economic interests regarding the protection of human and physical ecologies. The post–World War II end of colonialism and the emergence of new nations in Asia and Africa pointed to the development of new states, but also to the problems of nation-building in contexts of extreme ethnic variety. Even the Soviet Union became engaged in the plethora of nations and ethnic populations of Central Asia and Eastern Europe. Only during the last decade have social and political scientists been able to view these widespread phenomena from a perspective that enables us to see the full implications of ethnic and race relations as a foundational issue for political and economic order. Relationships between indigenous peoples in the United States were marginated and isolated. Their cultures were articulated in folkloric and touristic ways when interaction with mainstream America occurred.

Such traditional relations were challenged during the civil rights era. Moreover, the celebration of the Bicentennial of the American Revolution in 1976, the empowerment of Native Americans, and their victories in the courts and in legislative authority produced a new threshold from which the renegotiation of relationships could begin. With new cultural confidence and economic capacity, most notably in the gaming industry, the descendants of native peoples entered a new epoch of American pluralism. Some may argue that the reclamation and revival of tradition and power are unique social and political events. A wider view suggests that native populations are but another manifestation of an ethnic group's articulation of its power and the pursuit of its agenda within the contexts of the American legal and economic order. Acute popular consciousness of indigenous peoples was heightened when attempts to celebrate the 500th anniversary of Christopher Columbus's voyage of discovery encountered strong resistance from advocates of Native Americans.

On the international level another front of resistance emerged in the struggle against apartheid in South Africa. While many Americans viewed the South African situation through the simplistic lens of color consciousness, its impact on the larger arena has become apparent. The development of a new South African regime increased awareness of indigenous peoples. The exploration of roots and new remedies for the conquest that turned many into a permanent underclass has awakened indigenous people, and a code of international conduct in protection of cultural rights has entered international law.

The following articles represent a cross section of the current experience of indigenous ethnic groups, their forced accommodation of a high-tech world, the environmental and cultural effects of rapid change, and the challenges to a renewal of their identifying traditions. The indigenous ethnic populations invite us to recall their struggles and to find ways of shaping and sharing the new sense of pluralism offered within the American experience and the spiritual sources of ethnic identity that people encounter as the legitimacy of ancient practices widens.

Indigenous ethnic communities have encountered a complex array of historical, social, cultural, and economic forces. As a result, in the late twentieth century, the traditions of indigenous ethnic groups have been renegotiated by yet another generation. The North and South American economies and pluralistic cultures, as well as those of other continents, are a challenging stage for their quest for self-sufficiency as well as for the preservation of a unique cultural legacy. Current indigenous ethnic leaders challenge past perceptions. They find it increasingly difficult to strike a balance between traditional values and new demands. Native Americans have increasingly interfaced with the American legal system at the state level on issues of land use and gaming, which represent part of this current redefinition. Finally, however, they are challenging themselves to be themselves, and examples of indigenous self-help reveal insights into how personal leadership and service to the community weave the social fabric of civil society.

Ethnicity is built upon the truth and strength of a tradition. Senses of family and community and an unwillingness to give up claims have led to standoffs with many forces within America. From this perspective, this unit details ways in which an ethnic group retrieves its rights and heritage to preserve an ancient culture from extinction.

The expansion and profitability of Native American gambling casinos, their attendant impact on state and local economies, and the tax exemptions enjoyed by these ventures appear to be headed toward contentions that may spill over into new issues of public order. On the international level, the discussion of human and cultural rights of peoples guaranteed in the United Nations and the traditional mode of state sovereignty indicates that a fragile accommodation between indigenous people and the mainstream societies at whose margins they exist may be entering a new phase. Their unequal relationship began with the consolidation of large territorial political and economic regimes. Under scrutiny are personal rights and group rights, pluralistic realms that ensure transnational solidarity, and cultural and religious challenges to those in authority fueled by the passion for power at those intersections between modernity and tradition—the large-scale institutional versus the local and culturally-specific community.

Indigenous Ethnic Groups

New Answers to an Old Question:

Who Got Here First?

By JOHN NOBLE WILFORD

SANTA FE, N.M.—For most of the 20th century, the solution to the mystery of the original Americans—where did they come from, when and how?—seemed as clear as the geography of the Bering Strait, the climate of the last ice age and the ubiquity of finely wrought stone hunting weapons known as Clovis points.

According to the ruling theory, bands of big-game hunters trekked out of Siberia sometime before 11,500 years ago. They crossed into Alaska when the floor of the Bering Strait, drained dry by the accumulation of water in a frozen world's massive glaciers, was a land bridge between continents, and found themselves in a trackless continent, the New World when it was truly new.

The hunters, so the story went, moved south through a corridor between glaciers and soon flourished on the Great Plains and in the Southwest of what is now the United States, their presence widely marked by distinctive stone projectile points first discovered near the town of Clovis, N.M. In less than 1,000 years, these Clovis people and their distinctive stone points made it all the way to the tip of South America. They were presumably the founding population of today's American Indians.

People may have arrived tens of thousands of years sooner than believed.

Now a growing body of intriguing evidence is telling a much different story. From Alaska to Brazil and southern Chile, artifacts and skeletons are forcing archaeologists to abandon Clovis orthodoxy and come to terms with a more complex picture of earliest American settlement. People may have arrived thousands to tens of thousands of years sooner, in many waves of migration and by a number of routes. Their ancestry may not have been only Asian. Some of the migrations may have originated in Australia or Europe.

The Clovis-first paradigm "has become increasingly improbable," said Dr. Robson Bonnichsen, an archaeologist at Oregon State University in Corvallis, opening a recent conference here titled "Clovis and Beyond" at which archaeologists looked beyond the shards of old theory in search of new explanations.

"Clovis was not the only culture in America 11,000 years ago," Dr. Bonnichsen said.

Two discoveries—the remains of a pre-Clovis camp at Monte Verde in Chile and the skull and bones of the Kennewick Man, possibly as old as 9,300 years and bearing little physical resemblance to later American Indians—are primarily responsible for the profound shift in thinking. Freed from the restrictive Clovis model, archaeologists and other scholars have aired a wide assortment of alternative explanations for the initial occupation of America.

"Monte Verde puts the peopling of America in a new light," said Dr. David J. Meltzer of Southern Methodist University in Dallas. Two years ago, Dr. Meltzer was a member of a blue-ribbon panel of archaeologists, including some resolute skeptics, who inspected the Monte Verde site, which had been excavated by Dr. Tom D. Dillehay of the University of Kentucky. The visitors took a close look at the stone, wood and bone artifacts, remnants of hide-covered huts and a child's footprint. These were judged to be clear evidence that humans had reached southern Chile 12,500 years ago, more than a millennium before the first signs of Clovis hunters in North America.

After years of stout resistance from many establishment archaeologists, the Clovis barrier had finally been breached. Monte Verde was not only the first confirmed pre-Clovis site, but it was nowhere near the Bering Strait and bore little resemblance to the Clovis culture. It seemed time to examine more seriously other migration hypotheses.

Because the ice-free corridor on the eastern flank of the Rockies did not open before 13,000 years ago, and does not appear to have had many plants or animals to feed travelers, many scholars have revived speculation of coastal migration routes.

Some of the early people may have come from northeast Asia in hide-covered boats, hugging the southern shore of the Bering land bridge, putting in from time to time for food and water. They could have continued down the west coast of North America long before the glacial corridor was available to them. They could have traveled great distances in relatively short periods, conceivably reaching South America much faster and more easily than by any land routes. Prehistoric people at least as early as the Australian colonists some 50,000 years ago had boats capable of open-sea navigation.

Coastal migration is an attractive idea, archaeologists at the conference said, because it could explain the existence of Monte Verde and other possibly pre-Clovis sites in several places in South America and why their cultures, by Clovis times, bore few similarities to North American settlers. Perhaps, Dr. Meltzer said, "there were more, rather than fewer, migratory pulses to the Americas."

Establishing a coastal migration was once thought to be hopeless. At the end of the ice age, melting glaciers raised sea levels and inundated what had been ancient shorelines. But recent artifact discoveries off British Columbia, in the Channel Islands off California and along the coast of Peru have bolstered arguments favoring coastal routes as one of many migration theories.

"Clovis first and Clovis everywhere was a regional North Ameri-

can phenomenon, and a late one at that," said Dr. Ruth Gruhn of the University of Alberta in Edmonton, reflecting a view long held by a few archaeologists working at South American sites. "North Americans have been discounting South American evidence because it did not fit their models."

Monte Verde also inspired researchers in North America to dig deeper. They have found possibly pre-Clovis remains in South Carolina and Virginia and are beginning to reinterpret findings at the Meadowcroft rock shelter, a site near Pittsburgh.

This was how Dr. Albert Goodyear, a University of South Carolina archaeologist, discovered likely pre-Clovis traces at the Topper site near the Savannah River. "I had stopped a little below the Clovis stratum," Dr. Goodyear explained. "You don't look for what you don't believe in. But in light of Monte Verde, I thought, maybe this might be a place to look for pre-Clovis."

Increasing evidence of early Clovis, and possibly pre-Clovis, remains in the Eastern United States has raised eyebrows. Perhaps the hunters who came through the ice-free corridor went east first, then moved west. An even bolder idea is attracting debate: perhaps ancestors of the Clovis hunters arrived not by the Bering land bridge, but from Europe by boats skirting the ice of the North Atlantic.

Dr. Dennis Stanford of the Smithsonian Institution, a leading proponent of the possible European connection, cited as evidence the stylistic similarities between the stone tools of Clovis and those of the Solutrean culture from Spain and southwestern France, dated from 20,000 to 16,000 years ago. The idea has drawn little support from most archaeologists.

But if Monte Verde encouraged thinking about multiple migrations, the discovery of the Kennewick Man, a skeleton found in 1997 in Washington State and dated between 8,000 and 9,300 years old,

raised unsettling questions about the origins of the first Americans. Were they all from Asia? Are American Indians actually direct descendants from the first migrants?

Early descriptions of the Kennewick skull led to reports that the man was Caucasoid and possibly European. After a more careful analysis, the skull appeared to be longer and narrower than those of modern American Indians. Dr. Joseph Powell of the University of New Mexico reported last month that its physical affinities appeared to be closer to those of South Asians or Polynesians than either Europeans or American Indians.

At the conference, Dr. Douglas Owsley of the Smithsonian Institution and Dr. Richard Jantz of the University of Tennessee at Knoxville reported that close examination of the craniums of several other skeletons and mummies found in the Americas produced similar results. The evidence, they said, suggested that either more than one group of people migrated into the New World or the settlers underwent significant physical changes in the time after their arrival. It is even possible that the first migrants became extinct, replaced by subsequent groups.

The issue is central to a legal case pitting American Indians, who claim Kennewick Man as an ancestor and want his remains turned over to them for reburial, and anthropologists, who are seeking access to the skeleton for more detailed studies, including DNA tests of the man's genetic background.

Another skeleton, of a woman being called Luzia, which was found in Brazil, has prompted speculation of another origins scenario. The skeleton, estimated to be possibly 11,500 years old and thus older than any previous human bones in the Western Hemisphere, appeared to be more Negroid in its cranial features than Mongoloid.

Dr. Walter Neves of the University of Sao Paulo said this suggested that some of the first people in South America might have originated in

Europe and Australia as possible cradles for the Americas.

Australia, or at least South Asia. Last month, he said Luzia might have belonged to a nomadic people who began arriving in the New World as early as 15,000 years ago. They may have come across the Pacific, but more probably, he said, they were a branch of Southeast Asians, some of whom settled in Australia as the Aborigines while others navigated northward along the Asian coast and then across the Bering Strait.

It may be a long time before the shattered Clovis-first hypothesis is replaced by a single new paradigm. In the meantime, some Clovis partisans are not giving up without a fight.

In the current issue of the magazine Scientific American Discovering Archaeology, Dr. Stuart J. Fiedel of John Milner Associates in Alexandria, Va., which conducts archaeological excavations under contract, said that Dr. Dillehay's Monte Verde report was riddled with errors and omissions that "raised doubts about the provenience of virtually every" artifact excavated there. Monte Verde, he concluded, "should not be construed as conclusive proof of a pre-Clovis human occupation in South America."

Dr. C. Vance Haynes Jr. of the University of Arizona, one of the staunchest defenders of the Clovis orthodoxy, said that, though he had been a member of the panel of experts that authenticated Monte Verde's pre-Clovis credentials, he now had serious second thoughts. After further study of the evidence, he said, "To my surprise, I found these data to be inadequate and therefore unconvincing."

The attack on Monte Verde, published just before the conference here, raised cries of foul. Many archaeologists complained that Dr. Fiedel's review was biased and ignored material that did not support his critical thesis. They deplored his tactic of airing his critique in a popular magazine rather than a peer-reviewed journal.

In a defense of Monte Verde, also published in the magazine, Dr. Dillehay acknowledged that some errors had crept into the 1,300-page report and would be corrected, but none of them undercut an interpretation of the place where pre-Clovis hunter-gatherers camped 12,500 years ago. At the conference, he called Dr. Fiedel's review "ungrounded accusations" and one more example of North American archaeologists' dismissal of South American sites because they lacked the familiar Clovis stone-tool technology.

"The half-century-long emphasis on Clovis projectile points and related durable lithic artifacts," argued Dr. James M. Adovasio of Mercyhurst College in Erie, Pa., who excavated the long-disputed Meadowcroft site and thus sees himself as another victim of Clovis chauvinism, "has actually served to mask rather than elucidate the nature of late ice age adaptations in the New World."

Warming to the attack, Dr. Adovasio charged that evidence of "soft technologies" such as cordage, netting and basketry was seldom given its due at many early American sites. The result, he said, was a failure to appreciate fully the way of life of the first American colonizers.

"Nets suggest a subsistence strategy carried out by both sexes and all age groups in stark contrast to the traditional model based on highly mobile groups of spear-wielding, mammoth-killing macho men," Dr. Adovasio said to another round of hearty applause.

The loss of a paradigm has thus plunged American archaeology into a new period of tumult and uncertainty over its oldest mystery, one critical to understanding how modern humans spread out through the world. For their entry into America was the last time in history when people occupied an entirely new land, alone and with little more than their own ingenuity and an eye on far horizons.

"We're going to have to open our minds," Dr. Michael B. Collins of the University of Texas said at the conference. "We're going to have to explore some ideas that may not get us very far. We're going to have to be tolerant of each other as we explore these ideas. My God, this is an exciting time to be involved in research in the peopling of America and the earliest cultures of the Americas."

12th Session of UN Working Group on Indigenous Peoples

The Declaration Passes and the US Assumes a New Role

GLENN T. MORRIS

Glenn T. Morris is the Executive Director of the Fourth World Center for the Study of Indigenous Law and Politics, at the University of Colorado at Denver. He is also co-editor of the Fourth World Bulletin and Associate Professor of Political Science at CU-Denver.

After nearly nine years of debate, deliberation and revision, the United Nations Working Group on Indigenous Peoples (UNWGIP), at its 12th Session (25-29 July 1994), completed preparation of the Draft Declaration on the Rights of Indigenous Peoples and sent the document on to higher levels in the UN system. Over 160 indigenous peoples' organizations, forty two state members, nine specialized agencies of the United Nations, and dozens of interested nongovernmental organizations, totaling nearly 800 individuals, participated in the 12th Session. The Declaration was forwarded to the UN Sub-Commission on Prevention of Discrimination and Protection of Minorities. At its 46th Session (in August 1994), the Sub-Commission agreed to transmit the Declaration to the UN Commission on Human Rights for discussion at its annual meeting in February 1995. For final adoption as an instrument of emerging international law, the Declaration must ultimately be accepted by the UN General Assembly.

The 12th Session was notable for several important developments that this article reports in some detail. First, there was a significant debate about the Declaration's treatment of the right to self-determination; the ensuing discussion of the issue left momentous questions unresolved. Second, several other major issues that will have great bearing on the rights of indigenous peoples were postponed to future discussions in which they will be detached from the text of the Declaration. And third, the United States Government assumed a new and decidedly more dynamic role among the states that have actively participated in developing the Draft Declaration.

Self-determination

Discussion of the right to self-determination for indigenous peoples has always provoked passionate and oppositional controversy at Working Group sessions. In the initial drafts of the Declaration, the right was not mentioned explicitly at all. In subsequent drafts, at the insistence of indigenous peoples, the right was expressed, but was often accompanied by limiting language or provisions. At the 11th Session (1993), indigenous delegates proposed that reference to the right to self-determination for indigenous peoples should be modeled after the language already found in the International Covenant on Civil and Political Rights and the Interna-

From the *Fourth World Bulletin*, Fall 1994, Winter 1995, pp. 1-7, 28-29, 32. © 1995 by the Fourth World Center for the Study of Indigenous Law and Politics. Reprinted by permission.

tional Covenant on Economic, Social and Cultural Rights. That proposal was accepted, and Article 3 of the draft now reads:

> Indigenous peoples have the right of self-determination. By virtue of that right, they freely determine their political status and freely pursue their economic, social and cultural development.

Some states, notably the United States and Canada, have publicly opposed Article 3, and they can be expected to introduce dramatic revisions of it, or try to completely delete it in the future.

The major objection to self-determination stems from the fear by some states that explicit recognition of that right, in the language of the human rights covenants, will allow indigenous peoples and nations to exercise a right of political independence separate from the states that surround them. Through this exercise, states fear the dismemberment of their claimed territories and the emergence of new, independent indigenous states. This fear is especially pronounced in cases where indigenous enclaves are entirely surrounded by states or where indigenous territories contain valuable natural resources.

Most states assert that relations, especially territorial and jurisdictional relations, between themselves and indigenous peoples are internal, domestic matters that are beyond the scope of international law. The inclusion in the Declaration of a right that would allow indigenous peoples to be recognized to possess juridical character, with rights recognized in international forums, is viewed as an attack on the sovereignty and territorial integrity of current U.N. members.

Conversely, most indigenous peoples argue that they have never given their informed consent to be integrated into the states that came to surround them, that they have not been party to the establishment of international legal principles to the present, and that they have been (and continue to be) denied the opportunity to decide for themselves their political status. In essence, they argue that they are in a state of internal colonial bondage, and they advocate an extension of international standards of decolonization to apply to their cases. In that regard, indigenous delegates have regularly stated that the right to self-determination is a major cornerstone of the Declaration, upon which other provisions of the document must rest.

Indigenous delegates have consistently argued that under the right to self-determination, complete independence is only one of several available options. They maintain that most indigenous peoples around the world do not aspire towards political independence, and would choose some variation of autonomy, short of independence, within the current state system. However, during the 12th Session, several states (Brazil, India, Myanmar) repeated their steadfast opposition to any recognition of a right to self-determination for indigenous peoples. Others, such as Denmark, expressed support for the self-determination provision.

Upon their arrival at the 12th Session, some indigenous representatives were surprised to find that the Declaration had been altered, without their consultation, from the form that had been concluded at the 11th Session. Of particular concern was the addition of Article 31, which recognizes "autonomy" or "self-government in internal and local affairs" as a specific form of the exercise of self-determination. Miguél Alfonso Martínez, the Latin American regional member of the Working Group and the author of Article 31, had reasoned that Latin American state governments were unlikely to accede to the open-ended interpretation of self-determination expressed in Article 3. He wrote and appended Article 31 to the Declaration in the hope that it would provide essential safeguards for Latin American indigenous peoples but not alarm the state governments of the region.

Serious discussion and disagreement developed over whether Article 31 would limit the right to self-determination expressed in Article 3. Some indigenous delegates (especially some Canadian and United States Indians, Native Hawaiians, Mapuches, Maoris, Nagas, and others) objected that the language of Article 3 was perfectly clear, and any attempt to modify the meaning (as they interpreted the intent of Article 31) might later be construed as a limitation of the right to self-determination, that "autonomy" might result as the maximum (or at least the preferred) extent of the exercise of the right for indigenous peoples. They argued that Article 31 is therefore superfluous and should be deleted.

The opponents of Article 31 also suggested that certain states, notably the US and Canada, are hostile to Article 3 and can be expected to amend it significantly or even delete it from the Declaration, at future forums. If Article 3 is indeed eventually deleted, Article 31 will remain as the only articulation of what self-determination means. According to the opponents, Article 31, read alone, is an incomplete and inadequate protection of the right of self-determination for indigenous peoples.

The proponents of Article 31, on the other hand, maintained that the article should be read as an extension, not a limitation, of Article 3, and that local and regional autonomy would result as the *minimum* standard of self-determination that states must recognize for indigenous peoples. They suggested that for many indigenous peoples who must deal with states that fail to provide even minimal recognition of indigenous rights, Article 31 might provide a crucial safeguard against violations of fundamental human rights.

In future deliberations over the draft, the substance of the right to self-determination for indigenous peoples will remain of central importance. In the eyes of many indigenous peoples, the integrity of the entire instrument rests in the willingness of the international community to recognize the right of indigenous peoples to control their political, economic, social and cultural destinies. In contrast, the concerns of states over the freedom of indigenous peoples to exercise their right to self-determination is intimately linked to the belief that states possess a basic right to protect their own sovereignty and territorial integrity from competing indigenous claims. The ultimate success of the Declaration may therefore rest in the ability of the contending sides to assuage the fears of the other, by finding the common ground that satisfies the interests of all concerned.

Future Deliberations over the Declaration

According to modified UN rules of procedure, the discussion of the Draft Declaration at the Working Group level had been open to all UN members, all interested indigenous delegates, and all governmental and non-governmental organizations with an interest and a contribution to make to the efforts of the Working Group. With the conclusion of the Working Group's discussion, however, the Declaration was transmitted to the Sub-Commission and then to the Commission on Human Rights, where the procedures for participation are considerably more restrictive.

To participate at the Sub-Commission or the Commission, delegates must be credentialed by those respective bodies, and the application for credentialing must come through a nongovernmental organization (NGO) that possesses consultative status within the UN Economic and Social Council (ECOSOC). To date, only twelve indigenous NGOs, primarily representing indigenous peoples of the Americas, have received consultative status.

During the 12th Session, both indigenous representatives and states expressed doubts that in future forums in which the Draft Declaration is discussed, indigenous peoples who are not affiliated with the recognized NGOs, or who are otherwise not credentialed, will be included in the discussions. This issue is of special concern to peoples from India and other parts of Asia and the Pacific, the Russian Federation, and Africa, because many of them are not currently members of credentialed NGOs.

The issue of who will be able to participate in future discussions becomes especially important when considering the probable course for the Declaration. According to a number of state observers at the 12th Session, once the Draft reaches the Commission on Human Rights, it will be sent to another working group, within the Commission itself. Unlike the discussions at the previous Working Group, which were directed by international legal experts (as opposed to delegates representing the interests of states), the Commission working group may well be directed by appointed delegates whose primary concern will be the protection of their governments' interests.

While the Draft is in the Commission's working group, it will be subject to a comprehensive review and reconsideration. Provisions that might seem problematic to states are susceptible to complete revision or removal. Indigenous representatives expressed concern that a limitation of their participation in this process may endanger the progress that has been made over the past ten years, and it may weaken the most important international legal instrument affecting indigenous peoples ever to appear.

Indigenous delegates have previous experience upon which to base their wariness. In 1989, during the debate over revision of International Labor Organization (ILO) Convention 107, only credentialed indigenous representatives could participate, and then only on a limited basis, while a number of important persons and perspectives were completely excluded. To many indigenous peoples, the ILO rules determining participation were totally arbitrary. Consequently, indigenous delegates now insist on more open participation at the Human Rights Commission and successive fora that deal with the Declaration.

Members of the Working Group itself have also recommended relaxation of the rules of procedure in the Human Rights Commission's discussion of the Draft. The Australian government promised that it would introduce a measure to allow indigenous participation, regardless of consultative status, and it proposed that any meetings of the Commission working group be convened immediately prior to the meeting of the Working Group on Indigenous Peoples, so as to maximize the opportunity for indigenous participation. Australia's proposals were endorsed by a few other countries, particularly Sweden, Denmark and Norway.

The Role of the US at the 12th Session and Beyond

The United States delegation to the 12th Session took a new and decidedly more active role in the deliberations of the Working Group and the discussion of the Draft Declaration. Until the 1994 meeting, the United States has participated mostly as an observer, relying on the lead of countries such as Canada and Australia to fashion and advance the interests of state members at the Working Group.

For several years, some indigenous delegates to the Working Group have become convinced that the most prominent governments from English-speaking countries (Australia, Canada, New Zealand and the United States) have coordinated their participation in international forums concerned with indigenous peoples' rights. Rudolph Rÿser, Director of the Center for World Indigenous Studies, has charted a succession of joint meetings between those governments. According to Rÿser's analysis, Canada has played a particularly active role, one that is considered by many indigenous delegates to be especially hostile toward any expanded recognition of indigenous rights. Australia, conversely, has played a role that is publicly more sympathetic to indigenous claims, one that has even supported limited usage of terms like "peoples" and "self-determination." New Zealand and the United States, says Rÿser, have taken approaches that vary between those of Canada and Australia, while the US delegation's public posture has ranged from indifference to hostility.

Affirming Rÿser's analysis, the changing agenda of the United States has been revealed in an unclassified internal State Department memorandum of July 1993. In this document, State Department officials acknowledge that for the first dozen years of the Working Group's existence, the US "invested little effort in [it]." By 1993, however, the US attitude toward developments at the Working Group apparently had changed significantly. The memo explains that the Working Group and the Draft Declaration are now at a stage where it is important for the US to "try to shape the text [of the draft] to reflect US interests before it goes to the Commission [on Human Rights]."

Of major concern to the US is the question of what impact the application of the principles of collective rights and self-determination of indigenous peoples might have for the United States and international law. It is clear from the memo that the US opposes extending the right of self-determination, as it has been interpreted in the international human rights covenants, to indigenous peoples. The memo asserts that self-determination "is most commonly understood to mean the right to establish a sovereign and independent state, with separate personality under international law. Like many other countries, the United States could not accept the term in any contexts implying or permitting this meaning."

Addressing an issue closely related to self-determination, the State Department is critical of using the term "peoples" (with an "s" at the end) in conjunction with the word "indigenous." According to the memo, "the term [peoples] implies that such groups have the right to self-determination under international law." The document expresses concern about "the risks and uncertainties of extending the legal concept of self-determination to indigenous groups." It emphasizes that the recognition of indigenous collective rights expressed in the Draft Declaration is troublesome, because as a general rule, "the United States . . . does not recognize the existence of collective rights under international law . . ." and "we generally do not think it desirable to incorporate such rights into future legal instruments."

While the memo lends general support to the concept of a declaration for the protection of indigenous peoples, and while it even questions some basic assumptions about generally accepted notions in State Department circles (e.g., "recognizing carefully defined group rights need not *per se* be a BAD THING," and "should we oppose a tightly drawn treaty saying that a defined collective group has a defined legal right to practice their culture or religion opposable against their [sic] government?"), it also makes very clear that the security and integrity of the current state system is of preeminent importance.

The flavor of the 1993 memo was integrated into the US intervention at the 12th Session, where the use of the term "peoples" was deliberately avoided, and instead, the terms "people," "populations," "tribe," and "tribal," were used sixteen times. The delegation (led by Miriam Sapiro, from State's Legal Affairs Office, and John Crook, Counselor for Legal Affairs at the US Mission in Geneva) also provided further insight into the US position regarding indigenous self-determination. The memo suggests that US indigenous policy can be used as a working model for the effective implementation of indigenous rights on an international level, given that the essence and extent of self-determination for indigenous peoples should basically mean "self-governance and autonomy . . . within an existing state." Of course, this implies that US indigenous policy does not apply to "non-historic" or non-federally recognized Indian nations, Alaskan or Hawaiian Natives, Chamorros, Samoans, or other indigenous peoples that have never been given any pretense whatsoever in the realm of "self-governance" or "autonomy."

Equally revealing of the true US policy, at unofficial meetings during the 12th Session, Crook and Sapiro made clear that the semantic debates over such terms as "people" versus "peoples" were less important to them than was some resolution of the substance of the right to self-determination itself. Sapiro asked several times, "What does Article 3 mean?" And at one session Crook even called the semantic debate "stupid." However, the term proved important enough that the US delegation has made a conscious, deliberate decision to refuse to use the term "peoples" at all. The apparent implication is that if the term self-determination can be interpreted, in any context, to recognize the right of indigenous peoples to independent political existence, then the United States will oppose it.

The current US position on the Declaration can be identified in a plank of the "Clinton-Gore Plan" (the campaign platform of 1992) and also in a statement by President Clinton on 29 April 1994, both of which affirmed "government-to-government" relationships between indigenous nations and the United States, while placing the treatment of indigenous self-determination solely within the domestic jurisdiction of the United States. Some indigenous delegates have observed that the use of the term "government-to-government" by the United States constitutes an attempt to reduce indigenous issues to "internal" status and to degrade the international (i.e., nation-to-nation) relationship that is embodied in the hundreds of treaties concluded between the US and various Indian nations. Others have observed that the quality of "self-determination" accorded to only the recognized "historic tribes" of the US is truncated by the language of the Indian Self-Determination and Education Act of 1975, which limits the exercise of self-determination to decisions concerning the allocation of appropriations distributed by the federal government.

Sapiro and Crook stated in the Session that the United States plans to play a more active role in the future of both the Draft Declaration and the Working Group. They appeared confident that the Draft would pass through the Sub-Commission in August 1994 (which it did), and that it would then be transmitted to a working group in the Commission on Human Rights, after February 1995. The delegation suggested that in future months very serious discussion and debate of the Draft will take place, especially over such controversial matters as collective rights, self-determination, control of territories and natural resources, and development matters, and that the US will play an active role in both the procedural and substantive aspects of these debates. The inference must be that, because the US and other states disagree with the wording of some key provisions of the Draft Declaration, significant changes might reasonably be expected at the Commission level.

In a briefing held in Washington DC, on 20 January 1995, John Shattuck, Assistant Secretary of State for Human Rights, reiterated that the US position regarding the Draft Declaration, at the February 1995 meeting of the UN Human Rights Commission, will be "supportive," and that the United States will follow Australia's lead in creating an open-ended working group within the Commission. Shattuck and his aides repeated that the US perceives human rights primarily pertaining to individuals, not to groups, that the US wants a clearer definition of "indigenous peoples," in order to determine to whom the rights in the Declaration apply. Shattuck also said that his office was committed to open discussions concerning the Declaration (to be held in the US), in various forums with indigenous groups and other NGOs.

The key features of US policy continue to be: that the US considers individuals and not groups to be the subject of human rights; that questions involving indigenous peoples are basically domestic matters to be negotiated between states and indigenous peoples; that the right to self-determination should be read more narrowly than it was in the past, and should not normally be read as a recognition of the right of independent political existence for indigenous peoples; and that any political and economic sovereignty rights of indigenous peoples are inferior and subordinate to the overarching sovereignty of existing states. Undoubtedly,

the basic position of the United States on these questions will play an important and enduring role in the consideration of the Draft Declaration and in the future of the Working Group.

Whatever the role of the US in future deliberations of the Working Group, a serious amount of work remains unfinished and will have to be resolved in the coming years. These issues are, in summary, the scope and substance of the right of indigenous peoples to exercise self-determination, the international legal status of treaties between indigenous peoples and states, and the responsibilities of states and the United Nations in assuring that indigenous peoples and their territories are not sacrificed in the pursuit of national and international economic development.

Indigenous Self-Determination and U.S. Policy

Commentary

As explained in the [first part] of this issue article, there has recently been a major shift in the posture of the United States Government regarding the Draft Declaration on the Rights of Indigenous Peoples and the UN Working Group on Indigenous Peoples (UNWGIP). Some have applauded the U.S. awakening in the indigenous-rights arena, replete with its dubious interpretation of the language of "self-determination," as a welcome and positive change. Unfortunately, we are unable to share that optimism.

In our view, the position shift should be viewed cautiously as perhaps the latest reflection of a long tradition in U.S. policy, which is characterized by massive contradictions of legal and moral obligations.

American Indians, more than any other indigenous peoples, should understand the implications of U.S. posturing on human rights. The possibility or probability that the U.S. will support or promote the Draft Declaration on the Rights of Indigenous Peoples can and should be measured in relation to the attachment of the U.S. to other, comparable pieces of international legislation on human rights.

It should be understood that the Declaration on Indigenous Rights, even when finally concluded, will not create any immediately binding legal obligation on any state, because it is not a treaty. Subsequent to its adoption by the UN General Assembly, the Declaration may eventually be transformed into a Convention, just as the 1948 Universal Declaration on Human Rights was put into force in the form of two competing (or complementary) human-rights covenants, in 1976, but this development will take many years, if it happens at all. Present U.S. support for the Draft Declaration, therefore, can be understood to be virtually risk-free, as far as immediate legal obligations are concerned.

More importantly, the United States has consistently refused to participate in international human-rights institutions over the past fifty years. The U.S. Senate, which must ratify all treaties

to which the country might become state-party, rejected all opportunities for the U.S. to accede to the 1948 Genocide Convention, until 1986. Similarly, it refused to ratify the 1966 International Covenant on Civil and Political Rights (which codifies that set of human rights expressed in the U.S. Bill of Rights itself), until 1992. Only last year, in 1994, did the Senate ratify the 1965 International Convention on the Elimination of All Forms of Racial Discrimination. But did ratification in these very few cases indicate that the United States would actually abide by the terms of the agreements? No, because whenever the Senate has ratified human-rights treaties, it has appended "provisions" and "reservations" that have made international laws subordinate to the laws of the United States. There is little reason to believe that the treatment of the Declaration on Indigenous Rights will be different.

The stated U.S. position should not be regarded as an insignificant policy change in an obscure area of international human-rights discourse, nor should it be viewed in isolation from the evidence of U.S. behavior when indigenous rights are obviously at stake. Rather, the policy statement should be viewed as intimately related to several other important foreign-policy areas that are implicated by past and present indigenous (or "nationality") conflicts around the globe. For example, the U.S. supported a Tibetan rebellion against Chinese occupation in the 1950s and 60s, but when President Nixon decided to play the "China card" against the USSR, in 1972, the Tibetans were abandoned to be slaughtered and exiled by the Chinese Army. Similarly, the U.S. supported Iraqi Kurds in their rebellion against Saddam Hussein, in 1973 (the prelude to the events of the Gulf War in 1991), but when U.S. interests in the region shifted, the Kurds, too, were abandoned to be slaughtered by the thousands. On the other hand, because of the strategic importance of Turkey, the U.S. virtually ignores the fate of Kurds in that country.

In another, similar policy contradiction, the U.S. supported and instigated Ukrainian secessionist rebellion against the

USSR until 1991, when President Bush strangely attempted to persuade Ukraine *not* to seek independence, after all (of course, he was too late). Bush's address to the Ukrainians, in which he reversed forty-five years of policy to warn of the "excesses of suicidal nationalism, was labeled his "Chicken Kiev Speech" by *New York Times* columnist William Safire, marking the first evidence of a major dispute within the ranks of U.S. conservatives on indigenous nationality policy generally and the policy applied toward Russia, in particular.

It is difficult to underestimate the cynicism of U.S. policy on human rights. At the Vienna World Conference on Human Rights, in July 1993, President Clinton and Secretary of State Christopher swore before the world that the United States was prepared to join the International Covenant on Economic, Social and Cultural Rights. That promise could not have been less believable, considering the fact that the ESC Covenant has always been understood as the major human-rights statement of socialist regimes, led by the former USSR, and so it hardly could have been expected ever to gain approval in the Senate. Clinton and Christopher also preached human rights to the Chinese government and threatened to withhold Most-Favored Nation (MFN) trading privileges unless China reformed its behavior according to Western precepts of "democracy"—and then reversed themselves, when China indicated that it was not about to be pressured on human-rights issues.

Meanwhile, within the U.S. itself, indigenous human-rights issues go largely unacknowledged and unaddressed by the public, because of the myth that the U.S. is the world's leader in observance of human rights. This myth probably explains why, though people in western Europe, Russia, and elsewhere are aware that President Clinton has refused to deal with the worldwide campaign to grant clemency to the American Indian political prisoner Leonard Peltier, Americans themselves hardly know his name. The illusion that the U.S. alone is the hegemonic arbiter of good and evil may account for its pursuit of the forced relocation of Diné on the Hopi Partitioned Lands, while it forbids the UNWGIP to discuss that issue, lest the U.S. scuttle that forum.

As a measure of the current U.S. foreign policy on rights of indigenous/nationality peoples, Chechnya is an illustrative case, since Russia remains the "centerpiece" of U.S. foreign policy in the post–Cold War era. U.S. reaction to Russia's most recent invasion of Chechnya (there have been several over the past 300 years) has been typically full of contradictions. Although members of the Clinton Administration have condemned Russia's brutal military *tactics* against the Chechens, there has been virtually no challenge to the legitimacy of the basic Russian claim over Chechen territory. President Clinton is clearly supporting Yeltsin's regime, in its attempt to fend off opponents, including the fascistic Vladimir Zhirinovsky, who has no sympathy for Chechens and wants to re-establish a Russian empire. The Clinton Administration believes that Yeltsin represents the best present hope that Russia will become a pro-Western capitalist enterprise. That hope is contingent on territorial integrity, however, and Chechen secession would probably seal Russia's doom, by tapping the wellspring of endemic separatism in the complex Russian Federation. Such separatism could bring on a period of chaos and, given the genuine possibility of a military coup, precipitate another Cold War.

The absence of official criticism and opposition from the U.S. Government has been matched in the U.S. mainstream media. The *New York Times,* for instance, has repeatedly supported Russia's suppression of Chechen self-determination and encouraged Washington to "quietly counsel [Yeltsin] to apply force carefully," because the Chechen claims "cannot be allowed to stand" (*NYT,* 14 December 1994). This, despite the *Times'* own acknowledgment that the Russians have, in the past, occupied Chechnya but never subdued it—because the Chechens have resisted and rebelled continually against Russian domination, twice earlier in this century.

The U.S. State Department (the agency that is constructing the policy on indigenous peoples' rights) agreed with the Times, giving Russian territorial claims and military actions higher legitimacy than those of the Chechens. State Department official Mike McCurry succinctly stated the U.S. position on 14 December 1994 (also later affirmed by President Clinton and Secretary of State Christopher) that "Chechnya is an integral part of Russia, and events in Chechnya, because of that, are largely an internal affair." Vice President Al Gore underlined the Administration's stance by saying that the US is "not going to challenge Russian territorial integrity [on the Chechen question]" (Associated Press, 9 January 1995).

As the *Times* concluded, the U.S. statements gave "Mr. Yeltsin a green light for military intervention" (*NYT,* 28 December 1994). Apparently, neither the U.S. nor the *Times* will object to the general principle of an established state invading a stateless people's territory. The feeble concern that they do raise is rather that the invasion was bungled—it was not done quickly or quietly or effectively enough, and it was not executed cleanly out of television camera range.

Ironically, Zbigniew Brezinski (Jimmy Carter's National Security Adviser), recently joined a few Republican members of Congress and a smattering of conservative newpaper editors in condemning U.S. policy for complicity in the denial of Chechen self-determination, in a column in the *Washington Post* (8 January 1995). Brezinski claims that Chechnya "could become the graveyard of America's moral reputation," because the U.S. refuses to come to the assistance of a "freedom-seeking" people that "dared to reach out for independence." His defense of the "helpless Chechens . . . who are not Russian and do not wish to be Russian," while laudable under normal circumstances, rings hollow when one recalls his lack of defense of the freedom-seeking Tibetans against China, or of the freedom-seeking East Timorese against Indonesia, and the pounding of the freedom-seeking Kurds by Iran, Iraq, and Turkey, during his watch at the White House. His commentary represents the depth of contradictory sentiments within both conservative ranks and the policy community at large.

In a most telling distortion in his column, Brezinski claims that the U.S. vilification of an indigenous or nationality struggle (of the Chechens), and justification of oppression (by the Russians) "has never happened before." In addition to the cases mentioned above, Brezinski seems to have forgotten the decades of U.S. opposition to the African National Congress, the IRA, the Eritreans, the PLO, the Polisario Front in the Western Sahara, and the Naga Nation struggling for its independence from India. The list of freedom-seeking peoples engaged in nationality and indigenous struggles that have been opposed by the United States could fill pages. It is precisely the United States' own history of opposition to self-determination struggles that should give pause to those who are watching the new U.S. agenda unfold on the indigenous-rights stage.

The justification applied by the U.S. to the Chechen case, that the survival of a state (Russia) and its territorial claims are more important than the survival of an indigenous people, can easily be observed in other serious cases at this very moment. The government of Myanmar (Burma) is waging a relentless and brutal military attack against the Karen Nation, killing hundreds and forcing tens of thousands of refugees to flee their homeland into Thailand. Not surprisingly, neither the United States, nor any other major power, has submitted any meaningful challenge to Myanmar's attacks. In November, just three months ago, the State Department claimed that it was taking a "conciliatory approach" toward the Burmese military regime, as far as human rights in general were concerned (especially the imprisonment of Nobel Peace Prize laureate Aung San Suu Kyi), but made no attempt to address the question of indigenous rights in particular. The U.S. maintains extensive trade relations with the Ne Win regime; the petroleum, natural gas, timber, weapons, and narcotics industries are all doing big business in Burma. Meanwhile, the U.S. supports, either actively or tacitly, the open relations between the Ne Win regime and China, Thailand, and Japan.

Rather than support the application of the principle of self-determination to the Chechens or the Karen—lest it set a precedent for other freedom-seeking peoples—the United States and other states of the world would prefer to protect the "sovereignty and territorial integrity" of the chauvinistic and human-rights-abusing governments of Russia and Myanmar out of political or economic expedience. Rather than examine the claims of the Karen or the Chechens, that they have never given their consent to be integrated into the Burmese or the Russian states, and that they have long-standing political and territorial claims of their own, the governments of the world side with the oppressor's invasion in the name of regional stability and order. Similar examples of expedience over principle can be cited from Chiapas to the Western Sahara, from Indonesia to Eritrea.

The self-determination of the peoples of Eritrea was ignored, even actively opposed, for over three decades by the major powers of the world, led alternately by the U.S. and the Soviet Union, in the interests of protecting Ethiopia's sovereignty. At the same time the U.S. was assuaging Israel's fear that the Red Sea might be completely bordered by states hostile to its existence. The Eritrean spirit of freedom prevailed despite prohibitive odds, surviving drought and over thirty years of military oppression from the Ethiopian government that was alternately supported by both the United States and the Soviet Union. Eritrea's seat in the United Nations, which can be celebrated as an enormous monument to the perseverance of the Eritrean people, should also serve as a constant source of shame to the world community that consistently rejected a legitimate claim of self-determination in favor of the territorial integrity claims of a corrupt Ethiopian government. Eritrea would still not be seated at the UN if it had to rely solely on the international community's embrace of high-sounding principles respecting the self-determination of peoples. Eritrea's seat would not exist had the Eritreans not mobilized the military might necessary to liberate their homeland and to defend and protect their claim to self-determination.

The lessons of the Chechens, the Karen, and the Eritreans should serve as important lessons to other indigenous peoples and nationalities. If the international community has a choice between the legitimacy of indigenous peoples' claims for territory, treaty rights, economic sustainability, or self-determination, versus the claims of a state, any state, for continued survival, indigenous peoples can be virtually certain that the statist claim will be supported consistently. For the United States, consolidating global hegemony is the preeminent national interest at this time. U.S. hegemony can be managed successfully only with a limited number of sovereign states in the system. The U.S., therefore, judges it imperative to forestall any possibility, real or imagined, of a wave of secessionism.

The United States clearly does not take international human-rights obligations seriously, despite its charade of being the world's bastion of respect for rights. Neither is it ever likely to accept the Declaration of Rights for Indigenous Peoples as a constraint on its own policy towards the indigenous peoples enclosed by its borders. At this point in history, there is no reason to believe that increased U.S. interest in indigenous peoples' rights is anything more than self-serving political posturing. The U.S. has made it clear that it opposes any meaningful recognition of the right to self-determination for indigenous peoples; it opposes any serious assertion of territorial or natural-resource control by indigenous peoples; it opposes recognition of the international standing of treaties between indigenous peoples and states; and its recommendation for the protection of indigenous rights rests solely within the domestic jurisdiction of the very states that have historically attacked, dismembered and sought to destroy indigenous peoples. Does this record bespeak an indigenous-rights policy that should be applauded?

American Indians + Welfare State Liberalism =

A Deadly Mix

by Hendrik Mills

An article of faith among Indian activists and their liberal allies today is that any problems experienced by Native Americans are caused by their unjust, rapacious treatment at the hands of whites, including a continuing "cultural genocide." This victimology is reinforced by many romantic beliefs about Indians, including the conviction that they are less materialistic, more spiritual, more in tune with the earth and inclined to care for the environment than other Americans. These sorts of beliefs, widespread in areas distant from Indian country, have served to justify a great web of public programs for Native Americans.

Unfortunately, these seemingly generous programs have resulted, to a shocking degree, in social disintegration on the nation's reservations. That's because they are based on a false understanding of what the real obstacles to Indian progress and happiness are today.

Never mind "cultural genocide." A much more straightforward picture of the kinds of problems plaguing Native Americans today can be seen in a recent, sadly typical story from the Great Falls, Montana *Tribune*. It reported that a four-year-old Indian girl had been struck and killed by an auto at the intersection of Cheyenne Avenue and Dull Knife Drive in the town of Lame Deer. Speed was not a factor, and the 49-year-old woman driving the car was not to blame.

The first problem was that the four-year-old was not being escorted by any parent or other adult. She crossed the street alone while returning from a Boys & Girls Club she had visited with her brother and sister.

The second problem was that three broken street lights blackened the intersection. "It was dark," Highway Patrol officer Tim Lytle said. "Had the lights been working, it would have made a big difference." Area residents told Lytle that vandalism to street lights in the area was a recurring problem. The culprits? Indian juveniles.

The simple elements of this tragic story—crime, and a lack of parental supervision and involvement with children, resulting in premature death—crisply capture conditions in many Native American communities today. I know because my family and I have lived for five years on and near the Fort Belknap Indian Reservation in north central Montana. I haven't always been skeptical of the "Indian-pride" point of view. In October 1991, I was one of those protesting against Columbus Day at a rally in downtown Denver sponsored by the American Indian Movement. When my wife and I initially decided to move to, and work in, Indian country, it was because we sympathized with Native American claims.

Initially, it was the goings-on in the schools here in Harlem, Montana, that forced me to re-examine my beliefs. Until the 1970s, white and Indian children had peaceably attended these schools together and had received solid educations. But in recent years, the local schools have been plagued by indiscipline, violence, and drastically lowered academic standards. Only a few local white parents still have their children in Harlem public schools. Instead they drive them daily to neighboring towns where they attend public schools in which discipline and the work ethic are still intact. As I began to investigate, I met former teachers who told horror stories of Indian parents coming into the school to curse at teachers because their child had been assigned "too much homework" or had been disciplined for fighting in school. Parents told me of racially motivated playground and street violence against their children.

How could this have happened? It was in answering that question that my radical-leftist illusions began to die. I queried many residents of our area, both old-timers and young, Indian and non-Indian, on and off the reservation. I read widely, in-

From *The American Enterprise,* November/December 1998, pp. 57-59, 77. © 1998 by the American Enterprise Institute. Reprinted by permission.

cluding *Indian Country Today,* a national Indian newspaper, and other writings by Indians, as well as many other books and journals. And I discovered it was my own generation that, in the 1960s, set in motion the processes of racial separatism and social and economic change that ultimately resulted in the chaotic schools and other social failures in Indian country.

The main demands of Indian militants and their political allies since the 1960s have been: (1) enlargement of the reservations; (2) federal dollars to remedy unemployment and poverty on the reservations; (3) recognition of Native American sovereignty (the idea that each reservation is a self-determining nation); and (4) official support for an Indian culture separate from the rest of America. Only the first demand has been largely denied.

The request for federal funds has been granted in spades. It is widely believed that Native Americans have been forgotten and impoverished by the actions—or inaction—of mainstream America. In fact, present-day Indians are surrounded by a cradle-to-grave system of benefits enjoyed by no other racial group in America. The U.S. Indian Health Service provides free health care with no co-payment whatever to all Indians living on or near reservations—everything from filling cavities, to intensive care after a heart attack, to reconstructing facial contours injured in a barroom brawl. Through the Department of Education's "impact aid" program, school districts with a large number of Indians receive millions of dollars of extra annual aid, to cover everything from routine operating expenses to the running of bilingual Indian-language programs. The "impact aid" program doesn't just fill the coffers of the school district, it also mandates that the local tribal council must agree to the school district's budget in order for the federal money to be granted.

Tribal colleges, set up on almost every reservation, provide two-year community college curricula right where the students are. Scholarships and living stipends are the rule, not the exception, for Indian students attending tribal colleges.

"Treaty money"—a lump sum often exceeding $10,000—is given to Indian youngsters of many tribes when they reach the age of majority. This is justified as a settlement of various historic claims that activists, beginning in the 1960s, asserted against the U.S. government.

Indians who live and work on reservations here in Montana are also exempt from many kinds of taxes: new-vehicle licensing taxes, county taxes, state income tax, and in some cases federal income tax. Gambling laws that ban or restrict casinos off-reservation often do not apply on the reservation, which is why there has been an explosive growth of Indian gambling casinos.

Head Start is a fixture on all reservations, providing federally funded child care for every Indian child, as well as an array of health care, feeding, and educational services. Welfare is freely available; the Montana state welfare authorities re-

Hendrik Mills is a Montana writer and school teacher with extensive experience on Indian reservations.

cently announced that all Indians on reservations in Montana would fall under the "hardship exemption" to the recent welfare reform law, thereby exempting them from the law's work requirements.

Many other programs likewise transfer cash, goods, and services to Native Americans. Back when many of the government Indian programs were begun in the 1970s, there was a great increase in the number of self-described Native Americans; so the U.S. government instituted the "⅛ rule" to determine who would be eligible for federal benefits. This rule states that a person who possesses at least "⅛ blood quantum" is an Indian, and Indians are issued wallet-sized cards specifying their blood quantum, e.g. "$3/16$ Assiniboin, $5/32$ Gros Ventre." Nowhere, therefore, is the linkage between race and government payoffs more mechanistic, strained, and ultimately harmful than it is for Indians.

Pitiful stories of Indian poverty are often told to support continued expansion of government programs. But lack of money is not the main component of Indian poverty today. The owner of a taxi service in Havre told me and my co-workers one day that he gets a lot of business from Indians on the first day of every month, when welfare checks arrive. Someone asked, "Are they going to the grocery store to buy food?" He replied, "No, most want rides to the casinos."

At the local dump, one can regularly see discarded food thrown away by people who are supposedly in dire need. Fruit juice, canned fruit, macaroni, soup, rice, and beans are sometimes thrown by the case into municipal dumpsters by Indians who are allegedly so poor their children must be given extra tax-subsidized meals at school. The source of these discarded groceries is a U.S. Department of Agriculture "surplus" food distribution program that operates on reservations. Improvidence of this sort makes it impossible to solve Indians' problems by transferring resources to them.

Since the 1960s, government has taken on many of the traditional functions of parents on the Indian reservations. Many mothers and fathers have willingly ceded responsibility for their offspring to this rich uncle. An Indian Health Service dentist I know tells of parents bringing in pre-school children with their entire set of teeth rotted at the gumline. When the dentist asks them whether they have followed the advice given in every clinic not to leave a baby alone in a crib with a bottle of milk or soda pop propped before him, the parents sometimes respond, "You fix his teeth; that's *your* job!" Books and even toys are scarce in most reservation homes, but junk food and television are omnipresent.

Thanks to the progressive disintegration of the Indian family, parental negligence makes some children *de facto* orphans. An elementary school principal who works in Indian country told me about a little girl who came to school on a Monday morning with a staple embedded in her hand and an infection already begun. He had the staple removed and the infection treated by the Indian Health Service. He found out it had been in her hand all weekend, and no caring adult had been present in her home.

In the worst homes, Indian children are growing up without ever being socialized to acceptable norms. These are the promiscuous teenagers who produce fetal-alcohol afflicted babies. These are the young men who steal insulin syringes from their grandparents (a recurring problem on the nearby reservation) so they can shoot up the drug "crank." Crime, including murder and assault, is a serious problem in Indian country. While gang activity is growing, crime rates on reservations and nearby towns are typically two or three times as high as in non-Indian areas.

through the reservation at no cost to the reservation, was kept from working because they employed some non-Indians, and the state balked at paying for the privilege of repairing the reservation's road. The telephone company was held up in its attempt to install new phone lines to Indian residences because its linemen were non-Indian. Trucks delivering goods to Indian-owned stores on the reservation refused to pay the tax, and so delivery to these stores was delayed. I could tell many other similar stories of the accomplishments of the sovereign tribal governments.

Large numbers of Indian parents have abdicated their parenting responsibilities. This is linked to the comprehensive network of services provided by the government.

In many Indian extended families today, several serious older people are the only remaining source of cohesion. Grandmothers raising babies are now a common sight in Indian country, as fathers and mothers go to jail, wallow in crank or alcohol, and forget about their offspring.

Ironically, the many orphans and near-orphans in Indian country cannot be adopted by non-Indian families—due to a federal law intended to protect Indian children from cultural assimilation. This disastrous provision, the Indian Child Welfare Act, should be scrapped as soon as possible, so that the underage victims of rampant social decay can find stable and loving homes elsewhere.

There are bright spots. Responsible parenting seems to run in certain families on the Indian reservations. The Indians who operate working ranches or farms often seem to turn out successful children. In those households, children are given responsibilities and hard work from an early age, and they learn useful, satisfying skills. But the consensus in Indian country is that large numbers of Indian parents have abdicated their parenting responsibilities. In my opinion, this is linked to the comprehensive network of services provided by the government.

The activist demand for recognition of Indian sovereignty has been granted to a very significant degree in the last couple of decades. A reservation with a population well under 10,000 typically has dozens of tribal government positions that pay annual salaries in the $30,000–50,000 range. Unless you've lived and contended with these independent tribal bureaucracies, you can scarely imagine how inefficient they are. I wonder if Third World dictatorships have as many paper-shufflers presiding over so little economic activity.

One example may suffice: In 1996 our local tribal council flexed its sovereign muscles and imposed the so-called Tribal Employment Rights Organization Tax, a per-capita levy on every non-Indian working, even temporarily, on the reservation. A Montana road crew, repairing the main paved artery

Aside from matters of efficiency, there remains an important question of principle in the exercise of Indian sovereignty. Can any group be considered "sovereign" when most of its funding comes from an outside source? When sewers or schools or water plants are built in the rest of America, they are funded by local property tax levies. But there is relatively little economic production carried out by Indians on reservations, thus scarcely any local tax base. The main strategy for raising money followed by the tribal councils and the reservation school districts is simply to lobby the federal government. Many Indians have become quite adept at this, and the public opinion campaigns that go with it, skillfully wielding "victim" stories to maximize external public funding of their "sovereignty."

The proliferation of easy, make-work jobs reserved for tribal members has eroded the Indian work ethic. A young Indian man once came into the garage where I used to work as a mechanic, asking my advice about a stalled car. Later he brought it in for me to repair. Since he seemed bright and curious, I encouraged him to go to the vocational school 45 miles away to learn auto mechanics so that he could earn a living and provide a badly needed service on the reservation. His reply: "No man, that's too much work." I saw him a few months later driving a car with U.S. government plates, "working" for the federal Indian bureaucracy.

One elderly Montana businessman I know notes that many Indians now living on reservations in states of semi-unemployment once worked in skilled trades in places like Seattle's shipyards or Los Angeles's factories. It wasn't until the federal government began building subsidized housing and offering other benefits on reservations in the 1960s that many of these productive citizens came "home" to idle. The result has been the creation of a largely unproductive population intensely dependent on government favors.

A number of Indian parents do not work at all. Many others hold jobs whose salary would be impossible to attain, given their level of education and productivity, in the competitive world away from the reservation. Both of these examples discourage schoolchildren from working hard in school. Combine these disincentives with the breakdown of Indian parenting and with the prevailing notion on reservations that "America owes us," and one begins to see that the misbehavior of so many Indian children is almost a logical outcome.

I want to note that many Indians have "made it" in America. They have jobs, or are employers themselves. In our area of northern Montana, the largest wholesale distributor of gasoline and diesel is owned by an Indian named Ezzie Ereaux. The area's main tourist resort is owned and operated by an Indian family. One of the biggest ranchers and businessmen in our county is an Indian; his son holds an M.D. Another Indian family includes two M.D.s, a retired hospital administrator, and a hospital nursing supervisor. A local Indian girl recently won a full scholarship (not specifically targeted to Indians) to Montana State University. I hear from a fellow teacher that the greatest math talent in the area is a teenaged Indian boy.

Off our local reservation, many Indians work at jobs just like any other American. Indians who show the requisite reliability, punctuality, and willingness to work have no trouble finding and keeping positions. Banks, groceries, convenience stores, and ranches often have Indian employees. Indian-run ranches and farms are common on the reservation, although much of the economic activity consists of white farmers growing crops or raising cattle on land leased from Indian landowners.

Many Indians are successful, for the same reasons other Americans succeed: They have a work ethic, literacy, frugality and business acumen, and a command of standard English that allows them to play in the same league as other Americans. The sad thing is that many more Indians could be succeeding with them, instead of drowning in pathology—if only they were treated more like other citizens, and less like a race apart.

American Indians in the 1990s

The true number of American Indians may be unknowable, but a rapidly growing number of Americans are identifying with Indian culture. The Anglo appetite for Indian products is creating jobs on poverty-plagued reservations. Gambling and tourism are the most lucrative reservation businesses. Meanwhile, the middle-class Indian's urge to "go home" is growing.

Dan Fost

Dan Fost is a contributing editor of American Demographics *in Tiburon, California.*

When Nathan Tsosie was growing up in the Laguna Pueblo in New Mexico, he was not taught the Laguna language. The tribe's goal was to assimilate him into white society.

Today, Tsosie's 9-year-old son Darren learns his ancestral language and culture in the Laguna schools. He speaks Laguna better than either of his parents. "They're trying to bring it back," says Darren's mother, Josephine. "I'm glad he's learning. I just feel bad that we can't reinforce it and really teach it."

The strong bonds American Indians still feel to their native culture are driving a renaissance in Indian communities. This cultural resurrection has not yet erased the poverty, alcoholism, and other ills that affect many Indians. But it has brought educational and economic gains to many Indians living on and off reservations. A college-educated Indian middle class has emerged, American Indian business ownership has increased, and some tribes are creating good jobs for their members.

The census counted 1,878,000 American Indians in 1990, up from fewer than 1.4 million in 1980. This 38 percent leap exceeds the growth rate for blacks (6 percent) and non-Hispanic whites (13 percent), but not the growth of Hispanics (53 percent) or Asians (108 percent).

The increase is not due to an Indian baby boom or to immigration from other countries. Rather, Americans with Indian heritage are increasingly likely to identify their race as Indian on census forms. Also, the Census Bureau is doing a better job of counting American Indians.

Almost 2 million people say that their race is American Indian. But more than 7 million people claim some Indian ancestry, says Jeff Passel at the Urban Institute. That's about 1 American in 35.

"A lot of people have one or more ancestors who are American Indian," says Passel. "There's a clear trend over the last three censuses for increasing numbers of those people to answer the race question as American Indian. But it doesn't tell you how 'Indian' they are in a cultural sense.

"The strength of this identification in places that are not Indian strongholds is transitory. If it becomes unfashionable to be American Indian, it could go down."

People who try to count American Indians employ many different means that often confound demographers. Tribes keep tabs on enrollment, but the rules vary on how much Indian blood makes one a member. Some tribes are not recognized by the federal government. Local health services may keep one set of records, while federal agencies like the Bureau of Indian Affairs will keep another. Some Indians are nomadic; Navajos, for example, may maintain three residences. Rural Indians can be hard to find, and minorities are always more prone to census undercounts. A growing number of mixed marriages blurs the racial boundaries even further.

"I don't know what an Indian is," says Malcolm Margolin, publisher of the monthly *News from Native California.* "Some people are clearly Indian, and some are clearly not. But the U.S. gov-

INDIAN STATES

During the 1980s, Oklahoma replaced California as the state with the largest American Indian population. South Dakota dropped off the top ten list as New York moved into ninth place.

(population of the ten states with the largest American Indian populations, in thousands)

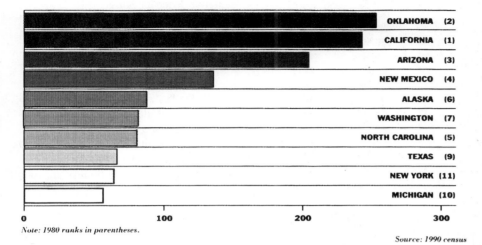

OKLAHOMA (2)
CALIFORNIA (1)
ARIZONA (3)
NEW MEXICO (4)
ALASKA (6)
WASHINGTON (7)
NORTH CAROLINA (5)
TEXAS (9)
NEW YORK (11)
MICHIGAN (10)

0   100   200   300

Note: 1980 ranks in parentheses.

Source: 1990 census

ernment figures are clearly inadequate for judging how many people are Indian."

Even those who can't agree on the numbers do agree that Indians are returning to their roots. "In the early 1960s, there was a stigma attached to being American Indian," Passel says. These days, even Anglos are proud of Indian heritage.

IDENTIFYING WITH INDIANS

When white patrons at Romo's restaurant in Holbrook, Arizona, learn that their host is half Navajo and half Hopi, they frequently exclaim, "I'm part Cherokee!" The host smiles and secretly rolls his eyes. More *bahanas* (whites) are jumping on the Indian bandwagon.

"In the last three years, interest in Indian beliefs has really taken off," says Marzenda McComb, the former co-owner of a New Age store in Portland, Oregon. To celebrate the sale of her store, a woman performed an Indian smudging ritual with burnt cedar and an eagle feather. Most of McComb's customers were non-Indian.

Controversy often accompanies such practices. Some Indians bristle at the shar-

ing of their culture and spiritual practices with whites. But others welcome people of any race into their culture. And many tribal leaders recognize that Indian art and tourism are hot markets.

Anglos are not the only ones paying more attention to Indian ways. Indian children are showing a renewed interest in their culture. Jennifer Bates, who owns the Bear and Coyote Gallery in California, says her 9-year-old son has taken an independent interest in Northern Miwok dance. "It's nice, knowing that we're not pushing it on him," she says. "He wanted to dance and make his cape. It's up to us to keep things going, and if we don't, it's gone."

The oldest generation of California Indians "grew up among people who recalled California before the arrival of whites," says Malcolm Margolin. These people have "something in their tone, their mood, their manners—a very Indian quality." Younger generations are more comfortable in the white world, he says, but they sense "something very ominous about the passing of the older generation. It's the sense of the younger generation that it's up to them."

The Zuni tribe is trying to revive ancient crafts by opening two tribal-owned craft stores—one in their pueblo in New Mexico, and one on San Francisco's

trendy Union Street. The most popular items are fetishes—small stone carvings of animals that serve as good-luck charms. "After *Dances with Wolves* came out, we weren't able to keep the wolf fetishes in stock," says Milford Nahohai, manager of the New Mexico store.

JOBS ON RESERVATIONS

Many Indians on and off the reservation face a well-established litany of problems, from poverty and alcoholism to unemployment. Many tribal leaders say that only jobs can solve the problem. Promoting Indian-owned businesses is their solution.

The number of Indian-owned businesses increased 64 percent between 1982 and 1987, compared with a 14 percent rise for all U.S. firms, according to the Census Bureau. "A whole new system of role models is being established," says Steven Stallings, president of the National Center for American Indian Enterprise Development in Mesa, Arizona. "Indians see self-employment as a viable opportunity."

In boosting reservation-based businesses, Stallings aims to create sustainable, self-reliant economies. In some areas, 92 cents of every dollar earned on a reservation is spent outside the reservation, he says. Non-Indian communities typically retain as much as 85 cents.

Stallings's center hopes to start by attracting employers to Indian country. The next step is to add retail and service businesses that will "create a revolving economy on the reservation."

This strategy is at work in Laguna, New Mexico. The Laguna Indians were hit hard in 1982, when the price of uranium plummeted and the Anaconda Mineral Company closed a mine located on their reservation. But the Lagunas have bounced back with several enterprises, including Laguna Industries, a tribal-owned manufacturing firm that employs 350 people.

Laguna Industries' clients include the Department of Defense, Raytheon, and Martin Marietta. Its flagship product is a communications shelter that U.S. forces used in the Gulf War. "It's pretty nice to see your own people getting in-

INDIAN INDUSTRIES

American Indian specialty contractors had receipts of $97 million in 1987.
But automotive and food-store owners may earn higher profits.

(ten largest industry groups in receipts for firms owned by American Indians and Alaska Natives)

rank	industry group	firms	receipts (in thousands)	receipts per firm (in thousands)
1	Special trade contractors	2,268	$97,400	$43
2	Miscellaneous retail	1,799	85,400	47
3	Agriculture services, forestry, and fishing	3,128	84,000	27
4	Automotive dealers and service stations	222	65,300	294
5	Food stores	301	54,300	180
6	Business services	2,532	48,600	19
7	Eating and drinking places	464	35,300	76
8	Construction	461	34,200	74
9	Trucking and warehousing	590	32,200	55
10	Personal services	1,719	26,500	15

Source: 1987 Economic Censuses, Survey of Minority-Owned Business Enterprises

INDIAN MARKETS

The 1990 census showed rapid increases among American Indians who live in large metropolitan areas. Some of the increases reflect an increasing willingness to declare one's Indian heritage.

(top ten metropolitan areas, ranked by American Indian, Eskimo, and Aleut population in 1990; and percent change in that population, 1980–90)

rank	metropolitan area	1990 population	percent change 1980–90
1	Los Angeles-Anaheim-Riverside, CA	87,500	5%
2	Tulsa, OK	48,200	41
3	New York-Northern New Jersey-Long Island, NY-NJ-CT	46,200	101
4	Oklahoma City, OK	45,700	82
5	San Francisco-Oakland-San Jose, CA	40,800	19
6	Phoenix, AZ	38,000	66
7	Seattle-Tacoma, WA	32,100	42
8	Minneapolis-St. Paul, MN-WI	24,000	49
9	Tucson, AZ	20,300	36
10	San Diego, CA	20,100	37

Source: 1990 census

volved in high-tech stuff," says welding supervisor Philip Sarracino, 44.

Laguna Indians are given first priority for jobs at the plant, but several middle managers are white. Conrad Lucero, a plant group leader and former tribal governor, says that non-Indian supervisors are often retirees who lend their expertise until Indians can run things on their own.

"I have an 8-year-old daughter," says Sabin Chavez, 26, who works in the quality control division. "I'm hoping to keep this company going, so our kids can live on the reservation. It's a long shot, but we have to believe in long shots."

High morale at Laguna Industries is tempered by the risks of relying on the government. The Lagunas realize that their dependence on military contracts makes them vulnerable to cuts in the defense budget. And in August 1994, the tribe's right to bid on minority set-aside contracts will expire—partly because the business has been so successful.

"We have to be able to meet and beat our competitors on the open market," Lucero says. The Lagunas may succeed: Martin Marietta Corporation has already awarded Laguna Industries a contract based on price and not minority status, says Martin Marietta customer representative Michael King.

Laguna Industries has not solved all the tribe's problems, however. Tribal planner Nathan Tsosie estimates that unemployment runs as high as 35 percent on the reservation. Much of the housing is substandard, water shortages could impede future development, and alcoholism still tears Indian families apart. But Tsosie has an answer: "We just need to develop more. People leave the reservation to get jobs. If there were jobs here, they'd stay."

GAMBLING AND TOURISM

Indians bring some real advantages to the business world. The Lagunas show that a cohesive community can be organized into an efficient production facility. Other reservations have rich natural resources. But the biggest benefit may be "sovereignty," or the suspension of many local, state, and federal laws on Indian territory. Reservations have no sales or property tax, so cigarettes, gasoline, and other items can be sold for low prices. They can also offer activities not permitted off-reservation.

Like gambling.

"Bingo is a way for tribes to amass funds so they can get into other economic development projects," says Frank Collins, a Mescalero Apache from San Jose who specializes in development.

Bingo can be big business. One parlor on the Morongo reservation, just north of Palm Springs, California, draws 5,000 people a week and employs more than 140 people. The Morongo tribe's main objective is to develop as a major resort destination, says bingo general manager Michael Lombardi.

Lombardi won't say how much money bingo generates for the Morongos. He will say that 113 reservations allow some form of gaming, and he attributes bingo's popularity to the effects

THE BEST STATES FOR
Indians in Business

in lumber and tourism. And Alaska may rank first because its native American, Eskimo, and Aleut population received billions of dollars in a federal land claim settlement. These data do not contain businesses owned by Eskimos or Aleuts. But many of Alaska's Indians live in isolated towns where small businesses have a captive, all-native audience. —William O'Hare

This table shows how the states rank on the basis of business ownership among American Indians. States in the South may offer the most opportunity for American Indians, white midwestern states may offer the least.

The number of Indian-owned businesses in a state is not closely related to the business ownership rate. Business ownership rates are calculated by dividing the number of Indian-owned businesses by the number of Indians and multiplying by 1,000. The top-ranked state, Alaska, is one of only five states with more than 1,000 Indian-owned firms. But the state that ranks last, Arizona, has the seventh-highest number of Indian-owned businesses.

Statistical analysis also indicates that the pattern of business ownership among American Indians is not driven by the rate of growth in a state's Indian population during the 1980s, or by a state's overall level of business ownership.

There appear to be strong regional biases in patterns of Indian business ownership. The business ownership rate was 12.2 Indian-owned firms per 1,000 Indians in the South, 10.3 in the West, 9.6 in the Northeast, and only 7.4 in the Midwest.

One clue to a state's business ownership rate among Indians could be the share of its Indian population living on reservations. The lowest-ranking state, Arizona, contains seven of the ten most populated reservations in the U.S., including a large share of the huge Navajo reservation (1990 Indian population of 143,400 in Arizona, New Mexico, and Utah). South Dakota, ranking 47th, contains the large and economically troubled Pine Ridge, Rosebud, and Standing Rock reservations. Indians living on a reservation have limited entrepreneurial opportunities. Another factor that may be related to the Indian business rate is the state's general economic health: several states near the bottom of the ranking, Kentucky, Nebraska, and Michigan, have experienced weak economic growth during the 1980s.

But the most powerful predictor is probably the business skill of a state's Indian tribes. Third-ranking North Carolina is home to one branch of the Cherokee tribe, which has large investments

William O'Hare is Director of Population and Policy Research Program, University of Louisville.

INDIAN OPPORTUNITY

(states with more than 100 American Indian-owned businesses in 1987, ranked by business ownership rate)

rank	state name	number of firms 1987	American Indian population 1987	business ownership rate*
1	Alaska	1,039	28,700	36.2
2	North Carolina	1,757	75,600	23.2
3	Texas	872	57,500	15.2
4	Virginia	188	13,300	14.1
5	Colorado	343	24,600	13.9
6	California	3,087	225,600	13.7
7	Louisiana	221	16,600	13.3
8	Massachusetts	132	10,700	12.4
9	Kansas	225	20,000	11.3
10	Florida	348	30,900	11.3
11	Maryland	123	11,300	10.9
12	Pennsylvania	139	12,800	10.8
13	Georgia	122	11,400	10.7
14	New Jersey	131	12,800	10.3
15	New Mexico	1,247	126,400	9.9
16	Illinois	182	19,600	9.3
17	Montana	405	44,700	9.1
18	Oklahoma	2,044	229,300	8.9
19	Oregon	306	34,500	8.9
20	North Dakota	208	24,300	8.6
21	Wisconsin	306	36,300	8.4
22	Ohio	149	17,700	8.4
23	Washington	602	72,300	8.3
24	Nevada	146	17,700	8.3
25	New York	425	54,800	7.8
26	Missouri	133	17,500	7.6
27	Minnesota	333	45,400	7.3
28	Michigan	304	50,900	6.0
29	South Dakota	267	49,000	5.5
30	Utah	109	22,700	4.8
31	Arizona	843	189,100	4.5

* Number of American Indian-owned firms per 1,000 Indians.

Source: Bureau of the Census, 1987 economic census, and author's estimates of 1987 Indian population

of Reagan-era cutbacks in the Bureau of Indian Affairs budget. Lombardi says then-Secretary of the Interior James Watt told Indians, "Instead of depending on the Great White Father, why don't you start your own damn business?"

Indian culture also can create unique business opportunities. On the Hopi reservation in northern Arizona, Joe and Janice Day own a small shop on Janice's ancestral property. They swap elk hooves and cottonwood sticks, useful in Indian rituals, for jewelry, and baskets to sell to tourists.

The Days would like to credit their success to their shrewd sense of customer service. But they confess that the difference between profit and loss may be their wildly popular T-shirts, which read "Don't worry, be Hopi."

Not long ago, Hopis had to leave the reservation to go to school or find work. Today, the tribe has its own junior and senior high school and an entrepreneurial spirit. But small schools and small businesses won't keep people on the reservation. The Days still make a two-hour drive to Flagstaff each week to do their banking, laundry, and shopping. "The first Hopi you can get to build a laundromat is going to be a rich man," says Joe Day.

The Days lived in Flagstaff until their children finished high school. At that point, they decided to come "home." Janice's daughter is now an accountant in San Francisco, and she loves the amenities of the big city. "But who knows?" Janice says. "She may also want to come home someday. No matter where you are, you're still going to end up coming home."

THE URGE TO GO HOME

"Going home" may also mean renewing a bond with one's Indian heritage. While the population in 19 "Indian states" grew at predictable levels during the 1980s, the Urban Institute's Jeff Passel says it soared in the non-Indian states.

For example, Passel estimated the 1990 Indian population in Arizona at 202,000 (the 1980 population of 152,700, plus the intervening 58,600 births and minus the intervening 10,300

> ## "Instead of depending on the Great White Father, why don't you start your own damn business?"

deaths)—a figure close to the 1990 census number (203,500). But in Alabama, a non-Indian state, Passel found a huge percentage increase that he could not have predicted. Alabama's Indian population grew from 7,600 in 1980 to 16,500 in 1990, a 117 percent increase. Higher birthrates, lower death rates, and migration from other states do not explain the increase.

Passel explains the gap this way: "The people who are Indians always identify themselves as Indians. They tell the census they are Indians, and they register their newborns as Indians." These people are usually found in the Indian states. "People who are part Indian may not identify themselves as American Indians. But they don't do that consistently over time."

Today, for reasons of ethnic pride, part-Indians may tell the Census Bureau they are Indian. At the hospital, they may identify themselves as white to avoid discrimination. This is most common in non-Indian states, which Passel generally defines as having fewer than 3,000 Indians in 1950.

California ranks second only to Oklahoma in its Indian population, but its mixture of tribes is unique in the nation. Some Indian residents trace their roots to native California tribes, says Malcolm Margolin. Others came west as part of a federal relocation program in the 1950s. In California cities, Cherokees, Chippewas, and other out-of-state Indians congregate in clubs.

"What has happened is the formation of an inter-tribal ethic, a pan-Indian ethic," Margolin says. "People feel that America has a lot of problems. That cultural doubt causes them to look for their ethnic roots, for something they can draw strength from. And for Indians, it's right there. It's ready-made."

RALLYING CRY

Indians Hear A High-Tech Drumbeat

By Daniel B. Wood
Staff Writer of The Christian Science Monitor

DANIEL B. WOOD

ORGANIZER: *Tom Goldtooth uses a cell phone to call the shots at a native American protest in California's desert.*

WARD VALLEY, CALIF.

HUNDREDS of butte-desert miles from any sizable town, a protest is building. A lone-Indian chant is punctuated by scuffling feet and shaking rattles, while demonstrators lift hand-held signs: "Low-level dump/High-level hazard" and "We can't pick up and move like others can."

The scene has played out in scores of settings across the West, ever since the United States government targeted Indian reservations in the late 1980s as favorable sites for nuclear and other waste disposal. But this protest, like many of the others, includes a new element that is tipping the balance in native Americans' favor: the spirit of collective empowerment nudged forward by modern technology.

"We are seeing the result of years of coalition-building coming together with the aid of new ways to communicate to very remote, rural populations," says Tom Goldtooth, founder of the Indigenous Environmental Network.

Leaning over the hood of a faded blue Chevy, Mr. Goldtooth works a bank of portable cell phones with the urgency of a lobby receptionist. He directs protesters at two base camps a mile away; he choreographs the arrival of tour-bus-size contingents of sympathizing tribes from Texas to Oregon. He fields questions from the press about the protest in front of him, as well as one he just left in New Mexico.

Using cell phones, fax machines, and the Internet, a national native American movement is coalescing, helping disparate tribes communicate, educate, mobilize, and stand up for themselves.

From New York to Washington State and from Florida to California, coalitions made up from 552 federally recognized tribes are demanding enforcement of existing laws and the creation of new ones. Via phone or e-mail, they are asking far-flung tribes to show up at protests, write to local and national lawmakers, send money, appear at hearings, and visit Web sites to bone up on issues and strategy

"This is a sea change in the way tribes see themselves as activists on issues".... from environment to health care, says John Dossett of the National Congress of American Indians in Washington.

Native Americans' connections with one another—and with the rest of the world—have grown exponentially in the past 25 years. Back then, Alaska tribes were not aware of major federal legislation affecting them until a year after Congress passed it, Mr. Dossett says. "Now they know what each other is doing and can lend support in dozens of ways," he says.

The trend toward intertribal solidarity and activism got a big push between 1990 and 1993, when the hazardous-waste-disposal industry began targeting Indian reservations as potential dump sites for high- and low-level radioactive waste. From the companies' perspective, reservations have the advantages of being exempt from many state and local environmental regulations, are often far from population centers, and need income. Nationally, unemployment is 37 percent on the 56 million acres of land held in trust by the US for Indian tribes.

In response to such efforts, 25 tribes met in 1990 at the first Protecting Mother Earth Conference in Dilkon, Ariz. The next year, Goldtooth founded the Indigenous Environmental Network with members from nearly 50 tribes, and other coalitions have followed.

Counting victories

Besides a string of victories in slowing or stopping illegal waste dumping at remote sites, native American coalitions have halted archaeological digs at sacred Chumash burial sites in California, blocked a highway abutting Seneca land in northeast New York over state taxation issues, and forced the shutdown of a coal-burning power plant and cyanide-leached gold-mining operations in Montana.

One of the most publicized victories for the Indians came in 1993, when 30 tribes used railroad ties, barrels, and fencing to block US efforts to dump sludge on the Torrez Martinez reservation just south of here.

The new tribal solidarity has also won greater attention from government officials. The US, for example, has ap-pointed formal liaisons to interact with the tribes as the sovereign nations they are, much as it does in its dealings with state and county entities.

"The movement of native Americans to communicate among themselves and fight with a louder voice has really taken off in the last few years," says Robert Bullard, director of the Environmental Justice Resource Center at Clark Atlanta University.

The communication hurdles are high, he says. About two-thirds of the nation's 1.9 million native Americans live on rural reservations. Despite the economic gains from Indian gambling enterprises, the vast majority of tribes have fewer financial opportunities and a lower quality of life than does American society at large.

Here is isolated Ward Valley—where Nevada and Arizona meet California—more than 30 tribes from a dozen states are laying plans this week to stop test drilling by the US Interior Department. The department says the tests are needed to determine if Ward Valley is an appropriate site for a nuclear-waste dump.

"Throughout our histories we have not always seen eye to eye on everything with other tribes," says Gjrjle Dunlap, newly elected chairwoman of the Chemehuevi Indians, many of whom have come to protest at Ward Valley along with nearby tribes. "But we have seen that if we do not stand together for this issue, we all lose."

In another California case concerning Chumash burial grounds threatened by developers near San Semeon, Calif., members of several tribes have appeared at protests and hearings as far away as Ventura County. Such tribes include the Salanian Tribe, the Hollister tribe, and Esalen Tribes of northern California.

"We did extensive research about our rights and customs and presented it in unison; it was very powerful," says Quili Coe, a spokeswoman for the Chumash Indians. "Our opponents have been much more willing to take us seriously and try to understand us as a network than as individual tribes."

Mobilization of multiple tribes on a wide range of issues includes activists once considered out on the fringe. Vernon Foster, executive director of the American Indian Movement's Arizona chapter, brought members of several tribes to Ward Valey to advise local tribes in the event of physical confrontation with local law officials.

"Now we are in the era of high-tech attack," says Mr. Foster, sitting in a Chevy Blazer at a support camp for the Ward Valley demonstration. For Foster, an earlier 15-day standoff with federal authorities on Torrez Martinez tribal land just miles south of here was a turning point in tribal solidarity.

Foster says the new solidarity has helped win public-relations and legal battles from Minnesota to Arizona over the term "squaw," often used to name geographical sites from parkways to mountain tops. In Minnesota, the term—which native Americans consider to be derogatory—is banned, and in Phoenix, officials are voluntarily changing the name of a nearby mountain as well as of a highway that cuts through the city.

Tribes have also united to stop archaeological digs on sacred burial grounds area, he says.

"In the 1970s and 1980s, Indians were protesting on the outside of courthouses and legislatures," Foster says. "Now we are being taken inside the courthouses all the way to Congress."

Some of this newfound networking includes Indian efforts to gain access to official corridors of power—via the controversial practice of using tribal dollars to make contributions to political parties and candidates. Indeed, Interior Department chief Bruce Babbitt is currently being investigated for his decision to disallow a tribal request for a gambling venue that was opposed by another, some say more politically connected, tribe.

Back at the grass roots, meanwhile, the fight over nuclear-waste disposal has

PHOTOS BY DANIEL B. WOOD

'We are in the era of high-tech attack. . . .
In the 1970s and 1980s, Indians were protesting outside courthouses and legislatures. Now we are being taken inside the courthouses all the way to Congress.'

—*Vernon Foster,*
AIM Arizona chapter

'We have seen that if we do not stand together for this issue, we all lose.

—Gjrjle Dunlap of Chemehuevi Indians

been as much internal as external. Tribes have stood to gain hundreds of millions of dollars if they would agree to allow the US to bury nuclear waste on their land. But so far, all have resisted.

"Due to networking, among the more than 500 Indian nations that were approached, only a handful even considered [the proposal]," says Bryan Angel, executive director of Green Action, an environmental activist group. "Most of those who considered it voted it down after pressure from the coalitions that have been formed. Considering the lure of incredible sums of money for very poor tribes, that is amazing."

Limited gains?

Not all native Americans, however, see greater unity among Indian nations. Carey Vicente, former chief judge of the Jicarila Apache Tribe, says "My impression, living on a reservation for the last several years, is that there is not much of an effective activist movement." He

mentions a decade-long protest of uranium strip mining near the Grand Canyon.

Likewise, Shoshone Indians in Nevada have spent more than a decade enlisting the help of 25 Nevada tribes to protest the Yucca Mountain site as the burial grounds for spent nuclear fuel—without victory in stopping the project.

"It's been a nightmare dealing with the bureaucracy of the federal government," says Anita Collins of the Nevada Indian Environmental Council. "They really don't understand how to communicate with native Americans."

But that may be changing, according to Commanche leader La-Donna Harris, director of Americans for Indian Opportunity, one of several Indian coalitions in Albuquerque, N.M. The Pentagon, which has been the target of many Indian protests over abandoned munitions dumps and bombing areas, is creating a formal liaison to deal with tribal issues.

"The DOD has seen the light and is beginning to educate itself about what

TAKING A STAND; *Antinuclear protest at Ward Valley, Calif.—a remote corner of California that abuts Nevada and Arizona—epitomizes the new spirit of intertribal cooperation among native Americans in the West.*

tribes are all about, what our rights are," says Ms. Harris. "That is a major turnaround—and it's indicative of what's possible in a whole new era for native Americans."

Key Points to Consider

❖ In what regards does the case that occurred in late 1990–2000 of Elian Gonzalez, the six-year-old Cuban refugee, provide material for a case study in ethnic politics?

❖ How does attention to historical background and its expression in current culture promote both understanding and tolerance?

❖ When do ethnic and racial issues foster understanding? Tolerance? The appreciation of the particular? Does ethnic humor and comedy contribute to or confound ethnic group relations?

❖ What strengths and weaknesses do strong bonds of ethnic communities possess?

❖ In what respects is Hispanic/Latino American culture becoming part of mainstream American culture? What can be expected for relationships between Hispanic ancestry populations and the newest immigrants from Spanish-speaking countries?

❖ Are Hispanic voters in California, Texas, Florida, and New York the crucial electoral difference for the presidential election? Explain.

❖ Attention to and discussion of specifically ethnic entertainment and the paucity of ethnic entertainers in mainstream programing has entered a new level of concern: the development of cross-over roles for Hispanic actors and actresses has emerged on the agenda. Does this pathway of expressing ethnic group interests suggest that assimilation and ethnic particularity need not be exclusive? Is this perspective an example of pluralism that expresses personal freedom and the endorsement of options that are open to persons with more than one cultural competency?

 **Links** | **www.dushkin.com/online/**

These sites are annotated on pages 4 and 5.

The following collection of materials on Hispanic/Latino Americans is a composite of findings about ethnicities. The clustering of these ethnicities and nationalities, as well as their relationship to the Spanish language, seem to be sufficient evidence of the commonalities that constitute the shared expression of this complex of memory and contemporary politics. Yet the use of "Hispanic" and "Latino" that differentiates them from Anglo-American foundations, and their social expression as they search for a cultural and political terrain, are but the surface of the process of intergroup dynamics in the United States. Are Portuguese-speaking groups Hispanic?

The articles in this unit propose angles of vision that enable us to view the process of accommodation and change that is articulated in political practice, scholarship, advocacy, and art. The issues presented provocatively shift traditional perspectives from the eastern and midwestern mindset toward the western and southwestern immigration to the United States.

The Immigration Act of 1965 induced a process not unlike the period of large-scale eastern and southern European immigration between 1880 and 1924. This immigration includes scores of various ethnic groups. Cultural/geographic descriptions are not the clearest form of ethnic identity. Hispanic/Latino Americans are not a single ethnic group. The designation of various ethnic populations whose ancestry is derived from Spanish-speaking countries by the words "Latino" and "Hispanic" is a relatively recent phenomenon in the United States.

Hispanic was used in the 1970s and Latino was added to the U.S. Census in 1990. The cultural, economic, and political differences and similarities of various Hispanic/Latino communities, as well as the wide dispersal of these communities, suggest the need for care in generalization about Latino and Hispanic American populations. Does geographic location in the U.S. significantly influence personal and group issues?

The realities of these groups—whether they are political refugees, migrant workers, descendants of residents settled prior to territorial incorporation into the United States, long-settled immigrants, recent arrivals, or the children and grandchildren of immigrants—present interesting and varied patterns of enclave community, assimilation, and acculturation, as well as isolation and marginalization. Hispanic/Latino American linkages to Central and South American countries and Spain, the future of their emerging political power, and their contributions to cultural and economic change within the United States are interesting facets of the Hispanic/Latino American experience.

The Hispanic/Latino experience is a composite of groups seeking unity while interacting with the larger arena of ethnic groups that constitute American society. Convergent issues that bridge differences, as well as those that support ideological and strategic differences, bode a future of both cooperation and conflict.

What issues bind Hispanic or Latino groups together? What values cause cleavages among these populations? What does bilingualism mean? Is bilingualism a freedom-of-speech issue? Is bilingualism a concern of non-Spanish-speaking persons in the United States? What are the implications of establishing an official public language policy?

Competition and conflict over mobility into mainstream leadership positions are aspects of American society that may be exacerbated by the misuse of ethnic indicators. Nonetheless, indicators of social cohesion and traditional family bonds are apparently noncompetitive and nonconflictual dimensions of robust ethnic experiences. Thus, fears that Hispanic/Latino Americans may not relish competitive pressures are assuaged by the capacities of family and community to temper the cost of any such failure. This complex dynamic of personal and group interaction is a fascinating and fruitful topic for a society seeking competitiveness and stronger community bonds. Cast in this fashion, the American dilemma takes on a new and compelling relevance.

Specific Hispanics

SUMMARY Los Angeles, New York, Miami, Chicago, and Houston are well-known Hispanic markets. But just below the big five are dozens of smaller Hispanic centers. This first-ever look at 12 Hispanic groups reveals the top towns for Colombians, Brazilians, and others. The rapid growth of specific Hispanic groups is destined to attract attention from marketers.

Morton Winsberg

Morton Winsberg is professor of geography at Florida State University in Tallahassee.

Most marketers are familiar with the three biggest Hispanic-American groups. Since the U.S. census first counted Hispanics in 1970, those who identify Mexico, Puerto Rico, and Cuba as their country of origin have comprised about three-fourths of the total U.S. Hispanic population. Hispanics from other Latin-American nations and cultures are less well-understood, but they constitute one-quarter of an estimated $170 billion consumer market. And because Hispanics of all kinds often live together in small areas, each country of origin can form a visible and desirable target market.

Among all Hispanics, the share of Mexicans has fallen from 62 percent of all U.S. Hispanics in 1970 to 61 percent in 1990. The Puerto Rican and Cuban shares have remained at about 12 percent and 5 percent, respectively. Hispanic Americans who don't have origins in these three countries are a small share of the nation's total Hispanic population, but they have been growing. Their numbers grew by slightly more than 2 million between 1970 and 1990. Immigrants of the new wave have been fleeing civil wars in Nicaragua, El Salvador, Guatemala, and Colombia. Others come for jobs or to rejoin family members already here.

The 1970 and 1980 censuses identified just four categories of Hispanics: Mexican, Puerto Rican, Cuban, and "other." The 1990 census provides much more detailed information, identifying 12 nations of Hispanic origin, as well as "other" Central Americans and "other" South Americans. These data provide the first opportunity to understand where specific Hispanic groups live.

Many of the smaller Hispanic subgroups never show up on marketers' computer screens. Language barriers and the lack of large ethnic neighbor-

> **Immigrants have always settled in America's largest cities, and today's immigrants are not much different.**

hoods can make it hard to reach them with specially designed messages. Also, many Hispanic immigrants do not plan to become U.S. citizens or permanent residents. But rapid growth will inevitably lead more businesses to target Hispanic diversity. In ten years, America's Little Havanas will get a lot bigger.

BELOW THE BIG FIVE

Immigrants have always settled in America's largest cities, and today's im-

migrants are not much different. Six of the 12 Hispanic subgroups identified in the 1990 census have more than 80 percent of their populations in the nation's 20 largest cities, and 3 others have between 70 and 79 percent.

Mexican Americans are the only exception to the urban rule, because many of their ancestors never immigrated. Many Mexicans became U.S. citizens in the 19th century following the acquisition of Mexican territory by the United States. Almost all of this land was and still is rural or small cities. Many Mexicans who immigrated to the U.S. in recent years have settled in these same southwestern states. Here they normally reside in cities both large and small, as well as in rural areas.

Hispanics, like immigrants who came earlier, tend to concentrate in one or two major urban areas. New York City and Los Angeles early became a popular destination for Hispanics, but more recently, many have chosen Miami, Washington, D.C., and San Francisco. An example of an unusually high concentration of a Hispanic group in one city is the 77 percent concentration of people of Dominican origin in the New York urbanized area. Greater New York also has 60 percent of the nation's Ecuadorians and 44 percent of Puerto Ricans. Los Angeles has 49 percent of the nation's Guatemalans and 47 percent of its Salvadoreans. Miami is home to 53 percent of Cuban Americans.

Several U.S. places have Hispanic populations that rival or even surpass the largest cities in their countries of origin. New York's Puerto Rican population is now more than double that of San Juan. New York also has the second-largest urban population of Dominicans in the world, and the third-largest Ecuadorian population. The Mexican, Salvadorean, and Guatemalan populations of urban Los Angeles are surpassed only by those of their respective capitals: Mexico City, San Salvador, and Guatemala City.

Eighteen percent of all Hispanic Americans live in Los Angeles, and 12 percent live in New York. These two urban areas rank among the top-5 for 11 of the 12 Hispanic groups. Miami is on the top-5 list for 9 Hispanic groups, Washington, D.C., for 6, San Francisco for 5, and Houston and Chicago for 4.

The census also reveals many smaller areas with large and growing populations of specific Hispanics. For example, San Antonio and San Diego have the fourth- and fifth-largest Mexican-American communities in the nation, and Philadelphia has the third-largest Puerto Rican population. Tampa and Fort Lauderdale have the fourth- and fifth-largest concentrations of Cubans, and the Massachusetts areas of Boston and Lawrence have the third- and fourth-largest Dominican groups.

Chicago is the only midwestern urban area to come up on any of the top-5 lists, but it comes up a lot. Chicago has the country's second-largest Puerto Rican population, the second-largest Mexican population, and the third-largest Guatemalan and Ecuadorian populations. As a whole, Chicago has the fourth-largest Hispanic population of any urban area, at 4 percent of the national total.

TWELVE HISPANIC GROUPS

Laredo, Texas, is not big as urban areas go, with 99,258 people in 1990. But 94 percent of Laredo residents are Hispanic, and the overwhelming majority are of Mexican origin. The census count of Hispanics, also mainly Mexican, is 90 percent in Brownsville and 83 percent in McAllen, two other Texas border towns. Several border towns in other states have equally high shares of Mexican Americans.

Perhaps the most exotic place where Mexicans congregate in large numbers is in the Bay City-Saginaw metropolitan area in Michigan. Mexicans first came to Bay City-Saginaw to work on the local cucumber farms. The descendants of these farm laborers now hold urban jobs, many in the local foundries.

Puerto Ricans began immigrating to the U.S. after World War II, and now they are a significant presence in the industrial cities of New York and southern New England. When older residents of these cities had achieved middle-class status and moved to the suburbs, they left behind entry-level jobs in manufacturing and service, and low-cost housing. The Puerto Ricans who took those jobs established the barrios of New York City.

While less affluent Puerto Ricans came to the U.S. for jobs, many middle-class Cubans fled their native country for political reasons. Cubans soon became closely identified with southeastern Florida, but now they are found in several other Florida towns. In the university towns of Gainesville and Tallahassee, for example, many second-generation Cuban Americans live as students.

Dominicans are a major Hispanic force in New York City and several New England industrial towns. They are only 2 percent of the nation's 1990 Hispanic population, but they are 15 percent of Hispanics in New York, 22 percent in Providence, and 35 percent in Lawrence, Massachusetts. Dominicans are flocking to the Northeast for the same reason Puerto Ricans did several decades ago: jobs. Hondurans and Nicaraguans, who have also immigrated largely for economic reasons, are settling in more bilingual areas on the Gulf of Mexico.

Hondurans are most numerous in New York, Los Angeles, and Miami, and Nicaraguans are most common in Miami, Los Angeles, and San Francisco. But both groups are dwarfed by the enormous numbers of other Hispanics in these large urban areas, so their largest concentrations emerge in unexpected places. Although Hondurans are less than 1 percent of the nation's Hispanic population, they are 20 percent of Hispanics in New Orleans. Nicaraguans are also well-represented among New Orleans Hispanics, and they are visible in nearby Baton Rouge and Port Arthur. Salvadoreans are just 3 percent of the nation's Hispanic population, but 25 percent of Hispanics in Washington, D.C.

Panamanians are perhaps the most geographically diverse of any Hispanic group. They are disproportionately represented in the local Hispanic population in towns near large military installations such as Fayetteville, North Carolina (Fort Bragg); Columbus, Georgia (Fort Benning); Clarksville, Tennessee (Fort Campbell); Killeen, Texas (Fort Hood); Seaside, California (Fort Ord); and naval installations in Norfolk, Virginia; and Tacoma, Washington. Many who identified their ethnic origin as Panamanian in the 1990 census were military personnel once stationed in the former Panama Canal Zone.

People of South-American Origin began moving in large numbers from New York City or coming directly from their homelands to coastal Connecticut towns during the 1980s, attracted to a growing number of service jobs that were not being filled by the local population. Housing was also more affordable than in New York City.

The affluent Connecticut town of Stamford is particularly attractive to South Americans. Its Hispanic population includes large proportions of Colombians, Ecuadorians, and Peruvians. In nearby Norwalk, Colombians are 20 percent of the city's Hispanic population.

MARKETING ATTENTION

So far, few U.S. corporations have paid attention to the special needs of "other" Hispanics. Mainstream marketers "are resistant enough to work with Hispanic marketing in total," says Nilda Anderson, president of Hispanic Market Research in New York City. "They are not going to do focused marketing."

One problem is a lack of marketing information. Recent census results and private research have improved the data on smaller Hispanic groups, says Gary Berman, president of Market Segment Research in Coral Gables, Florida, but few data were available until the 1990s.

Another problem is that Hispanic immigrants are less likely than previous generations of immigrants to live in ethnic-specific neighborhoods. In Miami, for example, newly arrived Cubans are often neighbors to Nicaraguans, and

TWELVE FLAGS

Hispanics of all types cluster in New York

Central Americans in San Francisco, Colombians

San Francisco

San Diego

Houston

Los Angeles

San Antonio

(top-five urbanized areas for Hispanics by country of origin, 1990)

OVER AMERICA

and Los Angeles. But you can also find lots of
in Chicago, and Peruvians in Washington

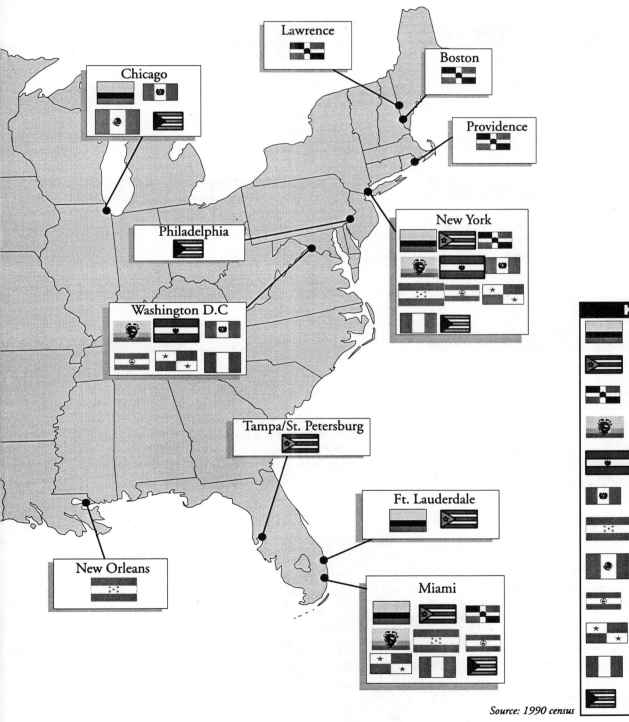

KEY

Flag	Country
	Colombia
	Cuba
	Dominican Republic
	Ecuador
	El Salvador
	Guatemala
	Honduras
	Mexico
	Nicaragua
	Panama
	Peru
	Puerto Rico

Source: 1990 census

Little Quitos and Little

Mexico

top-five urbanized areas	population	share
U.S. total	13,393	100%
Los Angeles	3,066	23
Chicago	538	4
Houston	528	4
San Antonio	524	4
San Diego	414	3

El Salvador

top-five urbanized areas	population	share
U.S. total	565	100%
Los Angeles	265	47
New York	62	11
Washington, DC	52	9
San Francisco	43	8
Houston	39	7

Puerto Rico

top-five urbanized areas	population	share
U.S. total	2,652	100%
New York	1,178	44
Chicago	1,464	6
Philadelphia	107	4
Miami	68	3
Los Angeles	51	2

Dominican Republic

top-five urbanized areas	population	share
U.S. total	520	100%
New York	403	77
Miami	23	5
Boston	16	3
Lawrence, MA	12	2
Providence, RI	9	2

Cuba

top-five urbanized areas	population	share
U.S. total	1,053	100%
Miami	559	53
New York	154	15
Los Angeles	55	5
Tampa-St. Petersburg	32	3
Ft. Lauderdale	24	2

Colombia

top-five urbanized areas	population	share
U.S. total	379	100%
New York	152	40
Miami	53	14
Los Angeles	27	7
Ft. Lauderdale	12	3
Houston	10	3

Nicaraguans may live next to Venezuelans. The city's celebrated "Little Havana" neighborhood is defined by its Cuban-owned businesses, but census data do not show an extreme overrepresentation of Cubans living in the area adjacent to those businesses.

Whatever their nation of origin, most Hispanic immigrants quickly acquire two basic American tools: a car and a telephone. Miami's Cubans may go to Little Havana to shop, socialize, and eat, just as Miami's Nicaraguans go to the

> **The most exotic place where Mexicans cluster may be Bay City-Saginaw, Michigan.**

Sweetwater district to buy copies of *El Diario La Prensa* and loaves of *pan Nicaraguense*. But when the trip is over, they return to homes scattered all over the city.

Another problem is that many Hispanic immigrants are not interested in owning a home, buying a new car, or otherwise participating as full-fledged American consumers. New York City is home to about 10,000 foreign-born Brazilians, for example. But "most Brazilians are in New York only to save money

San Juans

Mexicans are by far the largest Hispanic-American group, but 77 percent of Dominican Americans live in one urban area.

(top-five urbanized areas for Hispanics by country of origin, population in thousands; and share of segment, 1990)

Guatemala

top-five urbanized areas	population	share
U.S. total	269	100%
Los Angeles	133	49
New York	27	10
Chicago	15	6
San Francisco	11	4
Washington, DC	9	4

Peru

top-five urbanized areas	population	share
U.S. total	175	100%
New York	54	31
Los Angeles	27	15
Miami	16	9
Washington, DC	11	7
San Francisco	9	5

Nicaragua

top-five urbanized areas	population	share
U.S. total	203	100%
Miami	74	37
Los Angeles	37	18
San Francisco	25	12
New York	14	7
Washington, DC	8	4

Honduras

top-five urbanized areas	population	share
U.S. total	131	100%
New York	33	25
Los Angeles	24	18
Miami	18	14
New Orleans	9	7
Houston	5	4

Ecuador

top-five urbanized areas	population	share
U.S. total	191	100%
New York	115	60
Los Angeles	21	11
Chicago	8	4
Miami	8	4
Washington, DC	5	3

Panama

top-five urbanized areas	population	share
U.S. total	92	100%
New York	27	29
Miami	7	7
Los Angeles	6	6
Washington, DC	4	4
San Francisco	2	2

for the return to Brazil," says Maxine L. Margolis, an anthropology professor at the University of Florida in Gainesville. In her book *Little Brazil,* Margolis tells the story of a local television news program called "TV Brasil." When it began, Brazilian-owned businesses were eager to sponsor it. But the ads failed to attract new customers, she says, because many Brazilians spend only what they must and save everything else.

Perhaps the biggest problem is the size of "other" Hispanic groups. "TV Brasil's"

producers tried to persuade the Coors Brewing Company to advertise by claiming that 200,000 Brazilians lived in New York City, according to Margolis. But Coors turned them down anyway, claiming that the market was too small.

These obstacles may scare most businesses away, but the few that do target "other" Hispanics are rewarded with a growing source of loyal customers. As the airline of Colombia, Avianca focuses its U.S. advertising on Colombians, says Alberto Gil, a marketing analyst for the

airline in New York City. The city's five boroughs are home to about 86,000 Colombians, according to demographer Frank Vardy at the Department of City Planning.

Avianca advertising runs primarily on Spanish-language television, radio, and in newspapers circulated in New York. "We don't care so much about whether the [medium] has a high rating for all Hispanics, but for Colombians," he says. The airline gauges Colombians' interests by asking its customers to name their favorite publications, radio stations, and TV shows.

The airline also focuses on a 20-block area in North Queens that is the geographic heart of Colombian settlement in New York City. Travel agents in that neighborhood receive special attention from the airline, says Gil. "We are a symbol for [Colombians]," he says. "We are Colombia in the United States."

Colombian politicians are well aware that New York-based expatriates form a powerful voting bloc. In past elections, polling places for Colombian elections have been established at the Colombian consulate and in Queens, says Javier Castano, a reporter for the Spanish-language newspaper *El Diario*. Colombian presidential candidates occasionally travel to New York City at election time, and politicians from many countries buy

The affluent Connecticut town of Stamford is particularly attractive to South Americans.

advertising in *El Diario* and other New York media.

Immigrants follow well-worn paths when they come to the United States, and these paths do not change rapidly. If immigration from Latin America continues at its current rapid pace, America's Little Havanas, Little San Juans,

and other Hispanic enclaves will eventually grow to the point where targeting "other" Hispanics makes sense to mainstream marketers. Investing small amounts of time and money on specific Hispanics today could yield big payoffs tomorrow.

—*Additional reporting by Patricia Braus*

Behind the Numbers This study examines 1990 Hispanic populations in urbanized areas, defined by the U.S. Census Bureau as "one or more places (central place) and the adjacent densely settled surrounding territory (urban fringe) that together have a minimum of 50,000 persons." In 1990, the census identified 397 urbanized areas. For more information, contact the author at (904) 644-8377 or the Census Bureau at (301) 763-4040.

Latin U.S.A.

The Young Hispanics

Hispanics are hip, hot and making history. By 2005, Latinos will be the largest U.S. minority; they're already shaping pop culture and presidential politics. The Latin wave will change how the country looks —and how it looks at itself.

BY BROOK LARMER

STROLLING ALONG NORTHWEST EIGHTH Street in Miami—a.k.a. Calle Ocho—is like taking a trip through another country. But last week the sights and sounds of Calle Ocho were both intensely foreign and undeniably American. A crowd of angry Cuban exiles marched down the street denouncing the U.S. Coast Guard's use of force to round up six Cuban refugees near a local beach the day before. From the sidelines, other Latinos looked on: prim Honduran clerks at an evangelical bookstore, spiffed-up businessmen at an Argentine steakhouse, sweaty construction workers eating Salvadoran *pupusas*. Merengue music blasted indifferently from the Do-Re-Mi music shop. But the elderly Cubans playing dominoes in Maximo Gomez Park stood and joined in with the protesters: "Libertad! Libertad!"

Could this be the face of America's future? Better believe it. No place in the United States is quite so international as Miami; even the Latinos who run the city joke that they like it "because it's so close to America." But Miami, like New York and Los Angeles, is ground zero for a demographic upheaval that is unfolding across America. Like the arrival of European immigrants at the turn of the century, the tide of Hispanic immigrants—and the fast growth of Latino families—has injected a new energy into the nation's cities.

Latinos are changing the way the country looks, feels and thinks, eats, dances and votes. From teeming immigrant meccas to small-town America, they are filling churches, building businesses and celebrating their Latin heritage. In a special NEWSWEEK Poll of Latinos, 83 percent said being Hispanic was important to their identity. They are overwhelmingly Roman Catholic; 42 percent go to church once a week. They've become a potent, increasingly unpredictable political force: 37 percent of 18- to 34-year-old Latinos say they are independent, about twice as many as their Hispanic elders. In America, a country that constantly redefines itself, the rise of Latinos also raises questions about race, identity and culture—and whether the United States will ever truly be one nation.

The numbers couldn't be clearer. Fueled by massive (and mostly legal) immigration and high birthrates, the Latino population has grown 38 percent since 1990—to 31 million—while the overall population has grown just 9 percent. And with more than a third of the Latino population still under 18, the boom is just beginning. By the year 2005, Latinos are projected to be the largest minority in the country, passing non-Hispanic blacks for the first time. By 2050, nearly one quarter of the population will be Latino. "The [African-American] civil-rights slogan was 'We shall overcome'," says Christy Haubegger, the 30-year-old founding editor of the bilingual magazine Latina. "Ours is going to be 'We shall overwhelm'."

They may just have the muscle to back that up—particularly in politics. Though they accounted for only 6 percent of those who voted in the 1998 midterm elections, Hispanics are clustered in 11 key states, with a total of 217 out of the 270 Electoral College votes needed for the presidency. And neither party has a lock on this new force. "Latinos are the soccer moms of the year 2000," says Gregory Rodriguez of the New America Foundation. Is it any wonder that Al Gore and George W. Bush were both on campaign stops in Florida and California last week, eagerly greeting voters in Spanish?

The driving force behind the Latino wave are members of a cohort that is sometimes called Generation Ñ (following story). These young Hispanics—the Latin Gen X—are influential not simply because of their huge numbers. They are making their mark—and making all things Latin suddenly seem cool. Jose Canseco, a 35-year-old Cuban-American, and Dominican-born Sammy Sosa, 30, lead the great American home-run derby. Ricky Martin, 27, and Jennifer Lopez, 28, top the pop-music charts. Actors Benjamin Bratt, 35, and Salma Hayek, 30, are quickening the national pulse.

Is the rest of America ready? Hip Anglos on both coasts are dancing salsa, learning Spanish and dabbling in Nuevo Latino cuisine. And every fifth grader seems to know the lyrics of "Livin' La Vida Loca." But many Latinos doubt whether America can easily move past the stereotypes that depict them as illegals, gangbangers or entertainers. "Don't try to understand Latinos through [Ricky Martin]," says Manuel Magana, 21, a University of Michigan senior. "It's like trying to figure out Americans by listening to the Backstreet Boys."

Latinos can't be neatly pigeonholed. They come from 22 different countries of origin, including every hybrid possible. Many are white, some are black, but most are somewhere in between. Some Latino families have been in the United States for centuries, since the days when much of the Southwest was still a part of Mexico. Others, like the six Cuban refugees, swam ashore last week. (The Coast Guard freed them a day later.) Many Latinos are assimilating into cycles of urban blight; 40 percent of Latino children now live in poverty, the highest rate ever. But millions of Hispanics are also moving into the middle class, speaking English, inter-marrying and spending cash—lots of it. U.S. Latinos pump $300 billion a year into the economy.

Not everybody has been eager to give Latinos a big *abrazo*. When California voters

Latino Americans: The Face of the Future

Their numbers are growing—and fast. Today there are 31 million Hispanics in the U.S. By 2050 the population is projected to hit 96 million—an increase of more than 200 percent. And Hispanics are younger than the rest of the nation: a third are under 18. A look at Latinos in America:

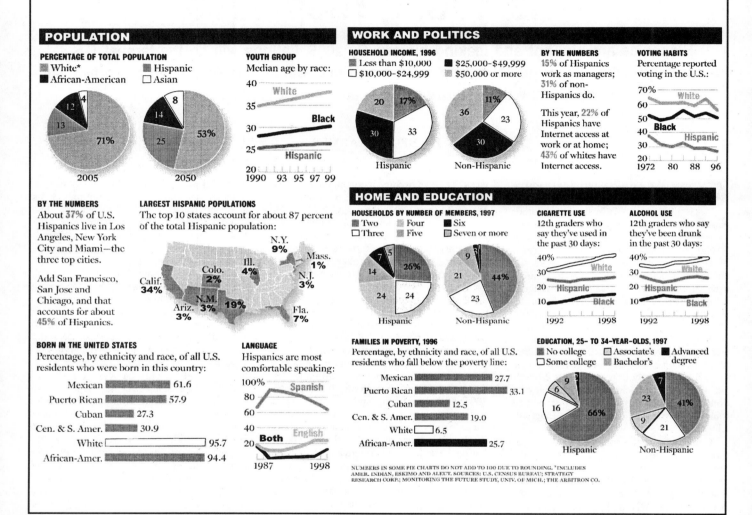

POPULATION

PERCENTAGE OF TOTAL POPULATION
White* · Hispanic · African-American · Asian
2005: 71%, 12, 13, 4
2050: 53%, 14, 25, 8

YOUTH GROUP
Median age by race: White, Black, Hispanic (1990 93 95 97 99)

BY THE NUMBERS
About 37% of U.S. Hispanics live in Los Angeles, New York City and Miami—the three top cities.

Add San Francisco, San Jose and Chicago, and that accounts for about 45% of Hispanics.

LARGEST HISPANIC POPULATIONS
The top 10 states account for about 87 percent of the total Hispanic population:
N.Y. 9% · Mass. 1% · Ill. 4% · N.J. 3% · Colo. 2% · Calif. 34% · N.M. 19% · Ariz. 3% · Fla. 7%

BORN IN THE UNITED STATES
Percentage, by ethnicity and race, of all U.S. residents who were born in this country:
Mexican 61.6
Puerto Rican 57.9
Cuban 27.3
Cen. & S. Amer. 30.9
White 95.7
African-Amer. 94.4

LANGUAGE
Hispanics are most comfortable speaking: Spanish, Both, English (1987–1998)

WORK AND POLITICS

HOUSEHOLD INCOME, 1996
Less than $10,000 · $25,000-$49,999 · $10,000-$24,999 · $50,000 or more
Hispanic: 17%, 20, 30, 33
Non-Hispanic: 11%, 36, 30, 23

BY THE NUMBERS
15% of Hispanics work as managers; 31% of non-Hispanics do.

This year, 22% of Hispanics have Internet access at work or at home; 43% of whites have Internet access.

VOTING HABITS
Percentage reported voting in the U.S.: White, Black, Hispanic (1972 80 88 96)

HOME AND EDUCATION

HOUSEHOLDS BY NUMBER OF MEMBERS, 1997
Two · Four · Six · Three · Five · Seven or more
Hispanic: 26%, 24, 24, 14, 7, 5
Non-Hispanic: 44%, 23, 21, 9, 3

CIGARETTE USE
12th graders who say they've used in the past 30 days: White, Hispanic, Black (1992–1998)

ALCOHOL USE
12th graders who say they've been drunk in the past 30 days: White, Hispanic, Black (1992–1998)

FAMILIES IN POVERTY, 1996
Percentage, by ethnicity and race, of all U.S. residents who fall below the poverty line:
Mexican 27.7
Puerto Rican 33.1
Cuban 12.5
Cen. & S. Amer. 19.0
White 6.5
African-Amer. 25.7

EDUCATION, 25- TO 34-YEAR-OLDS, 1997
No college · Associate's · Advanced degree · Some college · Bachelor's
Hispanic: 66%, 16, 6, 9
Non-Hispanic: 41%, 21, 9, 23, 7

NUMBERS IN SOME PIE CHARTS DO NOT ADD TO 100 DUE TO ROUNDING. *INCLUDES AMER. INDIAN, ESKIMO AND ALEUT. SOURCES: U.S. CENSUS BUREAU; STRATEGY RESEARCH CORP.; MONITORING THE FUTURE STUDY, UNIV. OF MICH.; THE ARBITRON CO.

---

passed propositions limiting immigrant rights and Washington tightened federal immigration policy in the mid-1990s, Latinos took it as a call to arms. The best weapons of defense were citizenship and the vote. Between 1994 and 1998, Latino voting in nationwide midterm elections jumped 27 percent even as overall voter turnout dropped 13 percent. The 2000 presidential election may show even more dramatic increases: Latino leaders aim to register an additional 3 million voters by then.

Latinos have long leaned Democratic (Clinton got 72 percent), but their vote is alluring these days precisely because it is up for grabs—and Generation Ñ seems intent on keeping it that way. Gore edged out Bush among all Latinos polled, 29 percent to 28 percent, but Generation Ñ voters favored Bush by a margin of 9 percent. Nobody understands how Latinos can swing an election more than Nevada Sen. Harry Reid, a Democrat. During his tight 1998 race, Reid's friend, boxing promoter Bob Arum, persuaded Oscar De La Hoya to join the campaign. The charismatic boxer did two fund-raisers, a public rally and several Spanish media spots. "He's the reason I'm in the Senate now," says Reid. Don't believe him? The senator won by just 428 votes.

Latinos are flattered to be considered hot commodities, whether as voters, consumers, employees or entertainers. But their aspirations, and their importance to American society, run much deeper than mere social acceptance. They are not "crossing over" into mainstream America; they are already here, getting more influential by the day, so the rest of America must learn to adapt as well. "Something tremendous is happening," says 30-year-old novelist Ixta Maya Murray. "This generation of Latinos is going to change the way America looks at itself." On the last Independence Day of the millennium, a new nation is being born.

With VERONICA CHAMBERS, ANA FIGUEROA, PAT WINGERT *and* JULIE WEINGARTEN

Article continues—

Generation Ñ

Raised on rock and Ricky Martin, the Latin Gen X is cruising the American mainstream, rediscovering their roots and inventing a new, bicultural identity—without losing anything in the translation

BY JOHN LELAND AND VERONICA CHAMBERS

EL CONQUISTADOR, IN THE TRENDY SILVERLAKE section of Los Angeles, is a hard place to find, set off from the street by a doorway of hanging straw. But once you're inside, the Mexican food is authentic and excellent. Over shrimp tacos and *albóndigas,* a traditional meatball soup, Olivia Armas and her husband, Rod Hernandez, begin an affectionate round of teasing. Olivia, 29, is the daughter of Mexican immigrants; Rod's family came to Los Angeles from Mexico two generations ago. From the time they met as undergraduates at UCLA, she has ribbed him about his shaky command of Spanish. "I didn't know what to make of him," she says. "I thought, 'Oh my God, he's a wanna-be Chicano who can't speak Spanish'." Now, as Rod, 31, gropes for the Spanish word for haircut, Olivia rolls her eyes. He returns the dig. Olivia's family's idea of cuisine, he says with a laugh, includes cow innards, organs— "parts of the animal that I had never seen before. I have to beg her to not make me eat that stuff. I say, 'Honey, can we please have pasta tonight?'"

In their gentle jousting, Olivia and Rod are performing a cultural balancing act that has become daily life for millions of young Latinos: the fine art of living in two worlds at once without losing anything in the translation. Largely bilingual—often more fluent in English than Spanish—they belong to a growing generation of truly bicultural Latinos, coming into their 20s and 30s with demographic clout, educational skills and cultural juice their parents never imagined. Where previous Hispanic generations crossed geographic borders, they cross cultural ones, sometimes three or four times in one sentence. Raised on rock *and* Ricky Martin, the Brady Bunch *and* "Qué Pasa U.S.A?," they navigate an extraordinarily complex web of relationships: with their elders, with Anglos and with each other, inventing identity in the interstices. "For our

parents, being Latino was a negative in this country," says Nely Galan 35, president of entertainment at the Spanish-language TV network Telemundo. "For us it's a plus. We get to be 100 percent American when we want to be but we can switch and say, 'I'm not even American today; I'm totally Latin. I'm going to a Latin club, I'm listening to Latin music, I'm speaking in Spanish'."

Unlike their anglo peers, they do not live in the shadow of a more populous baby boom. The Latino population is young and getting younger. "This generation is going to permanently change things," says Rudy Acuña, founding chair of Chicano Studies at Cal State Northridge. "Past generations have always assimilated. This time around, there are enough of them to say, 'We aren't going to make it *your* society. We want to make it on our own terms'."

Bill Teck, 31, set out to name this new power generation. Growing up in Miami, the son of Cuban and American parents, he felt left out of the Generation X rubric, especially the slacker part. "If you're the first generation born and educated in the U.S., you really can't have a slacker mentality." Nothing if not entrepreneurial, he coined the

> In a NEWSWEEK Poll of Latinos, 49% of those under the age of 35 say they have it better than their parents did

term Generation Ñ pronounced EN-yay, the extra flavor unit in the Spanish alphabet— and copyrighted it in 1995 as a full-service brand. The following year, in the first issue of Generation Ñ magazine, he published a letter that was part come-on, part manifesto. "If you know all the words to [the merengue hit] 'Abusadora' and 'Stairway to Heaven'," it ran, "If you grew up on café, black beans and 'Three's Company'. . . . If you're thinking of borrowing one of your father's guayaberas. . . . You're Generation Ñ." As peers in California toyed with their own rubric, Generation Mex, a cohort—or at least a marketing target—was born.

Better versed in American pop culture than their parents, Ñ's can also be more assertively Latin. In a special NEWSWEEK Poll, Latinos over 35 were most likely to identify themselves as American; those under 35 were more likely to identify as Hispanic or Latino. Often generations removed from the immigrant experience, many Ñ's are now rediscovering—and flaunting—their roots. The son of migrant farm workers, Jaime Cortez, 33, has an Ivy League education—and a San Francisco apartment full of traditional guayabera shirts. "We get them pressed when we go out," he says. "More and more, you see literary, educated guys doing things that immigrants wanted to get away from." By his lights, such reclaiming is vintage Latin. "America has this weird optimism that dictates that we have to leave the past behind. My generation of Latinos doesn't feel that way at all. We know we come from a rich history and culture, and we want to celebrate that. I think that's our defining trait."

The cultural mix, though, is not all salutary. Like other immigrant groups, Latinos in the second and third generations begin to absorb the worst of America: poorer health and diet, higher delinquency and dropout rates, more divorce and domestic abuse. Latino girls recently passed blacks with the

Critical Más: 20 for 2000

There's more to Generation Ñ than crossover pop stars. Here are some other young Latinos to watch:

KORY ARVIZU-JOHNSON
ENVIRONMENTAL ACTIVIST

PHOENIX, ARIZ., AGE 20. She started Children for a Safe Environment at the age of 9 and has been fighting to keep hazardous waste and pollution out of minority neighborhoods ever since. "Poor people shouldn't always be the ones dumped on," says Arvizu-Johnson, who is of Mexican-American and Native American heritage.

MARC ANTHONY
SALSA SINGER

NEW YORK, AGE 30 His CD, "Contra la Corriente," won a Grammy this year. Of Puerto Rican descent, he is recording his first English-language pop album.

CARLOS CARDONA
INTERNET ENTREPRENEUR

MIAMI BEACH, AGE 23 Cardona got the idea for yupi.com, an Internet portal site, while introducing his father to the Web in 1996. Now it's the most-visited Spanish-language site, drawing 6 million visitors a month.

LUIGI CRESPO
POLITICAL ORGANIZER

WASHINGTON, D.C., AGE 27 As the executive director of the Republican National Hispanic Assembly, the Peruvian-born Crespo aims to bring more Latinos into the Republican fold. "Our Hispanic ideals are very conservative," he says.

TED CRUZ
LAWYER

WASHINGTON, D.C., AGE 29 The first Latino to clerk for the chief justice of the United States, in 1996–97. His father emigrated from Cuba in 1957 and, Cruz says, "Education opened the American dream to him. We're failing to provide that education now, especially to poor minorities."

OSCAR DE LA HOYA
BOXER

LOS ANGELES, AGE 26 The undefeated welterweight camp and Olympic gold medalist grew up in East L.A., the son of Mexican immigrants. After he moved to upscale Bel-Air, De La Hoya says, "people in the barrio thought I abandoned them. But that's not the case anymore. They know I'm opening doors for my people."

JUNOT DIAZ
AUTHOR

NEW YORK, AGE 30 His critically acclaimed "Drown" (1996), a collection of stories about his childhood in the Dominican Republic and New Jersey, established him as one of the strongest voices of Generation Ñ. A Guggenheim Fellow, he's working on his first novel.

LYSA FLORES
MUSICIAN, ACTRESS

LOS ANGELES, AGE 25 She recorded her punk-inspired 1998 CD "Tree of Hope," on her own label, and is a stalwart in L.A.'s "Chicano alternative" music scene. Flores appears in the Telemundo series "Reyes y Rey," and is a fund-raiser for environmental and Latino causes.

JOHN LEGUIZAMO
ACTOR

NEW YORK, AGE 35 In his off-Broadway shows "Mambo Mouth," "Spic-O-Rama" and the Tony-nominated "Freak," the Colombian-born actor turned Latino stereotypes into real characters with heart. He plays an Italian in Spike Lee's "Summer of Sam."

REBECCA LOBO
BASKETBALL PLAYER

NEW YORK, AGE 25 The WNBA star, whose great-grandfather was Cuban, is injured and out for the season. But the kids wearing pint-size number 50 New York Liberty jerseys won't forget their 6-foot-4 hero.

JUAN MALDACENA
PHYSICIST

CAMBRIDGE, MASS., AGE 30 A MacArthur Foundation "genius" grant winner, this Argentine physicist's specialty is "string theory."

FAUSTO MEZA
MEDICAL STUDENT

GALVESTON, TEXAS, AGE 29 As coordinator of the National Network of Latin American Medical Students, the Ecuadoran-born Meza works to get more Latinos into medicine.

YXTA MAYA MURRAY
NOVELIST

LOS ANGELES, AGE 30 Her lyric novels explore society's rough edges. "Locas" was about female gangs in East L.A. Her latest, "What It Takes to Get to Vegas," is set in the Mexican-American boxing scene.

SOLEDAD O'BRIEN
TELEVISION JOURNALIST

NEW YORK, AGE 32 The NBC news correspondent-anchor is a one-women melting pot. Her Cuban-born mother is black, her father is Irish-Australian.

JOHN D. OLIVAS
ASTRONAUT

HOUSTON, AGE 33 A fourth-generation Mexican-American, he will finish the year-long NASA Astronaut Candidate program in the fall, making him the ninth Latino astronaut.

ALEX PADILLA
CITY COUNCILOR

LOS ANGELES, AGE 26 On June 9, Padilla became the youngest Latino (he's Mexican-American) to win a seat on the L.A. City Council.

ALEX RODRIQUEZ
BASEBALL PLAYER

SEATTLE, AGE 23 A-Rod, as Mariner fans call the Dominican-American shortstop, is the first 40-40 infielder—40 home runs and 40 stolen bases in one season—in major league history.

ROBERT RODRIGUEZ
FILM DIRECTOR

AUSTIN, TEXAS, AGE 30 His debut film, "El Mariachi," was made for only $7,000 and won him a Sundance Audience Award. A Mexican-American, his most recent film was the teen thriller "The Faculty."

SHAKIRA
SINGER

MIAMI, AGE 22 Her gutsy 1998 rock album "Donde Estan Los Ladroness" won her a zealous following among young Latinas. She's currently working on an English version with Gloria Estefan. A native of Colombia, she wants to show the world that Latinos "don't just do ranchero and salsa. We can do good rock."

BILL TECK
MAGAZINE EDITOR

MIAMI, AGE 31 The second-generation Cuban-American founded Generation Ñ magazine, and coined the term. "It's about saying, 'Wait a minute. We're not all Generation X'."

THOMAS HAYDEN *with* JUDY GANELES *and* RUTH TENENBAUM

45% of older Latinos say premarital sex is wrong; 40% of younger Latinos share that view

highest rates of teen pregnancy, more than double that for whites. "The longer [families] have been in the United States, the better the kids speak English and the higher their self-esteem,' says Michigan State sociologist Rubén Rumbaut. "But they also do less homework, have lower GPAs and lower aspirations." The reasons for this pattern are complicated and little-studied, says Rumbaut. Children's superior English skills may upset the family order. Also, second- and third-generation Latinos, who grow up with higher expectations than their immigrant parents, may be less resilient when they encounter discrimination.

In a monasterial Spanish mansion above Los Angeles, though, life is large. The salsa star Marc Anthony is talking to Jennifer Lopez about boats. "I'm getting an 83-foot yacht," he says, his slender arms carving the air to suggest nautical heft. "With four bedrooms." Both raised in New York City, the children of Puerto Rican parents, Lopez and Anthony have come to this hilltop manse to shoot the video to "No Me Ames," a Spanish-language duet from her hit album, "On the 6." The video calls for Anthony to die from an unnamed illness, then for his spirit to watch over the grieving Lopez. "It works in Spanish," says an assistant, sheepishly. "In English it's too corny." Lopez, for her part, sees it more "like a foreign movie, like 'Life Is Beautiful'." But for now, during a break, she is worried about that boat. "That's expensive upkeep," she says. Anthony shrugs. "You only live once."

At its best, the new wave of Latin-based music now riding the charts reflects the generation's bicultural lives. Though Latin audiences are in large part regionally divided—tropical grooves in the East, Mexican sounds in the South and West—young stars like Ricky Martin and the Colombian rocker Shakira break down the divisions by mixing a variety of pop styles, Latin and Anglo. "We are made of fusion," says Shakira, 22. "It's what determines our identity: the way in one mouthful we take rice, *plátanos,* meat." Her own music combines Alanis Morissette, reggae and Mexican mariachi sounds. As Bill Teck says, she's what you put on your CD changer between Sarah McLachlan and El Gran Combo. The musicians' breakthrough, for many Latinos, has become a measure of collective success in North America. "When I was growing up, it really wasn't cool to be Hispanic," says Adan Quinones 22, a real-estate broker in La Puente, a suburb of L.A. "There was pressure to act white. Now, everyone wants to be Latino. If Ricky Martin

has helped bring that about, then I certainly admire him."

The attention from Anglo audiences is not always gratifying. Anthony, 30, bristles over a recent magazine article that featured jalapeño peppers beside his picture. Jalapeños are Mexican. I've never eaten one in my life." The singer, who starred in Paul Simon's ill-fated musical "The Capeman," can work up a head of steam. "This whole 'crossover wave' thing really displaces me," he says. "Like I'm coming in and invading America with my music. I was born and raised in New York, man."

At the Third Spanish Baptist Church in the Bronx last month, Elizabeth Malave 30, and Adalberto Santiago, 31, said "I do" in front of 100 of their closest friends and family. Except they didn't say, "I do," they said, *Sí, acepto.* Elizabeth is a community health counselor, one of the growing numbers of Latina professionals; Adalberto delivers produce for a local distributor. In their menu of fried sweet plantains and roast pork, the couple bowed to the traditions of their Puerto Rican elders. But they also began a break. "My parents have a very good relationship," says Elizabeth, "yet we all know who the head of the household is. My dad makes the decisions, and that's how it works." In her own marriage, she says, "Berto and I are partners."

Many young Latinas are rejecting the traditional roles that their mothers embraced. "The main difference between our generations is that women are less tolerant," says Ana Escribano, 30, a student at Florida International University who works part-time at Generation Ñ. "Less tolerant of the machismo. Less tolerant of the cheating and doing everything for men." The result is often a culture clash between mother and daughter. The poet and writer Michele Serros, 33, a fourth-generation Mexican-American, calls

By exactly the same measure, 54%, Latinos young and old say their heritage is very important to their lives

herself a "Chicana Falsa" because she felt she didn't live up to ethnic expectations. The women in her family, she says, lived at home until they were married, and wouldn't dream of being on their own. "I grew up on TV, idolized Mary Tyler Moore and 'That Girl'." Her mother and aunts especially "would have never considered dating outside the race." Though her family accepts her Anglo husband, they don't understand why she kept her maiden name. "They think it is disrespectful [toward] my husband."

Such trailblazing can sometimes call for a new wardrobe. "A lot of Latin women like to dress in a feminine way: cinched waists, clothes that celebrate our bodies," says Yvonne Neira-Perez, 25, program coordinator for the nonprofit Hispanic Heritage Awards. On a June afternoon in Washington, D.C., she is dressed in a preppy blue shirt and khaki pants. "In school here, and now in work, I realized that people don't take you seriously when you look that way. I've had to change my look."

Many Ñ's are also wrestling with an even more deeply entrenched tradition: religion. Like their parents, young Hispanics are overwhelmingly Roman Catholic. But their faith is more fluid. In their home in San Francisco, Rod Hernandez and Olivia Armas have a traditional big red felt Virgin of Guadalupe over the bed, and they were married in the church. Their future children, they say, will be baptized. Yet they call themselves "cultural" Catholics. "We respect and honor Catholic traditions, but don't approve it," says Olivia. Enrique Aguilar, 25, says most of his friends feel the same ambivalence. Born in El Salvador, Aguilar came to the United States in 1981, during the revolution, and now manages and co-owns a wireless-accessories company in San Antonio. Although he is a practicing Catholic, he feels less devout than his parents. "In El Salvador there is so much hardship that you have to lean on religion or you will go crazy," he says. "But here we have so much opportunity. We believe in the religion, but we also question it much more."

As some take advantage of these opportunities, though, many are left behind. To get to her classes at Michigan State University, Rosa Salas, 21, drives first past the Mexican-American community in North Lansing, where children walk to a school that is falling apart. A few minutes later, she passes the brand-new high school in neighboring Okemos, where white Anglo kids surf the Internet. "I've got my sociology books in the car so I can discuss race and ethnicity with all the other white kids in my class who never had to deal with race," she says. The trip is a daily reminder that Latinos still trail the rest of the country economically and still have to deal with Anglo prejudice. "I'm tired of people thinking that I just came over the border," says Salas. "I'm tired of people asking me if I got my green card or if I eat tacos every night."

Many face prejudice from other Hispanics as well. With their jumble of races and national origins, Latinos can be as color conscious as anyone else, says the Dominican-born author Junot Diaz. "Dominicans are anti-Haitian because of anti-African feelings; Puerto Ricans treat Dominicans like Americans treat Puerto Ricans." At the very hip Miami nightclub La Covacha recently, the crowd is energetic, well dressed and universally fair-skinned. Though Miami has a growing Central American community, it is not represented here, either in the clientele or staff. This is no accident, admits promoter Aurelio Rodriguez, a former Armani model. "I'm catering to an upscale South American crowd," he says. "There's big discrimination against Nicaraguans. [They're] considered lower-class."

In Generation Ñ this tension is showing signs of easing. Among other reasons, the threat of recent movements to end affirmative action and restrict immigrants' access to some social benefits has fostered a broader solidarity. At a June press conference by the boxers Oscar De La Hoya and Felix Trinidad to promote their Sept. 18 title fight, most fans hold the national line. Puerto Ricans scream for Trinidad, Mexicans for De La Hoya. But a number switch camps. Amid the cheering, Omar Ortiz, 36, explains, "I'm Puerto Rican, but I'm for De La Hoya. He's proud of his culture, and that gives all Latinos pride."

These are the borders that Generation Ñ is crossing. Their elders may not always understand the new territory, but they are welcome there. In a quiet moment, Rod Hernandez's mother, Maria, takes stock of her son's generation. Maria Hernandez, 53, is a supervisor at the U.S. Bankruptcy Court in Riverside, Calif. Rod, she says, is better educated than she or her husband, and has also taught them things about Mexican history and art. For all Olivia's teasing, his Spanish is better than his parents'. And if his life is more chaotically American than theirs, it is in some ways even more respectful of its Latin roots. "My husband and I have always been comfortable with our heritage," Maria says. "But we were never as demonstrative about it as Rod and Olivia. They've taken it to a higher plane." In these and other ways, Generation Ñ is creating a new Latino America.

With ANA FIGUEROA, LYNETTE GLEMETSON, PAT WINGERT, JULIE WEINGARDEN, THOMAS HAYDEN *and* MARTHA BRANT

Hardliners v. "Dialogueros": Cuban Exile Political Groups and United States–Cuba Policy

MARÍA CRISTINA GARCÍA

THROUGHOUT UNITED STATES HISTORY various immigrant groups have tried to influence the politics of their countries of origin either by trying to shape United States foreign policy, or by recruiting men or money to aid political movements in their homelands. Irish, Jews, Poles, Mexicans, Filipinos, Latvians, among many others, have at different times tried to assist their homelands politically and economically. Whether they have migrated to the United States for economic or political reasons, immigrants and refugees maintain an active interest in their homelands, oftentimes for several generations. It is an emotional relationship that is not easily severed. The Cubans are among the most recent of such groups. What makes the Cuban community a particularly interesting case study is the level of their involvement in both United States and homeland politics. Despite being a largely first-generation community, they have one of the highest naturalization, voter registration, and political participation rates of any group to arrive in the latter half of the twentieth century. This increased involvement in the United States political process has had significant repercussions on United States hemispheric policy, the south Florida political landscape, and indeed, Cuba.

In looking at the political scene in south Florida, it is easy to assume that the Cuban immigrants who have settled there in such large numbers refuse to assimilate. Non-Cubans are perplexed, even angered, by the role of Cuba in public debate. In order to be elected to any political office in south

From *Journal of American Ethnic History*, Summer 1998, pp. 3–28. Reprinted by permission of Transaction Publishers.

Florida (regardless of one's ethnicity), one must hold the "correct" ideological position in the United States-Cuba policy debate. Local newspapers, both English and Spanish-language, are filled with stories of the "three C's": Castro, Cuba, and Communism. Over half a dozen Spanish-language radio stations offer round-the-clock commentaries on events taking place just one hundred miles from Florida's shores. These realities are the natural outcome of the Cubans' dominance in key institutions of the area, from universities to labor unions to the city commission. In just one generation the Cubans have transformed the cultural, economic, and political landscape of south Florida.

Despite these sociological indicators of success in the United States mainstream, the Cubans' "obsession" with Cuba symbolizes for many non-Cubans a refusal to assimilate. The Cubans may have the wealthiest Latino business community in the nation, their children may go on to college in large numbers, and they may have a high median income, but the fact that Cuba figures so prominently in their cultural and political life represents a "foreignness" that prevents them from being accepted as fully "American."

The Cubans, however, see no problem in being both "Cuban" *and* "American." They do not understand why United States citizenship should require forefeiting one's heritage. Instead, they challenge American definitions of "assimilation" and beliefs about "American-ness." Their insistence on dual identities is a product of their condition as exiles and refugees. The Cubans regard themselves as exiles, not immigrants: people who left their country not by choice but because they were pushed out. This identity was reinforced when the United States government granted the first arrivals in the 1960s refugee status. Those who arrived in the 1960s thought that their stay would be temporary. Exile movements had always been a part of Cuban history, and they perceived themselves as the most recent wave of people forced out of their country. Given the long history of United States interference in Cuban affairs, the exiles did not believe that the United States would tolerate a communist government so close to its shores; it would only be a matter of time before Castro was overthrown and they were able to return home. Interestingly, recent arrivals from Cuba in the 1990s also express a similar view: they believe that their stay in the United States will be temporary—not because they expect a United States invasion but because they believe that Cuba will eventually self-destruct. It is impossible to predict what percentage of the community will actually return to Cuba once there is

an acceptable change in government; however, their condition as first-generation exiles/refugees, together with Cuba's close proximity to south Florida and the continual influx of new arrivals guarantees that this community will always maintain an active interest in shaping the political realities in their country of origin.

The Cuban exile community in south Florida has attracted a great deal of attention for its highly conservative views regarding Cuba, and in particular, for dictating United States foreign policy towards their homeland. For almost forty years, the community has waged a war against Fidel Castro: a propaganda and paramilitary campaign, at times receiving financial and institutional support from the United States government, designed to discredit the Cuban leader and undermine his government. As the Cuban community has become more politically powerful over the years they have become key players in shaping United States foreign policy. Indeed, many analysts today claim that the Cuban exiles are partly the reason why the United States has failed to lift its thirty-eight-year-old trade embargo on Cuba despite intense international criticism and despite the policy's obvious failure to rid the island of the despotic Castro.

In analyzing Cuban exile politics the media—and many scholarly studies—have focused on the community's interventionist strategies: the secret paramilitary camps of the 1960s (some funded by the CIA); the terrorist groups of the 1970s; and the political action committees of the 1980s and 1990s. In recent years, the press has begun to focus attention on what they claim is a growing schism within the exile community between those who favor a political *rapprochement* with Cuba and those who maintain their hardline views. The press has interpreted, even celebrated, this schism as a "new" phenomenon, but it is not. As early as the 1960s a segment of the exile community had adopted a more tolerant view of the Castro government, and tried to serve as a mediating force between Cuba, the exile community, and the United States, hoping to ultimately bring some resolution to the conflict between the various parties. It is the conflict between these two segments of the exile community that is the subject of this article. Special attention will be focused on those who favor *rapprochement* if only because they have received comparatively less attention than the "hardliners."

The political views of the Cuban exile community in the United States have never been monolithic. Indeed, as far back as the nineteenth century, when the first Cuban expatriate communities were formed in cities such as Tampa, Key

West, New York, Philadelphia, and New Orleans, emigrés disagreed passionately about their country's political future. In the nineteenth century the Cuban expatriates were trying to redefine their relationship to Spain: Liberal reformists sought autonomy within the colonial system; annexationists, though nationalist in sentiment, regretfully concluded that political and socioeconomic realities on the island demanded that Cuba link itself to the United States; and the popular nationalists—the largest segment by 1895—argued that total and unconditional independence was the only acceptable goal. These expatriate communities in the United States played a critical role in shaping the political debate in the homeland, and most certainly in encouraging nationalist ideals in the final decades of the nineteenth century.[1]

In the decades following Cuba's independence, Cubans, cognizant of the fact that José Martí's revolutionary vision of a self-reliant nation based on social justice, racial harmony, and respect among classes had not been realized, continued to call and work for change. The political struggles of the 1930s through 1950s, culminating in the victory of Castro's July 26 movement, were all attempts to create a more just society as well as bring about greater political self-determination. Cubans living in the United States, exiles from the various political regimes on the island, also played a role in these struggles, following the tradition of their nineteenth-century forebears.

The elite and working-class Cubans who left Cuba after Castro's victory in 1959 became the most recent expatriate community to try to shape the political realities in the homeland. These post-revolutionary emigrés continue to debate passionately Cuba's future, and more specifically, what type of government should replace Castro-communism. They all claim to want democracy for their homeland, but they have different ideas of what democracy entails, their views shaped by the successes and failures of a century of Cuban politics. Some favor an authoritarian, non-communist government that will establish social and economic order, modeled, in part, after the Batista government that Castro's July 26 movement overthrew. Others advocate an open, multiparty electoral system, modeled after the United States or the parliamentary systems of other western democracies. In economics, some favor free-market capitalism, while others favor some variation of socialism that will address the social and economic inequalities that have plagued la pátria since the creation of the Republic. Some favor a perpetuation of their country's symbiotic relationship with the United States, while others, more staunchly nationalistic, demand political and economic independence. Represented within the post-revolutionary emigré population are supporters of the various political parties, factions, urban resistance and guerrilla groups of pre-1959 Cuba, as well as literally hundreds of new political organizations that have emerged in exile, each coalescing either around some charismatic individual or a particular political concern.

Opposition to Fidel Castro's government is the raison d'être of this exile community, and consequently, eliminating Castro's communist government has always been the number one concern in Cuban exile politics (as opposed to Cuban ethnic politics).[2] While some exile political groups actively engage in ideological discussions about Cuba's future and have tried to define a definite platform that would serve as a democratic alternative to the revolutionary government, the goal of most exile political organizations has simply been to overthrow Fidel Castro. It is seen as a panacea for the ills of Cuban society, in much the same way that the Generation of the 1930s idealistically, and erroneously, viewed Machado's overthrow as a panacea, and just as the student generation of the 1950s thought that Batista's overthrow would create a more democratic society. For most emigrés today, the details of shaping a post-Castro society is something that will be worked out later. Literally hundreds of groups emerged during the 1960s and 1970s to lead the "war against Castro": some of them functioned as paramilitary groups running raids against Cuba, but the majority were propaganda organizations dedicated to damaging Castro's reputation in the international arena. Some of these organizations continue to operate today. These "hardliners" consider rapprochement or any political/economic accommodation of the Castro government to be totally unacceptable.

The community's staunch anti-Castroism obscures the complexities of the Cuban emigrés' politics. They are labeled conservatives (even "fascists" and "reactionaries") by the European and Latin American Left because of their vocal opposition to the Castro government. However, a good number of the emigrés would probably identify themselves as liberals. Many claim to have supported traditionally liberal causes as universal health care and education, agrarian reform, the nationalization of public services, and workers' rights, which initially attracted them—they say—to Castro's revolutionary platform. Ironically, their disillusionment and ultimate break with the revolutionary government automatically shifted them to the opposite side of the political spectrum. Identifying the liberals in the domestic (United States) politics of the Cuban exile/Cuban American community is equally problematic. Cuban emigrés might support traditionally liberal causes associated with the Democratic party, such as health care reform, greater government controls and protections, and even abortion rights, but in Miami they vote overwhelmingly Republican, at least in national elections, because of this party's perceived stronger stance against communism. Domestic concerns are superceded by the determination to eliminate Castro. Even so, Democrats know that they should not write the Cuban vote off completely. In the most recent 1996 election, the Cuban vote in south Florida split with almost half of all votes going to the Clinton/Gore ticket. The Republicans' anti-immigration platform compelled the Cubans to take another look at the Democratic party, and the fact that Clinton maintained Reagan and Bush's hardline policy toward Cuba made that decision easier.

Given that this is a community of largely first-generation immigrants who harbor great resentment towards the government that displaced them from their homeland, and that imprisoned and executed tens of thousands of their countrymen, it is understandable that many are obsessed with the idea of eliminating Castro. Polls and surveys conducted in this community over the past thirty-five years show that a majority of Cuban exiles reject any political accommodation that will strengthen or perpetuate Castro's tenure and prevent democratic reforms. The most extreme hardliners oppose any contact with the Castro government at all, whether commercial, trade, or diplomatic, until Fidel Castro is dead or in exile himself.

At the same time, there is a segment of this community that rejects these views and favors *rapprochement*. They are called *dialogueros* because they favor any dialogue or communication with the Castro government that might lead to either reforms in the Cuban political system or a change in United States-Cuba relations, or both. The term *dialoguero* has become somewhat of a pejorative in this community due to the conservative exile radio commentators in Miami, who charge that all those who favor "dialogue" with the Cuban government are communists. It is a useful tactic for silencing discussion in this community since it instills fear of retaliation.

Most emigrés who today favor a political *rapprochement* with Cuba developed this perspective slowly, over time. While the exact percentage of the community that favors *rapprochement* is difficult to determine (for reasons that will be discussed shortly), the number of people who have vocally challenged community institutions that foster hardline views, such as the exile news media, has increased over the years. Separation from

homeland, family and friends, has led some emigrés to consider a more accommodationist relationship with the Castro government in hopes of being able to return to Cuba, even if just to visit. Others have come to favor *rapprochement* as a means of easing life for their relatives and countrymen back home, who find it hard to survive in post–Cold War Cuba. For others, it was the inability to topple Castro despite decades of effort that led them to consider other, more peaceful, alternatives. As Eloy Gutierrez Menoyo, former anti-Batista (and eventually anti-Castro) guerrilla fighter, recently explained: "Imagine a person who diets for that long without losing a pound. Anyone with common sense would change diets."[3]

THE FIRST DIALOGUEROS

Throughout the 1960s and early 1970s, young students and scholars of Cuban origin on various university campuses across the United States, and in Puerto Rico, gathered to discuss the revolution and its impact on their lives. They gathered formally, under the auspices of student organizations such as the Cuban Students Federation, or privately, in homes, churches, cafes, and businesses, to explore issues of identity, politics, and culture. Most had left Cuba as teenagers, and they now needed to define their relationship to their homeland and to the United States. They left one revolutionary state to enter another—an American society grappling with the counterculture, the Vietnam War protests, the feminist movement, and the Civil Rights movement. When the young Cubans questioned their identity and discussed issues of social justice, they had ample company. The radicalized milieu into which they entered encouraged introspection and rebellion.

These students and scholars came to many different conclusions about the Castro revolution. Some, outraged at the human rights abuses on the island, concluded that they had a moral responsibility to work for Cuba's "liberation," and they joined student paramilitary groups such as the *Directorio Revolucionario Estudiantil* (Revolutionary Students Directorate) and *Abdala,* which sought direct confrontation with the Castro regime. Others, influenced by the radicalized milieu of the sixties, and the cult-like status that Castro and Che Guevara enjoyed on some United States college campuses, developed a more tolerant view of the revolution. They came to interpret the revolution as an inevitable stage in Cuban history and politics, and not a betrayal of the Cuban people as many emigrés in Miami charged. A small number even came to support vocally the Castro government itself.

Many of these young students and scholars turned to writing as a means of exploring their relationship to the homeland. They founded journals (reflecting a variety of political positions) such as *Nueva Generación Joven ¡Cuba, Cuba, Va!, Krisis,* and *Areíto* to discuss issues relating to Cuba and its people both on and off the island. They wrote essays on Cuban history, the revolution, the sociology of exile, as well as on Cuban art, music, theater, and folklore. They contributed poetry, short stories, photography and artwork, and book and film reviews. Published in Miami and New York, these journals targeted the student generation and the young professional and working classes. The editorial staff took these cultural concerns seriously, and they were as idealistic as the names of their journals suggested. They believed that as the "Young Cuba" and the "New Generation" they could have an impact on their homeland, even from exile—just as the emigrés of the nineteenth century revolutionary wars had had on the intellectual and political climate in Cuba a century earlier. They viewed themselves as part of a historical continuum. Students and young professionals had always played a key role in shaping Cuban policies (best exemplified in the "Generation of the 1930s," which inspired a reformist movement on the island that culminated in the Castro revolution), and they perceived themselves as part of this reform tradition.

These journals became a vehicle to define their opinions and explore new perspectives. As one editorial in *Joven Cuba* stated:

> We the young people did not choose to leave Cuba. That was a decision made by our parent's generation. . . . We are not going to discuss the correctness of that decision now. . . . But it is now time for us to study Cuba and the revolution, and to form our own opinions. We did not know *la Cuba de ayer* ("the Cuba of yesterday"). Cuba and the rest of the world have changed much during the course of our formative years, and our views have inevitably evolved differently from that of our parents.[4]

Weary of the biased, and often libelous exile news media in Miami, the editors strove to make their journals a forum for objective discourse. They were willing to analyze both the accomplishments and failures of the revolution: a radical idea in a community where anger and resentment at the revolution colored all political discussion. As one editorial in *¡Cuba Va!* stated: "objectivity does not mean ignoring truths which we do not wish to confront, or which will force us to assume

difficult positions."[5] They turned a critical eye towards the emigré community, as well as Cuba. The editors criticized the exile community for its censorship and "terrorism of ideas": "symptoms of the same disease that plagued the homeland."[6] . . .

In 1978, several of those who comprised the "Grupo Areíto" recounted their personal and political formation in the anthology *Contra viento y marea* ("Against Wind and Tide"), which was published by Havana's *Casa de las Américas.* Through their testimonies they recounted their emigration experience as children and teenagers who left Cuba not of their own free will, but to follow their parents' wishes. They spoke of their alienation within American society, and "how against wind and tide, and contrary to all expectations and probabilities, they identified with Cuba, from the very cradle of exile and in the middle of North American society."[16] More than a collection of testimonies, *Contra viento y marea* explored the views of a particular segment of the emigré community, which until *Areíto,* remained voiceless. In 1978, Cuba awarded the anthology its most distinguished literary award, the "Premio Casa de las Américas": a gesture which was probably as much political as honorary.

Areíto's editorial views encountered a great deal of hostility in the exile news media, which called them *comunistas, infiltrados* (spies), drug addicts, and *vendepatrias* (sell-outs or traitors). One editorial in *Abdala,* the tabloid of the militant student group *Agrupación Estudiantil Abdala* stated:

> It doesn't surprise us that such detestable beings should exist: people who having the opportunity to choose between fighting for the liberation of their country or opposing tyranny should choose to follow Castro for reasons that only their unbalanced minds could explain. Traitors have always played a role in a country's history.[17]

During the mid-to-late 1970s, *Areíto*'s editorial staff was targeted by militant extremists who placed bombs in the homes or offices of several members; others were harassed by phone or accosted on the street.[18] Despite the unpopularity of its views, however, *Areíto* survived for over a decade. While other journals ceased publication by the mid-1970s because of financial difficulties or apathy, *Areíto* circulated well into the mid-1980s. For many emigrés, *Areíto*'s solvency was yet another proof that the staff had to be composed of *infiltrados* and that the Cuban government financed the journal. Author and former political prisoner Reinaldo Arenas called them "the official organ of the Cuban state police in New York."[19] The editors, however, credited subscriptions and fundraisers for their survival. In later years, the editors expanded their range of topics to include the revolutionary movements of all the Americas, especially the struggles in Chile, Nicaragua, and El Salvador. *Areíto's* circulation averaged some 3,000 subscribers of various nationalities. By the mid-1980s, however, the journal folded. In 1989 the journal resumed publication, albeit irregularly. . . .

In 1971, emigré scholars from the United States, Puerto Rico, and Latin America founded the *Instituto de Estudios Cubanos* (IEC) as a forum for all persons who wished to study Cuba "in a serious and responsible fashion, no matter what their political orientation."[25] Committed to pluralism, members ranged from the conservative to the Marxist. Most of the IEC members, however, fell into the political category known as "center-to-left." Most did not actively support Castro's communist government, but as scholars they aimed to establish a dialogue with other scholars on the island and to study the revolutionary process without political bias. Several members have carried out research projects on the island and, in 1980, the IEC sponsored one of its seminars in Havana. Cuban scholars from the island are regularly invited to participate in their annual meetings and do so if granted visas by the United States State Department, or if they do not object to the roster of those scheduled to make presentations. (Cuban scholars on the island boycott IEC meetings if intellectuals critical of the regime are scheduled to present; during the 1994 meeting, for example, several scholars from the island canceled at the last minute because the IEC scheduled presentations by several Havana-based dissenters.)

While pluralism is the hallmark of the IEC, the organization has, of course, encountered hostility from conservative exiles. Hardliners call IEC members "collaborationists" and many conservative scholars refuse to attend their conferences, claiming that the presence of Marxist scholars (both from Cuba and the United States) is ample proof that it is a pro-Castro organization. Militant Cuban exiles have made members targets. In 1978–79, when a number of IEC members participated in a *diálogo* in Havana, militant extremists made threats against their lives.[26] In 1988, when the organization sponsored a seminar in Miami on the pros and cons of reestablishing diplomatic relations with Cuba, extremists bombed the home of IEC director Maria Cristina Herrera. Despite these pressures from within the community, however, the IEC has endured. In 1994, the organization celebrated its twenty-fifth anniversary—an accomplishment due largely to the commitment of its members but to some degree, also to community support. Letters to the *Miami Her-* *ald* over the years revealed that many people in this community were grateful to the IEC and other institutions for trying to challenge the hold conservative institutions had on information. In recent years, membership and participation in IEC activities has increased, and the 1994 reunion was held in Miami once again, this time without incident.

CENSORING THE DIALOGUEROS

Since most Cuban exiles remained committed to the war against Castro, those who articulated accommodationist views, particularly within their own community, were regarded as enemies. Hardline institutions, such as the Cuban exile radio stations and tabloids, blasted the *dialogueros* (or *los comunistas,* as they called them), for their willingness to negotiate with the government that had displaced them from their country. Such rhetoric in the exile news media only inflamed the passions of the more militant Cuban exiles, who took more violent measures, harassing and even threatening the lives of those who supported any type of accommodation of the Castro government. By the mid-1970s, the militants were engaged in an all-out campaign to silence or eliminate the liberals in their community.[27]

This campaign to censor the dialogueros acquired urgency during the mid-to-late 1970s when it appeared that the United States and Cuba were actively moving towards *rapprochement.* During the Ford and Carter administrations, the United States negotiated a fishing rights and a maritime boundary agreement, lifted its ban on transferring American currency to Cuba as well as on using an American passport to travel there, and granted visas to Cubans to come to the United States on a temporary basis.[28] An unprecedented number of scholars, artists, writers, and scientists traveled to and from Cuba in the interest of cultural and scholarly exchange. The most important development, however, was the creation of American and Cuban "interests sections," which provided a limited diplomatic representation.

Hardliners, angered by these developments, concluded that they could only halt them if the community presented an image of unified opposition and pressured the United States government to abandon this course. Cuban exiles expressed their anger at the new United States policy through letters and phone calls to the exile news media, and they staged "anti-coexistence" rallies in cities such as Miami; Union City, New Jersey; San Juan; and Washington, D.C. But the community was not as solidly united in their opposition as many hardliners thought. It was not just university students and academics who were advocating a new approach to United States-Cuba relations. One *Miami Herald* poll in 1975 showed that, while slightly over half (53 percent) of Cuban exiles remained staunchly opposed to reestablishing diplomatic and trade relations with Cuba, the other half were at least willing to explore limited alternatives.[29] Among Cuban emigrés, 49.5 percent were willing to visit the island with Castro still in power—a surprising revelation to hardliners in this community who opposed any contact with the Cuban government whatsoever. Letters to the *Miami Herald* and other English-language news media (as opposed to the Spanish-language exile news media) revealed that a small percentage favored reestablishing diplomatic and trade relations. Polls and letters revealed a generational difference in attitudes. Cubans raised and educated in the United States, who were more likely to call themselves Cuban Americans than Cuban exiles, were more likely to favor accommodation than were their elders.

A handful of organizations emerged during the 1970s to lobby for *rapprochement,* among them, the Cuban Christians for Justice and Freedom, the National Union of Cuban Americans, and the Cuban American Committee. In 1979, the latter group sent a petition with over 10,000 signatures to President Carter requesting that the United States normalize relations with the Castro government.[30] The number of emigrés who joined these organizations was not significant enough to serve as an effective lobby, however—at least during the 1970s. Emigrés who favored the normalization of relations generally kept silent because they feared being branded *comunistas* in the exile press or by some radio news commentator. In the exile community, being branded a *comunista* or *infiltrado* inevitably affected careers and businesses. Hardliners interpreted the world in extremes: an accommodation of the Cuban government was an endorsement of Castro-communism. Hardliners could not understand why an *exilado* would choose to even talk to the individuals who had tortured, imprisoned, and executed thousands of their compatriots. Even the sending of medicine and food parcels to family members in Cuba (via third countries) was considered to be an act of treason.[31] Most of those who favored normalization of relations, then, kept quiet, out of fear, articulating their views only when they could be assured anonymity. Those who vocally supported *rapprochement* found their businesses boycotted, their property vandalized, and their families harassed.[32]

Despite these risks, in 1978, over 150 Cuban exiles, most of them businessmen, journalists, and academics from the United States and Puerto Rico, participated in a *diálogo*—a series of meetings in Havana with representatives of the Cuban government. These meetings in Cuba led to the easing of travel restrictions to the island: for the first time since the revolution, the Cuban government allowed exiles to return to their homeland for a limited period of time—usually one week—to visit family and friends. During the first year of the new policy (1979), over 100,000 emigrés returned to their homeland to visit, surprising Cubans, exiles, and Americans alike. . . .

. . . Liberal views were further silenced in the wake of the Mariel Boatlift of 1980, which brought 126,000 new refugees to the United States. News that the Cuban government had used the boatlift to rid the island of criminals and the mentally insane angered the exile community, who feared that their reputations as "golden immigrants" would be tarnished. Many of those with accommodationist views reconsidered their positions following *Mariel.* For many, the Cuban government's actions seem to support the hardliners' claims that Fidel had not changed and still could not be trusted.

Ronald Reagan's election in 1980 pleased the hardliners in the community and rekindled their hopes for Castro's overthrow. With Reagan in the White House, there was little chance of *rapprochement* and emigrés began plotting ways of pressuring the use of even more punitive policies towards the Castro government. Influencing foreign policy was possible due to the emigrés' growing clout in domestic politics. During the past decade, Cubans had registered to vote as soon as they became naturalized and their voting participation rate exceeded that of the general population.[35] In Dade County alone, they comprised 20 percent of registered voters by 1983, up from 8 percent in 1976. The Cubans' high turnout meant that theirs was a swing vote that could secure a margin of victory. Cubans voted Republican in national elections and more consistently so than any other ethnic group. Their loyalty to the Republican party had less to do with domestic policy issues, however, than with the Republicans' foreign policy agenda.[36] In the 1980 and 1984 presidential elections, Cubans in Miami voted for Reagan by over 90 percent. Outside of south Florida, in communities where Cubans were removed from powerful exile institutions and where their political attitudes were influenced by contact with more liberal Latino groups, Cubans still voted Republican but in smaller percentages (65 percent in New York and 68 percent in Chicago, for example).[37]

To take advantage of the new conservative climate in the country, in 1981, a group of wealthy Cuban businessmen in Miami, many of them Bay of Pigs veterans, founded the *Cuban American National Foundation* (CANF), a non-profit organization whose principal goal was to assist the Reagan administration formulate a "realistic" foreign policy towards Cuba.[38] The organization established its principal base in Washington, D.C., and concentrated its efforts on influencing congressmen through its political action committee, the "Free Cuba PAC." Since 1981 CANF has donated hundreds of thousands of dollars to the reelection campaigns of Democrats and Republicans alike;[39] in 1997 the Center for Public Integrity, a private organization that monitors the United States government, called CANF "the most powerful voice on U.S. policy toward Cuba."[40] For those who support a hardline policy toward Cuba, CANF's record is certainly impressive: CANF successfully lobbied for the creation of *Radio Martí* and "Television Martí," supposedly with the goal of increasing their compatriots' access to information on the island. CANF also successfully pressured the Reagan and Bush administrations to tighten the trade embargo against Cuba. In 1982, American tourists were once again prohibited from traveling to Cuba, with the exception of scholars, journalists, and emigrés wishing to visit their relatives on the island. In 1992, after intensive lobbying by CANF and other conservative exile groups, Congress passed the "Cuban Democracy Act," which imposed penalties on foreign subsidiaries of American corporations trading with Cuba.

THE 1990s: A RENEWED CALL FOR A 'DIÁLOGO'

The 1990s began with an escalation of hostilities between Cuba and the United States. The Bush administration, after witnessing the collapse of communism in the Soviet Union and the eastern bloc, and the defeat of the Sandinistas in Nicaragua, abandoned any plans—if it ever had any—of accommodating the United States's long-time foe in the Caribbean. By 1991, Cuba had already met many of the requirements that the United States had placed as conditions for renewing full diplomatic relations, among them, withdrawing its forces from Angola. Conservative political strategists argued, however, that it was foolhardy to strengthen the Castro government at the very time its collapse seemed certain. Instead, through the reinforcement of the United States trade embargo, the administration hoped to pressure democratic reforms, if not eliminate Fidel Castro once and for all.

After the dismantling of the Soviet Union, many political observers gave the Castro government only a few more months before it, too, fell. To the amazement of many, however, the Cuban government defied the odds. In 1990, in an effort to speed up democratic reforms, some Cubans on the island—and in Miami—began to call for a national dialogue (that would include the emigrés) to discuss and plan for the country's future. Despite Castro's continued rhetoric that Cuba would never abandon Marxism, they believed that the time was right to sit down with Cuban officials and negotiate for democratic reforms, perhaps even for multi-party elections. The chief proponent of the dialogue was the Havana-based dissident group the "Cuban Committee for Human Rights," headed by Gustavo Arcos Bergnes, a former member of Castro's July 26 movement who served more than ten years in prison for human rights activities.[41] . . .

By the mid-1990s, the two most important groups advocating dialogue and a new United States policy towards Cuba were *Cambio Cubano* ("Cuban Change") and the Cuban Committee for Democracy (CCD), both founded in 1993. *Cambio Cubano* was the brainchild of former revolutionary Eloy Gutierrez Menoyo (of the anti-Batista guerrilla group *Segundo Frente del Escambray*). Gutierrez Menoyo's "conversion" to *rapprochement* surprised many in the exile community. In the 1960s, he co-founded the anti-Castro paramilitary group *Alpha 66* in Miami—one of the oldest and most active paramilitary groups, which continues to operate today. Gutierrez Menoyo had served over twenty years in a Cuban prison for counter-revolutionary activities. During his years in prison he concluded that only through dialogue would there be a peaceful transition in a post–Castro Cuba. Since his release in 1987 he has dedicated himself to encouraging open exchange between Cubans of all political persuasions. Towards this end, Gutierrez Menoyo met with Fidel Castro in 1995. Some of his former counter-revolutionary colleagues have also changed their perspective; *Alpha 66* co-founder, Antonio Veciana, for example, has also come out in favor of a national dialogue.[44]

The Cuban Committee for Democracy, in turn, was founded by liberal Cuban emigrés, most of them businessmen, academics, and other professionals. Some were active in the youth journals of the 1960s, the pro-*rapprochement* activities of the 1970s, and the *dialogo* of 1978. A good number of the board members, including Marcelino Miyares, Maria Cristina Herrera, Alejandro Portes, and Marifeli Pérez-Stable are also participants in the *Instituto de Estudios Cubanos*. The CCD challenges the conservative hegemony of the Cuban American National Foundation, and serves as a foil to many of their hardline activities. With offices at the Brookings Institution in Washington, D.C., the CCD has sponsored symposiums and press conferences on United States-Cuba relations and has held various congressional briefings. In February 1994, the CCD decided to support several bills in Congress that favored the partial or complete lifting of the United States trade embargo against Cuba.[45]

It is difficult to estimate what percentage of the community the pro-dialogue organizations represents. In 1988, a poll conducted in Miami and Union City revealed that 41 percent of emigrés favored any accords that would lead to better relations between Cuba and the United States.[46] A *Miami Herald* poll three years later, however, revealed that only 28 percent supported a dialogue with the Castro government.[47] This apparent shift in opinion was explainable in light of the political events of the time: the collapse of the communist world, and the belief that Castro's fall was imminent, led many emigrés to abandon their accommodationist views, fearing that they would perpetuate Castro's hold on the country. However, a more recent poll conducted by Florida International University in 1995 yielded surprising results: while 84 percent of the community favored increasing sanctions on the island (57 percent favored a United States invasion), 68 percent saw a dialogue as an acceptable tactic to advance reform and 46 percent favored the establishment of a national dialogue between exiles, dissidents, and Cuban government representatives. The statistics appear contradictory, but FIU researchers claim that it reflects the emigrés' frustration with the political impasse and their willingness to consider any option that will permanently alter the situation in Cuba.[48]

Among the emigrés who support better relations with the Castro government are those who have families in Cuba. These emigrés want to be able to travel to their homeland on a regular basis without having to spend their life savings on inflated air fares, visas, and taxes. Groups such as the "Cuban American Committee for Family Rights" pressure the United States government to keep the channels of communication open. Cubans raised in the United States continue to be much more likely to hold a liberal position than do their first-generation elders, especially if they live outside south Florida, away from the powerful exile institutions that try to control public opinion. But even in Miami, the Cuban American generation is much more liberal than is the Cuban exile generation. Contact in the schools and workplace with other Latino groups who have immigrated to south Florida in large numbers, and

who do not share the Cubans' animosity towards Castro, has had a liberalizing effect on the Cuban American world view,[49] as has contact with more recent arrivals from Cuba, who are in a more realistic position to evaluate both the successes and failures of the revolution. The Cuban American generation is either apathetic or embarrassed by Cuban exile politics. If they are politically engaged at all, they are more likely to favor diplomacy over conflict.[50]

CUBA, CLINTON, AND THE EXILE COMMUNITY

. . . Ironically, Fidel Castro has proven to be the staunchest of "hardliners." While claiming to want dialogue that will lead to improved relations with the exile community and the United States, his actions over the past two decades have suggested otherwise. Whenever the United States has made some move towards improving relations, the Cuban government has responded in such a way as to prevent further developments. At the same time, few in Washington are committed to any real change in United States-Cuba relations. Despite numerous "fact-finding" trips to Cuba over the past few years, few congressmen have come out in favor of lifting the United States trade embargo because, according to the director of one Washington think-tank, "People on the Hill . . . are afraid to say anything because they fear the political power of the Miami Cubans, particularly the Cuban American National Foundation."[53]

Any move towards rapprochement is unlikely in the immediate future. In a recent move the Clinton administration issued a report stating that the United States is prepared to commit several billion dollars to help Cuba's transition to a free-market democracy; however, there are several conditions for this aid, among them the departure of Fidel Castro and his brother Raul from power, the release of all political prisoners, and a public commitment to free elections.[54] The hardline groups in Miami applaud the Clinton report, and its contents are repeatedly read over *Radio Marti*. Accommodationists, on the other hand, have called the move a "new Platt amendment" and warn that it will increase the social pressure on the island until it explodes.[55] Only the Cuban people have the right to determine their own destiny, they say, and the United States government is once again interfering in a nation's sovereignty, no matter how noble they may perceive their intentions.

As the exile community, and the United States and Cuban governments, continue to debate the pros and cons of hardline and accommodationist policies into the twenty-first century, the Cuban people on the island impatiently wait for change. The only guarantee is that the exile community will maintain an active role in that debate.

NOTES

The author thanks Daniel Bornstein, Walter Kamphoefner, Marifeli Pérez-Stable, Larry Yarak, and the anonymous readers, for their comments on this article. Some of the information that appears in this article also appears in my book, *Havana U.S.A.: Cuban Exiles and Cuban Americans in South Florida, 1959–1994.*

1. For a discussion of the nineteenth-century Cuban expatriate communities see: Gerald E. Poyo, *"With All and For the Good of All" The Emergence of Popular Nationalism in Cuban Communities in the United States, 1848–1898* (Durham, N.C., 1989); Louis A. Pérez, Jr., *Cuba and the United States: Ties of Singular Intimacy* (Athens, Ga., 1988); Louis A. Pérez, "Cubans in Tampa: From Exiles to Immigrants, 1892–1901," *Florida Historical Quarterly,* 57 (October 1978): 129–140; Nancy A. Hewitt, "Cuban Women and Work: Tampa, Florida, 1895–1901," unpublished paper presented at the meeting of the American Historical Association, Washington, D.C., December 29, 1987; Susan Greenbaum, "Afro-Cubans in Exile: Tampa, Florida, 1886–1984," *Cuban Studies/Estudios Cubanos,* 15 (Winter 1985): 59–72.
2. I make a distinction between Cuban exile politics and Cuban ethnic politics. Simply stated, exile politics concerns itself with the homeland—the political, social, and economic situation in Cuba—while ethnic politics concerns itself with domestic issues and life in the United States. The line between exile politics and ethnic politics often blurs, however, as demonstrated in local elections where, ironically, candidates must demonstrate an "ideologically correct" foreign policy.
3. Richard Lacayo, "Long Distance Calling," *Time,* 17 July 1995, pp. 22–23.
4. *Joven Cuba,* 3 (January 1974): 3–4. Translation mine. Unless otherwise indicated, all quotes were translated by the author.
5. "Documento-Respuesta," *¡Cuba Va!* 1 (Winter 1974): 30–32.
6. Editorial, *Krisis,* 1 (Summer 1975): 1.
7. Jose Prince, "Revista Nueva Generación," *Antorcha* September 1969, p. 8.
8. *Joven Cuba,* 1 (Febrero 1974): 1.
9. *¡Cuba Va!* 1 (Autumn 1974): 1.
10. "Nuestra carta de ciudadania cultural" *Areíto,* 7 (1981): 96.
11. See, for example, *Krisis,* I (Summer 1975): 1; and *Cuba Va!* 1 (Winter 1974): 30–32.
12. Related to the author by Marifeli Pérez-Stable, former board member of *Areíto.* For another interpretation, see Leonel Antonio de la Cuesta, "Perfil Biográfico," in *Itinerario Ideológico: Antología de Lourdes Casal,* ed. Maria Cristina Herrera and Leonel de la Cuesta (Miami, 1982), pp. 3–8. de la Cuesta writes that the journal's radical position prompted the defection of several sponsors.
13. Editorial, *Areíto,* 9(1984): 4–5.
14. Ibid.; see also "Nuestra carta de ciudadania cultural," *Areíto,* 7 (1981): 95–97.
15. "Nuestra carta de ciudadania cultural," *Areíto,* 7 (1981): 96.
16. Grupo Areíto, *Contra viento y marea* (La Habana, 1978), p. 14.
17. *Abdala,* April 1978, p. 3; for another example of exile press reaction, see "¿Quien es Lourdes Casal?" *Impacto,* 3 October 1973, p. 3.
18. Editorial, *Areíto,* 1 (January–March 1975), p. 3.
19. "La verdad sobre Lezama Lima," *CID,* September 1984, p. 26.
20. The original idea for the Brigade emerged in 1974 during a meeting of the Institute of Cuban Studies in Gainesville. Editorial, *Areíto,* 4 (Spring 1978): 2–3. For a discussion of the "Venceremos Brigade" see Henry Maurer, "With the Venceremos in Cuba," *Nation,* 2 July 1977, pp. 6–10; Sandra Levinson and Carol Brightman, *Venceremos Brigade: Young Americans Sharing the Life and Work of Revolutionary Cuba* (New York, 1971).
21. Editorial, *Areíto,* 4 (Spring 1978): 2–3.
22. "Declaracion de la Brigada Antonio Maceo," *Areíto,* 4 (Spring 1978): 4.
23. Barbara Gutierrez and Jay Ducassi, "City, Exiles Attacks Pro-Castro Brigade," *Miami Herald,* 29 October 1982, p. 1C; "In Defense of Miami's Antonio Maceo Brigade," *Miami Herald,* 5 November 1982, p. 22A; Roberto Fabricio, "Maceo Brigade like KKK to Cuban Exiles," *Miami Herald,* 30 October 1982, p. 1B.
24. *Cuban Studies Newsletter,* December 1970, p. 1.
25. Interview with María Cristina Herrera, Coral Gables, Florida, 19 March 1987.
26. Ibid.
27. For an analysis of Cuban emigré conservatism, see Carlos Forment, "Political Practice and the Rise of an Ethnic Enclave," *Theory and Society,* 18 (January 1989):47–81. Forment writes that the Cuban American enclave in south Florida is a product of Caribbean geopolitics and that Cuban American conservatism "was constructed during the early years of community formation as the result of the interaction between discourse and power."
28. Myles R.R. Frechette, "Cuban-Soviet Impact on the Western Hemisphere," *Department of State Bulletin,* 80 (July 1980): 79–80.
29. *Miami Herald,* 29 December 1975.
30. "El Exilio pide relaciones entre Cuba y Estados Unidos," *Areíto,* 5, 19–20 (1979):7–8; "10 mi exiliados piden Carter reanude relaciones con Cuba," *El Mundo,* 25 June 1979, p. 8.
31. See, for example, *¡Fe!* 15 December 1972, p. 1. Even burial in Cuba—which was allowed beginning in 1979—was strongly discouraged because such arrangements benefitted the Cuban government financially. Ana E. Santiago, "Más restos cubanos llevados a la isla," *El Nuevo Herald,* 4 April 1991, pp. 1A, 4A.
32. See, for example, issues of the *Miami Herald,* 2 April 1975; 23 July 1975; and 22 August 1978.
33. Jay Clarke, "Cubans in Miami Fearful," *Washington Post,* 23 May 1976, p. E1.
34. See U.S., Senate, *Hearings before the Subcommittee to Investigate the Administration of the Internal Security Act and Other Internal Security Laws.* 94th cong., 2nd sess., 1976. See also Edna Buchanan, "Foes Stalked Slain Exile," *Miami Herald,* 23 Feb-

ruary 1974, p. 1 B; "Acusa Nieves de agresión a lider Pragmatista," *Fe!* 7 April 1973, p. 3; "No Permitiremos que juege con Cuba un puñado de traidores," *Fe!* 15 June 1973, p. 2; Hilda Inclán, "Six Cuban Exiles Marked for Death by 'Zero,'" *Miami Herald,* 25 April 1974; "Dara Plazo a Torriente," *Fe!* 24 February 1973, p. 7; "Torriente es el farsante mas grande que ha parido este exilio corrompido y timorato," *Fe!* 19 May 1973, p. 10; "Nine Cuban Refugees Go on Trial in Miami Tomorrow, Putting Focus on Terrorists' Activities in South Florida," *New York Times,* 28 November 1976, p. 35.

35. Genie N.L. Stowers, "Political Participation, Ethnicity, and Class Status: The Case of Cubans in Miami," *Ethnic Groups,* 8 (1990): 76–77; Eleanor Meyer Rogg and Rosemary Santana Cooney, *Adaptation and Adjustment of Cubans: West New York, New Jersey,* New York: monograph no. 5, Hispanic Research Center, Fordham University, 1980, p. 18; Thomas D. Boswell and James R. Curtis, *The Cuban American Experience* (Totowa, N.J., 1983), p. 174.

36. As an example of the emigrés' suspicion of Democratic foreign policy, see the article "Hay Coexistencia si triunfan los Democratas," *Impacto,* 17 December 1971.

37. María de los Angeles Torres, "From Exiles to Minorities: The Politics of Cuban Americans," in *Latinos and the Political System,* ed. F. Chris García (Notre Dame, Ind., 1988).

38. Advertisement for the Cuban American National Foundation in *Girón* June 1982, p. 4.

39. Excerpt from the Report of the Center for Public Integrity, reprinted in "Cuban American Clout," *HeraldLink,* 24 January 1997.

40. "Study Highlights Clout of Miami Lobby on Cuba Politics," *HeraldLink,* 23 January 1997.

41. "Declaración de Arcos Bergnes," *El Nuevo Herald,* 16 June 1990, p. 8A.

42. The text of the document appears in "En aras de la unidad," *Fundación,* año 1, no. 3, 5–7. *Fundación* is a CANF publication.

43. Alfonso Chardy, "Cuban Vice-president Apparently Misspoke about Talks with Exiles," *Miami Herald,* 28 October 1990, p. 1 B; Alfonso Chardy, "Cuban Exile Groups Wield Increasing Clout," *Miami Herald,* 4 November 1990, 1B. See also the Miami magazine *Contrapunto,* June 1994, p. 30.

44. Lacayo, "Long Distance Calling," *Time,* 17 July 1995, pp. 22–23; Jon Elliston, "The Myth of the Miami Monolith," *NACLA Report on the Americas,* 29 (September/October 1995): 40–41.

45. Larry Rohter, "As Crisis in Cuba Worsens, Unity of Exile is Crumbling," *New York Times,* 6 October 1993, p. 1; "Welcome to Cuban Affairs," *Cuban Affairs/Asuntos Cubanos* (Newsletter of the Cuban Committee for Democracy) 1, 1 (Spring 1994): 2.

46. William M. LeoGrande, "A Party Divided and Paralyzed," *The Nation,* 24 October 1988, pp. 395–396.

47. Iván Román, "Hope for Speedy End to Castro Era Fading, Poll Shows," *Miami Herald,* 9 May 1991, p. 1B.

48. Mireya Navarro, "U.S. Policy a 'Betrayal', Cuban Exiles Protest," *New York Times,* 8 May 1995, p. A13.

49. For a discussion of ethnic politics in south Florida, see Alejandro Portes and Alex Stepick, *City on the Edge: The Transformation of Miami* (Berkeley, 1993).

50. There are exceptions, of course. At Florida International University, students founded two groups in the early 1990s to protest human rights conditions on the island. These are the groups "Hijos del Exilio Cubano" and the "Young Cuban Americans Freedom Foundation." In 1994, both groups, together with two other exile organizations, founded the free Cuba Foundation, with their own web page.

51. The two planes were operated by *Hermanos al rescate* ("Brothers to the Rescue"), an organization that assists the U.S. Coast Guard by patrolling the Florida straits to search for Cuban rafters. The Cuban government claimed that on at least three occasions members of Hermanos had violated Cuban airspace and dropped anti-Castro leaflets over the city of Havana; they also claimed that they had warned the Clinton administration that they would take action if the flights in Cuban air space persisted. This cold-blooded act, together with the callous glee demonstrated by the Cuban pilots who shot down the planes (recorded on tapes released by the Cuban government), prompted a public outcry not only in the Cuban exile community but in Congress and in the international community. Within days, the Helms-Burton bill that had stalled now sailed through Congress, and President Clinton signed the bill into law. See Christopher Marquis, "Castro Says He gave Order to Down Planes," *Miami Herald,* 3 March 1996, p. 1A.

52. The Helms-Burton bill, supported by CANF and other hardline exile political groups, seeks to force democratic changes in Cuba by further weakening Cuba's economy. The law tightens the U.S. embargo on Cuba by imposing harsher travel and trade restrictions, and discourages foreign investment in Cuba by allowing U.S. citizens and companies to sue foreign investors for compensation if these foreign investors use property once owned by them but confiscated by the revolutionary government.

53. Carol Rosenberg, "Congressional Travelers are Attracted to Cuba," *HeraldLink,* 14 January 1997.

54. The report titled "Support for a Democratic Transition in Cuba" was mandated as part of the Helms-Burton law of 1996. See Christopher Marquis, "Clinton: U.S. Ready to Finance a Free Cuba," *HeraldLink,* 28 January 1997.

55. The Platt amendment, drafted and passed by the United States Congress in 1901 and added to the appendix of the 1901 Cuban constitution, dictated the terms of the future political relationship between Cuba and the United States after the United States troops withdrew from the island. Among the many conditions established by Congress, the United States retained the right to intervene in Cuba "for the preservation of Cuban independence."

[**Editor's note:** Part of original material has not been included in this report. See *Journal of American Ethnic History,* Summer 1998, pp. 10–12, 13–15, 18–19, 21, 23–24 for missing text notes data.]

Unit Selections

Key Points to Consider

❖ Does the exposure of race profiling by law enforcement agencies and the end of affirmative action in educational policy indicate that public governmental programs are not responsive to the needs and desires of African Americans?

❖ Is race-based violence increasing? Defend your answer.

❖ Can any Democrat be elected President without massive electoral support of African Americans? Does a Republican presidential candidate need the support of African American voters to win? Explain.

❖ What are the most compelling issues that face African American communities? Is location an important variable in the formulation of your answer? What role will new African immigrants play in the African American community?

❖ What social, economic, and political conditions have supported the expansion of an African American middle class?

❖ What explains the persistence of an African American underclass? In what respect is this question related to integration? In what respect is attention to education an answer to economic and social integration of African Americans?

❖ Does the name "African Americans" augment the development of pluralism? Discuss in terms of Afrocentrism and integration.

❖ What effect will the Supreme Court's deemphasis on remedies for segregation and on other initiatives that use racial preferences have on race and ethnic relations?

❖ Nielsen ratings of top television shows among blacks and whites reveal a stunning and widening divergence. For example, the *Steve Harvey Show* ranks #1 among blacks and #118 among whites. Only *Monday Night Football, CBS Sunday Movie,* and *E.R.* appear to converge toward biracial appeal. *Friends,* #2 among white viewers, ranks #91 among blacks. What implications do these findings have for integration? For marketing and advertising? The paucity of African Americans in prime time, mainstream network programs has been recently deplored. What causes and remedies do you propose?

 **Links**

www.dushkin.com/online/

15. **National Association for the Advancement of Colored People (NAACP)**
   http://www.naacp.org

These sites are annotated on pages 4 and 5.

The 2000 U.S. Census appears to be heading toward a substantive redefinition of racial and ethnic diversity in as much as respondents will be able to select multiple racial/ethnic identities. Thus, the last vestige of the official separation of white and black demographics will emerge from the crucible of America's primordial problem of overcoming slavery and color consciousness.

A 1988 *New York Times* editorial suggests an appropriate introductory focus for the following collection of articles about an ethnic group that traces its American ancestry to initial participation as "three-fifths" persons in the U.S. Constitution and to its later exclusion from the polity altogether by the U.S.Supreme Court's *Dred Scott* decision. The editors of the *Times* wrote in the article "Negro, Black and African American" (December 22, 1988):

> The archaeology is dramatically plain to older adults who, in one lifetime, have already heard preferred usage shift from *colored* to *Negro* to *black*. The four lingual layers provide an abbreviated history of civil rights in this century.

The following glimpses of the African American reality, its struggles for freedom, its tradition and community, its achievements, and the stresses of building bridges between worlds reveal a dense set of problems. More importantly, they suggest pieces of authentic identity rather than stereotype. Becoming a healthy ethnic society involves more than the end of ethnic stereotyping. The basis of ethnic identity is sustained by authentic portrayal of positive personal and group identity. The cultivation of ethnicity that does not encourage disdain for and self-hatred among members and groups is an important psychological and social artifice.

Progress on issues of race involves examination of a complex of historical, social, cultural, and economic factors. Analysis of this sort requires assessment of the deep racism in the American mentality, that is, the cultural consciousness and the institutions whose images and practices shape social reality.

Discrimination and prejudice based on skin color are issues rarely broached in mainstream journals of opinion. Ethnic and racial intermarriage and the influence and impact of skin hue within the African American community raise attendant issues of discrimination and consciousness of color. This concern began in eighteenth- and nineteenth-century laws and practices of defining race that shaped the mentalities of color consciousness, prejudice, and racism in America. Other dimensions of the African American experience can be found in this unit's accounts of African American traditions and experiences of self-help and the family. New perspectives on the civil rights era can be gained from reflective accounts of the leaders who influenced the direction of social change that reconfigured race and ethnic relations in America.

As this debate continues, patterns of change within African American populations compel discussion of the emerging black middle class. The purpose and influence of the historically black university, the reopening of the discussion of the separate-but-equal issue in the courts, and the renewed attention to Afrocentric education are clear evidence of the ambivalence and ambiguity inherent in the challenges of a multicultural society. Earlier dichotomies—slave/free, black/white, poor/rich—are still evident, but a variety of group relations based on historical and regional, as well as institutional agendas, to preserve cultural and racial consciousness have complicated the simple hope for liberty and justice that was shared by many Americans. Issues of race and class are addressed in this section. Various approaches to Afrocentrism are explained and contrasted.

Questions on the future state of American ethnic groups raise profound issues. For example, an understanding of the changing structure of the African American family has stubbornly eluded researchers and parents who confront the realities of pride and prejudice. Does the continual discovery of prejudice and discrimination in corporations have implications for public policy? Should public policy sustain an ethnic model of family or direct the formation of family life that is consonant with public purposes and goals?

The civil rights movement has been over for more than 20 years, but many African Americans still face challenges in housing, employment, and education. Changing circumstances within the larger American society and the civil rights agenda itself have been affected by success and failure, and once-clear issues and solutions have taken on more complex structural, economic, and philosophical dimensions. The growing gap between blacks and whites in terms of education, financial status, and class and the growing crime and death rates of young black men paint a daunting picture of past policies and of this population's future. According to scales of mortality, health, income, education, and marital status, African Americans have emerged as one of the most troubled segments of American society.

To be sure, African Americans have made advances since the civil rights movement of the 1960s. They have made dramatic gains in education, employment, and financial status. Unfortunately, they still are portrayed as being part of an urban underclass when only one-third of their population is actually in this group. While not all African Americans are poor, those who are poor are in desperate situations. Will help come from the African American population that now constitutes part of the middle and upper classes of American society?

Scholarly differences of opinion concerning the composition of the urban underclass do not minimize the hardships that many endure. The growth of the underclass, its isolation from society, and society's inability to help it are tremendous obstacles that face our nation. Concrete strategies for improving this situation call upon both the public and the private sectors in areas of education, employment, and training. Suggestions for meeting future needs of this population and pragmatic policy responses also will help the general population.

The issues of race in the workplace and remedies for discriminating practices have been raised in the debate regarding the Civil Rights Act of 1991. Exploring ethnic and racial mobility and developing strategies that foster the breakdown of discrimination engage us in a web of baffling arguments and social, political, and institutional procedures.

10 Most Dramatic Events In
African-American History

Lerone Bennett Jr.

1. The Black Coming

A YEAR before the arrival of the celebrated *Mayflower,* 244 years before the signing of the Emancipation Proclamation, 335 years before *Brown* vs. *Board of Education,* a big, bluff-bowed ship sailed up the river James and landed the first generation of African-Americans at Jamestown, Va.

Nobody knows the hour or the date of the official Black coming. But there is not the slightest doubt about the month. John Rolfe, who betrayed Pochohontas and experimented with tobacco, was there, and he said in a letter that the ship arrived "about the latter end of August" in 1619 and that it "brought not anything but 20 and odd Negroes." Concerning which the most charitable thing to say is that John Rolfe was probably pulling his boss' leg. For no ship ever called at an American port with a more important cargo. In the hold of that ship, in a manner of speaking, was the whole gorgeous panorama of Black America, was Jazz and the spirituals and the black gold

*The Shaping of Black America

that made American capitalism possible.* Bird was there and Bigger and King and Malcolm and millions of other Xs and crosses, along with Mahalia singing, Duke Ellington composing, Gwendolyn Brooks rhyming and Michael Jordan slam-dunking. It was all there, illegible and inevitable, on that day. A man with eyes would have seen it and would have announced to his contemporaries that this ship heralds the beginning of the first Civil War and the second.

As befitting a herald of fate, the ship was nameless, and mystery surrounds it to this day. Where did this ship come from? From the high seas, where the crew robbed a Spanish vessel of a cargo of Africans bound for the West Indies. The captain "ptended," John Rolfe noted, that he needed food, and he offered to exchange his cargo for "victualle." The deal was arranged. Antoney, Pedro, Isabella and 17 other Africans with Spanish names stepped ashore, and the history of Africans in America began.

And it began, contrary to what almost all texts say, not in slavery but in freedom. For there is indisputable evidence that most of the first Black

immigrants, like most of the first White immigrants, were held in indentured servitude for a number of years and then freed. During a transitional period of some 40 years, the first Black immigrants held real property, sued in court and accumulated pounds and plantations.

This changed drastically in the sixth decade of the century when the White founding fathers, spurred on by greed and the unprotected status of African immigrants, enacted laws that reduced most Africans to slavery. And so, some 40 years after the Black coming, Black and White crossed a fatal threshold, and the echo of that decision will reverberate in the corridors of Black and White history forever.

2. The Founding of Black America

W HEN on a Sunday in November 1786, the little band of Black Christians arrived at Philadelphia's St. George's Methodist Episcopal Church, the sexton pointed to the gallery. The Blacks paused and then started up the rickety stairs with downcast eyes and heavy hearts. To the leaders of this group, Richard Allen and Absalom Jones, this was the ultimate indignity—to be shunted from the first floor to the gallery in a church Black men had helped build.

The group had barely reached the top of the stairs when a voice from the pulpit said, "Let us pray." Without thinking, the men plopped down where they were—in the *front* of the gallery. Allen was praying as hard as he could when he heard loud voices. He opened his eyes and saw a White sexton trying to pull Absalom Jones from his knees.

"You must get up; you must not kneel down here!" the White sexton said.

"Wait until the prayer is over," Jones replied.

The voices echoed through the church, and people looked up and beheld the incredible scene of a Black Christian and a White Christian wrestling in the house of the Lord over the color of God's word.

"Get up!" the sexton said. "Get up!"

"Wait until the prayer is over," Jones replied wearily, "and I will not trouble you any more."

Four or five White Christians rushed to the sexton's aid, and the struggle spread over the gallery. Before the issue was resolved, the prayer ended. The Black men stood up then and, without a word, streamed out of the church in the first mass demonstration in Black American history.

Richard Allen added a mournful postscript:

" . . . And they were no more plagued by us in the church."

They were no more plagued by Blacks in a lot of places. For the Philadelphia demonstration was the focal point of a national movement that created the foundations of Black America. On April 12, 1787, Richard Allen and Absalom Jones created the Free African Society which DuBois called "the first wavering step of a people toward a more organized social life."

Similar societies were formed in most major Northern cities. And on this foundation rose an intricate structure of independent Black churches, schools and cultural organizations. The movement climaxed in the 1820s and 1830s with the founding of Freedom's Journal, the first Black newspaper, and the convening of the first national Black convention.

3. Nat Turner's War

GOD was speaking, Nat Turner said later.

There was, he remembered, thunder and lightning and a "loud voice" in the sky. And the voice spoke to him, telling him to take up the yoke and fight against the serpent "for the time was fast approaching when the first should be last and the last should be first."

Nat Turner was numbered among the last. And although he was a slave in Southampton County, Va., it would be said of him later that he "made an impact upon the people of his section as great as that of John C. Calhoun or Jefferson Davis." A mystic with blood on his mind and a preacher with vengeance on his lips, he was an implacable foe of slaveholders. He had believed since he was a child that God had set him aside for some great purpose. And he decided now that God was calling him to rise up and "slay my enemies with their own weapons."

To this end, Turner, who was about 30 years old, chose four disciples and set his face towards Jerusalem, the county seat of Southampton.

On Sunday morning, Aug. 21, 1831, the disciples gathered on the banks of Cabin Pond on the property of Joseph Travis, who had married the widow of Turner's last master and who had therefore inherited Turner and death. Nat, who appreciated the value of a delayed and dramatic entrance, appeared suddenly late in the afternoon and announced that they would strike that night, beginning at the home of his master and proceeding from house to house, killing every man, woman and child.

At 1 a.m., Nat Turner and his army crept through the woods to the home of the luckless Joseph Travis. They were seven men, armed with one hatchet and a broadax. Twenty-four hours later, they would be seventy and at least fifty-seven Whites would be dead.

When, on Monday morning, the first bodies were discovered, a nameless dread seized the citizens. Men, women and children fled to the woods and hid under the leaves until soldiers and sailors arrived from Richmond and Norfolk. Some Whites left the county; others left the state.

Defeated in an engagement near Jerusalem, Turner went into hiding and was not captured until six weeks later. On Nov. 11, 1831, the short Black man called the Prophet was hanged in a field near the courthouse. Before climbing the gallows, he made one last prophecy, saying there would be a storm after his execution and that the sun would refuse to shine. There was, in fact, a storm in Jerusalem on that day, but Turner was not talking about the weather—he was predicting a major disturbance in the American psyche. The storm he saw came in the generation of crisis that his act helped precipitate.

4. Free at Last!

TO Felix Haywood, who was there, it was the Time of Glory when men and women walked "on golden clouds."

To Frederick Douglass, it was a downpayment on the redemption of the American soul.

To Sister Winny in Virginia, to Jane Montgomery in Louisiana, to Ed Bluff in Mississippi, to Black people all over the South and all over America, it was the Time of Jubilee, the wild, happy, sad, mocking, tearful, fearful time of the unchaining of the bodies of Black folks. And the air was sweet with song.

Free at last!
Free at last!
Thank God Almighty!
We're free at last.

W.E.B. Dubois was not there, but he summed the whole thing up in phrases worthy of the ages. It was all, he said, "foolish, bizarre, and tawdry. Gangs of dirty Negroes howling and dancing; poverty-stricken ignorant laborers mistaking war, destruction, and revolution for the mystery of the free human soul; and yet to these Black folk it was the Apocalypse." And he added:

"All that was Beauty, all that was Love, all that was Truth, stood on the top of these mad mornings and sang with the stars. A great human sob shrieked in the wind, and tossed its tears upon the sea—free, free, free."

Contrary to the common view, the emancipation of Blacks didn't happen at one time or even in one place. It started with the first shot fired at Fort Sumter. It continued during the war and in the Jubilee summer of 1865, *and it has not been completed.* For the slaves, who created the foundation of American wealth, never received the 40 acres of land that would have made freedom meaningful.

It was in this milieu that African-Americans embarked on a road called freedom. As the road twisted and turned, doubling back on itself, their enemies and their problems multiplied. But they endured, and endure.

5. Booker T. Washington vs. W. E. B. DuBois

THERE was a big parade in Atlanta on Wednesday, Sept. 18, 1895, and a huge crowd gathered in the Exposition Building at the Cotton States Exposition for the opening speeches. Several Whites spoke and then former Gov. Rufus Bullock introduced "Professor Booker T. Washington." The 39-year-old president of Tuskegee Institute moved to the front of the platform and started speaking to the segregated audience. Within 10 minutes, reporter James Creelman wrote, "the multitude was in an uproar of enthusiasm—handkerchiefs were waved . . . hats were tossed into

the air. The fairest women of Georgia stood up and cheered."

What was the cheering about?

Metaphors mostly—and words millions of Whites wanted to hear. Washington told Blacks: "Cast down your buckets where you are." To Whites, he offered the same advice: "Cast down your bucket [among] the most patient, faithful, law-abiding and unresentful people the world has seen. . . ."

Suddenly, he flung his hand aloft, with the fingers held wide apart.

"In all things purely social," he said, "we can be as separate as the fingers, yet [he balled the fingers into a fist] one as the hand in all things essential to mutual progress."

The crowd came to its feet, yelling. Washington's "Atlanta Compromise" speech made him famous and set the tone for race relations for some 20 years. One year after his speech, the Supreme Court rounded a fateful fork, endorsing in *Plessy* vs. *Ferguson* the principle of "separate but equal."

Washington's refusal to make a direct and open attack on Jim Crow and his implicit acceptance of segregation brought him into conflict with W.E.B. DuBois and a group of Black militants who organized the germinal Niagara Movement. At its first national meeting at Harpers Ferry in 1906, the Niagara militants said, "We claim for ourselves every single right that belongs to a free-born American, political, civil, and social; and until we get these rights we will never cease to protest and assail the ears of America."

So saying, the Niagara militants laid the foundation for the National Association for the Advancement of Colored People which merged the forces of Black militancy and White liberalism.

6. The Great Migration

HISTORY does not always come with drums beating and flags flying.

Sometimes it comes in on a wave of silence.

Sometimes it whispers.

It was like that in the terrible days of despair that preceded the unprecedented explosion of hope and movement that is called The Great Migration.

This event, which was the largest internal migration in American history and one of the central events of African-American history, started in the cracks of history, in the minds and moods of the masses of Blacks, who were reduced to the status of semi-slaves in the post-Reconstruction period. Pushed back toward slavery by lynchings, segregation and the sharecropping systems, they turned around within themselves and decided that there had to be another way and another and better place. The feeling moved, became a mood, an imperative, a command. Without preamble, without a plan, without leadership, the people began to move, going from the plantation to Southern cities, going from there to the big cities of the North. There, they found jobs in wartime industries and sent letters to a cousin or an aunt or sister or brother, saying: Come! And they came, hundreds and hundreds of thousands. The first wave (300,000) came between 1910 and 1920, followed by a second wave (1,300,000) between 1920 and 1930, and third (500,000) and fourth (2,500,000) waves, even larger, in the '30s and '40s.

In the big cities of the North, Blacks emancipated themselves politically and economically and created the foundation of contemporary Black America.

7. Brown vs. Board of Education

THE marshal's voice was loud and clear.

"Oyez! Oyez! Oyez! All persons having business before the Honorable, the Supreme Court of the United States, are admonished to draw near and give their attention, for the Court is now sitting."

The marshal paused and intoned the traditional words:

"God save the United States and this Honorable Court!"

It was high noon on Monday, May 17, 1954, and the Supreme Court was crammed to capacity with spectators. Among the dozen or so Blacks present was Thurgood Marshall, chief counsel of the NAACP, who leaned forward in expectation.

Cases from four states (South Carolina, Virginia, Delaware, Kansas) and the District of Columbia were before the Court, which had been asked by Marshall and his associates to overturn the *Plessy* vs. *Ferguson* decision and declare segregation in public schools unconstitutional. All America awaited the long-expected decision which would come on a Monday But which Monday? No one knew, and there was no sign on the faces of the justices that the issue was going to be settled on this day.

The Court disposed of routine business and announced decisions in several boring cases involving the sale of milk and the picketing of retail stores. Then Chief Justice Earl Warren picked up a document and said in a firm, quiet voice: "I have for announcement the judgment and opinion of the Court in No. 1— *Oliver Brown et al. v. Board of Education of Topeka*. It was 12:52 p.m. A shiver ran through the courtroom, and bells started ringing in press rooms all over the world.

Warren held the crowd in suspense, reviewing the history of the cases. Then, abruptly, he came to the heart of the matter:

"Does segregation of children in public schools solely on the basis of race, even though the physical facilities and other 'tangible' factors may be equal, deprive the children of the minority group of equal educational opportunities?" Warren paused and said: "We believe that it does." The decision was unanimous: 9–0.

The words raced across the country and were received by different people according to their different lights. Southern diehards like Herman Talmadge issued statements of defiance and promised a generation of litigation, but the implications of the decision were so enormous that many Americans were shocked into silence and wonder. In Farmville, Va., a 16-year-old student named Barbara Trent burst into tears when her teacher announced the decision. "We went on studying history," she said later, "but things weren't the same and will never be the same again."

8. Montgomery and the Freedom Movement

IT was a quiet, peaceful day in Montgomery, Ala., the Cradle of the Confederacy—but it was unseasonably hot for December 1.

The Cleveland Avenue bus rolled through Court Square, where Blacks were auctioned in the days of the Confederacy, and braked to a halt in front of the Empire Theater. There was nothing special about the bus or the day; neither the driver nor the passengers realized that a revolution was about to begin that would turn America and the South upside down.

Six Whites boarded the bus at the Empire Theater, and the driver stormed to the rear and ordered the foremost Blacks to get up and give their seats to the White citizens. This was an ancient custom, sanctioned by the peculiar mores of the South, and it excited no undue comment. Three Blacks got up immediately, but Rosa Parks, a mild-mannered seamstress in rimless glasses, kept her seat. For this act of defiance, she was arrested. Local leaders called a one-day bus boycott on Monday, Dec. 5, 1955, to protest the arrest. The one-day boycott stretched out to 381 days; the 381 days changed the face and heart of Black America, creating a new leader (Martin Luther King Jr.), and a new movement. There then followed in quick succession a series of movements (the Sit-ins and Freedom Rides) and dramatic events (Birmingham, Selma, Watts, the March on Washington) that constituted Black America's finest hour and one of the greatest moments in the history of the Republic.

9. Little Rock

THE GIANT C-119 flying boxcars circled the field, like grim birds.

One by one, they glided into the Little Rock, Ark., airport and debouched paratroopers in full battle gear. There were, in all, more than 1,000 soldiers, Black and White; and they were in Little Rock to enforce the orders of a federal court. For the first time since the Reconstruction era, the United States of America was deploying federal troops to defend the rights of Black Americans.

Escorted by city police cars, a convoy of olive-drab jeeps and trucks sped to Central High School where a howling mob had prevented the enrollment of nine Black students. The troops deployed on the double to block all entrances to the schools, and signalmen strung telephone lines and set up command posts.

Wednesday morning, Sept. 25, 1957, dawned bright and clear, and nine Black teenagers gathered at the ranch-style home of Daisy Bates, president of the Arkansas NAACP. At 8:50 a.m., there was a rumble of heavy wheels. The teenagers rushed to the window.

"The streets were blocked off," Daisy Bates recalled later. "The soldiers closed ranks... Oh! It was beautiful. And the attitude of the children at that moment: the respect they had. I could hear them saying, 'For the first time in my life I truly feel like an American.' I could see it in their faces: Somebody cares for me—America cares."

At 9:45, U.S. soldiers with drawn bayonets escorted six Black females and three Black males into Central High School, and the Rev. Dunbar H. Ogden, president of the Greater Little Rock Ministerial Association, said: "This may be looked back upon by future historians as the turning point—for good—of race relations in this country."

10. Memphis and the Triumph of the Spirit

THERE had never been a moment like this one.

Time stopped.

Everything stopped.

And every man and woman living at that terrible time would be able to tell you until the end of their time what they were doing and where they were on Thursday, April 4, 1968, when word came that Martin Luther King Jr. had been assassinated on the balcony of the Lorraine Motel in Memphis, Tenn.

The response in Black and White America was tumultuous. Performances, plays, meetings, baseball games were cancelled, and men and women walked aimlessly through the streets, weeping.

There were tears, rivers of tears, and there was also blood. For Black communities exploded, one after another, like firecrackers on a string. Some 46 persons were killed in uprisings in 126 cities, and federal troops were mobilized to put down rebellions in Chicago, Baltimore and Washington, D.C.

To counteract this fury, and to express their sorrow, Americans of all races and creeds joined forces in an unprecedented tribute to a Black American. President Lyndon B. Johnson declared a national day of mourning and ordered U.S. flags to fly at half-mast over U.S. installations at home and abroad. On the day of the funeral—Tuesday, April 9—more than 200,000 mourners followed King's coffin, which was carried through the streets of Atlanta on a wagon, borne by two Georgia mules.

Eighteen years later, the spirit and the truth of Martin Luther King Jr. triumphed when he became the second American citizen (with George Washington) to be celebrated in a personal national holiday.

Black America

T he heart of Chicago—Cook County, Illinois—is home to 1.3 million blacks, more than any other county in the country. Chicago's new African-American Marketing and Media Association has only 18 members, but president Ken Smikle is targeting another 300 black-owned or -operated advertising agencies, public relations firms, market research companies, television stations, magazines, and film production companies across the country.

"Chicago businesses are increasingly aware of the importance of black consumers," says Smikle. "People have to

learn to speak to this population, and the best way is to use the marketing expertise of local black professionals." In Chicago, these resources include six black-oriented newspapers and four radio stations.

The black population grew by 13.2 percent during the 1980s, faster than the national average of 9.8 percent but not as fast as the growth rate for Hispanics or Asians. Blacks now comprise 12.1 percent of all Americans. They live where whites live: the four most populous states (California, New York, Texas, and Florida) are also the top-ranking states for blacks.

Census data for blacks are not as accurate as data for nonblacks. The bureau counted between 97.5 percent and 98 percent of all Americans, according to estimates from its post-enumeration survey. But it counted only 94.2 percent to 96.3 percent of black women and 93.0 percent to 95.3 percent of black men. Census data are still the most accurate available, but they miss about 1 in 20 black Americans.

Most of the hot spots for black population growth are outer-ring suburbs of central cities, also the national focus of population growth. The black population of Gwinnett county, Georgia, north of At-

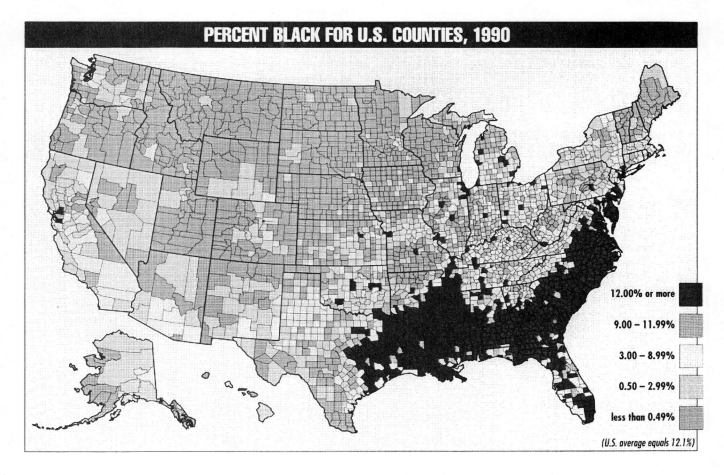

PERCENT BLACK FOR U.S. COUNTIES, 1990

12.00% or more

9.00 – 11.99%

3.00 – 8.99%

0.50 – 2.99%

less than 0.49%

(U.S. average equals 12.1%)

BIGGEST BLACK METROS

(metropolitan statistical areas ranked by size of black population in 1990)

rank / metro area	1990 black population
1 New York, NY PMSA	2,250,026
2 Chicago, IL PMSA	1,332,919
3 Washington, DC-MD-VA MSA	1,041,934
4 Los Angeles-Long Beach, CA PMSA	992,974
5 Detroit, MI PMSA	943,479
6 Philadelphia, PA-NJ PMSA	929,907
7 Atlanta, GA MSA	736,153
8 Baltimore, MD MSA	616,065
9 Houston, TX PMSA	611,243
10 New Orleans, LA MSA	430,470
11 St. Louis, MO-IL MSA	423,185
12 Newark, NJ PMSA	422,802
13 Dallas, TX PMSA	410,766
14 Memphis, TN-AR-MS MSA	399,011
15 Norfolk-Virginia Beach-Newport News, VA MSA	398,093
16 Miami-Hialeah, FL PMSA	397,993
17 Cleveland, OH PMSA	355,619
18 Oakland, CA PMSA	303,826
19 Richmond-Petersburg, VA MSA	252,340
20 Birmingham, AL MSA	245,726
21 Boston-Lawrence-Salem-Lowell-Brockton, MA NECMA*	233,819
22 Charlotte-Gastonia-Rock Hill, NC-SC MSA	231,654
23 Kansas City, MO-KS MSA	200,508
24 Milwaukee, WI PMSA	197,183
25 Nassau-Suffolk, NY PMSA	193,967

* New England County Metropolitan Area (NECMA)

lanta, increased 344 percent, for example, while its total population doubled during the 1980s, says planner Patrick Quinn. Gwinnett's affordable housing and job growth attract working families of all races; still, only 9 percent of its residents are nonwhite, compared with a national average of 20 percent.

Some metropolitan areas are disproportionately black, and some black hot spots are not suburbs. Baltimore is the 17th-largest metropolitan area in the U.S., for example, but it has the 8th-largest black population. New Orleans ranks 41st overall, but 10th in number of blacks. Among counties with 1990 black populations of 5,000 or more, the fastest-growing black county is in northern New York. The reason is Fort Drum, a military base that swelled from 3,600 soldiers in the mid-1980s to 11,000 soldiers last year.

The counties with the highest proportion of blacks remain in a southern region sociologists call the "Black Belt." Among the 50 counties with the highest proportion of blacks in 1990, Mississippi has 14, Georgia has 10, Alabama has 8, and South Carolina has 7. These counties are the former home of many blacks who now live in Cook County. Blacks who remain in the Black Belt have incomes that are among the lowest in the nation. In Jefferson County, Mississippi, 86 percent of residents are black, 23 percent of residents are unemployed, and the median household income ranks in the bottom 2 percent.

The share of blacks living in the south fell steadily for most of the 20th century, from 90 percent in 1990 to 53 percent in 1980. But in the wake of the civil rights movement of the 1960s, blacks began leaving the South in fewer numbers. And as southern cities such as Atlanta became economic powerhouses, the migration stream stabilized. Today, the South is still home to 53 percent of America's blacks, and the share who live in the Midwest is decreasing.

—Kathy Bodovitz

FASTEST-GROWING COUNTIES FOR BLACKS

(counties with black populations of 5,000 or more in 1990, ranked by percent change in black population, 1980–90)

rank / county	state	1990 black population	1980 black population	percent change 1980–90	rank / county	state	1990 black population	1980 black population	percent change 1980–90
1 Jefferson County	New York	6,501	274	2,272.6%	26 Fairbanks North Star	Alaska	5,553	3,006	84.7%
2 Gwinnett County	Georgia	18,175	4,094	343.9	27 Kenosha County	Wisconsin	5,295	2,886	83.5
3 Clayton County	Georgia	43,403	10,494	313.6	28 Hennepin County	Minnesota	60,114	32,986	82.2
4 Cobb County	Georgia	44,154	13,055	238.2	29 Montgomery County	Maryland	92,267	50,756	81.8
5 Arapahoe County	Colorado	23,279	8,446	175.6	30 Fairfax County	Virginia	63,325	34,985	81.0
6 Cleveland County	Oklahoma	5,271	2,132	147.2	31 Oneida County	New York	13,661	7,721	76.9
7 San Bernardino County	California	114,934	47,813	140.4	32 DeKalb County	Georgia	230,425	130,980	75.9
8 Essex County	Massachusetts	15,809	6,675	136.8	33 Collin County	Texas	10,925	6,260	74.5
9 Kings County	California	8,243	3,583	130.1	34 Worcester County	Massachusetts	15,096	8,724	73.0
10 Fort Bend County	Texas	46,593	20,420	128.2	35 Broward County	Florida	193,447	113,608	70.3
11 Denton County	Texas	13,569	6,173	119.8	36 Orange County	California	42,681	25,287	68.8
12 Johnson County	Kansas	6,917	3,161	118.8	37 Bristol County	Massachusetts	8,054	4,795	68.0
13 Prince William County	Virginia	25,078	11,597	116.2	38 Williamson County	Texas	6,861	4,111	66.9
14 San Luis Obispo County	California	5,727	2,726	110.1	39 Solano County	California	45,839	27,785	65.0
15 Virginia Beach (city)	Virginia	54,671	26,291	107.9	40 Sacramento County	California	97,129	58,951	64.8
16 Stanislaus County	California	6,450	3,124	106.5	41 Lehigh County	Pennsylvania	6,776	4,134	63.9
17 Riverside County	California	63,591	30,857	106.1	42 Henrico County	Virginia	43,827	27,096	61.7
18 Plymouth County	Massachusetts	16,520	8,144	102.8	43 Oakland County	Michigan	77,488	47,962	61.6
19 Norfolk County	Massachusetts	12,089	6,014	101.0	44 Sonoma County	California	5,547	3,466	60.0
20 Douglas County	Georgia	5,597	2,818	98.6	45 Washoe County	Nevada	5,680	3,552	59.9
21 DuPage County	Illinois	15,462	7,809	98.0	46 Clay County	Florida	5,513	3,470	58.9
22 Osceola County	Florida	5,902	3,012	95.9	47 Middlesex County	Massachusetts	40,236	25,358	58.7
23 Chesterfield County	Virginia	27,196	13,910	95.5	48 Howard County	Maryland	22,019	13,899	58.4
24 Kitsap County	Washington	5,107	2,704	88.9	49 Baltimore County	Maryland	85,451	53,955	58.4
25 Dane County	Wisconsin	10,511	5,688	84.8	50 Cochise County	Arizona	5,078	3,224	57.5

Source: 1990 census

Shock Therapy
A Racist Murder Leads Texas Town to Probe Its Bedrock Prejudices

Saddled With the 'R' Label, Jasper Opens a Dialogue Aimed at Reconciliation

Civility at the Traffic Lights

By Roger Thurow
Staff Reporter of THE WALL STREET JOURNAL

JASPER, Texas—The moment the sun came up on the first Sunday in June and pulled back the covers on a grotesque crime scene, America's scarlet letter was branded on the courthouse clock tower. R, for racist.

"What kind of sick city is this?" screeched one e-mail to the Jasper Chamber of Commerce. A black man had been chained behind a truck and dragged down a rural road, his body tearing apart as it bounced for two miles over the unforgiving pavement. Three white men were arrested. Somebody wrote all the way from Paris—France, not Texas—to say that the murder made him "feel ashamed to be a white person."

Citizens here protested mightily—"This isn't us," they cried, white and black alike—but they knew the letter was there to stay. They huddled in prayer on the courthouse square and decided that if they couldn't erase it, they would redefine it. R, for reconciliation. And so it is that out of that one random act of violence have come many random acts of kindness. Jasper, its nerves jangled, its complacency shattered, may now be the most race-sensitive place in the nation.

An auto mechanic, a white man, seeks out a former customer, a black man, and offers to make good for a misdeed from a couple of years back: He had charged for a new muffler and tailpipe when he actually installed used parts. "He told me that the only reason he had overcharged me was because I'm black," says Clifton Williams. "He said he was sorry."

Billy Rowles, the gregarious white sheriff, hears confessions in the most unexpected places—on front porches, in barbecue joints, on golf courses. "I've had

eight or 10 people tell me they now feel bad about using the 'N' word," he says.

Nancy Nicholson, a white city councilwoman, and Clyde Williams, a black councilman dab away tears as they recall the testimony of a white woman at a town meeting. After declaring that she had been prejudiced all her life, she hushed the crowd by recounting her moment of repentance. Not long after the murder, her young daughter scolded her for demeaning a black man. "That person never did anything to you," the child told the mother. Ashamed, the woman promised to never again judge another on the basis of color.

Civility and politeness are rampant. "The traffic light could be green," says Vickie Williams, who manages the predominantly black Pineview Apartments, a public-housing complex, "and they [whites] are still sitting there, waving at you to cross." Even players on the high-school and junior-high football teams are being coached to turn the other cheek when tempers flare on the field.

"We can't afford that someone from Jasper might start a fight," says Douglas Koebernick, the schools superintendent.

The hideous murder of James Byrd Jr., on a dark road in the piney woods just east of town, made Jasper an easy scapegoat for America's lingering racist legacy. But the reaction of the local residents—shocked into deep introspection by the brutality of the crime and the intense glare of the media—runs contrary to the often hostile response of other places that have been put on the hot seat by race crimes. Beyond the outbreak of good neighborliness, Jasper has responded with an ambitious series of town meetings, where repentance, re-

demption and economic development are on the same agenda—the town's version of South Africa's Truth and Reconciliation Commission.

For all this, though, Jasper remains on edge. This weekend, the courthouse square will be the scene of the annual Fall Fest, a spirited gathering that many expect will be a positive test of the town's newfound sensitivities. Yet next weekend, outside Ku Klux Klan groups are planning to stage a rally here. And if the Klan returns, it is likely that the New Black Panthers, a group that marched through town once before, will stage a countermarch.

Local residents, white and black alike, fear that these outside forces could find some recruits here. Beyond that, some blacks, who have long and quietly suffered the indignities of racial animosity, question the sincerity of their white Neighbors' contrition and tolerance.

"After Mr. Byrd's murder, you naturally feel bad. But feeling bad is one thing. It's what's in the heart that matters," says Theo James, a maintenance man at the Pineview apartments, where Mr. Byrd had been living. In the past, he's heard whites refer to Pineview derogatorily as "the hatchery." Today, he notes warily, these same people are saying hello and holding doors open for him.

"I don't know too many people who change their heart overnight," he says. "If you don't like broccoli, you don't like broccoli. Know what I mean?"

The Chamber of Commerce line is that Jasper always was a hospitable place; "Jasper, the Friendly Host," proclaimed a state travel magazine a few months before the Byrd murder. A town of about 8,500 people—with whites slightly outnumbering blacks, plus a small but growing Hispanic population—Jasper lives off the timber industry and the tourism value of nearby lakes brimming with bass. While some other east Texas towns tried to keep civil-rights advances outside their city limits, Jasper over the past two decades has been electing African-Americans to the City Council and the school board and elevating them to top business and civic posts, like administrator of the hospital and chairman of the Chamber of Commerce.

Law-enforcement officials, from the Federal Bureau of Investigation to the local police, believe the killing was an isolated incident. "We can't really blame Jasper for everything," says Joe Roy, director of the Southern Poverty Law Center's Intelligence Project, which tracks hate groups in America. "Jasper is more of a reminder that no matter how well we think we're handling our problems, there's always something out there."

Investigators say that rather than erupting from any impulses unique to Jasper (though two of the three men arrested had roots here), the murder may have had its genesis in the prisons where the accused did time, and where hate groups florish; indeed, the police are examining evidence that may link two of the suspects to white-supremacist groups. The three have been indicted for capital murder in the district court of Jasper County; they have pleaded not guilty and are awaiting trial early next year.

While defense attorneys say they will likely seek a change in venue, District Attorney Guy James Gray is hoping to keep the trial in the local courthouse. Even though that will keep the civic wound fresh, Mr. Gray is firm: "I don't want anybody in the world thinking that a Jasper jury couldn't do the right thing."

Turning the Other Cheek

Trying to do the right thing has been an obsession in Jasper since the June 7 murder. It began when the devoutly religious Byrd family, concerned about ugly retaliation or copycat crimes, called for healing between the races. As the Klan and the New Black Panthers flocked to town and raised the tensions, Walter Diggles, a prominent black citizen, huddled with Jesse Jackson at a

prayer service and urged him to praise the cooperation between the town's white and black leaders, and to commend the work of the white police chief, the sheriff and the district attorney, which Mr. Jackson did. In turn, white residents effusively lauded local black officials. Seizing the momentum, mayor R. C. Horn, an African-American, set up a task force to encourage interracial dialogue through a series of town meetings.

"Something like this happening in a small community hits close to home," says Mr. Diggles, executive director of the Deep East Texas Council of Governments. "It's something you read about in history, a lynching, and it happened here. It was a wake-up call. We had to respond."

Economics, if nothing else, demanded it. With the recent closings of a couple of timber plants, the unemployment rate in the area has swelled to over 12%. A similar drop in tourism—if outsiders would be afraid to even drive through Jasper, let alone sit and fish for a while at one of the many tournaments that regularly fill area hotels—would be disastrous.

Wynn Dee Baker, the Chamber of Commerce president, received a call from a woman in Louisiana who had been planning to bring a church youth group, with black and white children, for a camping and fishing trip.

"Is it safe?" she asked.

Ms. Baker, who is white, was taken aback. "To us, that's laughable, because we know it [the murder] was an isolated incident," she says. "We told her, 'It's the safest place in the world.' She came and they had a good experience."

For Jasper's citizens, the most profound experiences have come at the meetings of the reconciliation task force formed by the mayor, who is recovering from a mild heart attack suffered shortly after the murder. "We've had to ask some very hard questions of ourselves," says Sheriff Rowles. "We're talking about some things that are very tough to talk about."

Questionnaires are both handed out at the meetings and sent in the mail. How does the public perceive race relations in the community? Does racial discrimination exist? Is it widespread or isolated? Is there a level of fear in the community?

As the answers come in, people who have blithely lived side-by-side for years—the schools are fully integrated, as are many residential neighborhoods—are discovering tension, resentment and pat-

terns of segregation that went undiscussed until the Byrd murder. For instance, residents religiously flock to the high-school football games and pile into the home side of the bleachers. But there they sit, quite voluntarily, in white and black blocks.

The impression to visiting fans is that "we're really segregated," says the Rev. Ron Foshage of St. Michael's Catholic Church. This season, he and other members of the mayor's task force are spreading out to sit with fans of the opposite race.

Returned questionnaires and discussions at town meetings revealed another divide: Perceptions of race relations differ widely between white and black, reflecting the gap that stretches across America. White residents typically respond that relations are good, and that any trouble amounts to isolated incidents. Some complain about affirmative action, believing it gives blacks preference over whites. A few have also complained that another recent murder, where the victim was white and the suspect black, received far less attention than the Byrd murder.

Most African-American residents, on the other hand, point to their own experiences with discrimination and believe it to be fairly widespread, though they say they have rarely talked about it before. "Race relations were mostly hidden, or in the closet," wrote one.

Some blacks talk about brusque treatment in white-owned shops, others about being regarded suspiciously by the police or sheriff's deputies. They complain that most of the people they encounter in the service industry—bank tellers, restaurant servers, car salesmen—are white, or that whites are hired and promoted more quickly than blacks. Many recall the old community swimming pool being filled with cement rather than integrated.

Fear? It has ratcheted up since the Byrd murder, among both white and black. "Don't know who to trust or what to expect," wrote a black resident of fears "that someone will hurt me or my family because of hatred of our color." A white man said he fears retaliation from blacks. One white woman wrote of fearing "destruction of property or loss of life because of . . . recruitment of the lunatic fringe."

The unease is most palpable at the Rose Bloom Baptist Church, a long-standing black house of worship in a meadow off Huff Creek Road—the road along which Mr. Byrd was dragged, and where his head and torso were found. For weeks, bright-orange paint marked the evidence; the word 'head' was scrawled at the end of a driveway of a woman who is a Rose Bloom member. Just leaving the house, says her son, made his mother ill.

The orange has now been covered in black paint to match the pavement. The residents have asked the county to install streetlights, to eliminate shadows. But there is nothing to remove the psychological marks. "Many of our people are afraid to drive on the road after dark," notes the Rev. Jerry Lewis. At a recent Wednesday-night prayer service, only five worshipers knelt with him.

"There are too many signs of malice and hate out here," he says. "We're trying to draw a love picture for all the races."

An Open Dialogue

On a recent stormy night, with rain pounding down from a hurricane in the Gulf of Mexico, 13 citizens, black and white, gather at the Mount Olive Baptist Church for one of the task-force meetings. Councilman Williams conjures a sense of urgency to encourage discussion. "At no time in the history of Jasper have we had the chance to come together to voice our opinions," he says. "No disrespect to the white race, but never before had they felt the need to come to you and ask."

Cautiously, at first, they speak. A black woman says that when she was growing up, people would steal the family chickens in an effort to run them off their property. A man says his daughter was recently told by a white friend that her mother wouldn't allow any black children at her birthday party. Another woman suspects that blacks pay higher electricity rates. The schools are failing to teach tolerance, someone says. No, argues another, it's the parents who are failing their children; good race relations start at home. Everyone agrees the town needs to aggressively attract more industry and jobs, as well as trade school or a community college.

An elderly woman, quiet all evening, rises to speak, inspired by the singing of the church choir wafting through a vent from another room. "You can talk all you want," she says, "but only God can change your heart. Have all the town meetings you want, but if God isn't in it, it won't do you any good."

Just then, as if on cue, the choir begins singing "I saw the light, Lord." And Nancy Nicholson, the councilwoman, says, "I see you all, and I hear what you're saying, and I'm so sorry. God has a better plan for Jasper."

Throughout the series of task-force meetings, it is the whites who say the testimony has been most eye-opening. "At the beginning, I was, like, we don't have a problem," says Ms. Baker from the Chamber of Commerce. And this sentiment, she says, is largely shared by the predominantly white business community.

"But the more I go to the meetings," she continues, "the more I see how other people feel. They say things that you've never heard before, that I had never really thought about." She recalls one black person saying, "If you've experienced racial prejudice one time, it can be so strong you carry it with you for a long time.' As a white person, I haven't had that experience. I started thinking about it, that it would be a horrible feeling."

Sheriff Rowles started thinking, too, about the perception of race among the people he serves. He talked to his prisoners, to his friends, to strangers on the street. "As a police administrator, I'm disappointed that some of the black community, and, of course, some white people, don't have confidence in the officers to come to them with anything, to be able to talk to them. We need to spend more time in the various communities, being there as friends, not as officers. We need to just sit on the front porch and talk to them."

Even members of Jasper's Ministerial Alliance, which has been bringing black and white preachers, and their parishioners, together for more than a decade, are breaking new ground. Father Foshage recalls the meeting where the Rev. John Hardin of the Mount Olive Baptist Church rose to speak. "Rev. Hardin said, 'You all don't know the prejudices we've lived through.' I said, 'John, you never told us that before.' He said, 'But it's been there.' I know Rev. Hardin real well, but I never knew that."

Says Mr. Hardin: "I told Father Ron, 'You have to be black to understand.'"

Worries Over Children

Racial understanding also became one of the main assignments in the Jasper schools. Although schools were on summer vacation at the time of the murder, city leaders worried about what might happen when the children returned in mid-August. It became the task force's top priority.

Twelve days after the murder, teachers and staff were summoned back from their vacations for an all-day meeting, which spawned a series of sessions all summer. Every aspect of a school day was analyzed, from how to handle name-calling on the bus to adding more multicultural studies in the classroom. Teachers were refreshed on how to greet students: "Good morning, glad to see you." Principals were reminded, "At no time should a teacher use sarcasm." A video on racial tolerance became mandatory staff viewing.

When the schools opened for the fall semester, staff members felt prepared— and nervous. "It was very scary as we started out the year. But I feel great now," says Mr. Koebernick. "We've told the staff, 'Watch what you do, watch what you say.' It seems the parents have been telling their kids the same things."

So far, there haven't been any serious race-related incidents at any of the schools, whose enrollments—50% white, 42% black, 8% Hispanic—roughly reflect town demographics. Still, with the trial coming up, and the Ku Klux Klan threatening to make regular visits, Mr. Koebernick remains vigilant. "It keeps going though my mind that maybe the schoolchildren of Jasper were underestimated," he says. "Maybe the grown-ups were judging the children according to their own minds."

For Clara Byrd Taylor, Mr. Byrd's sister, Jasper is on the right track. "My brother didn't die for a cause," says Ms. Byrd, herself a teacher. "But since he did die, we don't want it to be for a legacy of the burning down of Jasper or more bloodshed, but for a legacy of more dialogue and more tolerance among the races."

Ms. Taylor, along with her parents and siblings, has formed the James Byrd Jr. Family Foundation for Racial Healing. One day, she hopes, they will build an education center in Jasper where people can study both the history of racism and virtues of reconciliation. America's scarlet letter, in both of its meanings, will hang on the front door.

"Maybe," she says, "we can make a difference in this little community and spread out to the rest of the world."

The Color of Justice

COURTS ARE PROTECTING, RATHER THAN HELPING TO END, RACIAL PROFILING BY POLICE.

DAVID COLE

It's no mean feat to find an issue on which President Bill Clinton, the Rev. Al Sharpton, Attorney General Janet Reno, many of the nation's police chiefs and NAACP president Kweisi Mfume agree, but at a Washington conference in June, they all expressed the view that racial profiling—the practice of targeting citizens for police encounters on the basis of race—needs to end. Clinton proclaimed profiling "wrong" and "destructive," and ordered federal agencies to gather data on the demographics of their law enforcement patterns. The consensus on profiling was underscored in August, when the National Association of Police Organizations, which staged a debate on the subject at its annual meeting in Denver, had to rely on a white separatist, Jared Taylor, to defend the practice.

Given the mountain of evidence that has piled up recently on racial profiling, the consensus is not surprising. Studies in Maryland, New Jersey, Illinois, Florida, Ohio, Houston and Philadelphia have confirmed that minorities are disproportionately targeted by police. On April 20 the New Jersey Attorney General's office issued a 112-page *mea culpa* admitting that its state troopers had engaged in racial profiling, offering statistics to support the claim and advancing a sophisticated analysis of the nature and scope of the problem. The next day North Carolina—yes, North Carolina—became the first state to pass a law requiring troopers to record and make public the racial patterns of their traffic stops. Connecticut followed suit with its own reporting law in June, and most recently, Florida Governor Jeb Bush has directed the Florida Highway Patrol to begin collecting similar data on January 1, 2000.

The press has covered the subject widely, recounting tales of black professionals stopped for petty traffic violations and investigating the arrest patterns of offending cops. While police departments are obviously at the heart of the problem, the cru-

cial role that courts have played in protecting and sustaining widespread racial profiling has been overlooked. The courts have not only failed to recognize that racial profiling is unconstitutional, but they have effectively insulated it from legal challenge. Where lawsuits challenging profiling have succeeded, it is only because political pressures compelled the police to settle.

The legal case against profiling should be easy to make. Defenders of the practice argue that it makes sense to target minorities because they are more likely than whites to commit crime. But the Constitution forbids reliance on racial generalizations unless they are the only way to achieve a "compelling purpose." Law enforcement is undoubtedly compelling, but racial sterotypes are hardly the only way to go about it. In fact, race is a particularly bad basis for suspicion, since most black people, like most whites, don't commit any crime. Annually at least 90 percent of African-Americans are not arrested for anything. On any given day, the percentage of innocent African-Americans is even higher. Thus, racial profiles necessarily sweep in a large number of innocents. In addition, when officers target minorities they miss white criminals. One need only recall the *Saturday Night Live* skit in which the black actor Garrett Morris and the white actor Chevy Chase walk through Customs. Morris, carrying nothing, is immediately surrounded by multiple Customs agents, while Chase pushes through an open wheelbarrow full of powder cocaine without a hitch.

Yet the Supreme Court has all but invited racial profiling. In 1996 the Court upheld the practice of "pretextual traffic stops," in which police officers use the excuse of a traffic violation to stop motorists when they are investigating some other crime. The same year, the Court allowed the police to use the coercive setting of a traffic stop to obtain consent to search. Together, these rules allow the police to stop and search whomever they please on the roads, without having to demonstrate

---

David Cole, legal affairs correspondent for The Nation, *is the author of* No Equal Justice: Race and Class in the American Criminal Justice System *(New Press).*

Reprinted with permission from *The Nation*, October 11, 1999, pp. 12-13, 15. © 1999 by The Nation Company, L.P.

probable cause. And where the police are freed from the need to justify their actions, they appear to fall back on racial stereotypes. In Maryland, for example, blacks were 70 percent of those stopped and searched by Maryland State Police from January 1995 through December 1997, on a road where 17.5 percent of the drivers and speeders were black. New Jersey reported that 77 percent of those stopped and searched on its highways were black or Hispanic, even though only 13.5 percent of the drivers were black or Hispanic.

At the same time, the Court has erected major barriers to lawsuits challenging profiling as racial discrimination. Dismissive of statistical evidence, the Court requires proof that individual officers acted out of racist motives in each case. Thus, the array of recent studies showing that minorities are disproportionately targeted do not establish a violation of the Constitution's equal protection guarantee. In fact, unless the police admit to racial profiling, the Court's intent standard is nearly impossible to meet.

Despite the courts, there's been more progress on profiling in the past decade than on any racial inequality issue in criminal law enforcement.

Even when a party can prove that he was profiled, the Court has made it very difficult to obtain a remedy that addresses the practice of profiling systemically. In *City of Los Angeles v. Lyons,* the Court ruled that victims of past police misconduct cannot obtain court injunctions against future misconduct unless they can prove that they will be *personally* subjected to the practice in the future. In 1994, a federal court in Florida dismissed a racial-profiling suit on these grounds even as it complained that the Supreme Court's *Lyons* decision "seemingly 'renders [the federal courts] impotent to order the cessation of a policy which may indeed be unconstitutional and may harm many persons.' "

An ACLU case now pending in Illinois illustrates just how difficult the courts have made it to challenge racial profiling. The Illinois State Police don't record the race of the drivers they stop, so the ACLU sought to obtain copies of ticketed motorists' license applications, from which they then planned to use Social Security or address information to develop racial data. The court ruled that the ACLU would have to pay Illinois $160,000 for that information.

Using last names as a rough proxy for ethnicity, the ACLU then showed that although Hispanics compose less than 8 percent of the state's population, they were 27 percent of those stopped and searched by a highway drug interdiction unit. The court replied that statistics aren't enough. The ACLU showed that the state police permit consideration of race, that their training materials focus on Hispanics as drug couriers and that state troopers admit they consider race. The court replied that the ACLU's claim still failed because the plaintiffs did not identify specific "similarly situated" white motorists who were not stopped and ticketed. When the ACLU pointed to a white lawyer who had been following a Latino motorist the day he was stopped, the court said the lawyer wasn't similarly situated, because her car was a different color and her license plate was from a different state.

Lawsuits have played an important role in the campaign against racial profiling, but not through any actions of the courts. The single most significant development to date on the profiling front was Robert Wilkin's decision in 1992 to sue when a Maryland state trooper illegally stopped and searched him and his family. Because, Wilkins, a Harvard Law School graduate and prominent public defender, was such a sympathetic plaintiff, Maryland quickly settled, agreeing to record the race of those it stopped and to provide that data to the court and the ACLU. That led to the first systematic evidence of a problem that until then had been largely a matter of anecdotes.

Another settlement, in Philadelphia, was also crucial. In 1996, civil rights attorney David Rudovsky and the ACLU threatened the Philadelphia police with a lawsuit sparked by media revelations of rampant police abuse. The city settled before the suit was filed, allowing plaintiffs access to racial breakdowns of police stops. There, as in Maryland, the data have provided critical evidence for charges of racial profiling.

Despite the courts, more progress has been made on racial profiling than on any other issue of racial inequality in criminal law enforcement in the past decade. There are many reasons for this. The issue has tremendous organizing appeal and has captured the attention of mainstream civil rights groups, such as the NAACP and the Urban League, which have all too often shied away from criminal justice issues. Unlike most law enforcement victims, innocent victims of racial profiling elicit public sympathy. The practice targets not just the disfranchised poor but rich and middle-class minorities, who are much more likely to have their complaints taken seriously. Everyone who drives understands the ultimate arbitrariness of who gets pulled over. And because most people see the world to one degree or another through racial stereotypes, it is easy to believe that police officers act on these bases.

Equally important, the relief that activists have requested, at least at this stage, seems nonthreatening: They ask principally for the collection and reporting of data. How police departments and the public will respond when the results come in remains to be seen. Profiling is not the work of a few "bad apples" but a widespread, everyday phenomenon that will require systemic reform.

It also remains to be seen whether the advances made on racial profiling will prove to be a wedge for more deep-rooted and lasting reforms directed at racial disparity in criminal justice, or merely an exception to the rule of laissez-faire. But one thing is certain: The courts will not lead. At one time, one could have looked to the federal courts, protectors of individual rights and leaders in the fight against racial discrimination, to play a significant role in the battle. But today's courts are cut from a different cloth. Faced with stark evidence, they would rather deny than confront discrimination.

Race, Politics and 2000

The affirmative action battleground shifts to the heartland

by David S. Broder
Washington Post Staff Writer

The national battle over affirmative action and racial preferences is moving into the heartland—and then, very possibly, into the presidential politics of 2000. Ward Connerly, the architect of initiative victories that knocked out programs designed to increase the number of minorities attending elite public universities or getting state government jobs and contracts in California and Washington, has targeted Michigan for his next big initiative campaign.

Meanwhile, a number of Republican presidential hopefuls are giving high visibility to their opposition to race-conscious remedies for past discrimination. Their stance is opposed by Vice President Gore and most Democrats, and could make affirmative action a significant issue in the next presidential campaign.

"Republicans should grow a backbone and grab this issue—but in a skillful way. This is not an angry white male thing," says John Carlson, the coordinator of the Washington initiative campaign.

The widening of the battleground comes as public opinion polls show white Americans have less sympathy for programs designed to aid racial minorities and are increasingly ready to say that the rules should be the same for all, regardless of race, sex or ethnicity.

Connerly, an African American businessman and University of California regent who spearheaded successful initiative campaigns against race preferences in California in 1996 and Washington in 1998, says Michigan is at the top of his list of target states for the 2000 election cycle.

A simmering dispute over admissions policies at the University of Michigan has produced a pair of lawsuits that are scheduled to be heard later this year, keeping the issue on voters' minds.

State Sen. William Bullard, a Republican who sponsored an anti-affirmative action constitutional amendment that died in the legislature last year, said in an interview that this year he will concentrate on organizing a signature drive to place such an initiative on the November 2000 Michigan ballot. Assuming a big-name sponsors' committee can be assembled this winter and adequate funds are in sight, Bullard said he expects the signature drive—limited to 180 days—would begin this spring.

Connerly said in an interview that he also has been contacted by people in Colorado, Florida, Nebraska and Oregon about possible initiatives in those states. After a meeting Jan. 20 with Republican Florida Gov. Jeb Bush, he released a report criticizing admissions policies at Florida's public medical and law schools. Connerly says that financial considerations dictate "we concentrate our resources and efforts in one or two states, rather than diluting them."

❖

MICHIGAN IS PARTICULARLY ATTRACtive for affirmative action foes, not only because the issue would be brought into a political swing state in another section of the country, but because Michigan—like California and Washington—has a prestigious state university whose race-conscious admissions policies have become the source of controversy. Class action lawsuits were filed late in 1997 against the undergraduate college of the University of Michigan and its law school on behalf of white applicants who say they are the victims of reverse discrimination. Preliminary motions have been disposed of, and the cases are set for argument this summer.

The university is strongly defending its policies, which have produced a campus where one of seven students is a member of a minority race. But a poll taken for the Detroit Free Press last October found only 27 percent of those interviewed supported the university admissions policy, while 47 percent were opposed and 26 percent were undecided. The language of the Connerly-backed initiatives provides that the state "shall neither discriminate against, nor grant preferences to, anyone on the basis of race, gender or ethnicity." In the Michigan poll, when voters were asked a question using the word "preferences" opposition rose to much higher levels.

While employment and contracting policies have direct economic impact on limited numbers of people, university admissions practices have provided the emotional fuel that powered Connerly's group to victory in the two West Coast states.

He had the strong backing of then-Gov. Pete Wilson, a Republican who is a 2000 presidential possibility, when his California initiative passed by 55 percent to 45 percent. In Washington state, where he faced adamant opposition from Gov. Gary Locke, a Democrat, most of the large newspapers and some of the state's biggest businesses, the Connerly-backed initiative passed by a surprisingly wide margin.

Carlson, the Seattle Republican political consultant and former talk show host who led the Washington initiative drive, says that even though opponents of Ballot Measure 200 raised three times as much money, the measure won more than 58 percent of the vote in a high-turnout year when Democrats made gains at every level of the ballot. Citing exit polls showing Measure 200 was backed by 80 percent of the Republicans, 62 percent of the independents

From the *Washington Post National Weekly Edition*, February 1, 1999, p. 6. © 1999 by The Washington Post Writers Group. Reprinted by permission.

and 41 percent of the Democrats, and 66 percent of the men, 51 percent of the women and 54 percent of union household members, Carlson says the issue can be a winner anywhere.

The breadth of support was consistent with the findings of a survey last summer by The Washington Post, the Henry J. Kaiser Family Foundation and Harvard University's John F. Kennedy School of Government. That survey found only 37 percent of respondents said the government "should do more" to help minority groups. In 1968, a similar question found 50 percent of the interviewees said government should do more.

Robert Blendon, the Harvard professor who served as an adviser on the project, says the shift in attitudes on the race question is one of the sharpest recorded over the last 30 years.

Both sides in the debate have found, however, that the wording of the ballot question goes a long way toward determining the outcome. Voters tend to have a positive reaction to the term "affirmative action" but a negative reaction to "preferences and quotas."

In a Houston referendum, Connerly's opponents, led by then-Mayor Robert Lanier, persuaded the city council's majority to rewrite the initiative language from a ban on "preferences" to discontinuance of "affirmative action," and the initiative was defeated by 55 percent to 45 percent.

A court subsequently invalidated the election results, because of the language change, and Connerly says he is waiting to see if the new council and mayor suspend the programs on their own. If not, he says, he will mobilize for another initiative—with his wording—in Houston.

Several of the Republican presidential prospects seem ready to follow the advice to "grab the issue." Former Tennessee governor Lamar Alexander said in a recent interview that the California and Washington initiatives "point the way" to sound national policy: "Government should stop making distinctions based on race. No discrimination, no preferences." Alexander says if any affirmative action programs continue, they should be based on class, not race.

❑

FORMER VICE PRESIDENT DAN Quayle calls for an end to affirmative action and the repeal of "all quota laws." Publisher Malcolm S. "Steve" Forbes denounces "quotas" and says, "In America, you should be judged as an individual, not as a member of a group." Texas Gov. George W. Bush says, "I'm against quotas and preferences." But when the courts outlawed a race-conscious admissions policy at the University of Texas, Bush backed legislation saving places at the university for the top 10 percent of the graduates of every Texas high school, a policy that could increase minority enrollment without explicit racial preferences.

By contrast, Vice President Gore supports Clinton administration affirmative action programs that include preferences in government contracts for minority firms. Gore had a spirited debate with Connerly on the issue during one of the round-table discussions that were part of President Clinton's 1997 race initiative. Gore and Clinton opposed the Connerly-backed initiatives in California and Washington. Gore made fund-raising forays into Washington to help those fighting Measure 200.

But the issue is not without its problems for Republicans. When language identical to that of the Connerly initiatives was offered as an amendment during debate on extension of the Higher Education Act last year, it was defeated in the House, 249 to 171. The margin of defeat came from 55 Republicans who joined all but five Democrats in opposition, while 166 Republicans supported the amendment.

David Bositis, a political scientist at the Joint Center for Political and Economic Studies, who has followed the issue for the leading think tank on minority affairs, says: "I would not be surprised to see Connerly's initiative pass in Michigan or most other places he might put it on the ballot. But I don't see white voters supporting Republicans because of this. The number of voters for whom affirmative action matters is very small. And when they pursue issues like this, it further solidifies [minority] opposition to the Republican Party."

Washington Post staff researcher Ben White contributed to this report.

Why Minority Recruiting Is Alive and Well in Texas

Out-of-state colleges, offering generous aid packages, capitalize on affirmative-action ban

BY JEFFREY SELINGO

> "The old adage in admissions circles was that Texas was not worth it, because students never left the state. Now they are, and that's all the more incentive to go down there."

AUSTIN, TEX.

CARRYING LARGE BOXES full of brochures and posters, Norris G. Williams weaves among students in the crowded corridors of Lyndon B. Johnson High School here. It's October, and a large wall calendar hanging in the guidance office indicates Mr. Williams will be one of a few-dozen college recruiters scheduled to pass through here before the new year.

As Mr. Williams makes his way to a meeting with students, a teacher passes him in the hall. "The University of Oklahoma, right?" she asks. "You got it," he says, flashing a big smile.

Mr. Williams is indeed well-known among high-school counselors and college recruiters in these parts. It's not because of his sharp suits or polished personality. Most don't even know him by name. They remember Mr. Williams because he's from the University of Oklahoma—considered by many here to be one of the top out-of-state "raiders" of Texas minority students.

In the wake of the 1996 *Hopwood v. Texas* decision that banned the use of affirmative action by Texas institu-

tions, dozens of mostly Midwestern colleges have stepped up their efforts to recruit black and Hispanic students here and elsewhere across the state. In the last two years, for instance, the number of out-of-state institutions requesting a schedule of college fairs in Texas has risen nearly 60 per cent.

"The old adage in admissions circles was that Texas was not worth it, because students never left the state," says Alan L. Cerveny, director of admissions and scholarships at the University of Kansas, where inquiries from Texas high-school students have more than tripled since 1997. "Now they are, and that's all the more incentive to go down there."

A BOOMING MARKET

Texas has become prime territory because of *Hopwood*, with public colleges in the state among a handful nationwide that cannot use race to decide whom to accept or whom to award scholarships to. What's more, the market is booming—non-white residents could account for more than half of the state's population by the end of the next decade.

The tough competition for minority students has rattled many of the state's college leaders, who not only selfishly worry about their own enrollments, but also about losing many of the best minds and future leaders from a growing minority population.

"Texas is being picked clean by other states," says Richard Whiteside, dean of admissions and enrollment planning at Tulane University, which has increased its outreach here.

College officials and legal experts link the raiding phenomenon to court rulings and political referenda that have limited affirmative action in several states. The result has created a bizarre recruiting market, in which opponents of affirmative action see their gains watered down as out-of-state colleges practice affirmative action in states that can't. Many say one set of rules, for or against preferences, is needed.

"National law should be, in fact, national," says Dan Coenen, a professor at the University of Georgia School of Law. "The Constitution shouldn't mean one thing in Texas and another in Georgia. The solution to that is for the United States Supreme Court to clarify what national constitutional law is."

While there's widespread agreement in Texas about the intense recruitment of minority students, the results are difficult to quantify. Recruiters touting out-of-state universities are reluctant to talk about their success rates, and most institutions typically categorize students by race or home states, but not both. However, a recent survey by Texas A&M University shows that one-third of the students accepted for fall 1997 by either the University of Texas at Austin or by Texas A&M turned down those offers and left the state for colleges elsewhere. More black students than white students left the state—40 per cent to 29 per cent. Hispanic students accounted for 25 per cent of those who left.

SETTING UP SHOP

Here in Texas, a few out-of-state institutions, including Indiana, Tulane, and Washington Universities, and the University of Iowa, have either opened admissions offices in cities with large minority populations, such as Dallas and Houston, or sent representatives there for extended periods. Some colleges have organized weekend visits to their campuses or dispatched staff members to Texas college fairs, even replacing local alumni.

Above all, out-of-state recruiters have wooed minority students with promises of money. It's aid they know Texas public colleges probably won't match, because of a 1997 legal opinion by the state's Attorney General banning race-exclusive scholarships. (A new Attorney General recently rescinded that decision, but at the same time warned colleges not to return to racially preferential policies.)

"When it comes right down to it, the decision on financial aid makes the difference for most minority students," says Ray M. Bowen, president of Texas A&M. "And Texas competes very weakly, so far."

Says Toniqua Huckaby, who took off for the University of Oklahoma after she graduated from a suburban Dallas high school in 1998: "O.U. gave me a scholarship that made tuition here equal to that of a state university in Texas."

Ms. Huckaby, who is black, isn't alone. Among the many pipelines that leave this oil-rich state, a new one seems to be carrying minority students directly to Norman, Okla., where nearly one-fifth of the University of Oklahoma's 4,700 minority students are Texas residents. No single out-of-state institution has more aggressively courted Texas minority students than has Oklahoma, according to interviews with more than a dozen high-school guidance counselors and college recruiters.

AHEAD OF THE CURVE

Oklahoma got an early start. When *Hopwood* was handed down, Texas admissions officials gathered for a workshop here on navigating the ruling.

Also in attendance was Mr. Williams, the director of Oklahoma's Minority Student Recruitment Services.

"They were kind of frantic," Mr. Williams says of Texas recruiters at the workshop. "I got the information about what direction I felt like they were going in, so I could see what we could do as far as O.U. was concerned. I wanted to have a strong presence at that particular time."

Soon after, Oklahoma opened an admissions office in Dallas and placed a full-time recruiter there. On the campus, the university drafted more of its minority students from Texas to serve as admissions representatives in the Lone Star State. And the university increased its budget for minority recruitment by about 25 per cent; this year, Oklahoma plans to spend some $50,000 to attract minority students from all over.

"It's not that we have anything against Texas or that we're trying to steal their kids," says Mr. Williams, an Oklahoma native who attended Wiley College, a historically black institution in Marshall, Tex. "We're trying to give them an opportunity to get a college education."

At Johnson High School here, in a small office where the bookshelves overflow with college catalogues and posters of campuses dot the walls, Mr. Williams tells three black students why the University of Oklahoma should stand out in their college searches. "People say this is a white university," Mr. Williams says as the students flip through an admissions brochure filled with plenty of white faces. "They're right." Then he passes around a poster listing nearly three-dozen minority-student organizations. "We have a lot of things going on to, let's say, 'blackanize' the campus for you guys," Mr. Williams adds.

The trip here for Mr. Williams is part of a three-month circuit around this state. During the day, he visits high schools. At night, he combs college fairs, bumping into many of his competitors. At one fair here last month, held at a University of Texas gymnasium, almost half of the 135 colleges represented were not from Texas. The Big 10 universities lined up in a row across from U.T. at Arlington. Emory University sent its dean of admissions and its athletics director to work its table.

ON THE ROAD AGAIN

In January, Mr. Williams intends to return to Texas to visit specific stu-

dents and work on parents at receptions in Dallas and Houston. Many other representatives from out-of-state colleges will do the same. Students here eagerly swap information about which college recruiters offer the best freebies, a raffle for airplane tickets to campus (Princeton University), a fajita dinner (Tulane), or an accordion folder for application papers (Boston University).

But getting minority students in Texas to actually apply to out-of-state colleges isn't easy.

For most, money is their biggest worry. An out-of-state college means non-resident tuition and living expenses that could far exceed those at many Texas institutions, particularly if students live at home. As a result, out-of-state recruiters know that they must allay cost concerns quickly if students and parents are going to stay through a sales pitch. And what are the recruiters telling them? That Texas is not always the cheapest option.

The recruiters, particularly from public colleges, say their prices are reasonable when compared with in-state rates at Texas's flagship campuses, U.T. at Austin and Texas A&M—at least once financial aid is factored in.

For example, because of housing costs, Texas residents actually pay $400 less to attend the University of Oklahoma than to enroll and live at U.T. at Austin, where annual in-state charges approach $12,000. Added to that, Oklahoma runs seven scholarship programs. This year, the university awarded some $3-million in grants to Texas students—about 16 per cent of its total aid budget, and a 42 per cent increase over 1996–97. The average award for a minority student from Texas was $4,052; for a white student, $3,207.

One scholarship includes a waiver of the difference in tuition for out-of-state residents, about $4,000 this year. In addition, the university awards other scholarships for leadership abilities or academic records to out-of-state students, although Mr. Williams says race is not a factor in those awards. Meanwhile, the University of Iowa offers a merit-based scholarship, worth $5,000 annually, exclusively for minority students. Students from Illinois, Missouri, and Texas account for nearly all of the 64 recipients of the award this year, university officials say.

"The money is giving me second thoughts about staying in Texas," says Sametria Holt, a high-school senior here, as she strolls around the recent college fair at U.T. She plans to major

Texas Colleges Seek New Ways to Attract Minority Students

AUSTIN, TEX.

WHEN LARRY R. FAULKNER visited the predominantly Hispanic John F. Kennedy High School last spring, he was greeted by cheerleaders in the parking lot, the marching band near the school's entrance, and members of the Reserve Officer Training Corps. crossing sabers outside the auditorium.

After all, it isn't every day that the president of the University of Texas at Austin comes to visit a school that has historically sent few students—if any—to the state's flagship each year.

"It was stunning," Mr. Faulkner says of the reception.

The visit to the San Antonio school was one of about 20 that Mr. Faulkner made last spring—all to city high schools with large minority populations. Never before had a president of U.T. at Austin embarked on such a tour, but neither had the stakes been so high.

Texas public universities are making broad-based attempts to stem the loss of minority students to out-of-state institutions following the 1996 *Hopwood* decision that forced them to give up affirmative action. In particular, over the past two years, the institutions have significantly adjusted how they raise and award money for scholarships.

The changes have resulted in part from the sweet aid packages that more and more out-of-state colleges have been offering to minority Texans.

TOUGH COMPETITION

It has become common for guidance counselors to wave such offers in the faces of respresentatives from Texas colleges. Says Spencer Bynes, director of the Houston Admissions Center for U.T. at Austin: "Counselors would ask me, 'How are you going to compete with that?' and I didn't have anything."

"I felt like a gunslinger with no bullets," Mr. Bynes says. "Now, we actually have bullets."

Both U.T. at Austin and Texas A&M now use an "adversity index" that factors in personal difficulties or challenges when awarding scholarships to students. As a result of the index, for example, Texas A&M significantly increased the number of minority students eligible for scholarships.

U.T. at Austin, meanwhile, in 1998–99 identified 49 Texas high schools where standardized-test scores and family incomes fell well below the state averages. The university designated up to six scholarships—$4,000 apiece—for each school. Nearly all of the schools were in the state's biggest cities, with concentrated populations of minority students. This fall, 95 students who received the award enrolled at U.T. at Austin; the university

plans to add 15 schools to the program in 1999–2000.

The scholarships are awarded only to seniors in the top 10 percent of their high-school class—a cohort the universities are required to admit under a 1997 state law. One of the oddities in that law, some say, has been that it opens the college door for many minority students and others whose parents never went to college, but doesn't provide the families with any financial aid.

"The effects of the 10-per-cent rule have not been dramatic," Mr. Faulkner says.

MORE NEED-BASED AID

An independent commission of Texas political leaders, educators, and business people has recommended that the state spend $500-million over two years on a new need-based-aid program. Lawmakers only allocated about one-fifth of that in their 1999 session.

"Access is important, but it can't be achieved in many ways without more financial resources," says state Rep. Henry Cuellar, a Democrat, who plans to push for more student-aid money in the next legislative session.

Alumni associations and fundraising foundations—both of which, as private, non-profit groups, were not constrained by the *Hopwood* ruling—have stepped in to offer race-exclusive scholarships. The Ex-Students

in sports medicine at Southwestern University, in Texas, but "if I could get more money somewhere else, I'd be willing to try something new."

Texas colleges have been pressing state lawmakers for more aid to help stem the exodus of minority students. While many lawmakers say the state should dedicate hundreds of millions of dollars to financial aid, a few are dubious of the colleges' claims that they're losing students.

Finding out who leaves and who stays is difficult because Texas only tracks highschool graduates that end up at one of the state's public colleges. And Texas high schools have been graduating, on average, 14,000 more minority students every year this decade, says Steve H. Murdock, a Texas A&M professor and the state's chief demographer.

What worries Texas college officials chiefly about the increased competition for minority high-school graduates is that, for a whole generation of talented minority students, the choice of a college could hinge on money.

A study released last year found that for black and Hispanic students who were accepted by Texas A&M or U.T. at Austin, but who chose not to attend, availability of financial aid was the most important factor in deciding where to apply and where to enroll. All other ethnic groups cited academic prestige as the biggest factor.

"Clearly, many of the Anglo kids going to A&M are able to make choices on prestige," says Mr. Murdock, one of the authors of the study. "Those factors may be important to Hispanic and other minority students, but economic necessities play paramount to them."

College leaders say they're frustrated they can't do more to keep minority students here. Privately, a few Texas presidents argue that their institutions are academically better than many other universities in the Midwest that have stepped up recruiting here. Except for going to an Ivy League campus or an elite public university, the presidents say, many of the minority students would be better off in Texas. They say, for instance, that U.T. at Austin and Texas A&M place better in national rankings, receive more federal research dollars, have more library holdings, and still attract a larger critical mass of black and Hispanic students than does, for example, the University of Oklahoma.

What is clear to many educators and politicians in this state is that the biggest loser in the raiding war is

Association at U.T. at Austin has raised some $4.2-million since *Hopwood* for minority scholarships. In September, it distributed about $800,000 to 200 students to help fill in the gaps in financial aid, says Jim Boon, the association's director.

Keeping minority students in Texas is not just about money—location matters for many, too. That's the key reason Mariel Fernandez, a freshman at Texas A&M, turned down offers from Georgetown, Harvard, Princeton, and Washington Universities.

"I didn't know if I was really ready to go so far away from home, that the one time I would be able to see my family was at Christmas and maybe spring break," says the lifelong San Antonio resident. "I really like the fact that I'm only three hours from home."

Even with more aid dollars and the advantage of location, Texas colleges still have work to do to stop the flow of minority students elsewhere, says Ray M. Bowen, president of Texas A&M.

"Even if *Hopwood* were to go away tomorrow, or if the financial-aid situation were to be resolved tomorrow, there's still going to be the residual question in the minds of families, 'Are my children welcome at these universities?'" he says. "If that happens, there's going to be several years where we would have to rebuild confidence and rebuild relationships." **—JEFFREY SELINGO**

Race-Blind Financial Aid? Texas's 'Adversity Index'

Texas A&M University and the University of Texas at Austin have devised an "adversity index" to increase aid for minority undergraduates. With the index, the universities provide scholarships for students who are from low-income families and low-achieving high schools. Here's how the index allowed Texas A&M to offer more aid to minority students this fall than they otherwise might have received.

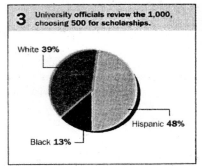

1 In-state freshmen are admitted.

White **89%**
Hispanic **9%**
Black **2%**

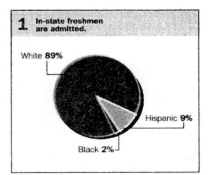

2 1,000 are deemed eligible for merit aid based on "adversity index."

White **65%**
Hispanic **27%**
Black **8%**

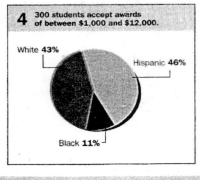

3 University officials review the 1,000, choosing 500 for scholarships.

White **39%**
Hispanic **48%**
Black **13%**

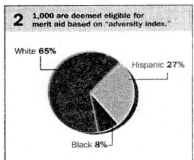

4 300 students accept awards of between $1,000 and $12,000.

White **43%**
Hispanic **46%**
Black **11%**

SOURCE: TEXAS A&M UNIVERSITY

Texas itself. President Bowen, of Texas A&M, says that decades ago, it was not unusual to see black and Hispanic Texans go on to achieve great things outside their home state. "We don't want to see a second wave of that," Mr. Bowen says. "You would like them to stay here, graduate from our universities, start their businesses here, and create a strong middle class. If that were to happen, Texas would be a much better place."

RESENTMENT FROM COUNSELORS

Several out-of-state recruiters, in turn, say they sense hostility here. They say that some counselors in this state—many of whom graduated from U.T. at Austin and Texas A&M—try to dissuade minority students from going elsewhere. A few years ago, Mr. Williams says, a counselor stuck him in a corner without a light during a college fair here.

Students and parents should judge a college for themselves, recruiters urge them. When one black student at Johnson High School called Norman "a cow town," Mr. Williams encouraged her to visit the campus. A 22-year veteran of Oklahoma, he knew that 80 per cent of those who visit eventually enroll. (For a fee, the university sponsors bus trips to the campus.)

The message from the recruiters resonates with at least some prospective minority students. Many of those who are open to leaving the state already picture an environment that is less hostile than the one they call "post–*Hopwood* Texas."

"When a professor at U.T.'s law school says blacks don't belong, why should I stay?" asks Alisia Darby, referring to comments in 1997 by Lino A. Graglia, who suggested that black and Hispanic students could not compete with white students at selective colleges. Ms. Darby, a senior at McCallum High School here, has her heart set on Spelman College in Georgia. "I just don't feel welcome in Texas."

* In-depth Information about the debate over affirmative action can be found on *The Chronicle*'s World-Wide Web site at: *http://chronicle.com/indepth*

Unit 6

Key Points to Consider

❖ In the last few years, has public attention to the activities of Asian Americans associated with campaign finance changed public perception of this ethnic group? Explain.

❖ The public passions generated during World War II have subsided, and anti-Japanese sentiment is no longer heard. Do you agree or disagree with this statement? Why?

❖ How can inclusiveness as an American value be taught? What approaches are most promising?

❖ What can be learned from examining Asian Americans' educational performance excellence and economic and cultural success in the United States?

❖ Chinese restaurants and enclave cultures have been a long-term feature of American diversity. Asian shopkeepers from time to time come into conflict with their neighbors in African-American comunities. Can you explain these social facts? What insight and recommendations does your explanation offer to the science and craft of conflict resolution?

 **Links**   # **www.dushkin.com/online/**

16. **Asian Community Online Network**
    http://www.igc.apc.org/acon/links/index.html

These sites are annotated on pages 4 and 5.

The following collection of articles on Asian Americans invites us to reflect on the fact that the United States is related to Asia in ways that would seem utterly amazing to the world view of the American founders. The expansion of the American regime across the continent, the importation of Asian workers, and the subsequent exclusion of Asians from the American polity are signs of the tarnished image and broken promise of refuge that America extended and then revoked. The Asian world is a composite of ethnicities and traditions ranging from the Indian subcontinent northeastward to China and Japan. The engagement of the United States beyond its continental limits brought American and Asian interests into a common arena now called the Pacific Rim. The most recent and perhaps most traumatic episode of this encounter was the conflict that erupted in 1941 at Pearl Harbor in Hawaii. Thus, examining the Asian relationship to America begins with the dual burdens of domestic exclusion and war. The cultural roots and current interaction between the United States and Asia form a complex of concerns that are explored in this unit's articles. Understanding the cultural matrices of Asian nations and their ethnicities and languages initiates the process of learning about the Asian emigrants who, for many reasons, decided to leave Asia to seek a fresh beginning in the United States.

The Asian American population growth since the immigration reform of 1965, the emergence of Japan and other Asian nations as international fiscal players, and the image of Asian American intellectual and financial success have heightened interest in this ethnic group in the United States. The variety of religious traditions that Asian immigrants bring to America is another dimension of cultural and moral importance. In what respect are non-Judeo-Christian-Islamic faith traditions issues of consequence? The aftermath of conflict and resulting analysis have riveted attention on the ethnic factor.

The details of familial and cultural development within Asian American communities compose worlds of meaning that are a rich source of material from which both insights and troubling questions of personal and group identity emerge. Pivotal periods of conflict in the drama of the American experience provide an occasion for learning as much about ourselves as about one of the newest clusters of ethnicities—the Asian Americans.

One of the first large-scale interactions between the United States and Asia was with the Philippine Islands and its population. This experience of war and empire and the attendant century-long process of military and defense relationships, as well as the exportation of institutions and cultural change, have forged a unique international-intercultural symbiosis. The role of the ethnic Chinese diaspora and the emergence of economic strength and political change in Asia suggest the globalization of the ethnic factor. Even the name of this American ethnic population has changed, as has its relationship to the islands and its ancestry. There is new politicization of the future of both an Asian homeland and the diasporic remnant. Its aspiring leaders are fashioning a new consciousness that is meaningful for its time and is inspiring actions that will articulate a most worthy future.

Asian Americans

Misperceived Minorities

'Good' and 'bad' stereotypes saddle Hispanics and Asian Americans

Pamela Constable

Washington Post Staff Writer

Richard Lopez, 29, a fourth-generation Mexican American businessman from San Bernardino, Calif., grew up in what he called a "Brady Bunch" suburb, and learned Spanish only to communicate with his great-grandmother. He is mystified when Hispanic newcomers complain of discrimination and angry when whites assume he needed special help to move up in American society.

"Nobody ever put a roadblock in front of me. I earned my way into college, and it offended me when people asked if I was receiving affirmative action," he says in a telephone interview. "I think a lot of the whining about discrimination is blown out of proportion. The biggest thing holding a lot of Mexicans back here is their resentment against those who succeed."

Ray Chin, 46, an insurance agent in New York's Chinatown, spent his teenage years washing bathrooms and delivering groceries in the city after his parents fled Communist China in the 1950s. Today he has earned the stature that often leads Asian Americans to be called the "model minority," a phrase he views as more curse than compliment.

"Yes, we can successfully join the mainstream, but once we reach a certain level, we're stifled by that glass ceiling," Chin says amid the din of a crowded Chinese restaurant. "People think we Asians can take care of ourselves, and they don't see the need to help us. But it's not true. We are still not included in things and we have to work three times harder to get to the same level as our co-workers."

No matter how much personal success they achieve, Hispanics and Asian Americans say they must fight stereotypes that can undermine their confidence or limit their potential. Whether "negative" or "positive"—the lazy, welfare-dependent Hispanic or the shy, technically oriented Asian American—such perceptions can be equally harmful and unfair, members of both groups say.

Worse, they say, is that ethnic minorities in the United States sometimes come to accept others' stereotypes about them, even when the facts and their experiences do not support those biases. For that reason, they may remain extremely sensitive to discrimination even when they have matched or surpassed white Americans in income and education.

Such contradictions—both in the views of other Americans toward Hispanics and Asian Americans and, at times, in the views of those groups about themselves—appeared throughout a nationwide telephone poll of 1,970 people conducted by The Washington Post, the Kaiser Family Foundation and Harvard University.

Yet there is also enormous diversity of opinion and experience within these two ethnic categories, other surveys and interviews show. The perceptions of Hispanics and Asian Americans about their opportunities and obstacles vary dramatically depending on their class, community and country of origin.

"It's very misleading to talk about the views of whites versus the views of minority groups like Latinos, because you cannot assume commonalty within those groups at all," says Rodolfo de la Garza, a professor of government at the University of Texas in Austin. He says it is crucial to know what language people speak, where they were born and how long they had been in the United States to accurately assess their views.

In a recent nationwide survey of 1,600 Hispanics by the Tomas Rivera Center in Claremont, Calif., for example, 71 percent of Hispanics from Central America said they believe that U.S. society discriminates against Hispanics, but only 42 percent of Cuban Americans agreed. Just over half of Mexican American respondents, by far the largest group of Hispanics in the United States, shared that view.

Poverty rates vary widely within both the Hispanic and Asian American communities, often depending on when, and from what country, members emigrated. In Los Angeles, unemployment is only 4 percent among Korean Americans, who flocked to the United States in the 1960s, but it is 21 percent among newly arrived Cambodian refugees. In New York, 32 percent of Dominican Americans are poor, but only 11 percent of Colombian Americans are.

For Hispanics or Asian Americans who live in the cocoon of urban ethnic enclaves, it may take a foray into other regions to make them appreciate the prejudice faced by others. Juan Santiago, 30, an office manager in the Bronx, N.Y., whose parents emigrated from the Dominican Republic, says he never experienced discrimination growing up in his heavily Dominican neighborhood. Then he went out to New Mexico as a foreman on a construction job.

Poll

HOW HISPANICS, ASIANS SEE THEMSELVES AND HOW OTHERS SEE THEM

Poll respondents were given a list of things some people have mentioned as reasons for the economic and social problems that some Hispanics and Asian Americans face today and were asked if each one is a major reason for those problems.

Is this a major reason for Hispanics' problems?	Hispanics who said 'yes'	Whites who said 'yes'	Blacks who said 'yes'	Asians who said 'yes'
Lack of jobs	68%	42%	74%	53%
Language difficulties	66%	56%	59%	59%
Lack of educational opportunities	51%	46%	63%	53%
Breakup of the Hispanic family	45%	28%	38%	22%
Past and present discrimination	43%	31%	58%	29%
Lack of motivation and an unwillingness to work hard	41%	25%	19%	32%

Those polled were asked the same question about Asians:

Is this a major reason for Asians' problems?	Asians who said 'yes'	Whites who said 'yes'	Blacks who said 'yes'	Hispanics who said 'yes'
Language difficulties	44%	44%	52%	37%
Lack of jobs	34%	31%	46%	43%
Past and present discrimination	20%	24%	41%	31%
Lack of educational opportunities	17%	18%	31%	31%
Breakup of the Asian family	14%	16%	27%	35%
Lack of motivation and an unwillingness to work hard	10%	22%	23%	20%

Polling data comes from a survey of 1,970 randomly selected adults interviewed in August and September, including 802 whites, 474 blacks, 352 Asian Americans and 252 Hispanics. The minority groups were oversampled to obtain large enough subsamples to analyze reliably. Margin of sampling error for the overall results is plus or minus 3 percentage points. The margins of sampling error for the four subsamples ranged from 4 percentage points for the white subsample to 7 percentage points for the Hispanic subsample. Sampling error is only one of many potential sources of error in public opinion polls.

"All the workers were Mexican, and the white owners had no respect for them. The work was very hard, the pay was very low, and there was no overtime," he recounts. "They tried to exploit me, too, but I knew my rights and I wouldn't let them. Until, then, I never really understood what discrimination was."

BUT LIFE INSIDE ETHNIC GHETTOS ALSO CAN CONfine and isolate, discouraging immigrants from joining American society at large and reinforcing others' misperceptions about them. In interviews, many foreign-born Hispanics and Asian Americans said they cling to immigrant communities, speaking to bosses and salesclerks in their native tongues and rarely meeting white Americans.

Yu Hui Chang, 35, a waitress in lower Manhattan, N.Y., says she and her husband work 12 hours a day in Chinese restaurants and rarely see their young son. Speaking through an interpreter in the cramped office of a Chinatown labor union, the Shanghai-born woman says she feels trapped in her community but is determined to succeed in her new country.

"It is very hard to be a woman in Chinatown," says Chang, who emigrated in 1982. "My life is nothing but working, working all the time. In China, I thought America was full of gold, and I still have the dream of taking that gold back home, but I can never save any."

Like Chang, the great majority of Asian Americans and Hispanics who responded to the Post/Kaiser/Harvard poll said they believe strongly in the American dream, but 46 percent of Asian Americans and 55 percent of Hispanics said they are farther from achieving it than they were a decade ago.

Both groups singled out hard work and family unity as keys to success here, and both singled out the same major obstacles: lack of good jobs, crime and violence, high taxes and the gap between their incomes and the rising cost of living. All agreed that learning English is crucial.

"You have to learn the language of the enemy to survive," says Juan Garcia, a Dominican-born man who manages a discount clothing shop in Washington Heights, a largely Hispanic section of Manhattan. "I've been here 13 years and my English is still poor, so I can't always defend myself," he adds in Spanish, describing his humiliation at being turned away from a fast-food counter when he could not explain his order.

Nonetheless, Garcia says he would not want to give up the comforts of American life. His son, 16, is studying computers and dreams of becoming a doctor. "Once you become civilized, you don't want to go back to a village with no lights or running water," he says.

Nationwide, the poll suggested that Asian Americans as a group think they have done much better economically than Hispanics think they have done. Asian Americans also have a far more optimistic view of their chances for success. Eighty-four percent of Asian Americans guessed that the average Asian American is at least as well off as the average white American, and 58 percent said they have the same or better chance of becoming wealthy.

Hispanics, on the other hand, tended to be more pessimistic and to believe others' critical views of them. In the poll, 74 percent of Hispanics said the average Hispanic is worse off than the average white, and 41 percent cited low motivation and unwillingness to work as a reason for their lack of advancement. Yet studies show that Hispanics have an unusually high level of participation in the work force.

"We are very susceptible to what others think about us, so we absorb those negative stereotypes in defiance of the facts," says Cecilia Munoz, Washington director of the National Council of La Raza, a Hispanic advocacy group. A 1994 survey by the council found that Hispanics have been most often depicted on TV and in films as "poor, of low status, lazy, deceptive, and criminals."

In the Post/Kaiser/Harvard poll, only one-quarter of white Americans cited unwillingness to work as a major obstacle for Hispanics; many more agreed with Hispanics that language problems and lack of educational opportunities are their biggest problems. In assessing the status of Asian Americans, whites cited only language difficulties as a major problem, suggesting that whites believe that Asian Americans face fewer barriers than Hispanics face.

More Hispanics say they thought they face the most discrimination as a group, but despite their relative economic success, more Asian Americans say they and their relatives and friends had experienced prejudice personally.

A majority of both groups agree that minorities should work their way up without special government help but also insist that government should protect their rights, for example by enacting tougher laws against workplace discrimination. And in interviews, many Hispanics and Asian Americans expressed deep concerns about a rising tide of anti-immigrant feeling.

Some specialists say the recent political furor over illegal immigrants has exacerbated a false impression that hordes of foreigners are arriving on U.S. shores. In the poll, the respondents guessed that 65 percent of Hispanics in the United States were born in foreign countries. According to the National Council of La Raza, only 33 percent of Hispanics were born in foreign countries.

"I see many Latinos trying to distance themselves from their roots as they react to the wave of anti-immigrant sentiment," says Harry Pachon, who directs the Tomas Rivera Center. "But I keep asking, how does an Anglo driving down the street pick out which Latino is native-born, which is a refugee, which is undocumented?"

IN OTHER WAYS, THE POLL SUGGESTED THAT MOST respondents are not especially hostile to either ethnic minority. Three-quarters said it "wouldn't make much difference" to the country if the number of Hispanics or Asian Americans were to increase significantly. Less than one-quarter said it would be a "bad thing" if either group were to grow substantially.

Yet the perception of growing xenophobia has created tensions between foreign-born and more established Hispanics and Asian Americans. Even in a community such as Jackson Heights, in Queens, N.Y., where Korean, Cuban, Vietnamese and Colombian immigrants live in tolerant proximity, second-generation residents expressed concern in interviews that illiterate or illegal newcomers are creating a negative image of all ethnic minorities.

"People have this idea that we are coming here in industrial quantities to invade America and go on welfare. The truth is that most of us were born here, we are working hard or going to school," says Mario Vargas, 22, a college student whose parents emigrated from Colombia. "But these days, the stereotypes are making it harder for the rest of us."

The challenge for U.S. Asians in the year 2000

By E. San Juan, Jr.

Part I

E. San Juan, Jr. is emeritus professor of English and Comparative Literature at the University of Connecticut, Storrs. He was 1993 Fellow at the Institute for the Advanced Studies in Humanities, University of Edinburgh, Scotland, and currently teaches Ethnic Studies and American Culture at Bowling Green State University, Ohio. He received graduate degrees from the University of the Philippines and Harvard University. His book Racial Formation/Critical Transformations *won awards from the Association for Asian American Studies and the Gustavus Myers Center for Human Rights.*

In this age of postality (postCold War, postmodern), one would expect that the public perception of Asian Americans—I prefer the term "U.S. Asians" to avoid any hint of unqualified acculturation or assimilation—would now be past stereotypes, myths, clichés. Not so. One textbook easily splices the narrative of the European "immigrant's quest for the American dream" with "the racial minority's" victimization by "discriminating laws and attitudes." In a revealing analysis of Judge Karlin's sentencing colloquy in the 1992 trial of Du Soon Ja, Neil Gotanda found that old paradigms are alive and well amid the reconfiguration of the planet's geopolitical map and the passing of the "American Century."

By the year 2020, the population labelled "Asian Americans" in this country will number 20.2 million. Filipinos now constitute the largest group (more than 2 million, up from 1,406,770 in the 1990 Census). And yet they still are considered pariahs: in the University of California at Berkeley, the treatment of Filipinos may be conceived as a symptom of benign "ethnic cleansing."

Given the heterogeneity of the histories, economic stratification, and cultural composition of the post-1965 immigrants and refugees, all talk of Asian pan-ethnicity should now be abandoned as useless, and even harmful, speculation. Not so long ago, Professor Roger Daniels stated the obvious: "The conglomerate image of Asian Americans is a chimera." This is more true today. No longer sharing the common pre-World War II experience of being hounded by exclusion acts, antimiscegenation laws, and other disciplinary apparatuses of racialization, Vietnamese, Kampucheans, and Hmongs have now diverged from the once dominant pattern of settlement, occupation, education, family structure, and other modes of ethnic identification. (We don't even reckon with the presence of Thais, Malaysians, Indonesians, Bangladeshis, not to mention the Pacific Islanders.) After 1965, one can no longer postulate a homogeneous "Asian American" bloc—except in fantasy. To use current jargon, the bureaucratic and totalizing category "Asian American" has been decentered by systemic contingencies to the point where today a cult of multiple and indeterminate subject-positions is flourishing. However, I have yet to meet a cyborg or borderland denizen of confirmed U.S. Asian genealogy.

Despite such changes, versions of the "melting pot" theory are still recycled to flatten out the politically significant mutations within a patriotic dogma of pluralism. A recent textbook entitled *Asian Americans* has no hesitation predicting that Asians will be easily assimilated in time. The trick is the promotion of toleration via consumerist "multi-culturalism," backed by the economic power of Japan and the Asian "Tigers." This accommodationism refuses to take seriously what I call the Vincent Chin syndrome: political demagoguery in times of social crisis can shift the target of scapegoating onto any Asian-looking "object" that can reactivate the sedimented persona of the wily, inscrutable, shifty-eyed foreigner in our midst. And multiculturalism is for the most part a refurbished version of white supremacy, the enshrined cooptative formula for peacefully managing differences among the subalterns.

In his 1972 pathbreaking book *Racial Oppression in America*, Robert Blauner repudiated the fallacy of subsuming the diverse experiences of subjugation of people of color under the immigrant model that privileges the teleology of Eurocentric assimilation in defining the character of the U.S. nation-state. But the specter of "American exceptionalism" has a way of being resurrected, especially in periods of crisis and neoconservative resurgence. Asian American panethnicity falls within this conjuncture. It is one specimen of the ideological recuperation of what I would call the Myrdal complex (the presumed schizoid nature of U.S. democracy preaching equality but institutionalizing exclusionary and oppressive practices) that plagues all utilitarian thought, including its radical and pragmatic variants.

Despite its reflection of a need for principled unity against institutional racism, pan-Asianism concealed the ethnic chauvinisms and class cleavages, hierarchy, and conflicts generated by the operation of U.S. racializing politics and its divide-and-rule policies. As Glenn Omatsu has pointed out, the "cultural entrepreneurs" of pan-Asianism turned out to be agents for opportunist electoral politics and brokers for the "get rich quick" ethos even while Asians (associated with the competitive power of Pacific Rim nations) are collectively perceived as a threat by blacks and other minority groups. They begot the post-1980s Asian neo-conservatives who glorify the "model minority" stereotype while nurturing the seeds for the Los Angeles explosion of April 1992.

The more profound motivation for pan-Asianism is the historically specific racism of white supremacy towards Asians. The historian Sucheng Chan notes: "In their relationship to the host society, well-to-do merchants and poor servants, landowning farmers and propertyless farm workers, exploitative labor contractors and exploited laborers alike were considered inferior to all Euro-Americans, regardless of the internal ethnic and socio-economic divisions among the latter." Instead of valorizing ethnicity or cultural difference per se, we need to concentrate on the "racialization" process, its ideological and institutional articulations, within the framework of the capitalist world system.

Part II

We need to attend to the national/international division of labor which provides the context to understand ethnicization as, in Immanuel Wallerstein's view, "the distinctive cultural socialization of the work force that enables the complex occupational hierarchy of labor (marked by differential allocation of surplus value, class/status antagonisms, etc.) to be legitimized without contradicting the formal equality of citizens before the law in liberal-democratic polities." Wallerstein points out that capitalism gains flexibility in restructuring itself to preserve its legitimacy, hence the unconscionable exploitation of the multicultural workforce in the Los Angeles garment industry, in the "free trade" zones of Mexico, the Philippines, South Korea, Malaysia and elsewhere. Ethnicity, then, is not a primordial category that testifies to the virtue of a pluralist market-cen-

tered system, but a means utilized to legitimize the contradictions of a plural society premised on racial hierarchy, also called a *Herrenvolk* democracy. What I would stress is precisely the need to analyze the racialization of ethnicized, class/gendered identities (initially enslaved, conquered, and colonized) to avoid the trap of multiculturalism as a discussion of formalistically reconciling cultural differences.

Recent scholarship on the ideological construction of "whiteness" in U.S. history should illuminate also the invention of the "Asian American" as a monolithic, standardizing rubric. It is clear that the diverse collectivities classified as "Asian American" manifest more discordant features than affinities and commonalities. The argument that they share similar values (e.g., Confucian ethics), ascribed "racial" characteristics, and kindred interests in politics, education, social services, etc. cannot be justified by the historical experiences of the peoples involved, especially those who came after World War II.

This does not mean that U.S. Asians did not and do not now engage in coalitions and alliances to support certain causes or cooperate for mutual benefit; examples are numerous. In fact, the insistence on pan-Asianism can only obscure if not obfuscate the enduring problems of underemployment and unequal reward ("glass ceiling"), occupational segregation, underrepresentation, and class polarization obscured by the "model minority" orthodoxy that props up the American Dream of Success.

Faced with the racial politics of the eighties and nineties, all talk about fashioning or searching for an "authentic Asian American identity" and "reclaiming" our history can only sound fatuous. More culpable is the view that in order

to transcend the Frank Chin-Maxine Hong Kingston misrecognition of each other, U.S. Asian artists should utilize their "ethnic sensibility to describe aspects of the Asian American experience that appeal to a common humanity"—a plea for commodifying the formerly "exotic" into plain American pie. The ubiquitous troupe of reconfigured "Lotus Blossoms" and "Gunga Dins," now of course sporting more fashionable trappings, still dominate the travelling roadshows of "Asian American" cultural production today.

Incalculable damage has been inflicted by a postmodernist skepticism that sometimes has claimed to be more revolutionary than rigorous research into internal colonialism, labor segmentation, national self-determination, and so on. One example of postmodernist chic is the notion of transnational subjectivity. It doesn't require Superman's x-ray vision for us to tell that the paragon of the diasporic subject as a postcolonial "hybrid" often masks the working of a dominant "common culture" premised on differences, not contradictions. Heterogeneity can then be a ruse for recuperative patriotism. The latest version is the theory of "multiple identities" and "fluid" positions of immigrants (for example, Filipino Americans) straddling two nation-states assumed to be of equal status and ranking in the world system; such identities are unique because they allegedly participate in the political economies of both worlds. This is obviously a paradigm based on the dynamics of market exchange-value whereby all goods and values can be made equivalent. The status of the transnational migrant, however, remains parasitic on the superior nation-state (the United States), belying its claim to autonomy and integrity. The fatal mistake of the transnational model is analogous to that of panethnicity: despite its gesture of acknowledging political and ideological differences, it assumes the parity of colonized/dominated peoples and the U.S. nation-state in contemporary global capitalism.

It is a truism that for all neocolonized subjects in the Western metropoles, the process of survival involves constant renegotiation of cultural spaces, revision of inherited folkways, reappropriation of dominant practices, and invention of new patterns of adjustment. All these embody the resistance habitus of peoples attempting to transcend subalternity. What is crucial is how and why a specific repertoire of practices is enabled by the structures of civil society, the state, and the disposition of the agents themselves. When Filipinos, for example, construct the meaning of their lives, they don't simultaneously conform to and resist the

The argument that they share similar values (e.g., Confucian ethics), ascribed 'racial' characteristics, and kindred interests in politics, education, social services, etc. cannot be justified by the historical experiences of the peoples involved, especially those who came after World War II.

hegemonic "free enterprise" ideology. This implies a reservoir of free choices that doesn't exist for most subjugated communities. Indeed the construction of Filipino identity as a dynamic, complex phenomenon defies both assimilationist and pluralist models when it affirms its anti-racist, counterhegemonic antecedent: the long-lived revolutionary opposition of the Filipino people to U.S. imperial domination.

New postCold War realignments compel us to return to a historical materialist analysis of political economy and its overdeterminations in order to grasp the new racial politics of transnationality and multiculturalism. With respect to the Asian/Pacific Rim countries whose destinies now seem more closely tied to the vicissitudes of unequal exchange as well as indebtedness to the World Bank-IMF, the reconfiguring of corporate capital's strategy in dealing with this area requires more astute analysis of the flow of migrant labor, capital investments, media manipulation, tourism, and so on.

There are over a million Filipinos (chiefly women) employed as domestics and low-skilled workers in Hong Kong, Singapore, Japan, Taiwan, Korea, and Malaysia. Their exploitation is worsened by the racializing process of inferiorization imposed by the Asian nation-states, the Asian "tigers," competing for their share in global capital accumulation. The Western press then reconfigures the Asian as neoSocial Darwinist denizen of booty capitalism in the "New World Order."

All these recent developments inevitably resonate in the image of the Asian—its foreignness, malleability, affinities with the West, etc.—that in turn determines a complex of contradictory and variable attitudes toward U.S.-domiciled Asians. Such attitudes can be read from the drift of the following questions: Is Japan always going to be portrayed as the scapegoat for the loss of U.S. jobs? Is China obdurately refusing to conform to Western standards in upholding human rights and opening the country to the seductions of market in-

dividualism? What about "mail order brides" from the Philippines and Thailand as possible carriers of AIDS virus? Are the Singaporeans that barbaric? And despite the end of history in this postCold War milieu, will the North Koreans continue to be the paragons of communist barbarism? Are Korean and Indian merchants really that greedy and clannish?

In effect, given the demographic and sociopolitical re-articulation of U.S. Asian collectivities, we have not even begun to address what Nancy Fraser calls the redistribution-recognition dilemma, that is, how political-economic justice and cultural justice can be realized together by transformative means instead of repackaging liberal nostrums so popular among people of color in the mainstream academy. In short, the challenge of a radical democratic critique still needs to be taken up as we confront the disintegration of panAsian metaphysics and transnationalist discourse amid the postCold War realignments of nation-states and North/South power blocs.

TRAPPED ON A PEDESTAL

Asian Americans confront model-minority stereotype

Thea Lee

THEA LEE is a staff editor at *Dollars & Sense.* Her great-great-grandfather came to the United States from China in 1850 to work on the railroad.

"Visit 'Chinatown U.S.A.' and you find an important racial minority pulling itself up from hardship and discrimination to become a model of self-respect and achievement in today's America. At a time when it is being proposed that hundreds of billions be spent to uplift Negroes and other minorities, the nation's 300,000 Chinese-Americans are moving ahead on their own—with no help from anyone else."
—U.S. News and World Report, December 26, 1996

"Asian Americans are our exemplar of hope and inspiration."
—Ronald Reagan
as quoted in the *New Republic,* 1985

In the mid-1960s, when relaxed restrictions dramatically increased Asian immigration to the United States, the popular press, politicians, and others assigned Asian Americans the role of "model minority." When the 1980 Census revealed that median family income for Asian-Americans actually surpassed that of whites by almost 13%, the stories resurfaced with renewed intensity. *Fortune* ran an article entitled, "Super-minority," and the *New Republic* chimed in with "America's Greatest Success Story."

The model-minority label, enviable though it might seem, has served Asian Americans badly. It obscures real differences among Asian Americans and exacerbates the resentment of other minority groups. The stories of spectacular achievement are presented as proof that Asian Americans either do not face or have overcome adverse racial discrimination. This not only denies Asian Americans legal and social protection against discrimination, but creates a backlash of its own—as majority or other minority groups lobby to offset their perceived advantage.

PLUS ÇA CHANGE...

Although the nation's 6.5 million Asian Americans still make up less than 3% of the total U.S. population, they are the fastest-growing minority group in the country. According to current estimates, the ethnic Asian population in the United States doubled between 1980 and 1990, as it did between 1970 and 1980. The rapid growth brings with it equally dramatic changes in its composition, rendering the old stereotypes ever more obsolete.

Filipinos recently overtook the Chinese to become the largest single Asian group in the United States (see table). The Japanese-American population remained relatively stable in the 1980s, while the number of Indochinese more than tripled. The number of Asian Indians and Koreans continued to grow at a steadily high rate, with each of those

Ethnic Asians in the United States
(in thousands)

	1980	1990*	2000*
Japanese	715	800	860
Chinese	810	1,260	1,680
Indian	385	680	1,000
Korean	355	820	1,320
Philippine	780	1,400	2,080
Vietnamese	245	860	1,580
Laotian	55	260	500
Cambodian	15	180	380
All Asians	**3,465**	**6,550**	**9,850**

* Projection

Source: *Pacific Bridges,* ed. Fawcett and Carino

From *Dollars & Sense,* March 1990, pp. 12–15. *Dollars & Sense,* a progressive economic magazine, One Summer Street, Somerville, MA 02143. (617) 628-8411. Subscriptions are $14.95 per year.

groups constituting a little over 10% of the Asian-American population.

Judged by standard measures of success, the achievements of Asian Americans—as a group—seem impressive. Their median family income in 1979 was $23,100, compared to the national median of $19,900. Moreover, a 1988 study by the Civil Rights Commission found that the hourly wages of most American-born Asian men exceed those of whites with comparable levels of education and experience. According to the 1980 Census, 34% of Asian Americans completed four or more years of college, compared to only 16% of the total U.S. population. And at elite universities, Asian Americans are even more disproportionately represented: in 1986, Asian Americans made up 12% of the freshman class at Harvard, 22% at MIT, and 27% at the University of California at Berkeley.

However, the economic and social reality of Asian immigrants is far more complex than these statistics indicate. Focusing on averages and success stories misses an equally striking case of Asian "over-representation": at the bottom of the barrel. Although Asian Americans are three to five times as likely as whites to be engineers and doctors, they are also two to four times as likely to work in food services or textiles. Many of the poorest Asian Americans are undocumented or paid under the table at sweatshops or restaurants; their incomes are likely to be under-represented by official figures. And offsetting their high educational attainment as a group is the fact that 6% of Asian Americans have not completed elementary school—three times the rate for whites.

To a large extent, deep differences among Asians from different countries, between recent immigrants and long-time residents, and between refugees and skilled professionals swamp the similarities, rendering generalizations misleading. For example, the median income of a Laotian family in 1979 was $5,000, compared to $27,400 for a Japanese family and $25,000 for an Indian family.

The stereotype of the successful minority hurts those Asian Americans who need the most help, because the success of some is used as an excuse to deny benefits to all. The most striking example is in college admissions. Most schools no longer consider Asians a "disadvantaged minority," excluding them from special consideration in the admissions process and in the awarding of financial aid. Some schools have gone a step further and rigged their admissions standards to handicap

Asian students. Patrick Hayashi, now the vice-chancellor in charge of admissions at Berkeley, testified that in the mid-1980s, people "seemed to be deliberately searching for a standard which could be used to exclude Asian immigrant applications."

THE AMERICAN DREAM?

Inappropriate and sometimes irrelevant comparisons contribute to racial tension between Asian Americans and other minorities. Black conservative Thomas Sowell, among others, has suggested that blacks would do well to follow the example of Asian Americans—work hard, get a good education, and achieve the American dream.

But American blacks face barriers quite different from those faced by Asian immigrants. Although both black Americans and early Asian immigrants endured legal and personal discrimination during their history in this country, Asian Americans at least came voluntarily. Furthermore, the 1965–75 wave of Asian immigrants consisted largely of highly educated, financially solvent professionals.

Another advantage of some Asian immigrant groups is that they have developed alternative ways to raise capital, ways that depend more on informal financial arrangements among families and acquaintances than on commercial banks. One such method is the rotating credit association.

Called *hui* in Chinese, *kye* in Korean, and *tanomoshi* in Japanese, these self-financing pools originated centuries ago to help families finance major expenses like weddings and fu-

would be one way of dealing with the inadequate and racially discriminatory lending policies of U.S. financial institutions. But the path is a risky one, due to its very informality: If the leader is dishonest, or if one member cannot pay her or his share, the other members can lose their entire investment. As the *Wall Street Journal* points out, "There is no deposit insurance covering these free-wheeling banks, only the integrity of the leader, and stories about crooked operators and defaulted contributions abound in Asian communities."

Moreover, rather than urging other minorities to emulate the circuitous path Asian Americans have taken, policymakers should work to lift the barriers in the U.S. economy—particularly in the financial system—facing all people of color and recent immigrants. Setting up one minority as the "good minority," and another as "bad" misses the point entirely. Both blacks and Asian Americans suffer from discrimination, albeit different kinds, and both have needs that are unmet by the U.S. economy and current policy.

DISCRIMINATION AND SUCCESS

At face value, the 1980 Census seemed to prove conclusively that Asian Americans no longer face discrimination in U.S. labor markets. If they earn more than whites, the argument went, then if anything they must enjoy a relatively advantageous position.

But upon closer scrutiny the Asian income figures reveal a more complex

---

The Asian income advantage evaporates when per capita incomes, rather than median family incomes, are compared.

---

nerals. The pools serve an important need once immigrants come to the United States, providing start-up capital to people who might be denied loans by conventional banks for lack of collateral or a poor credit rating. Up to 40 people participate, each contributing savings to a pool, which is loaned out to each participant in turn.

Should blacks, Latinos, and native Americans take a clue from Asian Americans, and set up similar institutions in their communities? That

picture, even beyond the differences among nationalities. For one thing, the Asian income advantage evaporates when per capita incomes, rather than median family incomes, are compared. Since Asian-American families tend to be larger than average, with more workers per household, per capita Asian income in 1979 was actually slightly lower than the U.S. average.

But lower income in itself is not proof of discrimination, any more than higher income is proof of its absence.

Other factors such as education, experience, and number of years in this country also need to be taken into account. A 1988 report by the U.S. Civil Rights Commission used 1980 Census data to compare annual income and hourly wages for Asian Americans in the six largest national groups: Chinese, Japanese, Filipino, Korean, Indian, and Vietnamese. Adjusting for levels of education, work experience, and geographic location, they tried to isolate race in order to see whether discrimination had occurred.

U.S.-born Japanese-American and Korean-American men were found to earn somewhat more annually than comparable non-Hispanic white men. Other Asian groups, however, fared less well. Measured annually, U.S.-born Chinese men earned 5% less, Filipino men earned 9% less, and Indian men earned 30% less than similarly qualified white men.

Asian women, both immigrants and U.S.-born, earn as much as or more than white women with similar characteristics, although they still earn substantially less than Asian or white men. The earnings gap between black and white women is also significantly smaller than the earnings gap between black and white men. This may occur because women tend to be clustered in lower-paying jobs than men.

Contrary to the stereotype, Asian men as a group work fewer hours per year than white men, although foreign-born Asian men tend to work longer hours than foreign-born white men. The Civil Rights Commission notes that the lower average hours of work "may reflect barriers to employment," such as seasonal or irregular work. Asian-American women, on the other hand, work more hours and weeks per year than white women and are more likely to be in the labor force.

TROUBLE AT THE TOP

Lumping Asian Americans together obscures the fact that within occupations and in some regions of the country, Asian Americans are clearly discriminated against. The most successful Asian Americans—those held up as examples of super-achievement—are routinely paid less and promoted less often than comparable whites. This effect grows as they climb higher, both in academia and in corporations.

U.S.-born Asian men are less likely to hold managerial positions than whites with comparable skills and characteristics. While Asian Americans make up 4.3% of professionals, they are only 1.4% of officials and managers. The stereotype of Asians as passive and technically oriented may impede their promotion to top managerial positions.

Even though Asian Americans are famous—or infamous?—for their relatively high investment in higher education, both as families and as individuals, they tend to receive a lower return on their education than whites. A study by Jayjia Hsia using 1980 Census data found that Asian-American faculty with stronger than average academic credentials and more scholarly publications were paid less than average. In sum, the labor-market position of Asian Americans—even those at the top—is hardly enviable. They invest heavily in education, only to catch up to whites who have invested somewhat less. They work for corporations, only to find that their bosses have already decided how far they can advance.

ONE WAY OUT

One way that Asian Americans have coped with limited upward mobility and relatively lower access to skilled union jobs has been to buy small businesses. Asian Americans have a high rate of business ownership compared to other minority groups—54.8 business owners for every 1,000 Asians or Pacific Islanders, compared to 12.5 for blacks and 17 for Latinos. The Korean, Chinese, and Japanese business rates are higher than that for all Americans (64.0 per 1,000).

Although they have provided some opportunities for recent immigrants, small businesses are notoriously difficult to run. A Los Angeles-based study showed that Korean-American-owned enterprises in that city are heavily concentrated in two labor-intensive and highly competitive industries: retail and selected services. These businesses are small, both in terms of the number of employees and the value of sales. Four-fifths of these firms hire five or fewer employees, and nine-tenths hire ten or fewer. Virtually all had sales under one million dollars. Typical of Asian-owned businesses in the rest of the country, their geographic locations are usually outside mainstream markets, in mostly minority communities with high crime and poverty rates. Like all small businesses, they are particularly vulnerable to business cycles, with a higher than average failure rate.

The visibility and the "foreignness" of Asian merchants in the inner cities make them easy targets for resentment. Edna Bonacich, a sociologist at the University of California at Riverside, points out that merchants of any race, by definition, make their livings by making a profit from their customers. Since many of these merchants live elsewhere, she argues, they also tend to reinvest their profits elsewhere. And since many of these Asian-owned businesses employ family members, they offer relatively few jobs to the community.

Bonacich argues that the Asian merchants act as "minority middlemen," and are themselves exploited by the corporations whose goods they sell. It isn't profitable for large chain supermarkets or department stores to sell in inner-city neighborhoods, so Asian immigrants fill the void. Their willingness to face the personal and financial risks involved in operating a business in high-crime areas allows large corporations a bigger market for their goods.

In recent years, black leaders in Harlem, Bedford-Stuyvesant, and elsewhere have led boycotts and protests against Asian merchants in their communities. This anger is misdirected. Asian immigrants buy stores in poor neighborhoods not to take advantage of residents, but because they can't afford the higher rents in more affluent neighborhoods.

WHO'S THE ENEMY?

Many Asian Americans, especially those whose grandparents or great-grandparents came to this country in the late nineteenth or early twentieth century, regard the glowing praise heaped upon the new "model minority" with some skepticism and irony. They may be the new darlings of the media, but for most of the earlier part of this century, Asian Americans were despised, feared, and legally excluded from many rights other Americans—black and white—took for granted.

In 1870, foreign-born Asians were singled out as the only racial group not eligible for U.S. citizenship. In 1882, the Chinese Exclusion Act virtually barred Chinese from immigrating to the United States. Additional laws passed in the early 1900s extended the ban to Japanese, Koreans, and Filipinos. In many states, Asian Americans could not legally own land or marry whites until after World War II.

In 1965, the U.S. government removed the last vestiges of anti-Asian discrimination from its immigration laws. Today, Asian Americans struggle more with stereotypes and ignorance than with legal discrimination. Confusion between Asian countries and people of Asian ancestry living in this country can lead to anger and sometimes violence from people frustrated over the outcome of the Vietnam war, the loss of U.S. jobs to Japanese firms, the increasing Japanese ownership of U.S. assets, or even the U.S. trade deficit with Japan.

This confusion cost 110,000 Japanese-Americans their homes, jobs, and freedom during World War II, when the war against Japan spilled over into a war against Japanese-American citizens. In 1982, the same confusion cost Vincent Chin, a Chinese-American man from Detroit, his life when he was beaten to death with a baseball bat by two men reportedly angered by the Japanese success in automobile markets.

Such incidents share roots in economic frustration. Given the current structure of the U.S. and world economies, there really aren't enough jobs,

housing, and resources for everyone, especially in poor neighborhoods. In the short run, it is easier for politicians to take sledgehammers to Japanese-built consumer goods than it is to improve the U.S. position in the world economy. It is easier for conservative economists or sociologists to compare blacks unfavorably to Asian Americans than it is to look at ways in which both face discrimination in U.S. labor markets. But it is important that progressives and organizers in minority and working-class communities resist these same quick-fix solutions.

Less Japan-bashing and more frequent acknowledgement of existing discrimination are a necessary first step to a more realistic assessment of the difficult and sometimes tenuous position of new immigrants and non-white Americans. The portrayal of Asian Americans as a super-minority not only dehumanizes Asian Americans, but creates unrea-

sonable expectations (much as the super-mom image does). And setting up one minority group against others inevitably creates inter-racial tensions, and sometimes violence. To the extent that blacks and Asians are squabbling over who gets to own ghetto grocery stores, neither is asking why conventional banks aren't lending to either one of them.

RESOURCES:

Jayjia Hsia, *Asian Americans in Higher Education and at Work,* 1988; U.S. Commission on Civil Rights, The Economic Status of Americans of Asian Descent: An Exploratory Investigation, October 1988; Minority Trendsletter, Winter 1987.

Unit Selections

28. **Who Are We?** Raymond A. Belliotti
29. **Italian Americans as a Cognizable Racial Group,** Dominic R. Massaro
30. **The Blind Spot of Multiculturalism: America's Invisible Literature,** Werner Sollors
31. **Mr. Dybek's Neighborhood: Toward a New Paradigm for Ethnic Literature,** Thomas Gladsky

Key Points to Consider

❖ The post-Nixon and post-Watergate era of ethnic data collection began with the 1980 Census. A considerable shift toward self-identification began, which allowed persons to claim specific and/or multiple categories. Does the earlier scheme of designating groups have any scientific or political merit? Does personal identification trump all other considerations? How does ethnicity of an earlier era suggest the tension between worlds of meaning discussed in this section?

❖ When the U.S. Commission on Civil Rights held hearings on issues related to Eastern and Southern European ethnic groups in the United States, leaders of these groups objected to the names Euro-Ethnic and Euro-American. They preferred specific ethnicities such as Polish-American and Italian-American. Comment on the idea that the legacy of multiple ancestral origins and ethnic identities of European Americans derived from an earlier era of immigration argues for a lack of relevancy and the marginality of these ethnic populations to the central ethnic issues of our time.

❖ What is a central ethnic issue? By what criteria do we decide the importance and preferential protection of one ethnic group vis-à-vis another group?

❖ What lessons can be learned from the experiences of eastern and southern Europeans?

 **Links** **www.dushkin.com/online/**

17. **American Immigration Home Page**
    http://www.bergen.org/AAST/Projects/Immigration/index.html
18. **International Migration as a Dynamic Process: Kybernetes**
    http://www.mcb.co.uk/services/articles/liblink/k/diamanti.htm
19. **Italian American Web Site of New York**
    http://www.italian-american.com/main.htm

These sites are annotated on pages 4 and 5.

In a very provocative book by Michael Novak, *The Rise of the Unmeltable Ethnics,* written at the beginning of the 1970s, the author makes the following observation: "Two forms of prejudice stamped the immigrants. Both had a peculiar 'northern' quality: one was racial and the other 'progressive.' According to one view, it was his race and religion that made the Southern European inferior. According to the other, it was his social and political backwardness." Although acknowledgment of ethnicity and cultural pluralism emerged as an intellectual and cultural force in the mid-1960s, its origins were formed even before the period of mass immigration to America.

The American experience from 1870 to 1924 addressed the influence of these groups and in so doing shifted American consciousness of itself. Even 100 years later, America's public mind continues to identify and divide its history as an immigrant-receiving country into two periods: The Old Immigration, meaning Northern Europeans, and the New Immigration, meaning Others—the Mediterranean and eastern European as well as Asian and Hispanic populations. One marker of this division can be found in the *Report of the Dillingham Commission* (1910), a congressional and presidential blue ribbon panel that warned America that the eastern European and Mediterranean character was less capable of Americanization than the Nordics and Teutonics who had peopled America

Mediterranean and eastern European immigrants and their religious traditions entered an industrializing economy that required their labor, much like plantation production in an earlier period required the indentured servant and the slave. But they also met a cultural and political climate of potent challenges and denials of their integrity and existence.

Moynihan and Glazer, in *Beyond the Melting Pot* (1964), the report of the Kerner Commission, and findings of the National Center for Urban Ethnic Affairs, confirmed that ethnicity was a salient factor. The descendants of Mediterranean and eastern European immigrants, even into the fourth generation, were just barely moving toward the middle class, were absent in the professions, and were rarely admitted to prestigious universities or colleges. More specifically, Italians and Poles, notwithstanding the absences of affirmative action and legal recourse, were no less than blacks and Hispanics/Latinos excluded from the executive suites and boardrooms of America's largest corporations, publicly regulated utilities, and philanthropies.

The emergence of interest in retracing the pathways of these immigrant groups and assessing their participation in intergroup relations in America are topics of many scholarly disciplines. The inclusion of the following articles is but a peek behind the curtain of this neglected dimension of race and ethnic relations in America. Apropos of the selection of articles and our attempt to understand current attention to this persistent cluster of ethnic Americans (the descendants of Mediterranean and eastern European groups, which have been ignored and neglected, mislabeled white-ethnics and/or Euro-ethnics) is Noel Ignatiev's provocative book, *How the Irish Became White.* The

Irish immigrants, though not a Mediterranean or an Eastern European American ethnic group, had a similar experience in America of being different from and perceived as racially apart from the American regime, owing to their conquered status in the British empire.

Because of the considerable fluidity of the immigrant experiences, as well as the complex processes of cultural identity and political use of cultural symbols such as race and ethnicity, the search for more analytical rigor in this field is far from complete. Some guide to discernable and measurable features of ethnic phenomena and characteristics that are attributes of ethnicity was developed in a fine collection of materials on this topic, *The Harvard Encyclopedia of American Ethnic Groups,* which lists the following markers of ethnic groups: common geographic origin, migratory status, language/dialect, religious faith(s), ties that transcend kinship, neighborhood, and community boundaries, shared traditions values, and symbols, literature, folklore, music, food preferences, settlement and employment patterns, special interests in regard to politics in the homeland and in the United States, institutions that specifically serve and maintain the group, and internal sense of distinctiveness and an external perception of distinctiveness. The contributions and concerns of various ethnic immigrant groups over many generations provided a deep weave and pattern to the material and social history of America.

Present concerns of these ethnic groups include language preservation, fair hearings for homeland interests, enclave neighborhoods, inclusion in ethnic studies, and their articulation of historical American expressions of fairness, justice, and equity, and the collection of accurate data among all ethnic groups in America. These values are thoroughly patterned into their world view and their appropriation of the expansive promise of the American icon—the Statue of Liberty. After all, it was this icon of the American promise that resonated in their hearts and minds in 1965, when a coalition of Mediterranean and eastern Americans in the national government, such as Emmanuel Cellers, Jacob Javits, Peter Rodino, John Brademas, Abraham Ribicoff, and ethnic, Catholic religious leaders, such as Msgr. Geno Baroni and Rev. Theodore Hesburgh, joined Protestant and secular organizations in support of the immigration reform proposed by President John Kennedy that ended the quota system and in support of the 1965 Voting Rights Act that ensured fair elections for the disenfranchised, especially Negroes in the South. This legislative coalition accomplished, through deliberative democracy, not the mandate of the Supreme Court or the edict of administrative regulation, a fundamental change that significantly altered the terms of race and ethnic relations.

The massive migration of peoples during the past 30 years, which has included significantly large Mediterranean and eastern European populations, has reengaged the immigrant factor in American politics and the ethnic factor among all Americans. Should ethnic populations be denied their distinctiveness through absorption into the mass of modernity, or can their distinctiveness accompany them into mainstream modern American identities?

WHO ARE WE?

In many parts of the U.S. the image persists of Italian Americans as largely blue-collar workers with little education and large families. But current research reveals a more accurate sociological portrait of the estimated 26 million Americans of Italian heritage.

By RAYMOND A. BELLIOTTI

IN the last census of 1990, Italian Americans constituted the fifth largest ethnic group in this country after Germans, British, Irish and African Americans. Myths and stereotypes of these Italian Americans abound because we have relatively little empirical research on their attitudes, attributes, and lifestyles. Four years ago, however, a comprehensive study of Italian Americans was released, although its findings were largely ignored by the national media.

A Profile of Italian Americans

In 1992, the National Italian American Foundation commissioned the National Opinion Research Center (NORC) at the University of Chicago to undertake a research project on Italian Americans. The study that resulted was called " A Profile of Italian Americans: 1972–1992." It compared Italian Americans to 14 other ethnic racial, and religious groups in the United States including Asians, African Americans, Jews, Hispanics and other Europeans. The 15 ethnic groups were compared in 80 categories, including education, income, politics, social habits, val-

From *Ambassador,* Number 23/30, 1996, pp. 18-21. Reprinted courtesy of *Ambassador* magazine, a publication of the National Italian American Foundation in Washington, DC.

A gathering of the Rossi and Scarboro families, founders of the successful Italian Swiss Colony wineries in California. Although the image of large and patriarchal families persists in the popular mind, the families of present-day Italian Americans actually differ considerably.

ues, attitudes, and general psychological well-being.

The NORC report revealed that the average Italian American still lives in the city he or she was raised in, has attended at least one year of college and has an average family income of about $33,000 a year. These facts indicate that Italian Americans slightly exceed the average when it comes to education and occupational prestige, and rank sixth out of the 15 ethnic groups in terms of average family income.

The Family

The NORC study also revealed that the contemporary Italian-American family differs considerably from the traditional, large and patriarchal stereotype of it in the popular mind.

In its structure, stability and birth rate, today's Italian-American family resembles a modern American middle-class family more than it does a traditional southern Italian one.

Compared to the other 14 ethnic groups in the NORC study, Italian Americans are raised in more stable families, mainly because of relatively fewer deaths, involuntary separations and divorces. From the 1970s to the 1990s, between 79 and 83 percent of the Italian Americans surveyed grew up in homes with both parents present.

The NORC study also found that, since the 1970s, the proportion of Italian Americans with unmixed ancestry (that is, with ancestors only from Italy) has fallen from 81 percent to 69 percent. Of the married Italian Americans in the study, only 33 percent had an Italian-American spouse, down from 68 percent before 1920. Nevertheless, the study found that Italian Americans still ranked fourth after Jews, Asians and Hispanics among those who married people of their own ethnic background.

Photo of the Italian Catholic Society of Washington D.C. in 1919. Even today, Italian Americans remain largely Roman Catholic. Nevertheless, the number of Catholics among them has declined over the last twenty years, from 81 percent to a present 70 percent.

When they do marry, Italian Americans tend to have fewer children than other minorities—one or two children—giving them the lowest birth rate (after Jews) of the 15 groups. This finding conflicts with the image of large Italian-American families, but corresponds to actual family patterns even for the parents of today's Italian-American adults, who were raised in smaller families than most other groups—about 3 children compared to the overall average of 4.0

In their social interactions (spending social evenings with friends or parents), Italian Americans rank higher than average—fifth among all groups. Most strikingly, they rank first in percentage of members who said they spend at least one evening a year in a bar, and second in percentage of drinkers. Traditionally, this high use of alcohol has not been a problem of Italian Americans because their alcohol consumption is culinary and social. Therefore, Italian Americans have manifested relatively high rates of alcohol use, but low rates of drinking problems. Recent trends, however, suggest that problem drinking among Italian Americans has reached or slightly exceeded national averages. In the late 1970s, 19 percent of the Italian Americans in the NORC survey reported that they sometimes drink more than they think they should. In the 1990s, this percentage moved up to 27 percent.

Politics

The NORC report found that Italian Americans, like Americans in general, have moved to the right over the last two decades. "In the early 1970s, only 17 percent [of Italian Americans] were Republicans," the report notes. "This number has doubled to 35 percent presently. Most of this increase has been at the expense of the Democrats. In the early 1970s, 45 percent of Italian Americans were Democrats. This number has since fallen to 32 percent. Likewise, the identification as Independents also

Two street scenes in New York's Little Italy in the 1970s: men conversing around a table as in a village in the "old country" and a bread delivery on Mulberry Street. Italian neighborhoods like this one, in big cities, are shrinking rapidly as more and more families leave in pursuit of social and economic betterment.

slipped slightly, from 36 percent to 33 percent," the study found.

In terms of political ideology, Italian Americans increasingly identify themselves as conservatives. This political shift to the right has brought Italian Americans to the center of the political spectrum, midway between liberal Democratic groups such as Jews and Blacks, and conservative Republican groups such as British and German Americans.

Values and Attitudes

Despite a tendency toward conservative politics, Italian Americans strongly support liberal social causes. They are more permissive on sexual matters than other Americans, somewhat more approving of nontraditional roles for women, and less likely to approve corporal punishment for children. Eighty-nine percent of the Italian Americans in the NORC survey said they would vote for a woman as president; 55 percent were pro-choice; and more

than 60 percent thought that the U.S. government should spend more on health, education, and the poor.

The picture of Italian Americans that emerges differs radically from a popular and firmly established perception of Italian American families as partriarchal, authoritarian, and insular.

Psychological Well-Being

The NORC survey also found that between 1972 and 1987 Italian Americans consistently expressed significantly less general happiness than the correlated national norms. They are less likely than other Americans to report that their lives are exciting, currently ranking next to the bottom among all groups, above only African Americans.

Since 1984, Italian Americans have expressed great satisfaction with friends, ranking first among the 15 ethnic groups in this category. Since 1972, Italian Americans have not differed much from the national averages on expressions of satisfaction with their families.

The overall conclusion that emerges is that while Italian Americans do not differ greatly from other groups in terms of earning power, professional stature, and family profile, their psychological well-being tends to be lower, except for their high satisfaction with friendships.

Religious Attitudes

Italian Americans still report the second highest percentage of Roman Catholic affiliation among all groups, although the figures have dropped from 81 percent to 70 percent over the past 20 years. Their strength of religious identification and church attendance are well below national norms. Italian-American Catholics are also somewhat more likely than other Americans to express so-called "progressive and compassionate" images of the Supreme Being, seeing him as a friend rather than as a king.

The overall picture suggests that Italian Americans are not more traditionalist, authoritarian, and patriarchal than other Americans in their religious beliefs, nor are they strong traditionalists in their faith.

Summary of the NORC Study

Tom Smith, who compiled the NORC report, concluded that Italian Americans are distinctive in various ways. "In many social, family, and religious attitudes, Italian Americans are moderate liberals, not patriarchs, traditionalists, or conservatives. This shows up in their support for equal treatment of women, sexual tolerance, and other progressive values. They also favor government spending for human services. In particular, Italian Americans are strong backers of governmental health care programs," Smith said.

Smith also noted that Italian Americans valued fulfilling friendships, were more satisfied with their friends, and more likely to socialize with them than any other group.

A superficial reading of the NORC survey results may lead to the conclusions that the distinctive features of Italian-American ethnicity have vanished. One might note a few interesting, marginal differences between Italian-Americans and national norms but conclude that Italian Americans on the whole have assimilated mainstream American norms.

Certainly when we examine two cardinal indicators of social position, education and occupation, we see that Italian Americans meet or slightly exceed national norms. Such indicators are important when assessing a

The editorial office of the Philadelphia newspaper, *L'Opinione*. Like the use of the Italian language, the once numerous Italian-language newspapers are largely a thing of the past. But Italian-American magazines and newspapers do exist today, and subscribing to them helps keep our ethnic heritage alive.

group's qualifications for places in the labor market, the extent to which mainstream culture has successfully instilled dominant American values, and correlations with income and wider social prestige.

This obvious interpretation is persuasive, but it may hinder a fuller understanding of who we are. First, it ignores how ethnic groups not merely internalize dominant norms, but also influence them. Second, it obscures class differences. We are never fully identified merely by our ethnicity. Socioeconomic class, gender, religion, occupation, generation, and primary leisure-time projects, among other things, also make us who we are.

The data in the NORC survey were not broken down by generation, socioeconomic class, and gen-

der. They may paint a broad picture of contemporary Italian Americans, but they fail to address numerous questions: What social differences, if any, exist between working-class Italian Americans and professional Italian Americans? Between Italian Americans who are city dwellers and those who live in small towns? Is the only remaining robust marker of Italian-American ethnicity the blue-collar culture we see caricatured drearily in the media?

We would expect that Italian-American ethnicity would be more obvious among members of earlier generations, older cohorts, inhabitants of the remaining Little Italys in the northeast, and recent arrivals to the United States. But the foregoing data obscure our full understanding of possible differences among Italian

Americans because the information is presented, understandably, at the highest level of generality.

Preserving Our Heritage

What do we have to do to keep our Italian-American heritage alive? At a minimum, we must initiate and participate in group and family events that remember, celebrate and transmit our cultural legacy. Such events permit us to keep faith with the past and reinforce solidarity.

Other appropriate ethnic behavior can include such commonplace actions as preparing and eating our traditional dishes, participating in specific holiday rituals, studying and speaking Italian, or even spicing English speech with Italian and dialect words and phrases, teaching our children about their ethnic history and background, practicing our customs and traditions, subscribing to an Italian-American magazine, newspaper, or newsletter; going to Italian-American films and plays; and attending Italian-American festivals and celebrations.

Less common but more ethnically intense actions include residing in an Italian-American neighborhood; producing an Italian-American newspaper, magazine or play; teaching or enrolling in an Italian-American studies course; engaging in concerted ethnically based political action; partaking in Italian-American religious societies; and participating in ethnic social and cultural clubs.

Ethnic social structures, such as families, neighborhoods, cultural clubs, and political organizations sustain a vital ethnic identity that does not degenerate into weak symbolic ethnicity or mere passive acceptance of Italian-American ethnicity. Such robust ethnic behavior recognizes certain debts of gratitude and obligations of legacy to those who preceded us, who lived the immigrant experience, who fought to survive and flourish, and who paved the way for us in today's American society.

Raymond A. Belliotti is a professor of philosophy at State University of New York at Fredonia. This article is based on his most recent book, Seeking Identity: Individualism versus Community in an Ethnic Context *(University Press of Kansas, 1995),* with permission of the publisher.

Italian Americans as a Cognizable Racial Group

Dominic R. Massaro

Dominic Massaro is a Justice of the Supreme Court of New York. A "Grande Ufficiale della Repubblica Italiana," he is chairman emeritus of The Conference of Presidents of Major Italian-American Organizations. In 1991 his treatise, Cesare Beccaria—The Father of Criminal Justice: His Impact on Anglo-American Jurisprudence *(Prescia: International UP 1991), garnered Italy's International Dorso Prize. Justice Massaro is the representative of the American Judges Association to the United Nations.*

Italian Americans are a cognizable racial group for purposes of the scope and application of civil rights laws. This view is confirmed by the sophistication of sociological definition and historical evidence, which is grounded in legal analysis and judicial interpretation. There are a number of citations, quotes, and references to which I will allude, including a limited amount of previous scholarship. Let me note at the onset that Italian Americans, more often than not, take umbrage at being defined as a minority group. Yet, a review of the relevant case law suggests that in no other manner can they hope for success in advancing legal claims that allege discrimination on the basis of national origin. Traditionally, civil rights legislation has provided virtually no protection against this form of discrimination. But the decision in *Scelsa v. the City University of New York* (CUNY) decided last November in Federal District Court in Manhattan— hereinafter referred to as *Scelsa*—accents the slow but steady erosion of the artificial distinction between "race" and "national origin" that has heretofore given rise to

ethnic minorities, including Italian Americans, receiving "different treatment under the law, as written or applied."

As an aside, you should be aware of what lies behind my view of *Scelsa*. In my position [as] Human Rights Commissioner, and in response to a growing number of complaints, I threatened mandamus against CUNY in November 1971; that is, I mandated that it release a statistical breakdown of Americans of Italian descent employed throughout the university system. Twenty years later, while on the bench as a non-partisan choice, I was invited to chair the Legislative Advisory Committee on Urban Public Higher Education. The Committee's central charge was to investigate and suggest redress for discrimination against Italian Americans at CUNY. Its final report, rendered 12 September 1991, contained a series of recommendations utilizing the special expertise of CUNY's Italian American Institute aimed at "underscor[ing] the University's commitment to the richness of diversity." Within a year, the Scelsa Court observed that CUNY sought "to sever the outreach, counseling and research aspects of the Institute . . . [and] shunt aside its Director."

However, what I found particularly disturbing was that, despite two intervening decades, only negligible changes had been made to remedy the woeful underrepresentation of Italian Americans in the work force. The release of these earlier statistics became the underpinning for critical reportage, academic study, the designation of Italian Americans as an affirmative action category by CUNY (the so-called Kibbee Memorandum), and legislative inquiry. The latter culminated in public hearings and provided the backdrop for the establishment of the John D. Calandra Italian American Institute of CUNY in 1979.

From a purely legal perspective, *Scelsa* presents us with a precedent-making judicial grant of extraordinary relief to Italian Americans; not only did the case galvanize Italian-American organizations, it placed the Italian American Legal Defense and Higher Education Fund that handled the action in the forefront of civil rights activity. By its very nature, injunctive relief is an extraordinary remedy; it is grounded in equity; that is, it is responsive to the demands of justice and right conscience. The manner in which it was granted and the fact that it was granted by the *Scelsa* Court is significant. A colleague stated it rather succinctly; namely that the decision "is a delight to those who are sympathetic to the plaintiffs' position and a nightmare to those favoring the defendants."

The petitioner, Dr. Joseph V. Scelsa, filed the action in both an individual and representative capacity (as director of the Calandra Institute). As dual plaintiff, he sought to bar CUNY from accomplishing three things: (1) "from employment discrimination against Italian Americans"; (2) "from relocating the Institute and transferring its operations to several different units of CUNY"; and (3) from removing him as the Institute's director. At the heart of his brief was the averment of discrimination in employment on the basis of national origin. The statutory prohibition against this type of discrimination is specifically proscribed by Title VII of the Civil Rights Act of 1964. Notwithstanding, the prohibition has been largely ignored by the courts and rarely used with success by plaintiffs seeking redress on this ground.

The *Scelsa* Court granted all three requests (or prayers as we say) by way of a preliminary injunction *pendente lite;* that is, pending trial, it barred CUNY from acting so as to prevent the further perpetration of a perceived wrong(s) until such time as the underlying issues are resolved. It concluded that the plaintiffs (Dr. Scelsa and the Institute) had "shown a balance of hardships tipping decidedly in their favor" and "irreparable harm" would otherwise follow. Significantly, the Court allowed Dr. Scelsa, equating his position as director of the Calandra Institute with representation of the Italian-American community of New York City to cross the litigation threshold to test the merits of the case. In doing so, the Court relied not only on the so-called "disparate impact" theory of Title VII, wherein a discriminatory effect may be shown vis-à-vis employment patterns, but, *sua sponte*: by its own initiative, it also invoked Section 1981 of the Civil Rights Act of 1866, our nation's first civil rights statute for jurisdictional purposes.

This Reconstruction era statute is far wider in scope than Title VII. It concerns the right to make and enforce both private and public contracts and provides broad federal remedies for the enjoyment of all benefits of a contractual relationship. The Court noted that "in grant[ing injunctive] relief to which the party in whose favor it is rendered is entitled," it may do so on such grounds "even if the party has not [specifically] demanded such relief in the party's pleading." Section 1981 was not pleaded in the moving papers. But the Court raised CUNY's two-decade-old awareness of Italian-American nonrepresentation and the university's pledge(s) to address and seek to correct this imbalance to the level of a contractual relationship with the Italian-American community. It noted:

> A Section 1981 violation may be established not only via presentation of evidence regarding defendant's affirmative acts but also by evidence regarding defendant's omission where defendant is under some duty to act.... The Court must find that CUNY's current policy represents either an attempt to renege on the promises of the past or, by denying that such promises were ever made or intended to be kept, a reaffirmation of the original findings of discrimination against an under-representation of Italian Americans that motivated the original Kibbee Memorandum....

Cited by the *Scelsa* Court is a case entitled *St. Francis College v. Al-Khazraj*, which was decided by the United States Supreme Court five years earlier in 1987. This also is significant. Due to the representative conferral granted to Dr. Scelsa because of the Calandra Institute's wider purposes, the citation espouses, on a stage even larger than employment, an opportunity for Italian Americans as a group to redress harms arising out of national origin discrimination. Discrimination on the basis of national origin has always been, and sadly continues to be, a destructive force in American society. As such, it is indistinguishable from racial discrimination. Notwithstanding, modern day civil rights legislation expressly prohibiting discrimination based on "race, color, religion, sex or national origin," has not been interpreted either administratively or judicially to afford protection to these victims of national origin discrimination. The clear and unambiguous language set forth in Title VII as advanced in *Scelsa* states that failure by an employer because of national origin "to hire ... or otherwise to discriminate against any individual with respect to his compensation, terms, conditions, or privileges of employment" is an unlawful employment practice. Yet the Act has a history of selective enforcement and it would appear that claims of national origin discrimination—either dismissed on procedural grounds or on the merits—have met with failure. A review of the regulations charting compliance with Title VII reveal that, notwithstanding the clear reference to "national origin," redress has primarily been defined within the context of racial classification for governmental purposes. Neither racial minorities nor ethnic minorities (including Italian Americans) have "melted" into Anglo conformity. Sociologists generally agree that thus far in the American saga, "acculturation" and not "structural assimilation" has proven to be the norm; and the diversity inherent in "cultural pluralism" has persisted well into the third, even the fourth generation. Public policy misconception of the process continues to ignore this reality and the legal definition of minority continues for practical purposes to be synonymous with skin color.

In light of this, no governmental compilation of ethnic data is either required or taken; thus, legal writers rightly contend that is all but impossible to prove the existence of discrimination based on national origin. Therefore, Italian Americans who are victims of discrimination must try to prove their case without the benefit of officially compiled statistics—an overwhelming task given essential Title VII procedural requirements. The need for statistical analysis in order to fulfill the initial legal burden of going forward to establish what we term a *prima facie* case was noted in *Scelsa*; nor did CUNY, despite good faith promises extracted in the 1970s to do so, maintain ongoing data on Italian-American recruitment and employment for affirmative action purposes. However, and in view of this failure, two statistical studies compiled by the plaintiff, Calandra Institute, were deemed "the best available evidence" by the Court. The *Scelsa* Court went further. By adopting the conception of race set forth in *St. Francis College* under the 1866 law, it eased the way toward addressing not only employment but an array of civil rights violations alleging national origin discrimination against Italian Americans by CUNY.

The Civil Rights Act of 1866 was an enabling statute for the Thirteenth Amendment. This post-Civil War enactment intended to confer the equality "enjoyed by white citizens" of the time—the white majoritarian Anglo or Nordic "race" then populating the country, the standard control group, if you will—upon all other persons and in all respects. The Supreme Court's decision in *St. Francis College*, relying on the 1866 Act, significantly expanded the definition of "race" for purposes that can find and have found expression in the modern day search for equal protection under the law by those claiming national origin discrimination.

In *St. Francis College*, the Court held that a white person may be protected from racial discrimination. It based its holding on a broad construction of the original intent of Section 1981 of the 1866 Act. Section 1981 of the Act states: "All Persons . . . shall have the same right . . . to make and enforce contracts . . . and to the full and equal benefit of all laws and proceedings. . . ." The Court rejected the counter argument that a Caucasian was barred from suing other Caucasians under the statute. Instead, relying heavily on the legislative history of Section 1981 and on the general conception of race during the nineteenth century when the statute was enacted, it observed:

[It] may be that a variety of ethnic groups . . . are now considered to be within the Caucasian race. The understanding of "race" in the nineteenth century, however

was different. Plainly, all those who might be deemed Caucasian today were not thought to be of the same race at the time Section 1981 became law.

In support of this reasoning, the Court examined two strands of evidence from the nineteenth century: dictionary and encyclopedia definitions of "race" and the legislative history of Section 1981. In considering nineteenth-century definitions of race, Webster's dictionary of 1877 proved insightful: "[t]he descendants of a common ancestor; a family, tribe, people or nation, believed or presumed to belong to the same stock." The Court also listed "races" found in nineteenth-century encyclopedias: the *Encyclopedia Americana* (1858) and the *Encyclopedia Britannica* (1878) that *inter alia* referred to "Italians" and various other ethnic "races." Similarly, a review of the legislative history of Section 1981 proved convincing to the Court. It too was "replete with references to the universality of its application"; that is, to all ethnic "races." This, combined with the nineteenth-century concept of race as illustrated by reference materials of the period, formed the foundation for the Court's holding:

Based on the history of Section 1981, we have little trouble in concluding that Congress intended to protect from discrimination identifiable classes of persons who are subjected to intentional discrimination solely because of their ancestry or ethnic characteristics. Such discrimination is racial discrimination that Congress intended Section 1981 to forbid, whether or not it would be classified as racial in terms of modern scientific theory.

The Court's opinion specifically rejected reliance on genetics and/or physical characteristics:

It is clear from our holding that a distinctive physiognomy is not essential to qualify for Section 1981 protection.

In making this finding, the Court defined the word "race" in its sociological, perhaps sociopolitical, rather than biological sense. "Race" in the sociological sense considers the concept that people differ from each other not primarily because of physical attributes, but because of differences rooted in culture. A review of the legislative history of the Act reveals that its supporters intended that its protection be liberally construed, encompassing the civil liberties of all persons without distinction as between race and national origin. Interestingly, the Court's research disclosed that only in this century have "races" been divided physiognomically, that is, "Caucasoid," "Mongoloid" and "Negroid," footnoting that many modern biologists and anthropologists . . . criticize [these] classifications as arbitrary and of little use in understanding the viability of human beings."

The *Scelsa* Court found that "[d]iscrimination on the basis of national origin is encompassed within the scope of activities prohibited by Section 1981." Italian Americans have benefited from this revised standard on a number of occasions prior to *Scelsa*, although not with the same potential for a sweeping remedy. The District of Maine in *DeSalle v. Key Bank of Southern Maine* in 1988 was the first Court to hold that Italian Americans are an identifiable class entitled to maintain an action under Section 1981 for purposes of discrimination. In *DeSalle*, the plaintiff had sued his former employer, alleging breach of contract and violation of civil rights on the basis of his Italian heritage. In accordance with *St. Francis College*, the Court held that discrimination based on a plaintiff's ancestry was actionable as a civil rights claim under Section 1981. The Court highlighted the references in *St. Francis College* to various ethnic "races." It concluded:

> The definition of race in the nineteenth century, when the legislative sources for Section 1981 were enacted, differed from the definition prevalent today; not all Caucasians were considered of the same race.... Section 1981 was designed to protect identifiable classes of persons, such as Italo-Americans, "who are subjected to intentional discrimination solely because of their ancestry or ethnic characteristics...."

In one of the few cases where a plaintiff prevailed on the merits is a 1989 national origin discrimination case. The Ninth Circuit, which is based in San Francisco, held in *Benigni v. City of Hemet* that Italian Americans are protected against discrimination for purposes of a companion Section 1982 of the 1866 Act, which concerns the right to hold property. The plaintiff, an owner of a restaurant, had obtained a jury verdict claiming that the defendant's police officers had discriminatorily harassed his business and customers, forcing him to sell his business at a loss. The Court of Appeals, in upholding the verdict, agreed:

> Elements of an intentional discrimination claim ... are present in this case because the evidence tends to show the discriminatory effect of greater law enforcement activity at [the plaintiff's business] than at other bars, and the discriminatory intent of singling out Benigni based on his Italian ancestry.

The Court cited *St. Francis College* for the interrelated proposition: "targets of race discrimination for purposes of Section 1981 include groups that today are considered merely different ethnic or national groups."

In another context, the Supreme Court has ruled that peremptory challenges in jury selection may not be used to further racially discriminatory motives. Under existing case law, a defendant must establish that he is "a member of a cognizable racial group" to make a *prima facie* or initial showing of discriminatory peremptory challenges. In 1989, *United States v. Biaggi* treated the issue. A motion to set aside a verdict on the ground that the prosecution had used its peremptory challenges discriminatorily to exclude Italian Americans from the jury was brought. In his moment of defeat, Mario Biaggi, the senior United States Congressman from New York City provided yet another service to an Italian-American constituency that extended well beyond the confines of his congressional district. Relying on characteristic Italian names ending in vowels to make the claim, it was argued that the prosecution had exercised certain peremptory challenges solely to strike potential Italian-American jurors. The Court held that Italian Americans constitute a "cognizable racial group" for purposes of raising objections to this form of challenge. The *Biaggi* decision followed two strands of reasoning: The first traced the meaning of "racially cognizable group"; the second traced the meaning of this term in light of *St. Francis College*. As to the first strand, the Court found:

> Italian Americans are "recognizable" and "distinct," and appear to have been "singled out for different treatment under the laws, as written or applied...." Italian Americans share a common ancestry in Italy, a common cultural and religious heritage here and there, and they often still share a common language. They are identifiable, in part, by their characteristic last names. The Court takes judicial notice that Italian Americans are considered in this district to be a recognizable and distinct ethnic group, commonly identified by their last names and by their neighborhoods. These qualities are sufficient to render Italian Americans no less cognizable than the other groups who have already been recognized for equal protection purposes.

The Court referred to three criteria useful in finding Italian Americans a cognizable racial group. They "(1) are definable and limited by some clearly identifiable factor; (2) share a common thread of attitudes, ideas or experiences; and (3) share a community of interests, such that the group's interests cannot be adequately represented if the group is excluded from the jury selection process."

Limiting its holding to the Eastern District of New York, which is based in Brooklyn, the Court held that Italian Americans satisfy these criteria to make "a sufficient showing to categorize [themselves] as cognizable." Moreover, it provided a detailed and illuminating discussion of its reasons for taking judicial notice of Italian Americans' cognizability:

> These observable, distinguishable names constitute a clearly identifiable factor separating Italian Americans from most other ethnic groups. These names emanate from Italian ancestors who immigrated to this country and who constitute a discrete resource from which Italian-American heritage has been passed down.
>
> Italian Americans share a common experience and background in their links to Italian families, Italian culture, and Italian group loyalties, and often share the same religious and culinary practices. The Court takes judicial notice that Italians have been subject to stereotyping, invidious ethnic humor and discrimination (" ... Italians ... continue to be excluded from executive, middle-management, and other job levels because of discrimination based upon their religion and/or national origin").... Like any group recently emigrated from a cohesive na-

tion, Italian Americans share numerous common *threads* of attitudes, ideas, and experiences, often including largely intertwined family relations in the country of origin. Finally Italian Americans have a community of interest; they generally share certain cherished values received through generations of Italian civilization and religion, including values relevant to moral culpability. Across the board exclusion of this group could not but impair the representation of these interests in juries.

Having concluded that Italian Americans are a cognizable racial group, the Court recounted *St. Francis College's* review of the nineteenth-century scholarly definitions of race and the legislative history of the 1866 Act. As to this second strand of reasoning, it found that the [l]egislative history of post–Civil War statutes provides corroborative support for the view that, at that time, "races" included "immigrant groups" coming from each foreign nation and, further, "[i]t can therefore be confi+

The *Biaggi* decision has since been cited with approval. Although the Court did accept the prosecution's racially neutral explanations for exercising the peremptory challenges, and denied the motion to set aside the guilty verdict, the decision is still crucial. It admirably recognizes discrimination against Italian Americans in various aspects of American society. Additionally it highlights for us that as an ethnic group, "Italian Americans are also shielded by the [Fourteenth Amendment's] equal protection clause's prohibition against discrimination because of ancestry."

In sum, Section 1981 grounds for seeking relief in cases of national origin discrimination illustrate a definite trend; namely an expanded equal protection jurisprudence where race can be and, in fact, has been equated with ethnicity or national origin. The Section provides an effective vehicle where injustice or inequity prevails against ethnic minorities. Moreover, Section 1981 filings are neither limited to the employment arena nor burdened with detailed procedural requirements that are a prerequisite to filings under modern-day civil rights legislation. Ethnics who have suffered discrimination as a result of their national origin in any area, would be well served in seeking judicial solicitude by alleging discrimination based on "race" under this statute—either alone or in conjunction with other statutory remedies.

In seeking social justice where right or entitlement within a sphere of cultural pluralism is denied, servitude in any form is alien to the espousal of a philosophy based on mutual respect and tolerance for differences. Indeed, it has been argued that the theory of Anglo conformity is inherently discriminatory: it requires assimilation into a majoritarian culture and inferentially emarginates other legitimate forms of cultural expression. Section 1981 relief, as we have seen from a reading of *Scelsa*, provides a wide avenue to redress this form of coercion. At the very least, it should suffice to assist plaintiffs who allege national origin discrimination in crossing the litigation threshold to test the merits of their cause before the Courts.

WORK CITED

Scelsa v. the City University of New York, 806 F. Supp. 1126 (S.D.N.Y, 1992).
St. Francis College v. Al-Kharaj, 481 US. 604 (1987).
DeSalle v. Key Bank of Southern Maine, 685 F. Supp. 282 (D. Me., 1988).
Benigni v. City of Hemet, 879 F. 2d 472 (9th Cir., 1989).
United States v. Biaggi, 673 F. Supp. 96 (E.D.N.Y, 1989).

The Blind Spot of Multiculturalism: America's Invisible Literature

Works by American writers in other languages have the potential to challenge the national and linguistic boundaries within which literature is often studied.

By Werner Sollors

NO MATTER WHERE WE STAND IN the canon wars, we assume that we know the outlines of American literature. But do we?

Consider the following excerpt from an American novel of the 1850s, in which the narrator comments: "A reliable writer from ancient Greece tells us that women once lived on the island of Lesbos who did not permit any man to touch them, since a whim of nature had given them the gift of being contented with each other." Then the following amorous dialogue ensues between two young women—Orleana (who has just been harassed by a drunken immigrant) and Claudine de Lessure (who has just left her husband):

"Do you really love me, Claudine?"

"Oh, how the fresh warmth of your proud neck confuses me! . . ."

"Claudine, Claudine, how tightly you are corseted!"

"Orleana, Orleana, how easily your clothes fall down!"

"Claudine, Claudine, how hard it is for me to get these things off!"

"Orleana, how pure and white your shoulders are!"

The dialogue is fairly sexually explicit, interrupted only by the narrator's explanatory comments claiming that this type of relationship between women may have been widespread in midcentury New Orleans. The chapter is entitled "Lesbian Love" and is taken from Ludwig von Reizenstein's little-known novel *The Mysteries of New Orleans*, serialized in a New Orleans newspaper in 1854 and 1855. As far as I know, this work is unlike anything else in American fiction of the period. But, until recently, it has been ignored by literary scholars—as have numerous other works.

For instance, many scholars now are interested in American slave narratives, but who has heard of Omar ibn Said? Yet his 1831 narrative—*The Life of Omar Ben Saeed, called Morro, a Fullah Slave in Fayetteville, N.C., owned by Garrison Owen*—is an early autobiographical document by an American slave in North Carolina, unfiltered by abolitionist rhetoric. Unlike Frederick Douglass—who, 14 years later, would represent the drama of his struggle against slavery in metaphors of Christian rebirth and draw an analogy between his search for freedom and his quest for literacy—Omar ibn Said draws on the Islamic education he received in Senegambia, in West Africa. He opens his narrative with chapters from the Koran and does not directly criticize slavery, but he complains about the man who bought him in Charleston: "a small, weak, and wicked man, called Johnson, a complete infidel, who had no fear of God at all." How many other Muslim slaves left written accounts of the New World? Would their perspectives challenge some generalizations about slavery in America?

And who among the many readers interested in women's literature today knows the memorable character Astrid Holm, the daughter of a stern businessman and a melancholy actress, who follows her father from Norway to Minnesota after her mother's death? In the 1887 novel *A Saloonkeeper's Daughter*, the Norwegian-born author Drude Krog Janson depicts Holm's attempt to make a life in a setting where none of the Old World maxims seem to apply anymore. The novel's lyrical style anticipates aspects of Kate Chopin's 1899 *The Awakening*, and the ending presents the companionship among women that some modern readers have wished to find in Zora Neale Hurston's 1937 *Their Eyes Were Watching God.*

WHAT do the three 19th-century texts that I have cited have in common, apart from the fact that they are relatively unknown, even to scholars who study American literature and culture? All were written in the United States, but in languages other than English—in German, Arabic, and Norwegian, respectively. The languages of these texts have excluded them from "American literature," for how could a work be considered "American" if it was written in a language that most Americans could not, and still cannot, read? At the same time, the texts' American settings and themes have excluded them from "German," "Arabic," or "Norwegian" literature. Yet works such as these have the potential to transform our understanding of both American literature and the literature of other nations—and even to challenge the national and linguistic boundaries within which literature is often studied.

In its explicit depiction of lesbian love, for example, Reizenstein's work is not merely different from anything in American literature of its time; it is also unlike German fiction of the period. Is there something in the transnational character of the works that may make their authors bolder than those situated firmly in one culture and language?

Omar ibn Said wrote his narrative in the Arabic of West Africa: His usage is rusty, and his Arabization of American place names (Fayd-il for Fayetteville) and an English-language cover page give his text more of a bilingual than a monolingual tone. The manuscript seems to be at home neither in the United States nor in the Arab-speaking world, even as it links elements of both.

Janson's novel contains some familiar themes of American-immigrant fiction: the differences between the Old World and the New, generational conflict between immigrant parents and children, the difficulties of courtship by "American" suitors. Yet the novel also has a specifically Scandinavian aura in its pervasive allusions to the ogres of Norse mythology and its evocation, in Astrid's love for the stage, of a particularly Norwegian ideal of serious dramatic art. Published in Copenhagen and Minneapolis, the novel calls attention to its transnational character in its original title, *En Saloonkeepers Datter*, which sandwiches an English term between two Norwegian words.

My three examples are hardly rare or exceptional. They are part of an enormous, largely uncharted, and invisible body of literature that one editor termed "non-English literature of the United States." A good number of the works were published before the founding of the United States, in colonies and territories that would later become part of the United States, in such languages as Spanish, Dutch, French, and Russian. Ironically, the long-outdated literary histories of American writing—from the *Cambridge History of American Literature* (1919) to the *Literary History of the United States* (1946)—offered a fuller treatment of American writing in "foreign languages" (a charged term, of course) than do comparable histories or anthologies published more recently.

The difference is all the more glaring because electronic library catalogues have made it far easier to do bibliographic research that can reveal how much of this work exists. In Harvard University's Widener Library alone, for example, a data-base search produced a list of more than 120,000 titles published in the United States in scores of languages other than English. These include works in many American Indian languages, as well as virtually every tongue spoken in the United States.

Who can say how many examples of aesthetically intriguing works such as Janson's novel, how many telling historical sources like Said's autobiography, and how many culturally fascinating scenes like that in Reizenstein's "Lesbian Love" are waiting to be rediscovered?

I first came across such texts 20 years ago, when I was assigned to write a broad comparative essay on "Literature and Ethnicity" for the *Harvard Encyclopedia of American Ethnic Groups* (1980). It became obvious to me that the essay would have to mention American Indian languages, French and Spanish texts from New World colonies, and immigrant literature in many tongues. That seemed natural to me.

After all, I did not grow up speaking English, and the first "American language" I studied at age 9 was (a no-doubt imaginary) Apache, the secret language that my cousin and I had memorized from the dialogues between Winnetou and Nscho-Tschi in Karl May's novels. (Later, when I began to learn English in my German high school, I was drawn to such "English" words as "wigwam" and "pow-wow.") After moving to New York in the 1970s, I became accustomed to children who asked each other what their "other language" was, and I studied the Spanish, Korean, and Chinese versions of such questions as "Do you need your diaper changed?" that were posted on the bathroom wall at my son's day-care center. Entering the many shops and little restaurants in which newspapers, posters, and broadsides were displayed, some printed in languages to which I had no clue, I got a sense of what the Romanian immigrant author Konrad Bercovici meant when he wrote *Around the World in Manhattan* (1924). That book takes readers to such places as Syria, Greece, China, and Africa—all without leaving New York City.

My essay for the encyclopedia (twice as long as had been requested) turned into the book *Beyond Ethnicity: Consent and Descent in American Culture* (1986). But, even though I did discuss examples of American writing in other languages in the book, I did not make language itself a central issue. Yet as I worked on the book, I was surprised by the relative neglect of the intersection of ethnicity and language by scholars in American studies and comparative literature. In the past 20 years, scholars have come to pay much attention to race, gender, and ethnicity; yet they have tended to ignore language as a defining part of American culture. I find this a prime blind spot in multiculturalism.

T ODAY, I'm happy to say, interest in the language issue is increasing among scholars. For example, the Longfellow Institute at Harvard, with which I am affiliated, was set up to stimulate new research in the subject, and during the past few years, the Andrew W. Mellon Foundation has helped the institute bring together an international and remarkably polyglot group of scholars and students to discuss non-English literature of the United States. A few panels at scholarly meetings have discussed this topic as well, and some works are being translated into English for publication in a new series.

Some recent research has been pulled together in a volume that I edited, published in August—*Multilingual America*. In it, scholars lay out some of the key questions that need to be asked. Why has intellectual life in the United States become so exceptionally monolingual? What has happened to the languages of America? What was it that brought about an end to many of them? Bans in schools on using languages other than English? The xenophobia engendered by World War I? Or the persistent cultural pressure to assimilate? And why are American students less and less familiar with languages other than English, even as the immigrant population grows? What would happen to literary study if works in "minority languages" were routinely included in national literary histories? Do we have to rethink what translations are, when we are dealing with bilingual texts and works in a mixture of languages?

We are just at the beginning of what is a daunting enterprise, but the moment seems right to undertake it. In our present transnational age, for example, the director John Sayles's new movie, *Men with Guns (Hombres Armados)*, was produced in the United States, but its dialogue is largely in Spanish and in American Indian languages, with only a few words of English spoken by American tourists. It may be that the end of the Cold War, the increased migration of people, and the growing need for international communication will combine to bring about the end of the fear of foreign languages in the United States.

In such a context, studying multilingual America may be a first step taking us not only "around the world in American literature," but also toward a literature without national boundaries.

Werner Sollors is professor of English and Afro-American studies, and chair of the American-civilization program, at Harvard University. He is the editor of Multilingual America: Transnationalism, Ethnicity, and the Languages of American Literature *(New York University Press, 1988).*

Mr. Dybek's Neighborhood: Toward a New Paradigm for Ethnic Literature

by Thomas Gladsky[1]

The difficulty of defining, describing, or even locating the ethnic writer appears to grow increasingly more troublesome. Even a casual glance at the introduction to *Ethnic Perspectives in American Literature*[2] reveals the problem. Turf wars, biological insiderism, and questions of definition haunt the essays offered in this 1985 collection of ethnic literary histories. The issue of authenticity, raised most recently in connection with Forrest Carter's *The Education of Little Tree*,[3] continues to complicate matters. In addition, current thinking about ethnic literature continues to be influenced by theoretical models that do not apply evenly to all ethnic groups and historical periods. Daniel Aaron's influential essay "The Hyphenate Writer and American Letters"[4] exemplifies this situation. Reflecting an opinion that had almost became axiomatic by the 1960s, Aaron confidently divides ethnic literature into three stages or phases. He describes the earliest ethnic writer as a "kind of local colorist," aiming to humanize stereotypes and win sympathy. In stage two, ethnic writers "lash out at the restrictions" and incur the risk of "double criticism." In the third stage, according to Aaron, the ethnic writer passes "from the periphery to the center" while continuing to possess a "double vision."[5] As Thomas Ferraro points out, Aaron's paradigm is rooted in the aesthetics of universality and modernism and in a commitment to the notion of literary evolution.[6] Moreover, his model fits only those groups which have a literary history that spans generations and that includes a substantial body of immigrant literature. In the case of cultural groups relatively new to the United States—Caribbean peoples, Southeast Asians, immigrants from the Indian subcontinent, or Euro-ethnics who have not developed a literary voice—this kind of paradigm presents difficulties. So too does the more recent effort of Werner Sollors to discuss literary ethnicity through consent and descent models.[7]

American writers of Polish descent are a case in point. Since the 1830s when Poles began to arrive in measurable numbers, the Polish experience has been chronicled almost exclusively by host-culture writers from Samuel Knapp, Willie Triton, Edith Minitier and Nelson Algren to such recent, influential works as James Michener's *Poland* and William Styron's *Sophie's Choice*.[8] Only since the 1960s have significant numbers of writers of Polish descent turned to their own ethnicity for material; and only recently have writers such as W. S. Kuniczak, Anthony Bukoski, Gary Bildner, Darryl Poniscan, Anne Pellowski, Richard Bankowsky, and Stuart Dybek begun to receive deserved recognition as the literary voice of an American cultural group.[9]

Unfortunately, Sollors' call to move beyond ethnicity—to interpret literary ethnicity through non-inclusive

---

[1]Thomas Gladsky is Dean of Graduate Studies at Central Missouri State University in Warrensburg, Missouri.

[2]Edward Ifkovic and Robert J. DiPietro, eds. *Ethnic Perspectives in American Literature* (New York, 1985).

[3]Forrest Center, *The Education of Little Tree.*

[4]Daniel Aaron, "The Hyphenate Writer and American Letters," *Smith Alumnae Quarterly* (July 1964), pp. 213–217.

[5]Carter, p. 214.

[6]Thomas J. Ferraro, "Avante-Garde Ethnics," in William Boelhower, ed., *The Future of American Modernism: Ethnic Writing Between the Wars* (Amsterdam, 1990), p. 18. In this article, Ferraro tries to reconcile modernism and ethnicity by examining Henry Roth and Henry Miller. In the process, he warns that Aaron assumes that modernism and universality are synonymous.

[7]See Werner Sollors, *Beyond Ethnicity* (New York, 1986), p. 198.

[8]Samuel L. Knapp, *The Polish Chiefs* (New York, 1832); Willie Triton, *The Fisher Boy* (Boston, 1857); Edith Minitier, *Our Natupski Neighbors* (New York, 1916); Nelson Algren, *Never Come Morning* (New York, 1942); James Michener, *Poland* (New York, 1983); William Styron, *Sophie's Choice* (New York, 1979).

[9]This is not to say that writers of Polish descent did not exist prior to the 1960s; but the publications of contemporary writers I have named and those included in anthologies such as *Of My Blood* (1980) and John Minczeski, ed., *Concert at Chopin's House* (St. Paul, 1987) indicate that a literary movement may be blossoming.

From *The Polish Diaspora: Selected Essays*, Columbia University Press, 1993, pp. 129-135. Reprinted by permission by East European Monographs.

models—tends to diffuse this literary phenomenon. As the first generation ready to record its own ethnic experience, contemporary writers of Polish descent must first make literary history before they can move beyond it. Without a recognizable literary tradition of their own and separated by considerable time and distance from their cultural roots, they must establish ethnic identity even while distancing themselves from it. They must bridge the chasm between modernity and the eccentricities of ethnicity, and they must balance between typicality and atypicality. They must, in addition, characterize both old and new ethnicities and transform the ethnic past, ethnic memories so to speak, into representations of the post-modern self in a trans-ethnic landscape. The literary ethnicity that results in such cases may be disappointing to readers who would look for an ethnic self frozen in images of first-generation transplant or in literary forms associated with the immigrant generation. Readers and scholars alike might also wonder what kind of ethnicity they are encountering, especially one which appears to renounce self-consciousness, cultural ethnocentrism, and traditional ethnic markers.

Although one might "read" a number of current ethnic writers this way, the work of Stuart Dybek represents both the limitations of traditional paradigms of ethnic literature and the special circumstances of the contemporary Euro-ethnic writer who resists such categories. Unlike many of his colleagues, Dybek is rather difficult to classify. Some readers associate him with region; some with issues of social class. A goodly number of the stories in *Childhood and Other Neighborhoods* and *The Coast of Chicago*,[10] his two collections of fiction, have no visible ethnic dimension. Other do. In some ethnicity hovers only along the edges, either in the form of urban trans-ethnicity or in the specific but shadowy outlines of Polishness and Polonia. His reviewers appear reluctant, however, to refer to Dybek's ethnic dimension despite the fact that he has from time to time connected his artistry to his Polish decent[11]; and despite the fact that most of his stories are set in ethnic Chicago neighborhoods where many of the characters have a Polish heritage of some degree or another.

Even so, Dybek's stories can hardly be described as "classic" examples of ethnic fiction. For one thing, the period of immigration has long ago ended for the people in his neighborhood. Consequently, he does not offer examples of assimilation and acculturation or generational conflict; nor are his protagonists defending their Old World heritage, or preserving ethnic rites of passage. For another, Dybek's protagonists—young, urban, outsiders—know little, if anything, about Poland or the cultural nuances of the immigrant generation from which they are descended. Moreover, Dybek ignores traditional cultural markets such as language, foods, religious feasts, folk music, dance, and allusions to Old World history and legend—all of which mark both host-culture literature about Polish Americans as well

as the work of earlier descent writers such as Monica Krawczyk, Helen Bristol and Victoria Janda. In what sense then, one might ask, does Dybek draw upon his ethnic roots and how does he represent the ethnicity of Americans far removed from their native grounds? What kind of ethnic literature is Dybek writing, if in fact we may even call it ethnic?

To begin to answer these questions, we must first recognize that as a contemporary writer of Polish descent, Dybek does not fit into the particular stages described by Aaron as appropriate to, let us say, Jewish American writers. On the contrary, Dybek operates on all three stages simultaneously. In other words, he must, of necessity, function as a local colorist, as a critic of both the ethnic experience and the mainstream culture, and as a writer who manages to stand one foot within the mainstream, the other on its edge.

To be sure, in Dybek's fiction ethnicity is a distinct and recognizable presence, in part because he supplies enough cultural details to establish particularity. On one level, he is a local colorist-information giver. For example, his characters have names like Swantek, Marzek, Vukovich, Kozak, and Gowumpe. Even those with Anglo names have a Polish frame of reference: grandmothers named Busha, churches named St. Stanislaus. Relatives call soup *zupa*; the neighbors listen to the *Frankie Yankovitch Polka Hour*; passers-by stammer in foreign-sounding English. In a few stories, Dybek "introduces" the Polish experience in ways similar to host-culture writers like Edna Ferber, Karl Harriman, and Russell Janney.[12] For example, in "Chopin in Winter," Dzia Dzia tells his young grandson about the music and life of Chopin and his own trek from Kraków to Gdansk to avoid being drafted into the Tsarist army, and in "Blood Soup," Dybek builds his story around peasant cuisine, mysticism, and old country temperament.[13] In virtually all his stories, Dybek artfully introduces some aspects of Polish culture even in those ostensibly about non-ethnic concerns. Here and there we run into *mazurkas*, Polish diminutives, Paderewski, Our Lady of Czestochowa, *babushkas*, and DPs, the standard reference for Old World Poles. Yet neither his characters nor narrators refer to themselves as Polish or Polish American. Polishness is understood and assumed; ethnicity, to paraphrase Carlos

---

[10]Stuart Dybek, *Childhood and Other Neighborhoods* (New York, 1986); Stuart Dybek, *The Coast of Chicago* (New York, 1991).

[11]Interestingly enough, Dybek's reviewers have concentrated on style, noting the grotesque, the bizarre, the fantastical, and the dark in his two collections of short stories, *Childhood and Other Neighborhoods* and *The Coast of Chicago*. Dybek has also been linked to regionalism—a Chicago writer in the style of Nelson Algran, as Howard Kaplan describes him. Dybek admits, in addition, to having more than a passing "interest in class."

[12]See, for example, Edna Ferber, *American Beauty* (New York, 1931); Karl Harriman, *The Homebuilders* (New York?, 1903); Russell Janney, *The Miracle of the Bells* (New York, 1946). All of these rely heavily on peasant folklore, stereotypical cultural characteristics, and the icons of Polish legend and history.

[13]See Dybek, "Chopin in Winter" and "Blood Soup."

Bulosan, is in the heart,[14] as Dybek implies that the postmodern ethnic self needs few labels and little or no introduction.

If anything, Dybek shows a generation resisting its ethnic impulses even as it rushes toward them. In one sense his young protagonists are not ethnic at all but modernists who, like Stephen Daedalus or Prufrock, wander city streets content with their own alienation and superior to the urban blight and social chaos that surround them. They are loners, eccentrics, budding intellectuals. They have no conscious sense of themselves as Polish American or as ethnic. They are consumed instead with adolescence, environment, friends, with life in deteriorating and changing southside Chicago. They prefer Kerouac, the White Sox, Edward Hopper and rock music to Sigismund, Silesia, and *szczowiowa*. Dybek best captures their state of mind in their rejection of Polish mysticism and parochial education. Frequently, he gives us post-adolescents turning their backs on the religion of their ancestors. The narrator in "The Woman Who Fainted" complains that "Perhaps I had already attended too many masses . . . and had come to resent the suffering, death, and, even more, the fear underlying religion."[15] In "Visions of Budhardin," the protagonist, in a rage of pent-up resentment, ravages the church which so callously ignored his childhood needs. But Marzek, in "Sauerkraut Soup," speaks for all Dybek's disillusioned Polish Catholics when he says: "I had already developed my basic principle of Catholic education—the Double Reverse: *(1) suspect what they teach you; (2) study what they condemn.*"[16] Marzek's statement serves not only as an indicator of protest and revolt, but also as a sign of the distance between the ethnicity of his generation and that of his immigrant ancestors who, "dressed in black coats and babushkas . . . sustained the intensity of their grief."[17] In this fashion Dybek functions as a critic of the perceived provinciality of his ethnic Chicago neighborhood.

Dybek's young ethnics are not happy. They thrive on melancholy, feast on loneliness, inhabit the "hourless times of night."[18] They are refugees from Edward Hooper's *Nighthawks.*[19] At the same time, they are acutely aware that they ache for something they cannot name "but knew was missing," as the narrator of "The River" phrases it; and that "things are gone they couldn't remember, but missed; and things were gone they weren't sure ever were there."[20] In part theirs is a rembrance of youthful things past. Dybek also implies, however, that this loss also involves the cultural past. For one thing, a reverential relationship between Old World Poles and their ethnic grandchildren occurs frequently in the stories. In "Blood Soup," "Chopin in Winter," and "The Apprentice," youngsters listed to, observe, attend to and assimilate cultural mores. As the title of "The Apprentice" implies, Stefan is initiated into grandfather's sense of history, displacement, fatalism, and the strangeness that defines the Polish temperament in Dybek's fic-

tion. For another, Dybek continually laments the disappearance of the Polish southside. As the narrator of "Blight" phrases it, "I was back in my neighborhood, but lost."[21]

Ethnicity is complex, pervasive, and dynamic in these stories. The neighborhood defies traditional national boundaries. In "The River," a Ukrainian kid fiddles a nocturne. The girl in "Laughter" is Greek. The upstairs neighbors in "Chopin in Winter" speak Czech. The eccentric teacher in "Farwell" comes from Odessa. Chicanos are almost as prevalent as Poles. The multi-cultural society that surfaces is, in fact, trans-ethnicity in the making. Dybek's protagonists are not Poles; they are not even Polish American by traditional definition. To paraphrase Michael Fischer, they have, paradoxically reinvented and reinterpreted themselves.[22] Theirs is a new identity—in part a fusion of consent and descent perfectly captured in a conversation between Dzia Dzia and his grandson in "Chopin in Winter." Grandfather is teaching the boy about the music of Chopin and mentions that Paderewski dearly loved Chopin. The boy, however, does not know Paderewski, a sign of his distance from his cultural heritage. Instinctively, Grandfather connects their dual heritages by asking, "Do you know who's George Washington, who's Joe Dimaggio, who's Walt Disney? . . . Paderewski was like them, except he played Chopin. . . . See, deep down inside, Lefty, you know more than you think."[23]

Lefty and all of Dybek's protagonists do indeed know more than they think. They know that ethnicity in America never stands still; that Polishness differs from generation to generation, and that when all is said and done "what they are" does not really matter in terms of the past. On a number of occasions Dybek looks at the new urban ethnic who accepts ethnicity while rejecting nationality. In "Hot Ice," for example, Eddie Kapusta arrives at this insight: "Most everything from that world had changed or disappeared, but the old women had endured—Polish, Bohemian, Spanish, he knew it didn't matter; they were the same . . . a common pain of loss seemed to burn at the core of their lives."[24] And in the same story, Eddie further discounts the significance of national origins when he admits to himself, "Manny could be talking Spanish; I could be talking Polish. . . . It didn't matter. What meant something was sitting at the table together."[25]

---

[14]See Carlos Bulosan's autobiography, *America Is in the Heart* (Seattle, 1943). Bulosan talks about America in metaphysical terms as a state of mind to immigrants and even the icons of Polish legend and history.
[15]Dybek, *Chicago*, p. 120.
[16]Dybek, *Childhood*, p. 127.
[17]Dybek, *Chicago*, pp. 154–155.
[18]*Ibid.*, p. 84.
[19]Edward Hopper, *Nighthawks.*
[20]Dybek, *Chicago*, p. 25.
[21]*Ibid.*, p. 71.
[22]See Werner Sollors, *The Invention of Ethnicity* (New York, 1989). p. xi.
[23]Dybek, *Chicago*, pp. 20–21.
[24]*Ibid.*, p. 154.
[25]*Ibid.*, p. 151.

In Dybek's fiction Chicanos and Americans of Polish descent often "sit at the table together": Ray Cruz and the narrator in "The Palatski Man," Eddie Kapusta, Manny, and Pancho in "Hot Ice," Ziggy, Pepper Rosado and the narrator in "Blight." The commingling of Latino and Slav is economic and sociological more than cultural—a product of shifting urban people and resulting neighborhood changes, the result of shared environment and social class. From this a new sense of ethnicity—an emblem of contemporary America—arises. On the surface, the new ethnicity appears to be nothing more than the camaraderie of friends thrown together by demographics. In reality, the union of Pole and Chicano represents the changing face of America and of Polish Americanness. Stanley Rosado is Pepper to some and Stashu to others, reflecting his Mexican father and Polish mother. When David, the descendant of Poles, goes to a bar with a friend, he drinks a Coco-Nana rather than vodka or *piwo* [beer]. The Mexican music on the jukebox sounds "suspiciously like polkas." David now listens to *"CuCuRuCuCu Palano"* on the radio, and Eddie Kapusta sings in Spanish. Tellingly, Eddie identifies more with Spanish than he does with the Polish language. He is stuck with the word *juilota* pigeon. It seems the perfect word because in it "he could hear both their cooing and the whistling rush of their wings." Equally telling, Eddie cannot remember "any words like that in Polish, which his grandma had spoken to him when he was little."[26] Eddie's relatives may likely turn out to be Hispanic in the sense that Richard Rodriguez, in *Hunger and Memory*, believes that he may become Asian.[27]

The Polish ethnic self, also addressed recently by Gary Gildner in *The Warsaw Sparks*,[28] assumes what some may regard as a strange identity. And Dybek emerges as a writer who eludes and absorbs traditional paradigms while suggesting a new one. To be sure, he does write about an identifiable ethnic group, supplying the preciousness of local color among the way. He is, at the same time, eager to resist the parochialism of ethnicity. His characterization of his young protagonists as romantic rebels, updated versions of Keats, Proust, Dosteyevsky and others whom they read, also leads him away from ethnic realism even though his fiction is rooted in region and in the cultural neighborhoods of southside Chicago. Without consciously trying, Dybek encompasses all three of Aaron's stages, functioning as a spokesperson for all generations of Americans of Polish descent and producing a multi-layered and multi-dimensional ethnic self. This self reflects the image of a trans-ethnic, transcends national origins but remains vital and where the ethnic and the modern self are not only compatible as Ferraro would argue, but are the essence of post-modernism and "a way of being American," as Andrew Greeley puts it.[29]

[26]*Ibid.*, p. 136.

[27]Richard Rodriguez, *Hunger of Memory* (Boston, 1982). Rodriguez speculates at one point about the course of American demographics and applies the changing cultural face of the nation to his own situation. He wonders if his presence in an Asian community might not naturally and inevitably lead to Asian descendants.

[28]Gary Gildner, *The Warsaw Sparks* (Iowa City, 1990).

[29]Andrew Greeley, "Is Ethnicity Unamerican?" *New Catholic World*, Vol. 219 (June 1976), pp. 106–112. Greeley disposes of the notion that ethnicity is "unamerican," arguing instead that ethnicity as Americanness is a "critically important phenomenon" (p. 111).

Unit Selections

Key Points to Consider

❖ Does the paucity of immigrant diversity in the South, except for Texas and Florida, and the substantial number of African Americans in all southern states explain the cultural content and intergroup dynamics of the South? Why or why not?

❖ In your opinion, are the issues of the South associated with the entire country? Explain.

❖ Does the 1998 racially motivated tragedy and murder of African American James Byrd Jr. in Jasper, Texas, revive images of lynchings? Expand your answer.

❖ What impact does the grouping of people into divisions such as black/white have? For self-identification? For government policy? For the law? For understanding pluralism in America?

❖ What stereotypes of American regions have you encountered? Discuss the tension between regional and universal values. Are universal human aspirations discoverable in regional forms? What prompts the divisions among persons from various traditions and prompts the capacity to overcome ethnic and racialist exclusion?

❖ Does whiteness provide a cultural legacy comparable to other ethnicities? If so, why do so few Americans identify themselves as "white"?

 **Links**   **www.dushkin.com/online/**

These sites are annotated on pages 4 and 5.

Ethnicity is often associated with immigrants and with importation of culture, language, stories, and foods from foreign shores. Appalachian, western, and other regional ethnicities are evidence of multigenerational ethnic cultural development within the American reality. The persistent, ongoing process of humanities expressed locally in unique and intriguing folkways, dialects, languages, myths, festivals, food displays, and other enduring monuments and visable signs of the past and public dimension of cultural consciousness that constitutes ethnicity. As this unit's articles illustrate, ethnic experiences may be less foreign and alien than most imagine them to be.

The American South has experienced considerably less immigration and undergone less urbanization than

Orne Jewett, Alice Walker, Flannery O'Connor, Maya Angelou, Robert Penn Warren, John Crowe Ransom, and Cleanth Brooks fashioned profound interpretative ground upon which fuller understanding of this regional clustering of group relations rests. This collection of articles is but a current aspect of this large tapestry. Moreover, southern culture has unique contemporary forms such as the emergence into the mainstream of Cajun/Acadian music and food, the claims of the revival of military tradition, and a form of revolutionary, political honor found in the New Republicanism of Newt Gingrich. An interesting demographic feature of the 73rd Congressional District that formed the core of his new Republican majority was its scant immigrant population.

The selection of articles included in this unit express

Percentage of Region	South	North-east	Mid-west	West
German	17.1	19.5	37.7	20.7
Irish	15.2	18.5	16.2	12.7
African-American	15.1	7.2	8.2	4.4
English/British	13.8	11.6	12.2	15.4
American/USA	9.2	—	3.7	2.6
Native American	4.8	1.5	3.2	3.7
Mexican	4.4	—	1.7	3.7
French	3.5	5.2	4.4	3.9
Scotch/Irish	3.1	1.5	1.8	2.2
Italian	2.9	14.8	4.1	4.3
Dutch	2.1	2.0	3.6	2.5
Scottish	2.1	—	1.9	2.7
Polish	1.6	6.9	5.8	2.0
White	1.1	—	—	1.0
Swedish	0.8	1.3	3.1	2.8
Acadian/Cajun	0.7	—	—	—

Source: 1990 U.S. Census

the North. Its persistent small towns, its ethos of agriculture, its rurality, and its isolation and independence from currents of northern intellectual and literary expression rooted in other traditions have differentiated its culture and arts and architecture, its folkways and learning. The South, unlike New England and much of the northern industrial states, has deeper ambiguities about the uprooting force of bourgeois and market-driven universalism. The absence of large-scale immigration and urbanization has limited its historical experience with diversity and pluralism. Southern regional culture is not homogeneous but does have embedded in it a particularity that is well worth exploring in more detail for its impact on ethnic and racial group formation. Their interaction in the context of the southern experience and the process of separation and integration is unique. The contextual character of group relations is well established in the social sciences as a powerful explanatory variable. In fact ethnicity as a local identity may be utterly and entirely contextual. The ongoing emergence of southern cultural and social histories produced by Lewis P. Simpson and Joel Williamson and the ongoing impact of the works of William Faulkner, Toni Morrison, Sarah

aspects of the southern legacy that includes the American founding, the strong experience of slavery and race consciousness, as well as the enduring influence of geographic and demographic isolation on traditions. Shaping the new South within this context is the ongoing work of each generation and its renegotiation of personal identity and group relations. The death of Alabama's former governor George Wallace is but one marker of that process. His historical meaning for the South and the country, as public person and myth, is worth pondering. Some additional perspective on this region is discernable from the comparative population patterns and the magnitudes of ethnic identification by regions of the United States as shown in the above table.

Interestingly, the South has by far the largest population of African Americans. The South and West are the only regions of the United States that have a measurable white population. The South has by far the largest percentage and absolute number of persons claiming the United States as their ancestry. In addition, unlike other regions with large immigrant populations and descendants of nineteenth century immigrants, over 15 percent of the population of the South provided no answer to the ancestry question on the 1990 Census.

Unsealing Mississippi's Past

In the name of segregation, the state ran its own spy agency. Now a generation later, the cause is lost, but a legacy of suspicion remains in the agency's newly opened files

By Paul Hendrickson

At 8 in the morning on the day last year when the files of the Mississippi State Sovereignty Commission were unsealed, a man named Richard Barrett stood on a walk outside the state archives and history building handing out filers. The message was: Mississippi's streets were safer, its schools better run, its patriots taller, in the days when the commission reigned and the state was a deeply segregated place.

Barrett is a white attorney, not a native Mississippian, just someone from the North who long ago fell in love with the state. He heads an organization called the Nationalist Movement. It's a movement for American patriots, he says. It's headquartered in the South, but its influence is spreading across the nation like moons of dark ink, or so he says, although he offers no membership figures.

This past January, before the national holiday honoring Martin Luther King Jr., Barrett went to York, Neb., to give a speech in support of the abolition of the "King Holiday, the Civil Rights Acts, the Voting Rights Act, Affirmative Action and miscegenation."

According to petitions to be handed out at the rally: "The King Holiday is the only tribute ever made officially to a hostage-taker, who ravaged our cities, debased our morality and demanded surrender of our nationality as a nation and as a people. It must be abolished, so that we will be one nation, indivisible."

A few days before going to Nebraska, Richard Barrett was sitting in his down-at-the-heels TV studio in south Jackson, where he produces and stars in a cable-access talk show called "Airlink." He was explaining why the Sovereignty Commission had been such a good thing. During its heyday, in the 1960s, it had protected the state against the forces of evil—the communists, the race mixers, the infidels who sought to destroy an American way of life—by keeping tabs on individuals and organizations. Richard Barrett would like to return to those days. "I eulogize the anti-communist patriots who fought for the Sovereignty Commission files," he said.

From the *Washington Post National Weekly Edition*, May 9, 1999, pp. 8-13, 20-25. © 1999 by The Washington Post Writers Group. Reprinted by permission.

RICHARD BARRETT: "THERE'S MORE OF ME IN MISSISSIPPI THAN YOU KNOW."

He said he was deeply worried about "the Africanization, the Mexicanization, the homosexualization of the country—these are all subversives, you know." He said it in the most civil tones, with a wreathing grin. He is a rumpled sort of man, and he was walking around in his socks. He apologized for not having a "beverage" to serve. He said he wished he could have "received" his guest in handsomer circumstances. But his work is so demanding.

He was asked if he thought of himself as bigoted.

"I call myself an American. I call myself a Nationalist. And then I call myself Pro-Majority. I think that's a term I coined." The wreathing smile. "What you would call segregationists I would call Pro-Majority Americans." He added, almost plaintively: "Stokely Carmichael. Vernon Dahmer. Medgar Evers. Martin Luther King: They should have been tried for conspiracy. These were subversives. These were people who deserve to be in the category of Ethel and Julius Rosenberg."

Vernon Dahmer is one of the heroes of the Mississippi civil rights movement, whose 1966 arson murder found its moment of justice only last August, 32 years later, when the former imperial wizard of the White Knights of the Ku Klux Klan, Sam Bowers, was convicted, by a jury of Mississippians, of ordering and masterminding the crime. Bowers is doing life.

Richard Barrett shook his head. That kangaroo court conviction was a moment of tragedy for the nation and for Mississippi, he said—no less than was the 1994 conviction of Byron De La Beckwith for the 1963 assassination of Medgar Evers. Beckwith is now in prison outside Jackson.

"Know what I did right before Christmas?" Barrett said. "Went to see him in jail. It was the kindly thing to do."

How was he?

"Frustrating, seeing a broken man like that. He looked bad, he's ill. He asked me, 'How is the pardon idea going?'"

Barrett's list of the infidels went on: RFK, JFK, Hubert Humphrey, LBJ: "All these people that pulled the trigger that has fueled 30 years of hate and violence in this country All the Sovereignty Commission was trying to do was put a hold on some of that in Mississippi."

Barrett himself is in the Sovereignty Commission files. But you can't read his file. His pages are in litigation from privacy suits. In Barrett's view, the commission got badly sidetracked in its final years. It was actually investigating the activities of the patriots! Shameful. Leftists were trying to seize control of Mississippi, is his explanation.

Before 124,000 documents were opened last year, Barrett went on the local ABC-TV affiliate and advised his fellow Jacksonians to evacuate the city. On the morning they were opened, handing out fliers, he found himself standing next to a friendly-looking man. Barrett stuck out his hand in greeting. The head of the American Civil Liberties Union in Mississippi identified himself. Barrett yanked back his hand as if somebody had touched it with a hot poker. "I know where that hand has been," Barrett said.

On the Web site of the Nationalist Movement, there is a lengthy piece titled "Who Is Richard Barrett?" Basic answer: "Voice of the common man."

"There's more of me in Mississippi than you know," Barrett said in January, just before he drove to Nebraska to exercise the right of free speech.

Sometimes, it seems God put Mississippi on Earth just for our moral contemplation.

No place else in America evokes the same complex set of memories and emotions as this flat, lush, heat-blistered paradise and place of sorrows. In the 1960s, Mississippi was

America at its worst—the hatred, the secrecy, the repression. The deadliest place in the United States, if you were a black person seeking to exercise your fundamental human rights, or a civil rights worker there to lend your hand. People died and people disappeared. The names of 40 martyrs are inscribed on the national Civil Rights Memorial in Montgomery, Ala.; 19 died in Mississippi. It was an American police state, something out of Chile or Argentina or East Germany. Our own magnolia-scented version of apartheid South Africa

Today, like other post-totalitarian societies, Mississippi is caught between memory and forgetting. Caught between folks who would like to put the past beyond limits and folks who believe that you have to honor the past, explore it, understand it, weigh it in your hand, before you can move forward. And that until you do, you can't begin to answer the question: Is Richard Barrett correct? How much is Mississippi still like him?

One place to begin is the files of the Sovereignty Commission. Three decades ago, in the paranoid pitch of civil rights, the commission guarded the gates of a closed society. Men with mellifluous speech and wonderful manners—who wouldn't have thought of leaving home without a fedora, or without pecking their wives on the cheek at the front door—climbed into their sedans and went downtown and turned in a day's work at the commission. It functioned from 1956 to 1973 and then went out of business for good in 1977. Together with the Citizens' Council and the Ku Klux Klan, it formed a triumvirate of repression. The difference was that the Sovereignty Commission was an official agency, funded by tax dollars.

It is the Orwellian creepiness of the name that seems compelling now, barely a generation later: a government bureau, in a sense no different from the Oil and Gas Commission, or the Swine and Poultry Commission, or the Board of Dental Licensing. Something created by an act of the legislature. An agency that had its offices in the state Capitol, a floor above the governor, and that was staffed by public servants (who in some cases were ex-FBI men). The governor, ex-officio, sat on its board and served as its chairman. The lieutenant governor was the vice chairman. The state attorney general and the speaker of the House of Representatives and various legislators and noted lawyers held seats.

Its mission was to wage war on the freedom movement, to keep the blackman down, and to monitor the activities of anybody and everybody suspected of wishing to alter the "Southern way of life." And according to William H. Barbour Jr., the federal judge overseeing the preservation and release of the files, "as the secret intelligence arm of the state, the commission engaged in a wide variety of unlawful activity."

The Closed Society is the title of a famous book about Mississippi in the '60s by a now-deceased historian named James W. Silver. The author wrote: "In such a society a never-ceasing propagation of the 'true faith' must go on relentlessly with a constantly reiterated demand for loyalty to the united front, requiring that non-conformists and dissenters from the code be silenced, or, in a crisis, driven from the community." It's no surprise, then, that Silver himself wound up the subject of surveillance by the good men of the Sovereignty Commission.

The act creating the commission in 1956, two years after the Supreme Court outlawed school segregation in *Brown v. Board of Education,* endowed vaguely defined powers: to "do and perform any and all acts and things deemed necessary and proper to protect the sovereignty of the state of Mississippi, and her sister states, from encroachment thereon by the federal government."

At first the agency functioned as a kind of semi-noxious propaganda and public relations bureau. But under avowedly segregationist Gov. Ross Barnett, as the '60s began, it grew and

was transformed into a home-grown CIA op.

The commission, PR-minded, had a traveling speakers bureau that described how its agents maintained files on "persons whose utterances or actions indicate they should be watched with suspicion on future racial attitudes." It even had a movie about itself that tried to get across the Mississippi Message, misunderstood, maliciously so, by outsiders.

It didn't commit murder and mayhem—not directly At the same time—as historian John Ditimer has pointed out in his 1994 book about Mississippi, *Local People*—the commission's officially sanctioned attack on human rights "fostered and legitimized violent actions by individuals not overly concerned with questions of legality and image." Which is to say those thugs who went nightriding in sheets.

It is now known that in 1964 a paid informant of the commission provided the license plate number of a blue Ford station wagon owned by the Council of Federated Organizations. COFO was a kind of umbrella organization of the vast 1964 voter-registration effort known as "Freedom Summer." The tag of that car was disseminated by the commission to sheriff's offices throughout the state. Months later, three civil rights workers—their names were Schwerner, Chaney and Goodman—were in that Ford when they were pulled over by Neshoba County Deputy Sheriff Cecil Ray Price and Klansmen. The three were murdered on the pond-still night of June 21, 1964, shot in the head, outside a place called Philadelphia Two days later the car was found in a sweet gum thicket out at Bogue Chitto Swamp, the tires burned off, the windows blown out. The bodies were found on August 4, 15 feet below a fresh earthen dam. For a long while, the car had been the only clue to the disappearance.

There are 87,000 indexed names in the commission' s files (although not 87,000 individuals; each variation on a name constitutes a separate entry). It's not possible to know what may have been destroyed—there's long

been a rumor that two trucks pulled away one night from the state Capitol. One took its contents to the state archives. The other went God knows where. Many folks wish the entire load had simply vanished.

"The past is the closed book, and they don't want to open it," said Bill Minor, maverick journalist and syndicated newspaper columnist. "That's the psyche of white people in this state. You and I may believe that if you ignore the lessons of history, you're doomed to repeat them. But the average person in this state doesn't believe it. We are some kind of microcosm for something in this country, and I can't quite figure it out.

"I sometimes think it's like original sin: Race is the original sin that many thousands, or millions, of Americans carry with them, but that down here we're just doomed to repeat. Nobody thinks those days could come back. Well, who says? If there are ripples, they're way under there."

How much hate remains in Mississippi? It seemed to me that one answer might lie in the files of the State Sovereignty Commission, and in some of the stories they contain. There's a force and documentary power to old declassified documents laid bare. Maybe there was once in the files half again, or twice again, as much paper as now exists. That's okay. What is there, I learned, writes its own parable.

Anybody can go in and read the files now. All you need do is walk past the monument to the Confederate dead out front of the Department of Archives and History near the state Capitol, across State Street from a big sign that says, "Welcome to Downtown Jackson. Best of the New South." You enter a room on the first floor and fill out a brief application. You log onto a Hewlett Packard Vectra XM2 computer, the hard drive of which bears a manufacturer's blue sticker: "Intel inside." You start punching up names.

Which is what I did on several January mornings this year. What I found said a lot about what Missis-

In the paranoid pitch of civil rights, the Sovereignty Commission guarded the gates of a closed society. With the Citizens' Council and the Klan, it formed a triumvirate of repression.

sippi was once upon a bigoted time. I learned that a person could get his or her name into the commission files if he or she bought the wrong book in a bookstore, or attended the wrong interfaith lecture, or even the wrong musical concert. (A Joan Baez performance at Tougaloo, one of the state's historically black colleges, would have been an instant cause for surveillance.)

Teachers, especially college teachers, could get into the files, because they had ideas.

Maybe somebody had lingered too long on a street corner on a Saturday morning talking to the wrong-colored person. He or she was ripe for the files.

It just depended. It was arbitrary, idiosyncratic, irrational in all its rationality.

The Files:

They once wanted to stop a man from applying to the state university in Hattiesburg, then known as Mississippi Southern University. This was March 1964. A year and a half earlier, in a night of bloodshed and death, James Meredith had integrated—with federal troops and U.S. marshals—Ole Miss up in Oxford. Now Southern, toward the bottom of the state, was in danger of falling. The director of the Sovereignty Commission—his name was Erie Johnston Jr., a big robust man—sent a memorandum to the school president, W.D. McCain. The memo was to be read out loud to the "subject" by either the president or the registrar, should the subject attempt to step onto the campus again:

"We have information that you are a homosexual. We also have sufficient information to prove it if necessary. If you change your mind about enrolling at an all white university we will say no more about it. If you persist in your application, we will give this information to the press and the Justice Department. We do not be-

lieve the government will back a homosexual in attempting to get admitted to a university."

This document is registered in the files under the number 1-70-0-24-1-1-1. It's one page long. There's a note at the bottom indicating a blind copy had been sent to the governor and lieutenant governor.

The Files:

Some collegians and two of their teachers got off a bus on July 5, 1961, in the semitropical antebellum river town of Natchez. They were from a college in New York. They were watched from the moment they stepped into the Trailways terminal. That evening the sheriff sent a Teletype to commission headquarters as well as to the director of the Mississippi Highway Patrol: "THESE SUBJECTS HAVE BEEN CONSTANTLY UNDER SURVEILLANCE SINCE THEIR ARRIVAL BY OFFICERS THIS DEPARTMENT. THEY HAVE MAILED TWO LETTERS SINCE THEIR ARRIVAL."

From the commission's report on the matter, filed a few days later, it was clear that the desk clerk at the Eola Hotel had listened to the group's phone calls and then phoned the sheriff. The postmaster was in on it also, and so was the local newspaper: "These subjects attempted to contact Mr. Jimmie Lambert of the Natchez Democrat Newspaper but were unable to see him."

From the report: "The subjects were identified as students and teachers at Adelphi College...." According to the Sovereignty Commission agent on the case, they "departed Natchez July 6, 1961, without causing any trouble or disturbance." They were headed up toward Little Rock, Ark., via Vicksburg. The local constabularies were alerted.

The Files:

In a county-seat town called Grenada, in north-central Mississippi, a

rumor was wildfiring about a white woman who'd given birth to a baby out of wedlock. The father was said to be black. A commission inspector named Tom Scarbrough motored up to Grenada to make a personal examination of the child's skin color and also of the size of the halfmoons on the baby's fingers, because that could be a telltale sign. He and the sheriff went out to the woman's house. The subsequent commission report ran for about 5,000 words: "I was looking at the child's fingernails and the end of its fingers very closely.... We both agreed we were not qualified to say it was a part Negro child, but we could say it was not 100 percent Caucasian."

The mother told them the father was an Italian. Apparently, they went away only partially satisfied.

There are other reports in the files where investigators are seeking to determine if someone is "colored." According to Mississippi law, if babies were "1/8 Negro" or more, they were black; if not more than "1/16 Negro," they were considered white.

The Files:

A preacher from Alabama was set to come to the capital city to speak before a ministerial association. This preacher was not yet globally known. His name was Martin Luther King Jr. This was September 1959. It was the opinion of a leader of the Citizens' Council that King and the several others who were coming to Jackson "should be harassed as much as possible." Possibly these individuals could be "arrested by the Police, taken down and fingerprinted and photographed."

The three-page commission memo indicated that a meeting had already been held between the leader of the Citizens' Council and the chief of detectives of the Jackson Police Department. Another meeting, with different people, had been held in the governor's office. Yet another meeting had been held with a person of authority at the Highway Patrol regarding the planting of a recording device on a "negro" informant who will have "the microphone in his pocket." It "will also be necessary" the memo added, "to secure some room or office space within a block of the meeting place where the recording instrument can be located and the speeches taken down or recorded."

The records were officially opened on March 17, 1998, bringing some closure to a battle in the courts that had begun in 1977, which was the year the state legislature had voted the commission out of existence. Legislators back then introduced bills to destroy all the records. Argument ensued and a bill was approved authorizing the files to be closed for 50 years. The ACLU and several other plaintiffs had other ideas. In 1989 a federal judge ordered that the records be unsealed. But it took another nine years, through various countersuits and appeals, until the order became reality. Some 7,700 pages remain in litigation.

In late March of this year, Judge Barbour announced that he had resolved privacy claims by 42 people named in the files. But the list of whose files will be released is still much in doubt, pending further appeals.

According to criteria established by Barbour, archivists assigned "state actor" or "victim" status to every name in the records. The actors were all those who'd worked for or complied with the commission or supplied information to it in its years of surveillance, while the victims were those who had been spied on.

Dave Ingebretsen is one of two full-time ACLU staffers for all of Mississippi—which is two more than there used to be. His office is in a pleasant old restored house a couple of football throws from where the files are sitting. He's originally from Chicago.

Is it a good thing for Mississippi? I ask.

"A very good thing," he says immediately "They got away with it because they were able to operate in secrecy.

You start here. You admit that. It's a sore. But the sore can heal."

The Sovereignty Commission, he points out, was never large—some shoe-leather investigators, some clerical staff, some publicity types. But everything it did, or tried to do, was hooked in with other official and semiofficial repressive bodies of the system, not least of which were local law enforcement agencies and the county-by-county chapters of the Citizens' Council. The council was in effect the white-collar Klan—respectable, middle-class, churchgoing men who used social ostracism and the economic squeeze as their weapons, rather than violence.

"What you get when you begin to read in those files," Ingebretsen says, "is not just the Sovereignty Commission, but the Sovereignty Commission working with every other state agency—doesn't matter, the Department of Agriculture or the folks who issue licenses to be a notary public—to infringe on the rights of people they didn't like. You just can't look at those files without coming away with a real sense of what the climate of fear was like back then. It's the story of a secret state agency and a rogue government denying ordinary folks their rights."

He doesn't say it with bile. "Mississippi is my home," he says. He wouldn't want to live anywhere else. Loves the weather, loves the land, loves the people. Some of the friendliest folks he's ever met anywhere.

It should be said that a lot of the spy work was bumbling and ineffectual and almost comic-absurd. In that sense the commission *was* a kind of corn pone Gestapo, or "KGB of the cotton patches," as journalist Bill Minor dubbed it. Often its reports amounted to a combination of scurrilous gossip, half-truths, bad information.

Ingebretsen: "Okay, the civil rights movement succeeded, and we all know that, but the fact is, people are still reluctant speak up in this state." He tells me this story: In south Mississippi several years ago, an elementary school principal had placed a camera in the boys' bathroom. Par-

ents found out that tapes were being made of their children, and being viewed. No one spoke out, not for two years. "Finally, one parent called me and said that the principal of his child's school had a box in the bathroom. I said, 'What?'"

According to Ingebretsen, the camera was in the bathroom from 1996 until last year, which is when his office found out and immediately stepped in.

"That's the darker legacy. People still reluctant to speak. It the fear."

In 1959, the emerging power in the Citizens Council—in the city of Jackson and across the state and in other Southern states as well—was William J. Simmons. If you watched episode 5 of the PBS documentary "Eyes on the Prize," you may remember a man in a dark suit with hooded eyes, a mustache and a big chunky head talking in a deeply pleasant drawl about the idea of a "supine surrender on our part" to those who would come in and wish to destroy Mississippi's way of life. *No way* was Bill Simmons's answer, no way in hell.

The Jackson chapter of the council was rumored to have built up by the late '50s a card file containing the racial views of nearly every white person in the city—and of course that information would have been traded with the Sovereignty Commission. One in-state observer wrote that the council had "created a climate of fear that has straitjacketed the white community in a thought control enforced by financial sanctions." Routinely, Simmons and other council members sat in on meetings of the Sovereignty Commission, and vice versa.

That was 40 years ago. Paper can come back to haunt. Bad things don't necessarily get interred with the bones, especially when some of them have been written down, and then opened up for anyone to read.

The proprietor of one of the capital city's loveliest bed-and-breakfast inns is picking up the telephone.

"Good afternoon. Fairview. This is Bill Simmons. May I help you?"

'You and I may believe that if you ignore the lessons of history, you're doomed to repeat them,' says a veteran journalist. 'But the average person in this state doesn't believe it.'

This voice wouldn't wish harm on flea.

I tell him I'm a reporter from out of town, that I've been down at the archives and history building scanning documents with his name on them. I say I'd like to come by.

"I have been retired from all that for a good many years," the voice on the phone interrupts agreeably. "My interest in that subject is historic, which is to say not very high. We're in the hospitality business now."

Fairview is Bill Simmons's boyhood home. It's on Fairview Street in one of Jackson's finest old neighborhoods, Belhaven. The inn, known for providing four-star hospitality, is an immense, white, wooden, six-columned affair. It's a three-minute drive from where the files now rest. Sometimes you can see Bill Simmons out walking in Belhaven, waving to neighbors, waving to folks he doesn't even know.

"Now we'd love to have you come over and stay with us," this voice on the telephone continues. "Folks seem to love our inn. They're comfortable here. Why don't you think about bringing your wife to Fairview on your next visit to Mississippi? I wouldn't be able to talk to you about the Sovereignty Commission though."

The receiver seems to be moving away from his lips.

But, sir, these documents . . .

"Oh, I don't think it really matters," he says. "I don't think there's anything in there of real consequence. Do you? I probably have a stack about three or four inches high with my name on it, don't I? That's all in the past, all in the past."

The thing about Mississippi is its ghosts. They are everywhere, wishing to rise up and greet you, disarm you with their seeming utter lack of guile. William Faulkner once told some students at the University of Virginia: "There is no such thing really as *was*

because the past *is* . . . . And so a man, a character in a story at any moment of action, is not just himself as he is then, he is all that made him, and the long sentence is an attempt to get his past and possibly his future into the instant in which he does something."

The something the former state-wide administrator of the Citizens' Council is doing is hanging up. Softly. It is ghostly, the sound.

In the end, it wasn't
enough just to read the files or to talk to folks in Jackson. If I wanted to understand what the climate of fear and oppression was really like back then, and to measure how much, if at all, things had changed, people told me, I had to go deeper, to find the heart of the old Mississippi.

Which is to say, I had to go to Greenwood.

Greenwood is on the eastern edge of the Delta–that flat, alluvial garden commencing in the northwest corner of the state, 200 miles long and 85 miles wide. The topsoil is 24 feet deep in some places. The reason the Delta bleeds the blues is because of the kind of dawn-to-dark stoop work that has gone on in its fields. James Meredith once said that you could almost hear the backs breaking and the vegetation growing as you drove down Delta back roads.

Greenwood has a population of 19,000 and cheerfully proclaims itself "Long-Staple Cotton Capital of the World." During the civil rights era, however, Greenwood was a town without pity. The Student Nonviolent Coordinating Committee once tried to tally all the violence that went on there within a matter of several weeks. The sheet reads like a war diary:

On Feb. 28, 1963, SNCC worker James Travis was machinegunned by three white men seven miles from Greenwood.

On March 6, 1963, three SNCC workers were shot at while sitting in a car outside the SNCC office. No one was hurt.

On March 24, 1963, the SNCC office was burned down.

On March 26, 1963, two shotgun blasts were fired into the home of SNCC worker George Greene. No one was hurt.

The brown Yazoo River curls through the middle of town. The county jail is on the top two floors of the stone courthouse, and prisoners stand behind its barred windows, looking down on pedestrians and cars. You can drive by the courthouse at midnight, and the prisoners are there, against their bars, the light shining from behind their backs the color of weak tea.

The gray steel girderwork of the bridge behind the courthouse carries you over to the white residential side. "The other side," Greenwood blacks call it. There, on Grand Boulevard, are some of the finest homes and tended yards in all of Mississippi. You come the other way on the bridge, to the south bank, and in no more than half a dozen blocks you're in the middle of hard Delta poverty. It's as if Chevy Chase and Anacostia were standing side by side, split by a swollen stream.

The mayor is white–but it's a predominantly black city council now. The president of the Lefiore County Board of Supervisors is black, and a majority of the board is black. The superintendent of Leflore County schools is black, and so is the superintendent of the city's schools.

But this is a city still segregated socially, bifurcated by color the way the river bifurcates the town. The city's public schools are 87 percent black, the county's 98 percent, while the private Pillow Academy has no black students.

This was the state headquarters of the Citizens' Council. Its founder, Robert Patterson, still lives in the

'We'd love to have you come over and stay with us,' says the voice on the phone. 'Folks seem to love our inn. . . . I wouldn't be able to talk to you about the Sovereignty Commission, though.'

Delta. You can get him on the phone. He's 77. Like William Simmons, he demurs–politely.

Greenwood was the home of Byron De La Beckwith. Emmett Till was kidnapped in this county and then killed–this was August 1955. Bob Dylan and Sydney Poitier and Harry Belafonte and Dick Gregory turned up in Greenwood in the '60s. James Forman, head of SNCC, wrote an eloquent piece of literature on scrap paper called "Letter From the Greenwood Jail." Stokely Carmichael and Bob Moses and Sam Block and Willie Peacock–names of history in black Mississippi–were all in Greenwood. There are people who've long worked for the D.C. government who were heroes on Greenwood's streets: Lawrence Guyot and June Johnson are two.

Marion Barry himself is from Itta Bena, right outside Greenwood.

So much beauty and history and heartache wrapped in one Delta county.

Gordon Lackey lives on the "other side," in a red brick rancher on East Barton Avenue. He used to have a motorcycle sales-and-repair business in his backyard. In old Associated Press wire stories from the '60s, Gordon Mims Lackey is identified as an alleged "kleagle," or organizer, of the Mississippi White Knights of the KKK. Lackey denies it all.

In 1966, he was subpoenaed to come to Washington as a witness before the House Committee on Un-American Activities. He took the Fifth on all questions related to alleged Klan activities or involvement. He prefaced or ended his refusals with remarks like this: ". . . with all possible respect for the committee."

He has me in, puts on the coffee. He's sitting on a stool in his breakfast nook. He's coughing and hacking and wheezing. All he was, he says, was "politically active" back then. He's 62,

on the other side of some bankruptcies and heart attacks. When I ask about the Sovereignty Commission files, he hoots the idea away.

"Sovereignty Commission? What were they doing, really? Bunch of bureaucrats. They just found out what we already exactly knew. . . . What about Ken Starr? He's around snooping on the president of the United States. What about Richard Nixon getting people to break into the office of Daniel Ellsberg's psychiatrist? How's that any different from what the Sovereignty Commission did? Somebody's gotta snoop in somebody's damn business. You ever seen it any different in America? That's all the Sovereignty Commission did. They never hurt anybody."

His best Greenwood friend for many years was Beckwith, he says. "Deelay," he calls him. There are old FBI reports from 1966 in which Lackey is allegedly telling a source for the Jackson office of the FBI that he, Lackey, had been involved in the shooting of Medgar Evers.

Lackey knows about that report. All bull, he says.

He leans close to my face, coughing, wheezing, dragging on his cigarette, swilling black coffee. His eyes are wide, there is a faint grin. "I never asked Deelay if he killed that damn nigger. And he never told me, neither."

But there are also Greenwoodians like Gray Evans. He, too, lives on the other side. It's as if his first name is a signal for where his mind is. "I knew things weren't right," he says slowly. He's a circuit judge; back then he was the city's prosecuting attorney. He is 71–a man who once loved to fish and hunt quail. But his arthritis and sciatica have him feeling poorly, and so what he loves to do now is have friends in and cook elaborate meals for them. "We didn't do right by a lot of those folks back then," he

says. "And yet I know in my heart I tried to stop some things that might have turned out deadly."

He wasn't in favor of unsealing the files. His feeling was that too many people on the wrong side of the equation would get tarred with the same brush. "I have no idea if I'm in there," he says. "I wouldn't be surprised. I'm not interested in finding out."

For the record, Senior Circuit Judge Gray Evans has one reference in the files. Nothing incriminating.

I go across the bridge, the other way. William McGee lives on West Henry Street. They call him Bud. He's a gospel deejay over at WNLA-AM in Indianola. He's got a kind of heh-heh, caving-in-on-himself chuckie. He's lived in Leflore County nearly all his life. You ask him if he likes it and he says, "I think I love Greenwood better than I love staying in Chicago. You speak to somebody in Chicago, they look at you like you're crazy."

He's in the files. I show him something written in his own hand that somehow got in. It is a kind of personal and informal affidavit, attesting to how he and others had suffered at the hands of Greenwood bigots. He signed it "William McGee, 202 Palace." That was decades ago. And so the shock now–it is all over his face–of discovery.

Bud is 58. It's a number to remember. On June 18, 1963, he was one of 58 blacks arrested in Itta Bena. They got jailed on made-up charges of disturbance and breach of the peace. They'd been singing for their freedom that night in Hopewell Baptist Church. Bud McGee had been leading the singing, and the song was "Ain't Gonna Let Nobody Turn Me Around."

The next day the prisoners, both men and women, were tried in groups, with no legal representation.

'Sure it's better now,' says William McGee, who appears in the files. 'But we're still on this side, they're still on that side. And you never know what's going on under the surface.'

It took an hour to get all of them in and out of the courtroom.

"How do you plead?" asked the justice of the peace to groups of 11 or 12.

"Not guilty."

Bang came the gavel. "Six months on the county farm, $500 fine."

The National Council of Churches got them sprung after nearly two months of hard labor.

Bud McGee is remembering this. He just got off work at the radio station. He's in a purple sweat suit, with a hood, and a Florida Gators baseball cap.

He takes me out to the old county farm on the edge of town.

"We'd get up in the morning. 'Make me a line!' the sergeant is yelling. Everybody'd jump up. They'd do a count outside. Then you'd go to work. We had the stripes on. We had kaiser blades. You'd go in the bushes along the side of the road for the bathroom. You had to tell the Shot, say, 'Taking a leak here, Shot.' 'Bumblebee here, Shot.' Shot says, 'You bigger than they are, boy. Finish your business.' Sometimes you have a good Shot, sometimes bad. You stay too long in the bushes, Shot would say, 'You better bring something back on a stick, boy.'"

Bud McGee is doing that little cave-in-on-himself laugh.

Did you pray, did you sing?

"Oh, we always sang. We sang on the way to the county farm in the bus when they were taking us there. They couldn't stop us from singing."

There seems so little bitterness in him. "Bitterness is against me," he says. "Bitterness'll make me sick. I think that's what happened to Stokely."

Is it better now?

"Lot better now. Sure, it's better now. But we're still on this side, they're still on that side. And you

never know what's going on under the surface."

On June 25, 1963, a week after Bud McGee and 57 others went to the county farm, Mac Cotton got arrested at the Greenwood courthouse on charges of loitering and failing to obey an officer. He had brought 200 people to the steps in an attempt to get some of them registered to vote. He had a five-minute trial and was sent to the county farm.

I go see Mac Cotton. He's in the files.

"Why aren't you riled up?" I ask at his seeming lack of anger about being spied on.

It's almost as if he doesn't get the question. He shrugs. His full name is Douglas MacArthur Cotton. He's 57. He's from Kosciusko, southeast of Greenwood, in another county, closer to Jackson. He doesn't get to Greenwood much now, but every time he does, so much memory rolls under the night.

"Why should I be riled up?" he says.

"But they were invading your rights."

"My whole existence was illegal in their eyes," he says. A pause. " 'Who are they to do that?' See, that would be the way you would think about it. You're a white person. You could get all riled up because you're coming from a different place. But me, I didn't have any rights in their eyes. I was lucky that's all they were doing. They could have come up and tap me on the head, shoot me. I was lucky all they were doing was snooping around."

"So you've never wanted to sue anybody over this?"

"If I did, it wouldn't be about being angry," he says. "It'd be about seeing that something like this didn't happen again."

At the county farm that summer, Mac Cotton went on a work and hun-

ger strike, and as a consequence was sent to Parchman state penitentiary He later signed an affidavit that was published in a book called Mississippi *Black Paper*. His testimony describes how he and several other prisoners were put in the "hot box," a room with a tiny ventilation hole, and then later, back in his cell, he was hung by his tied hands to the bars.

"They stood me on my toes and cuffed me to the top of the bars."

"I peed and [defecated] all over myself," Mac Cotton says. He is sitting in his living room. His wife, Mamie, is typing on a computer and listening in. "I think about this a lot. I think what God did for me. I was just kind of floating through the air after a time. After a while all of it was taken away. I imagine about after eight hours, I was removed from the pain of it."

I've brought along some pages from his Sovereignty Commission file. He hasn't looked at them yet. He's placed them face down on a coffee table, aligned their edges in a neat stack. "Almost makes me feel important. That they were watching me like that."

Mac Cotton's never been to the archives and history building. Maybe someday he'll go, he says. If he finds the time. Doesn't really add up to a lot of mystery for him. He pretty much takes it on faith they were doing what they felt they had to do.

On a Sunday this past January just like any Sunday of the year, Greenwood was at church. It was Martin Luther King Jr. weekend. It was unusually balmy. At the Episcopal Church of the Nativity, the rector preached on prophets and how they call into question things about ourselves we don't especially like. "They make us uncomfortable," the rector said, "and we drive them out." He told his flock they were self-evidently the brightest and best of their community—but it wasn't enough. He said it wasn't enough that they had done well professionally or financially. He said it wasn't enough they were comfortable in life. No, the gospel demands that a Christian live in such a way that God's love will embrace everyone in a community.

The priest spread his arms wide. There were no blacks in attendance at that 10:30 a.m. service. Martin Luther King Jr. wasn't mentioned by name.

That afternoon, there was a march through black Greenwood to commemorate King's birthday It started at St. Francis of Assisi Catholic Church and ended a mile or so away at Friendship Missionary Baptist Church. Old ladies sat in metal lawn chairs out front of shotgun shacks and waved. Kids rode their bikes along the parade's periphery. The size of the parade kept swelling as people hopped off their porches and fell in alongside the marchers. People sang "We Shall Overcome" and "If I Had a Hammer." A man with a bullhorn kept the parade moving. "We are in the process, and we will make it," he cried.

At Friendship Missionary Baptist, someone played an aching piano. Light came through the amber windows and fell on wood paneling. Hand fans bladed holy air. Babies squalled. A robed choir in front of a maroon velvet curtain sang hymns. Several preachers preached and some politicians orated. Someone in a beautiful falsetto voice sang the song that wonders, "Anybody here seen my old friend Martin?"

Except for a couple of Franciscan priests and nuns and myself, there were no whites in attendance. It could have been 1965, when a spy agency was in full cry. Much had changed in Mississippi since those days, I concluded. Richard Barrett was wrong—Mississippi is no longer much like him. The hate has gone mute. What remains is a deep sense of separation. Mississippi on the weekend of Martin Luther King Jr.'s birthday felt like a nation of strangers.

Paul Hendrickson, who writes for Style, is on leave working on a book about Mississippi. He is a 1999 Guggenheim Fellow.

WHITE GIRL?

Cousin Kim is passing. But Cousin

Lonnae doesn't want to let her go.

By Lonnae O'Neal Parker
Washington Post Staff Writer

I have a 20-year-old white girl living in my basement. She happens to be my first cousin. I happen to be black. Genetics is a funny thing. So are the politics of racial declaration.

My 5-year-old daughter, Sydney, calls her Cousin Kim. Kim's daddy calls my mother his baby sister. Kim's father is black. Her mother is white. And Kim calls herself white. At least that's what she checks off on all those forms with neat little boxes for such things.

She grew up in southern Illinois. Sandoval, population about 1,500. There were 33 people in her high school graduating class. Counting Cousin Kim, there was half a black. I used to think Kim lived in a trailer park. But one day she corrected me. We live in a trailer home, she said—"my mother owns the land."

The black side of Kim's family is professional. Lawyers, doctors, Fortune 500 company execs. We have an uncle who got a PhD in math at 21. The white side of Kim's family is blue collar. Less formally educated. Some recipients of government entitlement programs. Not to draw too fine a distinction, but color is not the only thing that separates us.

I brought Kim to Maryland to live with me after my second child, Savannah, was born. She is something of an au pair, if au pairs can hail from Sandoval.

Back home, Kim had run into some trouble. Bad grades, good beer. She came to D.C. to sort it all out. To find a

way to get her life back on track. And she came to get in touch with the black side of her family—and possibly herself.

She may have gotten more than she bargained for.

This is a story about how a close family can split right down a color line without ever saying a word about it. The details belong to Cousin Kim and me, but the outline is familiar to anyone for whom race is a secret or a passion or an issue or a decision. The story is scary in places. Because to tell it, both Kim and I have to go there. Race Place, U.S.A. It is a primal stretch of land. It shares a psychic border with the place where we compete for the last video,

parking space at the mall or kindergarten slot in that elite magnet school. Where we fight over soccer calls, and elbow each other to secure Tickle Me Elmos for our kids. It is the place where we grew up hearing black people smell like copper and white people smell like wet chickens. Where everybody knows that whites are pedophiles and gun nuts. And blacks smoke crack. Where interracial couples still bother us.

You've gotta pass through Race Place in order to make it to Can We All Get Along, but most everybody is looking for a shortcut.

For Kim and me, there are no shortcuts. We meet in the middle, from opposite sides of a racial divide. It is the DMZ and our shields are down. We may lose friends, black and white, for telling this truth so plainly. Still, alone together, we begin.

The First Time

Do you remember the first time somebody called you "nigger"?

I do. I was on vacation in Centralia,

"I hate the N-word. . . . I hate that the first thing they associate with that word is me."

Ill., where both of my parents were born and raised. Five minutes from where Cousin Kim grew up. It was the early 1970s, and I was maybe 5 years old.

Two white girls walked up to me in a park. They were big. Impossibly big. Eleven at least. They smiled at me.

"Are you a nigger?" one of the girls asked.

On the segregated South Side of Chicago where I lived, it was possible for a black child to go a very long time and never hear the word "nigger" directed at her. But I wasn't on the South Side, and after five years, my time was up.

I stood very still. And my stomach grew icy. My spider senses were tingling. Where had I heard that word before? "I, I don't know," I told her, shrugging my shoulders high to my ears.

The first girl sighed, exasperated. Then the other repeated, more forcefully this time, "Are you a nigger? You know, a black person?" she asked.

I wanted to answer her. To say something. But fear made me confused. I had no words. I just stood there. And tried not to wet my panties.

Then I ran. I turned quickly to look over my shoulder just in time to hear a rock whiz past my ear and plop into a nearby creek.

"You better git, you little Ne-gro!" somebody else, a white boy, yelled at me from a few feet away. I kept running, and this time, I didn't look back.

For the rest of the day, I harbored a secret. I harbored the shame for longer. I knew I was black. I had found out the year before. I remember because I had confronted my father, demanding to know when my blond hair and blue eyes would kick in. Like the Miss Breck shampoo girl on television. Like the superheroes on "Superfriends."

Only white people have blond hair and blue eyes, my dad said. "And we're black."

The wicked witch, the headless horseman, the evil stepmother and all the bad guys on "The New Adventures of Scooby Doo" wore black. Black eye, black heart, Black Death. Black ass. Mine was a negative, visceral reaction to the word.

Five years old was old enough to know I was black. It was old enough for somebody to call me a nigger.

And it was certainly old enough to feel like one.

That would be the first time.

One Black Drop

It is early June, and Cousin Kim and I are about to watch "Roots," the landmark 1970s television miniseries about a slave family. Kim says she's heard of the movie but has never seen it. So I go to queue the video in the cassette player, but first I make a cup of tea. And straighten the pillows on my couch. Then I check my voice mail.

I am puttering. Procrastinating. Loath to begin. Because I don't know if our blood ties are strong enough to withstand slavery. And I am scared to watch "Roots" with a white girl. Scared of my

anger. Scared of my pain. Scared that she won't get it. Scared of how much I want her to. Scared of the way race can make strangers out of family.

It has been nearly a year since Kim first came to live with me. She was a cousin I barely knew. She had visited my husband and me in the summer of 1994, when our daughter Sydney was a baby. The first time she had ever seen so many black people in her life, she would later say.

Before that, there were brief visits with my mom and quick kisses at my college graduation. Over the years, I heard much more than I ever saw of Cousin Kim. Kim's father had a black family. His kids were adults when Kim was born. Later, his wife died. And though they are now a public couple, my uncle and Kim's mom never married.

My girls adore Kim. And when she goes to get Sydney from school, the little black prekindergartners rush her at the door, greeting her with wide smiles and hugs and shouts of "Hi, Cousin Kim!"

This past year, we've laughed over sitcoms and shared private jokes. We've talked about old boyfriends, gone shopping and giggled over family gossip. Still, up to now, we've never been down that black-and-white brick road.

I was shocked to hear that Cousin Kim considered herself white. I found out only because she had to fill out some forms to get into community college. Because I asked her if they had a box for race. Then I asked her what she checked. I was ready to tease her pointedly for checking off "other." In between. Not quite either.

I was prepared to lobby—to drop science about the "one-drop rule." In slave days, that meant that if you had a drop of black blood, you were singing spirituals and working for somebody for free. Trying not to get beaten, and trying to keep your babies from being sold—even if the massa was their daddy. Color gradations were a legacy of the plantation system. And although light was favored, one drop gave us a common destiny. Shackled all of us darkies together.

Later, one drop meant that blacks were able to form a common cultural identity. To agitate for the common good. Because light mulattoes lynched as easily as dark Africans. But one drop also meant there have always been those who could pass. Who required writ, or testimony, or a declaration of intent to make them black. For whom race has always been a choice.

Cousin Kim would be one of these. Her eyes are bright blue-gray and her skin has only a suggestion of color. Generations of careful breeding have worked out all her kinks. To white folks, she looks

white. And mostly, that is how they treat her. Like one of their own.

Still, I was ready to cast her lot with the sisters. You know half-black is black, I was ready to say. I was ready for "other." I wasn't ready for "white." Or that familiar sting of rejection.

Passing Away

I have The Sight. Like my mother before me. Like most black people I know. It is a gift. A special kind of extrasensory perception. We may not be clairvoyant enough to determine the location of the rebel base. Or have the telekinesis it takes to shatter a glass ceiling.

But we can spot some Negro on you from three generations away.

It reveals itself in a flash of expression. A momentary disposition of features in repose. The curl of a top lip that seems to say "Nobody knows the trouble I've seen."

We have The Sight because we are used to looking at black people. Used to loving them. We know the range of colors black comes in. Because there's always somebody at our family reunions who could go either way. And because we are a worldly people, and we know how these things go.

The Sight is a nod to solidarity. It is a reaction against dilution and division. It is the recognition that when people face overwhelming odds, you need to know who can be compelled to ante up and kick in.

We use it to put a black face on public triumphs that look lily white. And to "out" folks who might act against our interests without sharing in the consequences.

No matter how many times she thanked "the black community" for embracing her music, we knew Mariah Carey was part black. And long before he opened his mouth, we saw something in Rock Newman's eyes, even though they are blue.

When people wanted to call actresses Jennifer Beals or Troy Beyer beautiful, we were eager to point out their black roots. Eager to claim New York Yankee Derek Jeter and Channel 4 newscaster Barbara Harrison. Old folks swear Yul Brynner was black and that was why he kept his head shaved. And speculation persists, despite the fact that Georgia representative Bob Barr has affirmed his whiteness.

Understand. It's not that we don't respect Tiger Woods's right to call himself a Cablinasian. We just don't think it will help him get a cab in D.C.

My cousin calls herself white and I see a side of me just passing away. Swallowed up by the larger, more powerful fish in the mainstream. And I wonder if that will be the future for my family, some who look like Kim—others who look like me but have married white, or no doubt will. And I wonder, ultimately, if that will be the future for black people. Passing themselves right out of existence. Swearing it was an accident. Each generation trading up a shade and a grade until there is nothing left but old folks in fold-up lawn chairs on backyard decks who gather family members close around to tell nostalgic tales that begin "Once upon a time when we were colored . . ."

And I think to myself, I wish there were some things that we just wouldn't do for straight hair. And I think of the struggle and the history and the creativity lost. And I trust that the universe will register my lament.

When my cousin calls herself white, I see red. And I hear echoes. "Well, I don't really consider myself black . . ."

Or maybe it is laughter.

The Real World

Cousin Kim is having a hard time with "Roots." Not her own, the movie. I'm not having an easy time myself.

She isn't ready for the stuff they left out of her history books. I am unable to restrain my commentary. Or my imagination. Sometimes my tears.

Ever heard of Calvert County, I ask Kim bitterly when a teenage African girl is sold at an Annapolis auction as a bed wench to Robert Calvert. Kim didn't know that Maryland had ever been a slave state.

There is a scene where kidnapped African Kunte Kinte won't settle down in his chains. "Want me to give him a stripe or two, boss?" the old slave, Fiddler, asks his Master Reynolds.

"Do as I say, Fiddler," Reynolds answers. "That's all I expect from any of my niggers."

"Oh, I love you, Massa Reynolds," Fiddler tells him. And instantly, my mind draws political parallels. *Ward Connerly*, I think to myself. *Armstrong Williams. Shelby Steele.* Hyperbole, some might say. I say dead-on.

"Clarence Thomas," I say to Cousin Kim. And she just stares at me. She may be a little tender yet for racial metaphors. I see them everywhere.

Kim is 20 in the way of small-town 20-year-olds all over the country. Her best-best friends are Jenny and Nikki and Theresa. They send letters, e-mail one another and run up my phone bill. She takes classes, takes care of my children and passes time painting her nails and watching "The Real World," on MTV.

I tease her about being Wal-Mart-obsessed.

Cousin Kim walked out of the movie "Glory" when she was in 11th grade. When Denzel Washington got lashed with a whip and cried silently. Couldn't handle it, she said. "I just didn't want to see it. I couldn't stand the idea of seeing someone literally beat." Avoidance and denial are twins in my family. In others as well.

When Kim was growing up in Sandoval, they didn't celebrate Black History Month, she says. "Not even Black History Week. We just had Martin Luther King Day."

The town was not integrated. Her father was the only black person she saw regularly. "And I don't consider him black," Kim says. My uncle is not one to disabuse her of that notion.

Kim's dad ran his own sanitation business. He was a hard-working, astute, sometimes charming businessman. A moneymaker. And my mother says people used to say if he had been white, he would have been mayor of Centralia. Of course, Kim has never heard this. In fact, "we've never had a conversation about race in my house," Kim says casually. And for a moment, I am staggered. But I am not surprised.

I have The Sight. Like my mother before me. Like most black people I know. It is a gift. . . . we can spot some Negro on you three generations away.

Making the Grade

My mama's people have always been color-struck. Daddy's, too, for that matter. Black folks know the term. It is part of an informal caste system that has always existed in the black community.

It is a form of mental colonialism. A shackle for the mind. A value system that assigns worth and power to those traits that most closely resemble the massa.

If you're light, you're all right. If you're brown, stick around. If you're black, get back, people used to say.

I am light; my husband is dark. When my daughter Sydney was born, everybody wanted to know who she looked like. They weren't asking about her eyes. They wanted to know what black folks always want to know when a baby who can go either way on the light-dark thing is born. Whose color is she? What kind of hair does she have?

The hair can be a tricky thing. Nothing for that but to wait a few months until the "grade" comes in good. But for color, we've got it down. We're a race of mad scientists, fervently checking the nail beds and ear tips of newborns to precisely determine where they'll fall over the rainbow.

My paternal grandmother was a very light woman with straight hair and black features. She had an inspection ritual she performed on all new babies in the family. A careful once-over to check for color and clarity before she pronounced judgment. I didn't know this until I introduced her to Sydney when she was about 6 months old.

She sat my baby on her lap. After a few minutes, she announced her findings. "Well, her color is good. And her hair ain't half bad considering how black that nigger is you married."

Hmmmm.

You know these days we try to stay away from divisive pronouncements on color, I wanted to tell her. We don't want to handicap our daughter with crippling hair issues.

But please. My grandmother might have hit me if I had tried to spout some nonsense like that. More to the point, particularly among the elders, there is a certain unassailable quality to the color caste logic. A tie-in with life chances. And my grandmother was nearly 80. So I took the only option available under the circumstances. I smiled sweetly and said thank you. Because, after all, this was high praise.

"Watch out for your children!" had been a favorite admonition passed down from my maternal grandmother. The one I shared with Cousin Kim. She wasn't talking about bad influences or oncoming traffic. She was talking about a kind of Breeders' Cup standard for black love. At least the kind that ended in marriage. Light skin, good-hair (a compound word), light eyes. That was the Triple Crown.

Early on, I learned there is a premium placed on my particular brand of mongrel.

I am Red, as in Red Bone. Or Yellow, for High Yellow. Or light, bright and damn near white.

I used to be able to break into a full genealogy incantation in an instant, with attention paid to the whites and Native

Americans in my family tree. Because that white girl was still running around my head asking me if I was black. Because black and ugly always came in the same breath.

But I credit white folks with my slow evolution toward racial consciousness.

We moved to a suburb of Chicago when I was 9. And we arrived squarely in a middle-class dream.

I had always been shy. A good student. With long hair. Teachers loved me. And always, a few black girls hated me. "White dog," they called me—no, wait, that's what they called my sister. I was a "half-white bitch." Theirs was a reaction. A rage. A demonstration of the only power they had, the only power perhaps they thought they would ever have. The power to bully. But back then, I didn't know that. I had "A Foot in Each World" but couldn't get my head into either.

I don't remember my moment of political and aesthetic epiphany. It was more of a slow dawn, I think. An incremental understanding of the forces that were working around me. Certainly, watching white folks pack up and leave the neighborhood in herds made an imprint. And when a white boy spat on me at a park, I took that very personally. But it was the trickle of small slights that accumulated over the years that combined to make one point very clear.

High Yellow was just a lighter shade of black.

To be in Chicago in 1983 when Harold Washington, a big, dark, deep-black intellectual, was elected mayor was to see the face of racism. To watch the way that hate contorts the features and purples the skin. White folks were rabid. Foaming at the mouth. A few white newscasters could barely read their copy. A flier circulated through my high school featuring a big-lipped black caricature chowing down on watermelon. The city would have to be renamed Chicongo, it said. And I understood.

Ultimately, race is political. And I am a partisan.

Sometimes I still hear that white girl ask me if I am black. And now I have an answer.

Pitch.

Cold.

Blacker than three midnights.

As black as the ace of spades.

I'm so black that when I get into my car, the oil light comes on.

I've decided that it is unhealthy for us to surrender to white sensibilities, including the ones that mock us from inside our own heads.

We have all been guilty of dumbing down our expectations of white humanity—like white folks can't process nappy hair—and it's time to help them raise the bar.

Playing the Race Card

Kim has a friend whose daddy was in the Ku Klux Klan. A poster-sized picture of a finger-pointing Klansman adorned her living room wall. "I felt like Clarice Starling in 'The Silence of the Lambs' whenever I went over there," Kim says. "Like the first time she went to the jail and saw Hannibal Lecter."

The father didn't ask if Kim was part black. Kim didn't tell. She just sat on the edge of the couch with her hands and legs folded. "I kept praying, oh God, he's going to see something on me and know that I am mixed." So she stared straight ahead. And she sucked her lips in a reverse pucker the whole time she was there. Trying not to make herself too obvious, she says. Trying not to look black.

When she was in fifth grade, Kim's dad took her to a basketball game. And the bleachers went silent. Then they got whispery. Some folks already knew her dad was black. After that, everybody did.

"They used to tease me," Kim says with a shrug. She is reluctant to talk. So I press her. "Let's see, it went something like this, "Nigger-lips, nigger-lips, nigger-lips." Kim won't look at me.

The grandparents of one of Kim's friends didn't like black people. They didn't know about Kim's daddy. When the girls visited these folks, they weren't allowed to watch "The Cosby Show" because the grandfather didn't want a black man in his living room.

"I hate the N-word," Kim says. It is late. We've finished another installment of "Roots," and Kim is unsettled. Ready to talk. Tripping over her pent-up thoughts. "Whenever somebody said 'nigger' in class, everyone would turn around and look at me. I *hate* that word. I *hate* that the first thing they associate with that word is me."

When she was a freshman at Sandoval High, Kim wore a T-shirt with Martin Luther King Jr. on the front and Malcolm X on the back. "They all looked at me as if to say 'Oh, my God, she really isn't white.' " She grins when she says this.

Around 1993, Kim says she started getting into the "movement." Started watching "Yo! MTV Raps" and "The Cosby Show." Started being hungry for black culture.

She gave a civil rights speech to her sophomore English class. Her teacher thought it was a little angry. That summer, when my daughter Sydney was a baby, Kim came to D.C. We toured the White House and saw the first lady. But it was the Father's Day tribute at a friend's house where a group of us read proclamations and praised all the things we loved best about black men that got her. That let her know there was a different world than where she came from.

Her mother said she seemed different when she returned. Kim says she's always been different. In a town where everybody knows everybody and the social hierarchy is simple and uncolored, Kim is an anomaly.

"I've never technically fit in Sandoval," Kim says. "I've never had the small-town mentality. Then, after I moved out here, I thought maybe I do. Maybe I'm just a little bit country."

"I'm really trying to figure out who I am."

Some of that goes with 20-year-old territory. It's a no woman's land. Biologically grown, legally not quite, emotionally uneven. But Cousin Kim's 20 is more complex than most. She's never tried to deny the fact that her dad was black. But she has never had the resources or the tools to embrace that side of herself. She is provincial. Unexposed. Underdressed as a black girl. Searching.

On the phone or when she goes home to visit, Kim is still white. But in my house, she is a real root sister. Neither are affectations. It's just the way her cards fall. Kim is, I suppose, the ultimate insider. Privy to our private jokes. The ways we laugh at white people. And at each other. A black spy in her world. A white fly on the wall in mine. A study in duality.

We have also had some growing pains in my house. And I am quick to assign blame. Quick to play the race card.

Cousin Kim smokes. I am hard pressed to name anybody else who smokes. Especially anybody young and black. I want her to stop, and I make the questionable leap. "You need to leave that nasty white girl [expletive] alone," I tell her. Initially when I said it, Kim just looked at me meekly. Now, she gives me the finger.

Ours is a jocularity. Aided by silent code. Reinforced by a power imbalance.

Reverse racism, I suppose some would call it. I don't think so. I believe white folks would know if blacks were ever to really reverse racism. We call them countermeasures. Cousin Kim, I ask her, if you hate me because I am black and I hate you because you killed my babies, is that the same?

It is a rhetorical question. Because in my house, we do not hate. We merely understand that there are those who do. So we strive for balance. We try not to resort to negative campaigning. Sometimes we succeed. Occasionally we fail.

But we always make the effort. Because fear leads to anger, anger leads to hate and hate leads to suffering. We do not need Yoda to tell us this. It is something people on the dark side have always known.

Killing Me Softly

A couple of months ago, Katie Couric made me mad. I had to vent with Cousin Kim. For a week, the "Today" show devoted a segment to tracing family histories. And Couric's roots go back to Alabama. When cotton was king and the Courics were part of the ruling family.

You could buy fertile land cheap, the segment said. And the Courics did. The family prospered and included a Civil War governor and a member of Congress.

Couric toured the family cemetery and recounted the stories behind the headstones. Then she said, "Slaves lie in unmarked but well-tended graves nearby."

That was it. No acknowledgment that these "slaves" were people her family bought and sold. That some of them might be her kin. That no matter how smart or talented or hard-working she is, her privilege was codified, her head start generations long. That it came at the expense of somebody else's freedom. No mention of any attempt to trace those other lives to see how they fared. Maybe that would have been too much to hope for. But how about an expression of regret. A mea culpa. An "I'm sorry—wish you were here."

Genealogy is about "our simple stories, not forgotten," Couric said. Interesting choice of words. Black families have stories, too. Ones we don't forget. That get passed down to our kids.

My great-grandmother shot a white man who tried to rape her in Mississippi, and the family had to scatter. My grandmother's family, who hadn't been able to get in on that fertile-land-for-cheap deal, was dirt poor and although she was the only one of her people to finish high school, there was no money for college. At 17, my mother sat outside a Birmingham train station crying because they told her she was too colored for the white side and too white for the colored side. On a family vacation, we were turned away from an empty motel lot because the manager said there were no vacancies. In college, when I told a white journalism professor I wanted to work at The Washington Post, he said, "Doing what? Sweeping floors?"

Cousin Kim, I say. Which is better? The kindly massa or the sadistic overseer? And Kim doesn't answer. Neither, I tell her. They are the same. Two parts of a whole. Today, folks won't just walk up to you and call you "nigger lips." Well, they might, but mostly it is the benign racists who are killing me softly. They don't recognize themselves in the mirror. They didn't mean anything by it. They harbor no ill will. They just don't care enough to step outside their comfort zone.

I understand that proclivity. Often I share it. Most of us are too self-involved to dig up the psychic pain of others. But when your family has owned slaves, indifference is a self-indulgence you forfeit.

More than 300 years of chattel slavery. 129 years of terrorism and de jure Jim Crow. Thirty-four years—one generation—of full legal enfranchisement. I don't know, seems a little corrupt for white folks to cry colorblind now. We go to the Race Place because these days, I find privileged indifference as culpable as malice aforethought. When you step on my toes, I may not retaliate in kind, but you must know that I will say ouch. Loudly. Such that it disturbs your peace. Then you say, "I'm sorry." Then help me heal. After that, we can all get along nicely.

Cousin Kim nods her head yes. I believe she really gets it this time. But perhaps that's just wishful thinking.

Black for Me

Cousin Kim and I have watched all six parts of Alex Haley's "Roots." And three parts of "Queen." Then we did an hour of WHMM's "Black Women on the Light Dark Thing." We have talked and we have shared. And still she is white. And I am as black as ever.

"We're lucky," the biracial woman Alice said in "Queen." "We can choose. Who'd choose to be black? Black is hard. White is so much easier."

Still.

I want my cousin to be black for me. For the little girl who ran from a rock thrown at her head. For all the niggers I have been. I want her to be black because I'm still afraid of casual monsters in white-girl clothes. Not because they might hurt me, but they might hurt my children. Not because they hate. But because they teach 5-year-old black girls to hate themselves. And black people of all ages to suck in their lips.

Cousin Kim still chooses white not only because she looks white, she says, but "because I was raised white," and because most white folks don't know the difference. Probably it is easier. Maybe to some people she is selling out—but I also know that is an option a lot of black folks would like to have.

If I'm honest with myself, maybe I'm one of them. At least sometimes, if I think about my husband or brother getting stopped by the police for speeding. Or maybe at Tysons Corner, when tears burn my eyes as I watch a sales clerk wait on everybody but me. My anger is hot and righteous. But I'd give it up for a simple "May I help you?" any day.

Every day the world lets me know I'm black. And I wonder what it would feel like not to carry that, just for a while. Probably guilty. Probably relieved. Probably a lot like Cousin Kim.

There are no easy choices, but I think I understand my cousin's. Maybe I did all along. I just had to tell our story to realize it. But understanding and acceptance are not the same. Cousin Kim is white but conflicted, and I still sting with rejection. So alone together, we linger.

The Magic Kingdom

Race. The final frontier.

The Race Place isn't crossed in a day. You can't pass through it in the time it takes to watch a miniseries. We traverse the Race Place in fits and starts, inch by inch, over the course of a lifetime. Or maybe two. Sometimes our progress is steady. And sometimes we are dragged for miles back to the beginning, chained behind a pickup truck, and have to start all over.

The overarching reality is that realities overarch. And jockey for head space.

The extremes are easy to condemn, but the vast middle is where most of us live. Where we raise our families. And where we hope that life's lessons land a little softer on the behinds of our children than they did on our own.

A few days ago, Cousin Kim said she got into an argument with her ex-boyfriend over "The Wonderful World of Disney." The characters in the old cartoons are racists, Kim said. Look at the crows in "Dumbo." "I won the argument," she says. "He told me 'Kim, you think too much.' "

Cousin Kim smiled. And I smiled. Because this is what I want for her. To think. To challenge. To recognize. To get it. If she does that, then maybe she doesn't have to be black.

Still, I can't help giving her a silent "right on, little sister." You just take your time. We're family. And I'll be here to hip-you-up if you ever change your mind.

THE UNBEARABLE WHITENESS OF BEING

They're Not Proud. They're Not Even Loud. A Race Rally of a Different Color.

By Karl Vick
Washington Post Staff Writer
CAMBRIDGE, Mass.

Paul Bauer is a white man. Quite a white man. So white he has freckles. So white his beard has grown in orange. "You won't see *me* on the beach during daylight hours," he says. "I'm just as pink as can be."

He is proud of his whiteness, but not in a white-pride way. No, definitely not. Bauer is troubled by the bad deeds his white ancestors did. And his ancestors were whiter than most.

Four hundred seventy-seven years ago, one of them set foot on Plymouth Rock. This was on his mother's side, Mom being a Warfield. (Dad is second-generation German, which is not only white, it is dangerously white; possibly Aryan.) In the United States of America it's Anglo-Saxons who first defined whiteness. And you don't get much more Anglo than the Pilgrims.

There were 101 of them on the Mayflower, splashing ashore on the chill cusp of winter, low on provisions and wearing the wrong clothes. They would survive to celebrate the first Thanksgiving, but as every schoolchild knows, it happened only because the friendly local Indians patiently demonstrated how to catch fish and plant corn.

The quarterly newsletter put out by the Center for the Study of White American Culture.

And here, centuries later, stands Bauer ("Like Eddie Bauer," he says, "but not as well dressed") with one finger firmly on the lid of his Starbucks cup so it won't spill on his "Father Sky, Mother Earth" T-shirt. The folding table he minds is stacked with literature from the Council for Native American Solidarity. The banner above his head bids, "Free Leonard Peltier," referring to the imprisoned Sioux the courts call a murderer and his supporters call a martyr.

Perhaps it has grown fashionable, when loved ones gather around the turkey, to include with the traditional prayer of thanks some passing acknowledgment of how wretchedly the white man has repaid the hospitality of his original hosts over the centuries. Perhaps the pangs are even genuine; sometimes they are just gas.

But rest assured there *are* people who feel very, very bad about all of this, people acutely, painfully, obsessively aware of all injustice past and present, real and perceived. Three hundred of these people, Bauer among them, gathered earlier this month on the fringe of Harvard University, and you'll never guess what they had in common.

The Second National Conference on Whiteness was not what you might think. It was not what just about everybody seemed to think.

"A lot of people say, 'Oh, you're going to a Ku Klux Klan meeting,'" says Carah Reed, who flew all the way from Orange County, Calif., for what was the furthest thing in the world from a Klan rally. The only hate being spewed at Episcopal Divinity School during three gray, rainy, introspective days was the self-loathing of committed liberals—anti-racism storm troopers who identify themselves as racists because they are, you know, white.

"One thing about white people, we tend to either be proud or ashamed of being white," says Jeff Hitchcock, executive director of the Center for the Study of White American Culture, the New Jersey nonprofit that organized the conference here. "Proud in a supremacist way, or guilty in a liberal way. Very seldom do you find the balance. It's either one or the other. And that's kind of psychotic."

So they gathered here to work it out. This year's conference drew six times as many attendees as last year's, evidence that whiteness is a topic of growing, serious scholarship. Some 90 percent of the people here are white, but they are multiculturalists at heart. They see society changing, becoming more ethnic, and they want to help it change.

But on another level this gathering appears to be a kind of purification ritual, the way the white attendees start out by copping to the very thing they are working against, ardently confessing that they harbor (somewhere within themselves) the same snap judgments and idiotic prejudices that everyone else harbors, but which surface in them only by sneaking past a watchfulness that puts the White House security detail to complete and utter shame.

"I have an ulcer, okay? I'm 23. I have an ulcer," a lad named Eric announces to his peers at a panel devoted to dissecting, among other evils, "adultism."

There are sessions on "Ableism and Racism," on "The Invisibility/Visibility of Arab Americans," on "The Vector of Whiteness" (subtitled "The Latino Case"). The sessions are pan-racial, as likely to be led by a stout black woman with a British accent as a fit graybeard from Boston.

But at the end of the confab, after all have had their say, it is obvious who will have to carry the freight. At the closing session Sunday morning, a Caucasoid fellow of about 60 reaches into a badly wrinkled paper bag, pulls out a bottle and throws back a hard slug of something. It is Pepto-Bismol.

The White Man's Burden: Rudyard Kipling, the English writer, adventurer and, many say, racist, coined the phrase in 1899. Kipling's poem went on about the grave responsibility of caring for "new-caught, sullen peoples/Half devil and half child." In this place, on this weekend, the White Man's Burden is something else altogether. The White Man's Burden is his own bad self.

Holding the Mayo

Martin Mull wrung about all the tang you can from vanilla in "The History of White People in America: Part I." The mockumentary, which aired on TV 10 years ago, profiled a typical suburban family, each member of which carried around a jar of mayonnaise the size of a chair. On a tour of the living room, Mull pointed out the stack of coasters, explaining that these will serve to protect the finish of a natural surface, "should any occur."

Who wants to be white? The pasty suburban kids lining up in baggy shorts to buy the latest Bone Thugs N Harmony disc? Their pasty dads who lined up for the latest Sly & the Family Stone album? *Their* pasty dads who faked a jazzman's heroin nod and debated bop?

"Whoever heard of a wise old white woman who gets a permanent once a week and talks on the telephone?" asks a woman named Myke, reading a poem at opening session of the whiteness conference. The poem is called "Wanting to Be Indian," and it has set heads to nodding. These nods are not terse; they are the kind that roll off the shoulders and involve a lot of neck. The sound that goes with them is a soft "hmmmmm," a throaty affirmation that translates to "how true."

It seems safe to say that no one in this sea of pale faces wants to be white. And in fact the room does not "feel" white. It does not feel like a New Hampshire Rotary club meeting on the day Pat Buchanan shows up to campaign. It does not feel the way the Roanoke Room or the Chesapeake Room or any dimly lit conference space in any hotel in America feels at 10 o'clock on a weekday morning, with the name tags lined up there beside the big stainless steel coffee urn and a stack of pastries on a perfectly round brown plastic tray; someone has sliced every Danish in half.

The big room at the Conference on Whiteness feels as though it has no color at all. The vibe here is of a deliberate wash, of identity being pulled back, conscientiously held at bay. Everyone in the room is in a receive mode, unwilling to project anything at all save the quietest, softest strength.

The people here—many of them women, many with long hair the color of steel—are practiced at this. It is what a lot of them do for a living: sit in a room with other people, thinking hard, feeling harder, withholding judgment. When the emcee, a fast-talking, short-haired woman named Meck Groot, asks how many are educators, a third of those present raise a hand. Afro-American studies. Women's studies. Multicultural advisory office. Another third call themselves activists or organizers. A little cheer goes up at the words, at the mere suggestion of a cause.

No one has to explain to this bunch what the "process room" is. (It's where you go "if you have an issue," Groot notes for the record.) No one has to say why the host starts with a "centering exercise." (It's to remind you "that you have a body, and it needs to be paid attention to.") A loosely structured workshop on "Modern Racism and Internalized Oppression" suits this crew like a peasant blouse, like a dashiki, like a Peruvian wool jacket that looks as scratchy as a hair shirt, maybe for a reason.

Colorless People

They are making history here. They are on the leading edge of something. Only five people in the entire group have ever taken a weekend to meditate on "whiteness." The concept is too new. Too slippery.

Here is a woman with a tortured expression on her face and a book in her lap. It is her journal. Look out. She's going to read from it.

"Whiteness," she says. "A strange, eerie, unreal thing. When you think about it."

Here is a muscular woman explaining why she is running a workshop on "White Folks Exploring Native American Cultural and Spiritual Traditions: Appreciation Versus Appropriation."

"One thing people ask us is, why are white people doing this workshop?" she says. She answers herself: "We're all experts. If a person is white, he's an expert on this."

And here someone who is not: a striking 28-year-old woman with hair the color of rust and skin the richest shade of sienna. She was born in the United States, grew up in Zimbabwe and has lived in the Boston area for eight years.

Her name tag reads: "Blessing."

"Coming back to America, I didn't identify with the African Americans," Blessing says. "I identified more with the white people. The African Americans seemed more like a different race. They weren't like me."

Her black friends noticed this, too. They said, "Oh, you're so white." They said she watches white TV shows.

" 'Seinfeld,' " she says. "I love it. It's one of my favorite shows."

Behind her, a man sneezes. She swivels toward him.

"Bless you," Blessing says.

"I make sure I watch it every Thursday," she goes on. "I can identify a lot with the situations. I mean, that's happened to me! But a lot of my black friends don't get it."

Blessing (last name: Tawengwa) is later called up to the front of the room with eight other people, most of them black. Each is to answer a question: "What does whiteness means to you?"

"It's a culture," Blessing Tawengwa says. "It's a socialization process. It's not color."

Wrong answer. (Well, no. There are no wrong answers. "We can process out here if you want to.") Every perspective has value here. But when it comes to fighting racism, certain perspectives are more useful.

An African American woman declares: "Whiteness to me is a threat."

"It's not a real human identity," says a black man.

"Definitely the absence of color," says another.

"Whiteness," says the woman who speaks last, a young Caucasian named Jane, "is potentially the one place of refuge I think I have in my life.

"The challenge for me is not to claim it."

And there it is. For the purposes of this discussion, white is not a color, not a pigment, not a race. It is a mantle that must be claimed—but also spurned.

Even the Center for the Study of White American Culture, which brought everyone together to talk about whiteness, at times seems to want no part of it.

Jeff & Charley

"Center for Study."

This is how Jeff Hitchcock has learned to answer the phone. It's what the executive director calls the "non-reactive" name for the Center for the Study of White American Culture, hard experience having taught him that if you utter the word "white" you will spend half the workday explaining what you are not.

He carries business cards that do it for him: "Not an organization for white people, as some people may infer . . ."

These are the same cards carried by the center's president, Charley Flint, but Charley Flint has less need of the explanation, being, as Charley Flint is, a black woman.

"I was named for my father," she explains.

They are husband and wife, Hitchcock and Flint, as well as salt and pepper. They have been together 22 years, which means that the officers of the Center for the Study of White American Culture are everything their group stands for: a harmonious multiracial society, living a day-to-day existence that tries to push whiteness "out of the center" of life to make room for a new way of doing things, one agreed upon by all parties.

In other words, Hitchcock and Flint put flesh on the bones of the issues that wisp around the rafters of the Episcopal center for three days. Together, they are specific.

For example: Their son goes to a public school. Most of the kids in the school are black—about 90 percent, Hitchcock says.

Flint says it's only 70 percent.

You could count the kids, of course, but the point is the disagreement. Despite all these years with a black partner, Hitchcock sees things with white eyes. Or at least with what his wife considers white eyes.

"I believe when blacks get to 10 or 12 percent, whites see more blacks," Flint says.

It might be one way of defining whiteness: Paranoia, or at least a looming sense of being outnumbered. (By 2050, non-Hispanic whites will be only a bare majority in the United States, the Census Bureau projects.)

There are other ways.

"Being on time for appointments, that's a white thing," says Christine Maguire. She thinks a moment.

"Making lists."

She is making one now. Folded onto a sofa in the lobby, taking a break, she has just finished leading a workshop on white people appropriating Native American culture—wannabes looking for purification in sweat lodges, or paying to watch a Hopi medicine man work. In the next room, people in another workshop can be heard producing their own random observations on whiteness.

"As white people, we want to know everything," a man says. "We want to be experts."

Maguire, whose ancestors were Scots, regards her list. "Very linear thinking, that's a white thing," she says.

"The list is hard to make for a couple of reasons. One is the very vagueness of "whiteness." If you begin, as everyone here seems to, with the premise that the majority group is the historical oppressor, and that the oppressor has established the society's norms and established its institutions, you can end up defining whiteness as everything around you, and all the usual ways of doing things. You may not have to reject society as we know it, but it might help to take a fresh look at it.

Hitchcock, for one, argues that by simply acknowledging that you are white, you are also acknowledging that you have privilege. You may not have asked for the privilege, but you do enjoy it, even if the privilege amounts to not being noticed.

"White people *never* think about a group identity," says Paul Marcus, one of the conference organizers, a son of small-town New Hampshire who now works for the Boston anti-racism group Community Change Inc. Marcus is white and therefore an expert. He believes that white people think of themselves as individuals, which is why they get their backs up when called racists: "Who, me? I don't think like that."

But blacks, he says, are more likely to identify with a group. Maybe it's a result of being seen that way by others. Maybe it's natural inclination of a population that feels aggrieved (this would explain Rush Limbaugh's Dittoheads).

In any event, Marcus points out, it begins to explain why whites and blacks spend so much time talking past each other when the topic is race.

Not that white people really *like* to talk about race.

"You know, white people do feel terribly self-conscious," says Hitchcock: " 'What if I say the wrong thing?' "

A Great White Hope

Uptightness. It is a hallmark of whiteness: Think of Richard Pryor doing his white guy, cutting the wattage by two-thirds and ratcheting up the sphincter factor. Think of Billy Crystal out on the dance floor in "When Harry Met Sally," doing "the white man's overbite."

The Ward Cleaver-Ed Sullivan archetype of whiteness is a parody of rigidity, and about the only place it survives today in public life may be the good old American workplace. (Who wants to be white? Quite possibly someone who isn't, when applying for a job.) It is an arid substitute for identity, the opposite of ethnicity. The archetype is such an easy target for satire because it is so obviously artificial.

And that artificiality turns out to be the central point of "Exploring Whiteness to End Racism," as the banner over the lectern in the Episcopal center reads.

The thinking here is that we might never have enshrined "whiteness" as a concept if people with lighter skin had not felt the need to feel superior to people with darker skin. And, in fact, scientists looking for something in the human genome that is as tidy as the categories on the U.S. Census survey are now concluding that there appears to be no gene for race.

"The idea of people, in 1997, buying into the concept of race is like the Flat Earth Society," says Lowell Thompson, one of the livelier wires at the conference.

A black man who works in advertising, Thompson has written a book called "The Invisible Man in the Gray Flannel Suit." At the conference he circulated a petition reminding President Clinton that he has "a chance to begin the next thousand years, as James Brown would say, 'on the good foot.' " But mostly he peddled his latest book, "White Folks." This, Thompson explains to a white man, is how black folks refer among themselves to the majority population. It's also the name of the Web site (*www.white-folks.com*) where Thompson posts his "White Folks Funnies," featuring Leroy Freud, the world's first "clinical whiteologist." (In the panel currently posted he has Woody Allen on the couch.)

The site is one of the few jackboot-free sites that come up when you type the word "white" in an Internet search engine. When Hitchcock of the Center for the Study (*www.euroamerican.org*) ran across it a couple of years ago the two struck up a relationship that resulted in the First National Conference on Whiteness. Held in New Jersey last year, it attracted about 50 pioneers, one-sixth the number who have turned out in Cambridge. At this rate next year's confab in Chicago may well push the study of whiteness somewhere powerfully near the mainstream, perhaps recasting a term now thrown around mostly by an extremist fringe that has made "white" a dirty word.

One of the enemy groups actually had the temerity to ask to be included on the program this year. It wasn't a militia wing, but a dubious pack of revisionists that goes by the name American Renaissance. Its Web site includes writings like a 1993 article summarized as follows: "American slaves had surprisingly positive things to say about slavery."

The antidote Hitchcock prescribes is itself enough to make your head hurt. But it begins with the blandly profound observation of author Robert Terry, who back in 1970 said that part of being white is not thinking about it. Therefore, says Hitchcock: "As you learn what it is to be white, that takes you out of the traditional experience of being white."

Standing there under the "Free Leonard Peltier" banner, Paul Bauer seems to know all this instinctively. He realizes that his heritage leaves him no choice but to be conflicted. He also realizes that the point of talking about whiteness is not to make white people feel self-conscious, which is uncomfortable. The point is to make them self-aware, which can lighten the load of that big jar of mayo.

"I personally prefer Miracle Whip Light," Bauer says. "But that's a neo-white thing."

Resolved: A conference titled "Exploring Whiteness to End Racism" is not going to end racism. But in the History of White People in America, it might show the way to Part 2.

Unit Selections

Key Points to Consider

❖ International events frequently affect the United States. In what ways can such events affect ethnic populations?

❖ Do regional, international organizations, and/or the United Nations have the capacity and the rightful authority to intervene in ethnic group conflicts and/or to prevent the wholesale destructions of ethnic groups within countries? Why or why not? Are there human rights that are beyond the claims of sovereignty? Explain. Are such judgments and mobilizations of military power influenced by concerns that are measurable in terms of economic and strategic benefits or are human and cultural rights simply important without regard to traditional criteria used in international relations? Defend your answer.

❖ Explain how the relationship of ethnic Americans to changes and challenges in the world arena provides strength or liability to American interests. Does conflict between ethnic interests and national interests present real or imaginary fears about U.S. activities in international affairs? Explain.

❖ How will increased immigration, technological advances, and a more competitive world market affect the relationships between ethnic groups?

❖ Should the claims of ethnic groups in the United States in defense of culture, territory, and unique institutions be honored and protected by law and public policy? Why or why not?

 **Links**

www.dushkin.com/online/

These sites are annotated on pages 4 and 5.

Since the breakup of the Soviet empire, ethnicity has reoriented the international arena. New national claims as well as the revival of ancient antagonisms are fragmenting Europe. War, the systematic expression of conflict, and its aftermath are also occasions for the use and misuse of ethnically charged political rhetoric. The rise of nationalistic political parties in Austria and France appeared to be unlikely given the expectations of European economic integration and the aspirations of the European Union. The presence of a politically relevant past and the invocation of religious warrants for group conflict have indicated the need for new approaches to peacekeeping and educational strategies for meeting and transcending group differences. The critiques challenging multiculturalism, the educational controversy regarding which should be the dominant expressions of our human commonality, and the various values and virtues found in all ethnic traditions pose challenges for economically and socially turbulent times. Whether these moments are crises of growth or decline will be measured by a host of indicators. Which of these indicators are the most salient is, of course, another question, whose answer depends on our selective invocation of historical materials and ethnic symbols as guides for contemporary analysis.

Ethnic relations have erupted into warfare in Africa, where conflicts have shattered emerging states and thus challenged the hopeful myth of postcolonial renewal as well as the racial/ethnic myth of black solidarity. But Africa's emerging countries are not alone: the Middle East, central Europe, Canada, Ireland and Northern Ireland, and the Balkans are additional venues of destructive conflict. Each of these simmering cauldrons—not melting pots—illustrates the stakes and consequences of unresolved conflict and distrust concerning land, religion, culture, leadership, and economic production and distribution. Each also shows the rewards and recognitions that fuel human passions, ambitions, and the will to dominate and to govern the affairs and destinies of various peoples that cohabit contiguous regions.

The winds of political change in the Middle East and eastern and central Europe reveal the saliency of ethnicity and the varied textures of group relations. In America the ongoing affinity of ethnic populations to the nations of their origin is expressed in subtle as well as obvious ways. The articles in this unit explain the transmission of ethnic tradition in music and suggest linkages between religion and ethnicity. The story of the interaction of ethnicity and religion is curiously exposed in the etymology of the Greek word *ethnikos* (i.e., the rural, Gentile, or pagan people of the ancient Mediterranean world). Though such philological roots no longer drive our principal understanding of ethnicity, the experience of social affinity and cultural affiliation elaborated in the following articles deepens our awareness and understanding of ethnicity—a changing yet persistent aspect of human identity and social cohesiveness.

The process of better understanding the multiethnic character of America and the world involves the coordinated efforts of formal and informal education, which are influenced by public and private institutions and the community-based voluntary associations that are the building blocks of society. This collection of articles addresses resistance to the challenges that are embedded in passionately held and politically potent traditions of ethnic opposition. The persistence of confusion, uncertainty, insensitivity, and violence toward and among ethnic groups is a sobering and stunning fact. Strategies for dealing with the tension and reality of bias are examined in this unit. Hatred and prejudice are frequently based on conscious manipulation of powerful images that profoundly shape personal and group identity. Exploring other societies is often a way of gaining fresh perspective on the American reality; differences and commonalities of the situations described in this unit are worth pondering.

Examination, for example, of the legacy of the civil rights laws crafted during the 1960s and the process of shaping a society grounded in exclusionary habits and institutions involves assessment on many levels—the social, the political, the ideological, and the economic. Even on the most basic level of public perception, most agree that progress has been made toward a society of equality and social justice, with increased hopes for decreased segregation in schools and neighborhoods. Yet differing views among ethnic and racial groups indicate that uniformity and a shared sense of the past and present are not generally common. Attempting to overcome such gulfs of misunderstanding before they lead to more serious forms of conflict is among the great challenges of the present.

Thus, the dramas of regional ethnic struggle and the growth of worldwide ethnic challenges to the constitution of human order itself are increasingly marked by episodes of blatant bigotry, intolerance, fanaticism, and zealotry. For those who can embrace the mystery of diversity, however, there is hope for the human condition in the twenty-first century.

Balancing Act

A Police Chief Typifies Macedonia's Attempts At Ethnic Pluralism

Albanian Muslim Bexheti Runs a Force in Which Slavic Christians Prevail

Maintaining Fragile Peace

By G. Pascal Zachary And John Reed
Staff Reporters of The Wall Street Journal

TETOVO, Macadonia—In Kosovo, Slavs and ethnic Albanians are killing each other. In Macedonia, they aren't. To understand the difference, meet one tough cop named Ismail Bexheti.

An ethnic Albanian and a Muslim, Mr. Bexheti runs a police force that is almost entirely made up of Slavic Christians. He is the first Albanian ever to be police chief here in Tetovo, though Albanians constitute 80% of northwest Macedonia's population and at least a quarter of the nation's two million people. His appointment, on Feb. 1, was roughly equivalent, in American terms, to naming a Black Panther Chicago's top cop in 1968. "Even if [Mr. Bexheti's job] turns out to be only symbolic, it can give Albanians a sense of belonging," says Gilles de Rapper, an anthropologist who has studied ethnic relations here.

Macedonia is the only former Yugoslav republic that has a substantial ethnic minority, has avoided communal bloodshed and is committed to pluralism. But the pursuit of this ideal may consume Mr. Bexheti, 40 years old. His new job, which forces him to sleep some nights on a moldy couch in his office

and to take constant calls while at home, "has destroyed my peace," he says.

From the start, Mr. Bexheti faced a rebellion of senior Macedonian officers who were mortified by the prospect of working for an Albanian. The squabble wounded Mr. Bexheti. "I don't trust most of my people," he says.

And they don't trust him. Last month, for instance, four Macedonian cops beat up an old Albanian refugee and threw him in jail after claiming that the man had attacked them with a knife. Mr. Bexheti decided the police story "defied logic." He investigated and quickly found that the officers carried Kalashnikoy rifles and were younger and more fit than the Albanian. And the knife couldn't be found. So Mr. Bexheti freed the refugee and tried to discipline the officers. But that so incensed other Macedonian cops that he couldn't punish the officers; he could only warn them not to beat anyone again.

Mr. Bexheti considers such compromises unavoidable. "I am not God," he says. "I can't see everything." He realizes that the gulf between Macedonians and Albanians is great, and not just on the police force. The two groups largely

lead separate lives. They live in different neighborhoods; their children attend segregated schools. Intermarriage is rare. Albanians fear Slavs are plotting against them, and Slavs generally see Albanians as dishonest and shiftless. So the country's effort to diversify its police is crucial to maintaining ethnic harmony.

Promoting Albanians

Ethnic Albanians now are just 3% of 9,000 police employees nationwide and 10% in Mr. Bexheti's predominantly Albanian northwestern region. Convinced that it needed more Albanian police, Macedonia early this year began giving top posts—and more police jobs—to Albanians in an attempt to win over its discontented minority.

The idea is to undo a perception of persistent bias. Ethnic Albanians say police are slow to give them basic documents, such as passports and birth certificates, that are quickly delivered to Macedonia's Slavic majority. They say they are more often the subject of police beatings, illegal searches, unwarranted arrests and political surveillance. In one major outburst in July 1997, police beat hundreds of protesting Albanians, following some into their homes.

Many Albanians, aware of Mr. Bexheti's appointment and proud of it, don't think he can make a difference in their lives. "From one flower, spring will not come—even if the flower is the chief of police," says Abdul Xhelil, who runs a sandwich shop near the police station.

Others insist that Mr. Bexheti is a tool of his Macedonian bosses in the capital city of Skopje, a 45-minute drive away. They cite his inability to hire people—that is done centrally—and his lack of control over his own budget. He can't, for instance, order spending on overtime without Skopje's approval. Critics worry that Mr. Bexheti's presence is designed to silence them. "Now it makes it harder for us to criticize the police because they can say the chief is Albanian," says Abdul Alieu, an ethnic Albanian and member of Macedonia's parliament.

The government denies any systematic discrimination against Albanians but agrees that its police must become more responsive. "I hope someday that a policeman will be seen as a protector of human rights instead of being feared by citizens," says Pavle Trajanov, Macedonia's minister of interior. Mr. Trajanov, who is Mr. Bexheti's boss, counsels patience. "We can't change police officers—or the citizens—overnight," he says.

Mr. Bexheti's experience illustrates the complexity of the situation. Soft-spoken and stylish, he is the youngest son of a successful local family. One brother is the mayor of a nearby city; another is a physician; and a third works as a government inspector. In 1983, at the age of 24, Mr. Bexheti attended a police academy in Skopje, then part of Yugoslavia. He joined the force in Tetovo, the Albanian enclave, as an ordinary officer.

After the breakup of Yugoslavia, and the independence of Macedonia in 1991, Mr. Bexheti gained his own command, of a small village outside Tetovo. One day he received an order from Skopje to begin ripping down the black-eagle flag of Albania, which many locals display in a show of cultural pride. Mr. Bexheti refused the order. He was stripped of his command, but to avoid making him into a martyr, he wasn't fired.

Back as a beat cop, Mr. Bexheti thought of quitting. "My friends encouraged me to stay," he says. "They said I could do a lot of good for my people," he recalls, as one of the relatively few Albanian officers. "But the job didn't do much good for me."

Languishing in the department, Mr. Bexheti was a pariah. The department's chief, a Macedonian Slav, not only refused to discuss problems with ordinary Albanians, he wouldn't even see Mr. Bexheti. Still, Mr. Bexheti kept a reputation for honesty, effectiveness and even heroism.

Natural Choice

In 1998, when the child of a prominent family was kidnapped, Mr. Bexheti learned where the child was being held from one of his many Albanian informants. He led a dramatic rescue, surrounding the kidnappers' hideout and saving the boy. He personally arrested one of the kidnappers, throwing him to the ground. Mr. Bexheti broke a leg.

When the government launched its affirmative-action plan early this year, Mr. Bexheti was considered the natural choice as chief. "He's clean, and he's not one of those Albanians who treats his own people worse just to show the Macedonians he's fair," says Arben Xhaferi, chief of the Albanian Democratic Party, the leading minority party in Macedonia, and Mr. Bexheti's political patron.

For a novice chief, Mr. Bexheti is a canny operator. Ordinary people can see him in his office, or run into him on the streets, at the Bolero cafe where he often sits outside drinking a cappuccino, or while driving his department-issue Volkswagen Golf. Everywhere he goes, it seems, people recognize him. "They know me, but I don't always know them," he says. If they have a police problem, he tells them to visit his office. If they say that Slavic police officers have sent them away—as some say happens—he replies, in his characteristically faint voice, "Tell them the chief sent you."

Inside the main station, a ramshackle four-story building left over from the communist era, Mr. Bexheti is decidedly less partisan. "I will not act only for Albanians," he told his Macedonian officers when he took office. Rather than issue orders, he has tried to coax them to try new approaches. He has also won fans by supporting a hefty pay hike for his men.

He doesn't mind an argument. Chain-smoking Marlboro Lights in his un-adorned office, he spends hours on the telephone with higher-ups in Skopje, lobbying for more Albanian officers. They have promised him 30 more, but won't say when. Such frustrations can make Mr. Bexheti reach for one of four bottles of liquor he keeps on the floor under his desk. Sipping a Johnny Walker one afternoon, he says, "I have a lot of plans but low means."

Modest Circumstances

With a salary of just $250 a month, he isn't getting rich, either. He lives in a four-room apartment, with his wife and three children, on the 10th-floor in a building with a balky elevator. Without the earnings of his wife, a schoolteacher, he would live less comfortably.

As chief, his hours are longer; he hardly sees his kids. Yet his presence has lifted the morale of the Albanian officers, who are playing important roles in monitoring refugee movements and their camps. Besides murders and theft, Tetovo has its drug-smugglers and extortion-gangs. But with the Kosovo war, the biggest task involves refugees. Elsewhere in Macedonia, where Albanians have virtually no role on the force, refugees have repeatedly complained of police brutality and even staged protests calling for NATO forces to replace Macedonian police at the camps.

In the Tetovo region, under Mr. Bexheti's watch, complains are far fewer, chiefly because he has stationed ethnic-Albanians in key spots. One evening this month, at a refugee camp two miles from the center of Tetovo, three cops listen to an old man explain why a family of eight should leave the camp with him, to live temporarily in his home. Two cops—the Macedonian Slavs—drift off, leaving the third man, an ethnic Albanian, to sort out the situation. There are 7,000 refugees in the camp, too many to allow them free movement. The family needs permission to leave, but the people who sign the forms are gone for the day. The Albanian cop sympathizes, and lets them go on the promise that they will take care of the paperwork later.

It is a risk, but worth it, he thinks. The refugees shake his hand, thank him and walk through the camp gate. He smiles, tears in his eyes. "I have been a policeman for 13 years," he says. "I am also an Albanian, and these are my people."

Don't expect this conflict to end anytime soon

Underlying NATO's resolve on Kosovo are guilt over earlier genocide in Europe and worry about a wider war

By David Walsh

The 20th century appears to be ending pretty much as it began. Refugees and misery are teeming out of the Balkans, the great tinderbox of Europe.

The faces of the ethnic Albanians, brutally ejected from Kosovo, seem to say it all. They look so much like the past that sympathy washes toward them from all corners of the earth. Memories of the dispossessed and displaced, of the pogroms and holocausts that have stamped our time, are all recalled to mind.

Even those of us who have lived in comparative ease throughout the cruelest century have become sensitized to the suffering entailed. Our complacency has been pricked by the awareness that we, too, could be reduced to the zero point of human existence. We, too, could be marched out of our houses and dispatched toward a stinking field beyond our frontiers without food, shelter, water or sanitation. The barrel of a gun can swiftly strip us of everything.

We can only wonder at the obtuseness of a regime that could fail to recognize its impact. How could Yugoslavian President Slobodan Milosevic and the Serbian government so totally misperceive the effect of a million refugees huddled in misery just beyond their borders? Especially when they became the focus of unrestricted media attention, and their harrowing stories overwhelmed all other considerations? How

CNS PHOTO

HUNGRY: Ethnic Albanians reach for food at a refugee camp

From *Our Sunday Visitor,* April 25, 1999, p. 3. Reprinted by permission of *Our Sunday Visitor,* 200 Noll Plaza, Huntington, Indiana 46750.

is it possible to maintain any sympathy for the Serbian cause, for its historic grievances and insecurities, even for the normal presumption to preserve the integrity of established borders?

TACTICAL BLUNDER

Milosevic has done more to delegitimize Serbian rule over Kosovo than any campaign for autonomy or independence could ever have accomplished. Neither the Albanian Kosovars nor the rest of the world recognize him as the legitimate government of the province. How was it possible for a man whom President Clinton avers as "not to be underestimated" to have so totally misread the world in which he lives?

This is one of the great unanswered questions of the current crisis. Milosevic has placed his small country of 10 million in an unenviable confrontation with the most powerful military alliance in the world. Sure, so far the NATO campaign has consisted of minutely calibrated bombing assaults on obvious targets. But the direction and intensity is expanding. With the introduction of tactical aircraft and helicopters, the conflict will be taken directly to Serbian units all over the region.

The avowed aim of NATO is nothing less than to erode Milosevic's military capability to the point that he can no longer project control over Kosovo. Introduction of NATO troops into a pacified province and the repatriation of the refugees would de facto render Kosovo an independent state. The only uncertainty is Western resolve, and Milosevic's own extraordinary brutality has hardened all wavering. Public opinion, the real threat he faces, is now so far ahead of political and military leadership that it has already proclaimed its willingness to commit troops and endure casualties in defense of the Kosovars.

It is a blunder of such staggering proportions that it could only come from a man who has never understood the experience of the century. How was it conceivable that America and Europe would sit idly by when so vividly reminded of the inhumanity against which they had struggled in two World Wars, a cold war and a string of lesser conflicts?

Certainly their idealism has been tempered by their aversion to discomfort. Western powers have seriously opposed brutality only when their own interests were also at stake. Milosevic is correct in his estimation of their unwillingness to sustain the significant casualties that a real Balkan war would entail. But the ability of NATO to inflict destruction short of an all-out military engagement is formidable, and it is even more so when directed against the finite resources of solitary Serbia. How many fuel depots, ammunition dumps, communication centers, bridges and infrastructures can the country continue to do without?

And all of this is before the extensive array of antipersonnel weaponry is directed against the military and paramilitary units and equipment. It is quite conceivable that Milosevic could be stripped of both his military assets and his capacity to control Serbia without a single NATO soldier setting foot on Yugoslav soil. The deliberately cautious tone of the daily briefings conceals the capacity and determination of a military giant to bring one puny rogue to heel.

Milosevic has failed to recognize the military capacity of the Western powers and their more impressive and indispensable will to use it. He did not count on the provocation of a unified public opinion that now virtually demands its leaders do something to reverse the depopulation of Kosovo.

In this, he not only miscalculated the impact of the global media to make the suffering of the Kosovars effective, but he also forgot the power that such images of mass exodus would have on memories formed by the upheavals of the 20th century. His own amnesia robbed him of the ability to foresee how intolerable the world would regard his actions.

MIGHT OR RIGHT?

Kosovo is not the last of the 20th-century horrors in which the world stood idly by; that dubious honor is best reserved for the Rwanda genocide. What we see in the reaction to Kosovo is a measure of the change wrought by such bitter experience. In a very real sense, humanity has become indivisible through the common bond of suffering. We cannot sit by when whole nations are force-marched out of their homes, not just because it might later happen to us, but because we would no longer be able to live with ourselves if we did nothing to defend them. Our own humanity is in the balance.

At the same time, we are only human. Moral outrage does not give us either the capacity or the authority to right all the wrongs of the world. We must do what we can to resist evil while straining mightily to commit as little evil as possible in the process. A bombing campaign may be a relatively cheap way of warfare, but it has two distinct advantages. It offers a reasonable change of limiting civilian destruction—an important requisite of the just-war mandate—and it minimizes alliance casualties, which would swiftly sap public support for the interventionist efforts.

Moral and practical considerations converge. The greatest temptation for idealists is arrogance, and there is no surer path to self-destruction. We may be temporarily on the side of the most aggrieved, but that does not mean that we can do no wrong.

Self-restraint must be gained through recognition of the limited capacity, wisdom and benefit of Western assumption of responsibility for the governance of other countries. Yugoslavs are the most appropriate to resolve their own problems. The Serbs, who are now the object of attack and demonization, are the ones to whom NATO and the Kosovars will have to turn to work out a lasting peace agreement. Again, the just-war exigence insists that war always be waged with the attitude of a peacemaker—that is, with the continuing exercise of military and rhetorical restraint and the recognition of the diminished moral authority of all combatants to negotiate peace.

Russia, in this sense, could still prove the one indispensable broker for a comprehensive settlement. That might be the final indignity for a triumphant NATO to swallow, but surely a small price to pay for putting human beings first.

David Walsh is a professor of politics at The Catholic University of America in Washington, D.C.

BELONGING IN THE WEST

Multiple challenges and concerns arise from the presence of ever-growing Muslim communities within Western society.

YVONNE YAZBECK HADDAD

When Daniel Pipes sounded the alarm: "The Muslims Are Coming! The Muslims are Coming!" in the November 19, 1990, issue of *National Review,* it was clear that Muslims were already here. Indeed, they had become an intregal part of the West. Since that time, Islam, particularly Islamic fundamentalism, has continually been depicted as the next enemy: as a force replacing communism as a challenge to the West.

Consequently, Muslims are often suffered from considerable prejudice. They have been accused of adhering to a religion that is devoid of integrity, that encourages violent passions in its adherents, that menaces civil society and is a threat to our way of life. Muslims are stereotyped as potentially bloodthirsty terrorists whose loyalty as citizens must be questioned. Not one promoter of political correctness has put them on a list of communities to be protected. But Muslims have been victims of hate crimes that include assault, murder, and the burning of mosques in both Europe and North America. As a result, their apprehension about their security and future in Western society has increased.

The Muslim encounter with the West dates back to the beginning of Islam. As Muslims spread into Byzantium and North Africa, they established their hegemony over large areas inhabited by Christian populations. While their expansion into western Europe was halted at Poitiers in 731, Muslims created a thriving civilization in different parts of Spain, Portugal, Sicily, and southern France between the eighth and fifteenth centuries. In the East, Ottoman expansion into Europe was not halted until the failure of the siege of Vienna in 1683. While a significant number of Muslims continued to live in eastern Europe, in Bulgaria, Romania, Albania, and Serbia, the fall of Grenada in 1492 and the Inquisition (which gave Muslims the options of conversion to Christianity, expulsion, or death) all but eliminated a Muslim presence in western Europe. Thus, the recent growth of the Muslim community in Europe and North America has been called the "new Islamic presence."

Indeed, since the sixteenth century, Muslims have encountered Western cultures as conquering and imperial powers, competing in their quest to subjugate Muslims and monopolize their economic resources. Consequently, some Muslims depict the West as bent on combating Islam not only through colonial conquest but through armies of missionaries. They perceive a West that is and ever has been eager to displace or eradicate Muslims. They find evidence in the Reconquista, the Crusades, and, more recently, in Palestine and Bosnia.

Living beyond the Islamic state

Muslim jurists have offered various opinions about whether it is permissible for Muslims to live outside the jurisdiction of an Islamic state. This issue has been raised during the last two decades, as some Muslim scholars have admonished Muslims to leave the West lest they lose their soul amid its wayward ways. Other jurists have insisted that as long as Muslims are free to practice their faith, they are allowed to live outside the house of Islam, while still others have said that it is Muslims' duty to propagate the faith in their new abode. Thus they not only have the opportunity to share the salvific teachings of Islam but must try to redeem Western society from its evil ways and restore it to the worship of God.

The question then is often asked: "Given their experience of the West, why do they come?" Surveys show that Muslims move to Europe and North America for the same reasons that other populations have chosen to come: for higher education, better economic opportunities, and political and religious freedom. Others are refugees, the by-product of Euro-American adventures in the world. Thus the first significant group of Muslims to come to France were North Africans and Senegalese who were recruited to fight in French colonial wars. Immigrants to Britain are from its former colonies and from the ranks of its Asian (Bangladeshi, Indian, and Pakistani) colonial civil servants expelled from Africa by the leaders of newly independent nations. In the Netherlands, the initial Muslim population came from the colonies of Indonesia and Suriname.

The majority of Muslims in Europe were recruited as temporary guest workers to relieve the shortage of labor in the post–World War II reconstruction. The host countries of Germany, the Netherlands, Austria, Britain, Switzerland, and France expected them to leave when their contracts expired. In the 1970s, a recession and growing unemployment prompted European governments to reduce imported labor. Some even provided financial incentives for the laborers to return to their homelands. This policy led to an unintended growth of the Muslim community, as many opted to bring their families and settle for fear that they would not have another opportunity.

Here Yet Apart

> Though an integral part of twentieth-century Western society, Muslims have lately been targets of considerable prejudice.

> Many argue that it may not be possible to lead a Muslim lifestyle beyond the borders of an Islamic state.

> Both Islamic and European governments have helped build mosques and Muslim centers in the West, in the hopes of blunting the rise of fundamentalism and aiding the assimilation of Muslim immigrants.

> Muslims ask whether Western society, which prides itself on liberal democracy, pluralism, and multiculturalism, will be flexible enough to provide for Islamic input into the shaping of its future.

In European nations with an official state religion, such as Britain and the Netherlands, Muslims have sought parity with Jews and Catholics who have been given special privileges. But to no avail. Thus, during the Salman Rushdie affair, Muslims sought implementation of the blasphemy law, only to find out that it operates only to protect Anglicanism. In Britain, for example, the school day starts with a Christian prayer. In courts, the oath is taken on the Bible. Town council meetings start with a prayer. Anglican clergy celebrate marriage that is automatically legal without having to go to the registrar. While Catholic and Jewish marriages are recognized, those performed by imams are not. Catholics and Jews obtain state funding to support their parochial schools, but Muslim requests for parity have been denied.

Muslims have fared differently in nations that have historically welcomed immigrants—the United States, Canada, Latin America, and Australia. Muslim migrant laborers began coming to America in the nineteenth century. While many returned, a few settled permanently and formed the nucleus of what is now the fourth and fifth American-born generation of Muslims. The largest number of Muslims came in the 1970s on a preference visa and were accepted

Muslim Legal Expectations

Kathleen Moore

When a truck bomb shattered the Murrah Federal Building in downtown Oklahoma City on April 19, 1995—the worst terrorist act ever on American soil—many in the media and federal law enforcement jumped to the conclusion that an "Islamic fundamentalist" was responsible. Similarly, the downing of TWA Flight 800 and the Olympic Park explosion in Atlanta set off allegations that "Middle Eastern-looking" terrorists were to blame. Those hasty conclusions have proved groundless. However, Muslim defendants have been convicted for the 1993 bombing of the World Trade Center, and a Muslim suspect has been arrested in connection with the attack on traffic near the CIA headquarters in January of that year.

Instantly attributing blame to unknown Muslim terrorists was not just the result of the media and law enforcement officials letting their imaginations run amok. Such images were also conjured up—and in some instances acted upon—by the general public. Some 200 incidents of anti-Muslim harassment were reported in the days immediately following the tragedy in Oklahoma.

Consequently, American Muslim communities mobilized to an unprecedented degree. Existing organizations, such as the American Muslim Council and the Islamic Society of North America, were joined by newly formed groups such as the Council on American-Islamic Relations (CAIR) to defend Muslims' civil rights. Public relations and lobbying efforts and press conferences highlighted not merely the Muslim presence in the United States but also the American Muslims' experiences as targets of discrimination. Thus the rights consciousness of this growing segment of the American population is largely being shaped by Muslims' responses to media distortions and perceived demonization of Islam.

The fears that motivate anti-Islamic sentiment appear to derive from a sense of insecurity that has lurked just beneath the surface of our national life since the fall of the Berlin Wall in 1989. The prospects for world peace would seem to be greater than at any other time in this century, but our doubts about the future seem nevertheless to escalate. This post–Cold War malaise has its consequences for those who fear they may come to take the unenviable place of the "Red menace" in the public mind. Of great concern to many Muslims is the prospect that they will be increasingly subjected to various forms of discrimination in Western countries as negative portrayals of Islam and Muslims take their toll.

The visible effects of these concerns and experiences of mistreatment can be seen in the emergence of rights-advocacy groups that have used a variety of legal strategies to assert Muslim rights. For instance, in the United States, CAIR has conducted media campaigns over the last two years or so to bring to public attention instances where women have been prohibited from wearing the traditional Islamic *hijab* (head scarf) at work. Cases of harassment involving Muslims who have been taunted with epithets relating to prevalent prejudicial stereotypes have been documented and financially supported through the legal process by these advocacy groups. In Britain, a few muslim activist have (so far, unsuccessfully) pressed the government for greater autonomy, particularly allowing Islamic courts to adjudicate issues of family law separate from the civil court system.

We are now witnessing the emergence of a distinctive Western Muslim identity, carved out of the secular social environment of the West. It would not be accurate, however, to assume that the Muslim identity being forged is uniform or monolithic. In fact, significant distinctions and disagreements exist within Muslim communities that are differentiated by sectarian, ethnic, regional, or generational traits. But it is meaningful to note that there are shared experiences and to recognize that the formulation of this identity is taking place under constraints imposed by the host societies. Muslim legal expectations and interpretations are thus voiced within particular contexts, in response to specific events, cultural characteristics, and historical pressures.

In an idealized sense, Muslims migrated to the United States and Britain with a centuries-old tradition in hand. In this legal framework are the classical traditions of Islamic jurisprudence that offer models for minority living. Historically, these models focus on three essential questions: First, under what conditions are Muslims allowed to live outside Muslim territory? In essence, the answer is only where religious freedom prevails. Second, what responsibilities do Muslim minorities have with respect to their host society? Here, answers are varied. Third, what is the relationship of Muslim minorities, living in places like the United States and Britain, to the global Muslim community as a whole? Again, answers are varied and problematic.

In general, the classical models suggest that if a Muslim minority does not encounter religious freedom and is unable to practice its faith, then it has the options of fighting back (*jihad*) or emigration (*hirah*).

Yet many see these traditions as out of touch with Muslim minorities' realities and in need of revision to fit today's circumstances. Recent calls have been made for the formulation of a "new" jurisprudence

as citizens and given voting rights. Predominantly members of the educated elite, they are doctors, professors, and engineers.

Islam is the second- or third-largest religion in various European nations. It is estimated that there are five million Muslims in France, organized in over 1,000 mosques and prayer halls. They constitute about 10 percent of the population, making Islam the largest religion after Catholicism and with more active adherin light of changing conditions. A variety of issues have been singled out by the British and American Muslim communities as being crucial.

Some issues are the product of the secular environment in which Muslims live. Do they have rights to religious freedom that require accommodation of their specific needs in the workplace, at school, or in the military? How will Muslims survive as a vibrant religious community in the West? Will they be able to freely and fully participate in its religious landscape and in defining the future as a pluralistic society? How can Muslim children be successfully integrated into the larger society, to function as hyphenated Americans or Britons without abandoning the faith? Can Muslims vote or run for political office in a secular society where the institutions of government are not based on Islamic values? What roles are women permitted to play in public life?

Attendance at mosques and Islamic centers (in the West) has gone up over the last decade or so. Mosques are now not only for prayer at the five prescribed times: They have become community centers and provide facilities for tutoring students in their school subjects, Qur'anic studies, marriage ceremonies, free counseling and mediation, and legal services.

In some of these places, Muslims are listening to those who warn from the pulpit that the encounter with the secular West is destructive and that the only option for Muslim survival is to remain marginal to public life. From this isolationist perspective, the Muslim minority should reaffirm a Muslim identity in isolation, untainted by the materialistic values of the West. This, it is thought, will have the effect of inviting others to Islam by providing an example of an incorruptible "city on a hill" in the midst of moral decay.

On the other side of the debate are the "accommodationists," who struggle to feel at home in the United States and Britain. Muhammad Abduh, an early twentieth-century reformer in Egypt, provides some insight into the accommodationists' position. Abduh gave a *fatwa* (religious legal opinion) permitting Muslims in South Africa to consume meat butchered for People of the Book (i.e., Christians and Jews) when no *halal* meat (i.e., food prepared or butchered in the Islamically prescribed way, similar to the Jewish tradition of kosher) was available.

Accommodationists advise cooperation with non-Muslims, provided that it benefits the Muslim community. As long as the Muslim who lives as minority is at liberty to maintain the "core" of the religion, he may adjust to the host society. Accommodationists argue that diet, as long as it is nourishing, need not comply with stringent Islamic strictures; attire, as long as it is clean and modest, need not be restricting (such as the so-called veil or head scarf is); and the architecture of mosques and Islamic centers need not slavishly imitate Middle Eastern styles as long as the buildings are accessible and functional.

In the last two decades the circumstances of Muslim minorities have come to the attention of various international Islamic organizations, such as the muslim World League, which has established a Fiqh Council, a body that engages in the interpretation of Islamic law to address minority concerns. The council represents a wide variety of Islamic legal schools and advocates what is being called "jurisprudence of necessity" (*fiqh al-darurah*) and "jurisprudence of minority" (*fiqh al-aqalliyah*) to respond to issues of Muslim life in a non-Islamic environment.

Some critics within Islam, though, see this as an effort to impose a "top-down" understanding of Muslim contingencies and reject it in favor of a "bottom-up" approach. Efforts at using American legal rules and then sanctifying them as "Islamic" because they are fair and just can be seen at the local level. For instance, American laws governing marriage, divorce, and child custody, where the woman would, arguably, have greater rights than Islam affords, have been sanctified in places where the *imam* (leader of the mosque) has sanctioned a civil marriage license or divorce decree obtained by a member of his mosque.

The secular legal system has had its effect on Muslim legal consciousness. For example, one leader of a large mosque community in an urban area in the western United States asserts that the process of working out a set of rules to govern Muslim life must be thought of as a jurisprudence of "minority," not because of any specific Islamic tradition but because Muslims are living in the United States, where a significant body of case law on minority relations already exists. To be labeled a minority entitles one to rights. The word *minority* may connote weakness or vulnerability, but it is also a recognized basis for making claims to resources and privilege in America. Thus, it is imperative to accommodate Islamic practices to fit the opportunities provided by the local customs and laws of the community in which they are now a permanent part.

Kathleen Moore is assistant professor of political science at the University of Connecticut.

ents than either Protestants or Jews. In Britain, the Muslim population is estimated at about two million, organized in over 600 mosques. The Muslim community of the United States is estimated at five million, about 10 percent of whom are involved in organized religion in over 1,250 mosques and Islamic centers. Canada has about half a million.

It is expected that Muslims will outnumber Jews in Canada and the United States by the first decade of the next century. The North American community is noted for its ethnic national, linguistic, and secretarian diversity. It includes over a million converts, mostly African Americans. While it is estimated that up to 18 percent of the slaves brought to America were Muslims, most had converted to Christianity by the beginning of this century. The conversion of African Americans to Islam is a twentieth-century phenomenon.

The Muslim experience in the West

The Muslim experience in the West varies according to the immigrants' background, the nations they came from, their reasons for leaving, and their educational attainments. The host country's policies are also influential: whether it welcomes foreigners and/or grants them citizenship rights, its perceptions of Islam, and its laws governing the relationship between religion and state.

During the eighties, various Muslim countries began laying Islamic foundations in the West by providing funds for the construction of mosques and schools and the teaching of Arabic and Islam. For example, in a two-year period, Saudi Arabia spent $10 million to construct mosques in North America. In Germany, Sweden, and the Netherlands—where there are large Turkish and Moroccan communities—the fear of the potential for growth of Islamic fundamentalism among the *marginalized guest* workers led to arrangements with the Turkish and Moroccan governments to supervise the religious affairs of the community. Both governments welcomed the opportunity to blunt the growth of fundamentalism and curtail its dissemination in their countries. The European governments paid for construction of Islamic centers and mosques and imported the religious leaders to lead prayers and provide religious instruction.

Two issues are of paramount importance for both the immigrants and host countries: security and cultural coherence. All nation-states have developed a myth of national identity that has been inculcated in schoolchildren through literature, art, music, assumptions, legends, and a particular understanding of history. These myths have shaped several generations of Europeans and Americans through the cauldron of two wars and created distinctive identities marking the way the West sees itself and what it takes for granted,

as well as what it identifies as alien, strange, and weird.

Educated Muslims who emigrated in the postwar period also have a preformed understanding of Western culture based on the experience of colonialism and neocolonialism. Their perceptions have been shaped by watching Western movies and television, which they perceive as imbued with drugs, violence, racism, and pornography. Muslims are repelled by what they see as a degenerate society with weak family values. They condemn premarital or extramarital sex and having children out of wedlock, both of which increase the fragility of marriage and hence the family bond. They believe that Western values concerning parents and children's duties toward one another are lacking. There is too much emphasis on individual freedom and not enough on corporate responsibility.

A primary concern for Muslim immigrants is surviving in what they experience as a hostile environment and safeguarding the welfare of their children. They are fully aware that Europe and the Americas have been shaped by secular Christianity. They seek to maintain the right to practice their faith according to its tenets as revealed to them by God. They are concerned about perpetuation of the faith among their children and preservation of Islamic values. In this context they have sought to have employers provide them with time off to fulfill their religious duties during the day, to attend the Friday prayer at the mosque, fast during the month of Ramadan, and celebrate the two major holidays (Eid al-Fitr and Eid al-Adha). Many are concerned about properly slaughtered meat (halal), while others seek the right to have their children excused from coed athletics and sex education (which they believe promotes promiscuity). They believe that religious freedom should provide the right to wear the head scarf (hijab) for women.

In France, the issue of wearing the hijab took on national significance when several female students were banned from wearing it on the grounds that such behavior is tantamount to proselytizing, a proscribed activity in the secular schools of France. For Muslims, the ban was seen as an anti-Muslim act, since Christians are allowed to wear a cross and Jews a yarmulke, both of which could then be interpreted as an act of propagating a faith.

The issue of the hijab has surfaced in other Western nations under different rubrics. For example, in Canada, feminists championed the banning of head scarfs, which they depicted as a symbol of oppression. Muslim girls who put them on insisted that it was an act of obedience to a divine injunction and therefore protected under the freedom of religion. More important, they viewed it as an instrument of liberation from being a sex object. In the United States, the Council on American-Islamic Relations reported that there was a 50 percent increase in 1996 in the number of incidents of discrimination against women who wear the hijab.

Islam in a plural society

The Western experience is also shaping new forms of Islamic organization and administration. The imam not only leads prayer and worship but acts as an ambassador to the host culture, attempting to build bridges to other faith communities and representing Muslims in interfaith events. Moreover, the mosque, besides being a place of congregational prayer, has become a social center where the community meets for a variety of events that help cement relationships and provide for community celebrations. In this center for Islamic knowledge and education Islam is taught to the next generation, which reflects on its meaning in the new environment. The mosque has become an island of security and a venue for the sharing of one's experiences. It is not unusual to see people clothed in their ethnic dress for Sunday services, taking advantage of a chance to affirm primary identity in an environment where individuals can be themselves without being under constant scrutiny for conformity.

Some Muslims contemplate the option of returning to their homeland, should conditions of life in the West continue to be unacceptable. Their children, however, have been reared and educated in the West. The West is their homeland. They are bicultural and possess an intimate experience and knowledge of Western society, as well as a knowledge about the culture of the parents as remembered and reinvented in the West. While immigrants struggle to maintain their identity; they are increasingly being challenged and changed as their children become more indigenized into the surrounding culture.

Some Western authors have continued to question whether Muslims are worthy of citizenship in a democratic nation or whether their presence will alter the place where they settle. While some continue to debate whether they belong *in* the West, it is evident that Muslims are part and parcel *of* the West. An estimated ten thousand Muslims currently serve in the armed services of the United States, for example. There are two Muslim chaplains, one in the Navy and one in the Army and plans have been made to appoint one in the Air Force.

Muslims in the West generally favor keeping a low profile for security reasons. They are the latest victims of chauvinism and xenophobia. Events such as the oil embargo of 1973, the Iranian revolution, the holding of American hostages for 444 days, and the Pan Am bombing have created concern among many westerners. Irresponsible and irrational actions such as the bombing of the World Trade Center have heightened fears of Islamic fundamentalism. This has exacerbated the fear of Islam and tapped into a history of misunderstanding and vilification. Thus, Muslims fear they are becoming the new villains on the block, replacing Jews, Gypsies, Italians, and African Americans as objects of odium.

Muslims continue to ask whether Western democracies are liberal enough to include Islamic input into the national consensus, or if they will insist on an exclusively Judeo-Christian culture. Will Western pluralism or multiculturalism be flexible enough to provide for Islamic input into the shaping of the future of Western society? Or will Muslims continue to be marginaiized, ostracized, studied, and evaluated, always judged as lacking, always the "other"?

Yvonne Yazbeck Haddad is professor of the history of Islam and Christian-Muslim relations at Georgetown University.

Histroy has stripped Africa's people of the dignity of building their nations on their own indigenous values, institutions, and heritage. The modern African state is the product of Europe, not Africa. To attempt at this late date to return to ancestral identities and resources as bases for building the modern African nation would risk the collapse of many countries. At the same time, to disregard ethnic realities would be to build on loose sand, also a high-risk exercise, Is it possible to consolidate the frame-

ultimate authority was an outsider, a foreigner. This mechanism functioned through the centralization of power, which ultimately rested on police and military force, the tools of authoritarian rule. This crude force was, however, softened by making use of traditional leaders as extended arms of state control over the tribes or the local communities, giving this externally imposed system a semblance of legitimacy for the masses. Adding to this appearance of legitimacy was the introduction of a welfare system by which the state provided

Ethnicity

AN AFRICAN PRECICAMENT

BY FRANCIS M. DENG

work of the modern African state while giving recognition and maximum utility to the component elements of ethnicities, cultures, and aspirations for self-determination?

THE CHALLENGE OF ETHNICITY IN AFRICA

Ethnicity is more than skin color or physical characteristics, more than language, song, and dance. It is the embodiment of values, institutions, and patterns of behavior, a composite whole representing a people's historical experience, aspirations, and world view. Deprive a people of their ethnicity, their culture, and you deprive them of their sense of direction or purpose.

Traditionally, African societies and even states functioned through an elaborate system based on the family, the lineage, the clan, the tribe, and ultimately a confederation of groups with ethnic, cultural, and linguistic characteristics in common. These were the units of social, economic, and political organizations and inter-communal relations.

In the process of colonial state-formation, groups were divided or brought together with little or no regard to their common characteristics or distinctive attributes. They were placed in new administrative frameworks, governed by new values, new institutions, and new operational principles and techniques. The autonomous local outlook of the old order was replaced by the control mechanisms of the state, in which the

meager social services and limited development opportunities to privileged sectors. National resources were otherwise extracted and exported as raw materials to feed the metropolitan industries of the colonial masters.

This new system undermined the people's indigenous system, which provided them with the means for pursuing their modest but sustainable life objectives, and replaced it with centrally controlled resources that were in short supply and subject to severely competitive demands. Development was conceived as a means of receiving basic services from the state, rather than as a process of growth and collective accumulation of wealth that could in turn be invested in further growth. The localized, broad-based, low-risk, self-sustaining subsistence activities gave way to high-risk, stratifying competition for state power and scarce resources, a zero-sum conflict of identities based on tribalism or ethnicity. Independence removed the common enemy, the colonial oppressor, but actually sharpened the conflict over centralized power and control over national resources.

Today, virtually every African conflict has some ethno-regional dimension to it. Even those conflicts that may appear to be free of ethnic concerns involve factions and alliances built around ethnic loyalties. Analysts have tended to have one

Francis M. Deng is a senior fellow in the Brookings Foreign Policy Studies program.

From *The Brookings Review,* Summer 1997, pp. 28-31. © 1997 by The Brookings Institution. Reprinted by permission.

of two views of the role of ethnicity in these conflicts. Some see ethnicity as a source of conflict; others see it as a tool used by political entrepreneurs to promote their ambitions. In reality, it is both. Ethnicity, especially when combined with territorial identity, is a reality that exists independently of political maneuvers. To argue that ethnic groups are unwitting tools of political manipulation is to underestimate a fundamental social reality. On the other hand, ethnicity is clearly a resource for political manipulation and entrepreneurship.

AFRICA'S RESPONSE TO THE CHALLENGE

After independence Africans were eager to disavow tribalism as divisive. Unity was postulated in a way that assumed a mythical homogeneity amidst diversity. Kwame Nkrumah of Ghana outlawed parties organized on tribal or ethnic bases. Houphouet-Boigny of Côte d' Ivoire coopted ethnic groups through shrewd distribution of ministerial posts, civil service jobs, social services, and development projects. Julius Nyerere, a scion of tribal chieftaincy, stamped out tribalism by fostering nationalistic pride in Tanganyika and later, Tanzania, born out of the union with Zanzibar. Jommo Kenyatta of Kenya forged a delicate alliance of ethnic groups behind the dominance of his Kenyan African National Union party. In South Africa, apartheid recognized and stratified races and ethnicities to an unsustainable degree. Post-apartheid South Africa, however, remains poised between a racially, ethnically, and tribally blind democratic system and a proud ethnic self-assertiveness, represented and exploited by Zulu nationalists, spearheaded by the emotive leadership of Chief Buthelezi.

Throughout Africa, the goal of safeguarding unity within the colonial state has preserved the stability of colonial borders while generating ethnic tensions and violence within those borders. Sudan offers an extreme example. The dominant North, a hybrid of Arab and African racial, cultural, and religious elements, is trying to resolve its identity crisis by being more Arab and Islamic than its prototypes. Worse, this distorted self-perception, heightened by the agendas of political elites, is projected as the framework for unifying and integrating the country, generating a devastating zero-sum conflict between the Arab-Muslim North and the indigenously African South, whose modern leadership is predominantly Christian.

The decision of the Founding Fathers of the Organization of African Unity to respect the colonial borders established a normative principle that has been followed with remarkable success. Secession movements have met with strong resistance from the OAU. Katanga tried to break away from the Congo

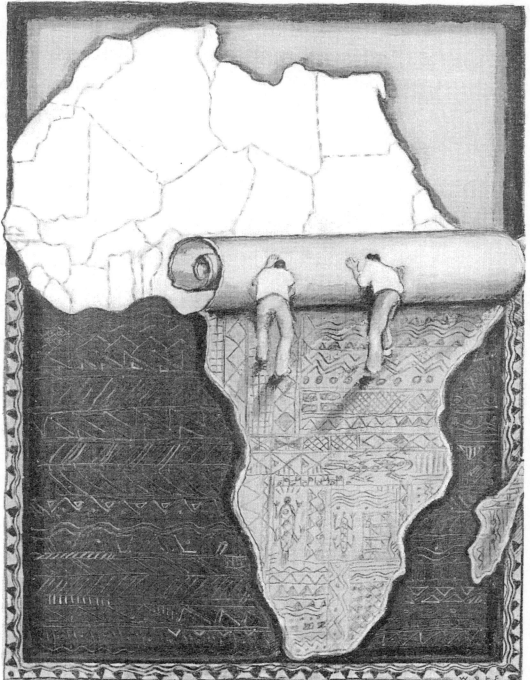

ILLUSTRATION BY ELIZABETH WOLF

(which became Zaire, now back to the Democratic Republic of the Congo) but failed. The secessionist Biafran war in Nigeria also failed. Somalia's attempt to take the Ogaden from Ethiopia was decisively thwarted. Southern Sudan struggled for 17 years to break away from the North and in the end settled for autonomy in 1972. When the fighting resumed in 1983, the stated goal was and remains the creation of a new Sudan that would be free from any discrimination based on race, ethnicity, culture, or religion.

Eritrea's breakaway from Ethiopia is seen not as a case of violating colonial borders, but of upholding them, since Eritrea had been a colony under Italian rule. Likewise, the de facto breakaway of Northern Somalia is seen as a restoration of colonial borders, since the North had been governed separately by the British. Even in the Sudan, often said to be a good candidate for partition, should the country be divided, the division might be rationalized as an extension of the British colonial policy that governed the Sudan as two separate entities, one Arab-Islamic and the other indigenous African with rudiments of Christian Western influences.

In most African countries, the determination to preserve national unity following independence provided the motivation

won their independence without negotiating an internal social contract that would win and sustain national consensus. The constitutions for independence were laden with idealistic principles developed outside the continent. The regimes built on them lacked legitimacy and in most cases were soon overthrown with no remorse or regrets from the public. But these upheavals involved only a rotation of like-minded elites, or worse, military dictators, intent on occupying the seat of power vacated by the colonial masters. Such leaders soon became their colonial masters' images.

At the moment, for the overwhelming majority of African countries the quest for unity underscores the intensity of disunity. As long as the Africans avoid confronting the issue of ethnicity and fail to develop norms and means for managing diversity within the framework of unity, peace and stability will continue to elude the pluralistic state.

MODELS OF ETHNIC CONFIGURATION

African governments have responded to the challenge in varying ways, ranging from pragmatic management to blind neglect and catastrophic mismanagement. The particular form the ethnic policies of a country take may in large measure be dictated

DEPRIVE A PEOPLE OF THEIR ETHNICITY, THEIR CULTURE, AND YOU DEPRIVE THEM OF THEIR SENSE OF DIRECTION OR PURPOSE.

behind one-party rule, excessive centralization of power, oppressive authoritarian regimes, and systematic violation of human rights and fundamental liberties. These in turn have generated a reaction, manifested in heightened tension and the demand for a second liberation. Managing ethnic diversity within the unity of the colonial borders is a challenge that African states are reluctant to face, but cannot wish away.

Ethiopia, after Eritrea's breakaway, can claim credit for being the only African country trying to confront head-on the challenge of tribalism or ethnicity by recognizing territorially based ethnic groups, granting them not only a large measure of autonomy, but also the constitutional right of self-determination, even to the extent of secession. Ethiopia's leaders assert emphatically that they are committed to the right of self-determination, wherever it leads. Less idealistically, it can be argued that giving the people the right to determine their destiny leads them to believe that their interests will be provided for, if only to give them a reason to opt for unity.

The only sustainable unity is that based on mutual understanding and agreement. Unfortunately, the normative framework for national unity in modern Africa is not the result of consensus. Except for post-apartheid South Africa, Africans

by the characteristics of its identity configuration.

A few states in Africa enjoy a high degree of homogeneity or, at least, a relatively inconsequential diversity. Botswana, for example, reflects exemplary cohesiveness, democracy, stability, and sustained growth.

Most African countries, particularly those in West Africa (possibly excepting Nigeria), Kenya, and southern African countries (exclusive of South Africa), fall into a second category. These countries face significant ethnic pluralism that is nevertheless containable through an effective system of distribution that upholds the integrity and legitimacy of the state. The way the nations in this group perceive themselves is consonant with the self-perceptions of their component groups.

A third group of countries, including Zimbabwe, Namibia, and modern-day South Africa, suffers racial, ethnic, religious, or cultural divisions severe enough to require special arrangements to be mutually accommodating in an ambivalent form of unity in diversity. Burundi and Rwanda, as well as Sudan, are candidates for this category though all also have aspects of the fourth, and final, category.

The fourth category the zero-sum conflict situation, consists of states embroiled in acute crisis with no collective sense of identification, no shared values, and no common vision for the nation. The framework of the nation-state is perceived as an imposition by the colonial invaders, now perpetuated by the dominant group whose identity defines the national character. Such definition might be explicit, as in apartheid South Africa, where race and ethnicity were factors in allocating or denying the rights of citizenship, or in the Sudan, where the identification of the country as Arab and Islamic carries inherent stratification and discrimination on racial, ethnic, and religious grounds. These conflicts are the most difficult to manage within the unity framework; depending on the particular circumstance of the case, they may call for fundamental restructuring and perhaps partition.

POLICY IMPLICATIONS FOR NATIONBUILDING

At present, most African countries are addressing the racial and ethnic identity issues through a pacifying system of distribution and allocation—a form of ad hoc pragmatic management rather than a strategic approach. What makes the issue of identity particularly acute for the continent is that it touches not only on politics, but also on economics and the organizational capacity for a self-generating and sustainable development from within.

There are four policy options for managing pluralistic identities. One is to create a national framework with which all can identify without any distinction based on race, ethnicity, tribe, or religion. This option, of course, best suits those countries that are highly homogeneous. The second option is to create a pluralistic framework to accommodate nations that are racially, ethnically, culturally or religiously diverse. Under this option, probably a federal arrangement, groups would accommodate each other on the basis of the principle of live and let live, but with a more uniting commitment to the common purpose of national identification. In the third case, for more seriously divided countries, some form of power sharing combined with decentralization, with identities being geographically defined, may be the answer. In the zero-sum conflict situations, federalism would expand into confederalism, paradoxically trying to reconcile unity with separation. Where even this degree of accommodation is not workable, and where territorial configurations permit, partition ought to be accepted.

THE ROLE OF THE INTERNATIONAL COMMUNITY

How are these options to be brought about? Deciding which option to adopt is, of course, in the first place part of the sovereign right of the people of the country. But regional and international actors also have a responsibility that cannot be abdicated in the name of national sovereignty. By its very nature, sovereignty implies a tension between the demand for internal solutions and the need for corrective remedies from the outside. In other words, the responsibilities of sovereignty require both internal and external accountability, which are inherently at odds, especially since the need for external involve-

ment is commensurate with the failure of internal systems. Given the ambivalence of the international system about intervention, this responsibility should belong first to the subregional and regional actors, with the international community, through the United Nations, as the ultimate resort.

The interconnectedness of the conflicts of neighboring countries means that preventing, managing, or resolving conflicts is becoming recognized as a matter of interest and concern not only to the countries directly involved, but also to the region as a whole. Regional awakening to the common threat of internal conflict is still nascent, but the importance of the shared threat is being increasingly realized, especially in view of the tendency toward isolationism in Europe and the United States, the only powers still capable of effectively intervening for humanitarian reasons or for the cause of peace, security, and stability in other parts of the world.

RECONCILING TWO CONFLICTING PATHS

Final accountability for the responsibilities of sovereignty must ultimately fall on the international community, more specifically the United Nations. The intervention of international financial institutions in the affairs of sovereign countries to ensure more efficient management of their economies has now become a truism. International concern with issues of governance such as democracy and respect for fundamental human rights, has also become widely accepted, despite the lingering resistance of vulnerable regimes. Beyond the issue of protection of minorities, long recognized as a legitimate concern for the international community, the politics and conflicts of identity and their impact on the prospects for peace, stability, development, and nation building must also be recognized as critical items on the agenda of a responsible and accountable sovereignty.

Insofar as the modern African state is the creation of European conquest, restructuring the continent, linking it to the international system, and reconceptualizing and reconstituting the state will require the cooperation of Africa's global partners. Outside actors can offer an objective and impartial perspective that can be pivotal to balancing the concerns of the internal actors. In addition, the international legitimacy of any new arrangements, which is necessary for building support from outside sources, can best be ensured by enlisting international partners in the search for effective solutions to these internal crises.

Post–colonial Africa stands poised between rediscovering its roots—its indigenous values, institutions, and experiences—and pursuing the logic of the colonial state in the context of universalizing modernity, primarily based on Western experience. The resulting tensions cannot be easily resolved. But an eclectic process that fashions a system in which ethnic groups can play a constructive role in the modern African state could significantly reduce the tension, foster cooperation, and facilitate the process of nation building.

Ethnicity Is No Excuse for Espionage

By E. V. KONTOROVICH

Jonathan Pollard has become the Jewish Mumia Abu-Jamal. Or rather, the campaign to commute the life sentence of the intelligence analyst turned spy—which has gained considerable impetus in recent weeks—has all the hallmarks of the "Free Mumia" movement on behalf of the Black Panther propagandist turned cop-killer.

Both movements rely on inflammatory appeals to ethnic solidarity and groundless charges of bigotry in the criminal justice system; both have the support of various Hollywood stars; and, above all, both defend felons whose guilt is beyond serious doubt. True, Pollard's supporters don't chant "No justice, no peace," but they have a sharper Web site.

But while Abu-Jamal's defenders come mostly from the extreme left, Jews of all stripes and persuasions have rallied to Pollard's defense. Now, 13 years after his imprisonment, the movement for his release has reached a fever pitch. Indeed, with Vice President Al Gore having visited Israel last week, there is talk of giving the spy to Jerusalem, to which he sold U.S. secrets, as a 50th birthday present for the Jewish state.

In recent weeks, all three major Jewish religious movements have pleaded Pollard's cause with President Clinton. The Conference of Presidents of Major American Jewish Organizations, representing more than 50 groups, signed on recently.

All these mainstream organizations have convinced themselves, and most of their members, that anti-Semitism, not espionage, got Pollard his stiff sentence. The president of B'nai Brith International, Tommy Baer, was quoted in New York Observer last month as saying the Pollard affair is "the closest thing to an American Dreyfuss case." Pollard himself has been busy conveying this impression.

The convicted spy contacted me from the Federal Correctional Institution in Butner, N.C., late last year, hoping I would pen a "J'accuse" on his behalf. Over the next few months, we had several telephone conversations. Pollard knows how to play journalists. He began by lavishly praising my writings on Israel and Jewish affairs. He suggested that since I was concerned about the plight of Israel, I would be sympathetic to his cause.

When the Pollard case first broke, American Jews were afraid that they would be suspected of comprising a fifth column. In a great American reversal, Pollard and his sympathizers, far from fearing accusations of dual loyalty, now enlist the support of many American Jews by playing on the guilt some may feel about not doing their share for Israel. Pollard, the argument goes, acted heroically to defend the Jewish state, and thereby took on the burden of all American Jews.

When I rebuffed Pollard's advances, he was puzzled.

"Can you explain how you've come to this position so quickly?" he asked. "Has someone gotten to you?"

Such paranoia seems to have infected not only Pollard but many of his defenders. "While Mr. Pollard remains in jail . . . no Jew can place complete trust in this country," columnist Anne Roiphe wrote last month. Pollard's supporters, however, understand that ominous hints about an anti-Semitic cabal spanning three presidencies is unlikely to sway President Clinton, who has already thrice denied Pollard's pleas. But their substantive arguments don't stand up to much scrutiny:

• *Disproportionately severe sentence.* "I was punished for treason, but I only committed espionage," Pollard told me as if he were proud of the latter crime. (In fact, the Constitution stipulates that treason is punishable by death.) Pollard's life sentence is harsher than the punishments of many other spies because, unfortunately, many have gotten off with pathetically light punishments. Pollard points to 13 spies convicted in recent years who have gotten lighter sentences. Peter Lee, for instance, spent one year in a halfway house for spying on behalf of China. But out of a group of convicts, one will always have the stiffest sentence, and that person will have some sort of ethnicity. Pollard's supporters simply seem to think that it shouldn't be "our guy." Instead of defining espionage down, the courts should make Pollard's sentence the new norm for spies.

• *Spying for Israel is not as bad as spying for other countries.* Surely Pollard's defenders who champion this view, like the esteemed moralist Dennis Prager, would not think adultery a less serious offense if committed with a close family friend. In any case, it's likely that Pollard did not spy "for" Israel, but for money: He got well over $60,000 in cash and jewels for his perfidy. The intelligence community says that Pollard did real damage to U.S. security; his defenders dispute this, but since these matters remain classified it's hard to draw an independent conclusion. Still, to excuse spying for "friendly" states would set a terrible precedent. An Arab-American intelligence officer, upset that America does not fully share classified information with, say, Syria or Saudi Arabia, both of which fought under our banner in the Gulf War, could take matters into his own hands and sell them this information.

• *Remorse.* Pollard's supporters claim he deserves leniency because he has made statements claiming to be repentant. While it is impossible to read the spy's mind, one should realize that he has every incentive to dissemble if it might help his situation. In my conversations with him, he refused to say, when I asked directly, that he would not do it all over again. Indeed, he seemed proud of his actions, and considers himself a martyr. In various interviews with journalists, he seems unable to restrain himself from bragging about the importance and nobility of his actions. He called the

U.S. a "foreign" country in a January interview with the Associated Press.

It's striking that, notwithstanding the weakness of these arguments, the American Jewish establishment has come together in favor of leniency for this spy. This seems to be yet another manifestation of the culture of victimhood pervading the country. Identity politics makes criminals into symbol of the larger social bias against their particular group. Giving these criminals lenient treatment thereby comes to be seen as a legitimate form of remedial preferential policy for the group.

The O. J. Simpson case is certainly the most celebrated example, but it seems everyone is getting on board. The World Trade Center bombers claim they are being picked on because America is anti-Muslim; Asian-Americans allege racism in the in-

vestigation of the role of a few Asians in illegal political fund-raising; last year, the Irish rallied to stop the deportation of six Irish Republican Army terrorists, winning political asylum for one bomber. Indeed, the prominent Brooklyn, N.Y. rabbi, Avi Weiss has praised the Korean community's show of support for Robert Kim immediately after his arrest for spying for South Korea, as an example that Jews should emulate.

By becoming the poster boy for a new victimhood delusion, Pollard may be doing a more lasting harm to America than he managed in his short career as a spy.

Mr. Kontorovich works at the Journal editorial page and is a contributing editor of the Forward.

Unit 10

Unit Selections

Key Points to Consider

❖ What signs have you seen of an increase in racist, anti-Semitic, anti-immigrant, and antiminority group acts that recent studies apparently confirm? Does anti-Catholicism still exist?

❖ What explains the fact that large population studies confirm that in the areas of ethnic, racial, and religious differences, Americans are more tolerant than ever?

❖ Why do teenagers commit 80 percent of all bias-related acts?

❖ What problems does conflict in ethnic and race relations pose for corporate and governmental institutions?

❖ What media images of race and ethnicity are dominant?

❖ What avenues are available for the authentic cultural resources of ethnic communities and traditions?

❖ How can multiethnic expressions of traditions intersect with the breakdown of community and the isolationist tendencies related to individual and personal achievement?

❖ How can the promotion of positive prototypes of ethnicity ever become as powerful as negative stereotypes?

❖ How can dialogue among conflicting parties about dilemmas that are essential to technological and economic change enable us to share and shape the burden of social change?

❖ Contrast local knowledge with national and local media as sources of information on race and ethnicity.

❖ Why should advocates of multicultural development and diversity argue for the following: (1) Fair and equal protection under the law; (2) The compilation of full and accurate data on the ethnic composition of the American population; (3) Corporate and governmental leaders who are focused on issues that do not exacerbate relations among persons because of ethnicity and race.

❖ What are the benefits of ethnic groups meeting regularly with other ethnic groups and engaging in friendly "What's your agenda" meetings?

❖ Who, if anyone, benefits from the persistence of ethnic tension and conflict?

DUSHKIN ONLINE Links   www.dushkin.com/online/

These sites are annotated on pages 4 and 5.

The increase in racial conflict and ethnic hatred on campuses and in marketplaces across the world are manifested in acts ranging from hateful speech to physical violence. Strategies for dealing with this problem include increased awareness through mandatory ethnic studies, the empowerment of targets of violence, and fostering social and cultural interaction in festivals, folk-arts fairs, and literary and political forums. Systematic knowledge about ethnic groups has not been a central scholarly concern. In fact, mainstream literary, humanistic, and historical disciplines have only recently begun to displace sociological attention to the pathologies of urban ethnicity as the primary contact and source of information and interpretation of ethnic traditions. The historic role that voluntary groups have played in the reduction of bias and bigotry also needs to be revalued and revitalized. Voluntary associations can take part in a host of state and local initiatives to improve intergroup relations. Schools and parents can help children understand commonalities and differences among and within ethnic traditions and groups. The incorporation of everyday experiences of families and a formal pedagogy rooted in accurate and locally relevant resources are essential building blocks for understanding diversity.

The reemergence of the discussion of race, ethnicity, and intelligence that is included in the selections found in this unit reveals the embeddedness of interpretive categories that frame the discussion and analysis of race and ethnic relations. The enormity of the educational effort that is required as we attempt to move beyond the ethnocentrism and racism that bred hatred and destructive relationships between persons and communities is revealed in a variety of ways. Philosophic reflection on the epistemological issues associated with explaining human variety is rarely invited. However, it is precisely at this intersection of social philosophy and science that the crucial breakthroughs in understanding are likely to appear. The continual mismeasures of intelligence and misreading of meaning indicate the long-term need for critical reformulation of the very idea of race. Scholarly differences of opinion concerning the composition of the urban underclass do not minimize the hardships that many endure. The growth of the underclass, its isolation from society, and society's inability to help it are tremendous obstacles that face our nation. Concrete strategies for improving this situation call upon both the public and the private sectors in areas of education, employment, and training. Suggestions for meeting future needs of this population and pragmatic policy responses also will help the general population.

At this time a variety of ways of measuring the development of race and ethnic relations and results are being proposed. Evidence cited by claimants to this knowledge and the attendant public criterion of credibility point to the expectation of a spirited debate. This unit challenges us to rethink the assumptions, contradictions, and aspirations of social-development models.

Understanding Cultural Pluralism

In the eighteenth century a disastrous shift occurred in the way Westerners perceived races. The man responsible was Johann Friedrich Blumenbach, one of the least racist thinkers of his day.

the Geometer of Race

STEPHEN JAY GOULD

Stephen Jay Gould, a contributing editor of Discover, *is a professor of zoology at Harvard who also teaches geology, biology, and the history of science. His writing on evolution has won many prizes, including a National Book Award, a National Magazine Award, and the Phi Beta Kappa Science Award. For* Discover's *November 1993 special section on ten great science museums, Gould wrote about the glass flowers at Harvard's Botanical Museum.*

INTERESTING STORIES often lie encoded in names that seem either capricious or misconstrued. Why, for example, are political radicals called "left" and their conservative counterparts "right"? In many European legislatures, the most distinguished members sat at the chairman's right, following a custom of courtesy as old as our prejudices for favoring the dominant hand of most people. (These biases run deep, extending well beyond can openers and scissors to language itself, where *dexterous* stems from the Latin for "right," and *sinister* from the word for "left.") Since these distinguished nobles and moguls tended to espouse conservative views, the right and left wings of the legislature came to define a geometry of political views.

Among such apparently capricious names in my own field of biology and evolution, none seems more curious, and none elicits more questions after lectures, than the official designation of light-skinned people in Europe, western Asia, and North Africa as Caucasian. Why should the most common racial group of the Western world be named for a mountain range that straddles Russia and Georgia? Johann Friedrich Blumenbach (1752–1840), the German anatomist and naturalist who established the most influential of all racial classifications, invented this name in 1795, in the third edition of his seminal work, *De Generis Humani Varietate Nativa* (On the Natural Variety of Mankind). Blumenbach's definition cites two reasons for his choice—the maximal beauty of people from this small region, and the probability that humans were first created in this area.

> *Caucasian variety.* I have taken the name of this variety from Mount Caucasus, both because its neighborhood, and especially its southern slope, produces the most beautiful race of men, I mean the Georgian; and because . . . in that region, if anywhere, it seems we ought with the greatest probability to place the autochthones [original forms] of mankind.

Blumenbach, one of the greatest and most honored scientists of the Enlightenment, spent his entire career as a professor at the University of Göttingen in Germany. He first presented *De Generis Humani Varietate Nativa* as a doctoral dissertation to the medical faculty of Göttingen in 1775, as the minutemen of Lexington and Concord began the American Revolution. He then republished the text for general distribution in 1776, as a fateful meeting in Philadelphia proclaimed our independence. The coincidence of three great documents in 1776—Jefferson's Declaration of Independence (on the politics of liberty), Adam Smith's *Wealth of Nations* (on the economics of individualism), and Blumenbach's treatise on racial classification (on the science of human diversity)—records the social ferment of these decades and sets the wider context that makes Blumenbach's taxonomy, and his subsequent decision to call the European race Caucasian, so important for our history and current concerns.

The solution to big puzzles often hinges upon tiny curiosities, easy to miss or to pass over. I suggest that the key to understanding Blumenbach's classification, the foundation of much that continues to influence and disturb us today, lies in the peculiar criterion he used to name the European race Caucasian—the supposed superior beauty of people from this region. Why, first of all, should a scientist attach such importance to an evidently subjective assessment; and why, secondly, should an aesthetic criterion become the basis of a scientific judgment about place of origin? To answer these questions, we must compare Blumenbach's original 1775 text with the later edition of 1795, when Caucasians received their name.

Blumenbach's final taxonomy of 1795 divided all humans into five groups, defined both by geography and appearance—in his order, the Caucasian variety, for the light-skinned people of Europe and adjacent parts of Asia and Africa; the Mongolian variety, for most other inhabitants of Asia, including China and Japan; the Ethiopian variety, for the dark-skinned people of Africa; the American variety, for most native populations of the New World; and the Malay variety, for the Polynesians and Melanesians of the Pacific and for the aborigines of Australia. But Blumenbach's original classification of 1775 recognized only the first four of these five, and united members of the Malay variety with the other people of Asia whom Blumenbach came to name Mongolian.

We now encounter the paradox of Blumenbach's reputation as the inventor of modern racial classification. The original four-race system, as I shall illustrate in a moment, did not arise from Blumenbach's observations but only represents, as Blumenbach readily admits, the classification promoted by his guru Carolus Linnaeus in the founding document of taxonomy, the *Systema Naturae* of 1758. Therefore, Blumenbach's only original contribution to racial classification lies in the later addition of a Malay variety for some Pacific peoples first included in a broader Asian group.

This change seems so minor. Why, then, do we credit Blumenbach, rather than Linnaeus, as the founder of racial classification? (One might prefer to say "discredit," as the enterprise does not, for good reason, enjoy high repute these days.) But Blumenbach's apparently small change actually records a theoretical shift that could not have been broader, or more portentous, in scope. This change has been missed or misconstrued because later scientists have not grasped the vital historical and philosophical principle that theories are models subject to visual representation, usually in clearly definable geometric terms.

By moving from the Linnaean four-race system to his own five-race scheme, Blumenbach radically changed the geometry of human order from a geographically based model without explicit ranking to a hierarchy of worth, oddly based upon perceived beauty, and fanning out in two directions from a Caucasian ideal. The addition of a Malay category was crucial to this geometric reformulation—and therefore becomes the key to the conceptual transformation rather than a simple refinement of factual information within an old scheme. (For the insight that scientific revolutions embody such geometric shifts, I am grateful to my friend Rhonda Roland Shearer, who portrays these themes in a [her] book, *The Flatland Hypothesis*.)

BLUMENBACH IDOLIZED his teacher Linnaeus and acknowledged him as the source of his original fourfold racial classification: "I have followed Linnaeus in the number, but have defined my varieties by other boundaries" (1775 edition). Later, in adding his Malay variety, Blumenbach identified his change as a departure from his old mentor in the most respectful terms: "It became very clear that the Linnaean division of mankind could no longer be adhered to; for which reason I, in this little work, ceased like others to follow that illustrious man."

Linnaeus divided the species *Homo sapiens* into four basic varieties, defined primarily by geography and, interestingly, not in the ranked order favored by most Europeans in the racist tradition—*Americanus, Europaeus, Asiaticus,* and *Afer,* or African. (He also alluded to two other fanciful categories: *ferus* for "wild boys," occasionally discovered in the woods and possibly raised by animals—most turned out to be retarded or mentally ill youngsters abandoned by their parents—and *monstrosus* for hairy men with tails, and other travelers' confabulations.) In so doing, Linnaeus presented nothing original; he merely mapped humans onto the four geographic regions of conventional cartography.

Linnaeus then characterized each of these groups by noting color, humor, and posture, in that order. Again, none of these categories explicitly implies ranking by worth. Once again, Linnaeus was simply bowing to classical taxonomic theories in making these decisions. For example, his use of the four humors reflects the ancient and medieval theory that a person's temperament arises from a balance of four fluids (*humor* is Latin for "moisture")—blood, phlegm, choler (yellow bile), and melancholy (black bile). Depending on which of the four substances dominated, a person would be sanguine (the cheerful realm of blood), phlegmatic (sluggish), choleric (prone to anger), or melancholic (sad). Four geographic regions, four humors, four races.

For the American variety, Linnaeus wrote "*rufus, cholericus, rectus*" (red, choleric, upright); for the European, "*albus, sanguineus, torosus*" (white, sanguine, muscular); for the Asian, "*luridus, melancholicus, rigidus*" (pale yellow, melan-

Scientists assume that their own shifts in interpretation record only their better understanding of newly discovered facts. They tend to be unaware of their own mental impositions upon the world's messy and ambiguous factuality.

choly, stiff); and for the African, *"niger, phlegmaticus, laxus"* (black, phlegmatic, relaxed).

I don't mean to deny that Linnaeus held conventional beliefs about the superiority of his own European variety over others. Being a sanguine, muscular European surely sounds better than being a melancholy, stiff Asian. Indeed, Linnaeus ended each group's description with a more overtly racist label, an attempt to epitomize behavior in just two words. Thus the American was *regitur consuetudine* (ruled by habit); the European, *regitur ritibus* (ruled by custom); the Asian, *regitur opinionibus* (ruled by belief); and the African, *regitur arbitrio* (ruled by caprice). Surely regulation by established and considered custom beats the unthinking rule of habit or belief, and all of these are superior to caprice—thus leading to the implied and conventional racist ranking of Europeans first, Asians and Americans in the middle, and Africans at the bottom.

Nonetheless, and despite these implications, the overt geometry of Linnaeus's model is not linear or hierarchical. When we visualize his scheme as an essential picture in our mind, we see a map of the world divided into four regions, with the people in each region characterized by a list of different traits. In short, Linnaeus's primary ordering principle is cartographic; if he had wished to push hierarchy as the essential picture of human variety, he would surely have listed Europeans first and Africans last, but he started with native Americans instead.

The shift from a geographic to a hierarchical ordering of human diversity must stand as one of the most fateful transitions in the history of Western science—for what, short of railroads and nuclear bombs, has had more practical impact, in this case almost entirely negative, upon our collective lives? Ironically, Blumenbach is the focus of this shift, for his five-race scheme became canonical and changed the geometry of human order from Linnaean cartography to linear ranking—in short, to a system based on putative worth.

I say ironic because Blumenbach was the least racist and most genial of all Enlightenment thinkers. How peculiar that the man most committed to human unity, and to inconsequential moral and intellectual differences among groups, should have changed the mental geometry of human order to a scheme that has served racism ever since. Yet on second thought, this situation is really not so odd—for most scientists have been quite unaware of the mental machinery, and particularly of the visual or geometric implications, lying behind all their theorizing.

An old tradition in science proclaims that changes in the theory must be driven by observation. Since most scientists believe this simplistic formula, they assume that their own shifts in interpretation record only their better understanding of newly discovered facts. Scientists therefore tend to be unaware of their own mental impositions upon the world's messy and ambiguous factuality. Such mental impositions arise from a variety of sources, including psychological predisposition and social context. Blumenbach lived in an age when ideas of progress, and the cultural superiority of European ways, dominated political and social life. Implicit, loosely formulated, or even unconscious notions of racial ranking fit well with such a worldview—indeed, almost any other organizational scheme would have seemed anomalous. I doubt that Blumenbach was actively encouraging racism by redrawing the mental diagram of human groups. He was only, and largely passively, recording the social view of his time. But ideas have consequences, whatever the motives or intentions of their promoters.

Blumenbach certainly thought that his switch from the Linnaean four-race system to his own five-race scheme arose only from his improved understanding of nature's factuality. He said as much when he announced his change in the second (1781) edition of his treatise: "Formerly in the first edition of this work, I divided all mankind into four varieties; but after I had more actively investigated the different nations of Eastern Asia and America, and, so to speak, looked at them more closely, I was compelled to give up that division, and to place in its stead the following five varieties, as more consonant to nature." And in the preface to the third edition, of 1795, Blumenbach states that he gave up the Linnaean scheme in order to arrange "the varieties of man according to the truth of nature." When scientists adopt the myth that theories arise solely from observation, and do not grasp the personal and social influences acting on their thinking, they not only miss the causes of their changed opinions; they may even fail to comprehend the deep mental shift encoded by the new theory.

Blumenbach strongly upheld the unity of the human species against an alternative view, then growing in popularity (and surely more conducive to conventional forms of racism), that each major race had been separately created. He ended his third edition by writing: "No doubt can any longer remain but that we are with great probability right in referring all . . . varieties of man . . . to one and the same species."

AS HIS MAJOR ARGUMENT for unity, Blumenbach noted that all supposed racial characteristics grade continuously from one people to another and cannot define any separate and bounded group. "For although there seems to be so great a difference between widely separate nations, that you might easily take the inhabitants of the Cape of Good Hope, the Greenlanders, and the Circassians for so many different species of man, yet when the matter is thoroughly considered, you see that all do so run into one another, and that one variety of mankind does so sensibly pass into the other, that you cannot mark out the limits between them." He particularly refuted the common racist claim that black Africans bore unique features of their inferiority: "There is no single character so peculiar

Blumenbach upheld the unity of the human species against an alternative view, then growing in popularity (and surely more conducive to conventional racism), that each race had been separately created.

and so universal among the Ethiopians, but what it may be observed on the one hand everywhere in other varieties of men."

Blumenbach, writing 80 years before Darwin, believed that *Homo sapiens* had been created in a single region and had then spread over the globe. Our racial diversity, he then argued, arose as a result of this spread to other climates and topographies, and to our adoption of different modes of life in these various regions. Following the terminology of his time, Blumenbach referred to these changes as "degenerations"—not intending the modern sense of deterioration, but the literal meaning of departure from an initial form of humanity at the creation (*de* means "from," and *genus* refers to our original stock).

Most of these degenerations, Blumenbach argued, arose directly from differences in climate and habitat—ranging from such broad patterns as the correlation of dark skin with tropical environments, to more particular (and fanciful) attributions, including a speculation that the narrow eye slits of some Australian aborigines may have arisen in response to "constant clouds of gnats . . . contracting the natural face of the inhabitants." Other changes, he maintained, arose as a consequence of customs adopted in different regions. For example, nations that compressed the heads of babies by swaddling boards or papoose carriers ended up with relatively long skulls. Blumenbach held that "almost all the diversity of the form of the head in different nations is to be attributed to the mode of life and to art."

Blumenbach believed that such changes, promoted over many generations, could eventually become hereditary. "With the progress of time," Blumenbach wrote, "art may degenerate into a second nature." But he also argued that most racial variations, as superficial impositions of climate and custom, could be easily altered or reversed by moving to a new region or by adopting new behavior. White Europeans living for generations in the tropics could become dark-skinned, while Africans transported as slaves to high latitudes could eventually become white: "Color, whatever be its cause, be it bile, or the influence of the sun, the air, or the climate, is, at all events, an adventitious and easily changeable thing, and can never constitute a diversity of species," he wrote.

Convinced of the superficiality of racial variation, Blumenbach defended the mental and moral unity of all peoples. He held particularly strong opinions on the equal status of black Africans and white Europeans. He may have been patronizing in praising "the good disposition and faculties of these our black brethren," but better paternalism than malign contempt. He campaigned for the abolition of slavery and asserted the moral superiority of slaves to their captors, speaking of a "natural tenderness of heart, which has never been benumbed or extirpated on board the transport vessels or on the West India sugar plantations by the brutality of their white executioners."

Blumenbach established a special library in his house devoted exclusively to black authors, singling out for special praise the poetry of Phillis Wheatley, a Boston slave whose writings have only recently been rediscovered: "I possess English, Dutch, and Latin poems by several [black authors], amongst which however above all, those of Phillis Wheatley of Boston, who is justly famous for them, deserves mention here." Finally, Blumenbach noted that many Caucasian nations could not boast so fine a set of authors and scholars as black Africa has produced under the most depressing circumstances of prejudice and slavery: "It would not be difficult to mention entire well-known provinces of Europe, from out of which you would not easily expect to obtain off-hand such good authors, poets, philosophers, and correspondents of the Paris Academy."

Nonetheless, when Blumenbach presented his mental picture of human diversity in his fateful shift away from Linnaean geography, he singled out a particular group as closest to the created ideal and then characterized all other groups by relative degrees of departure from this archetypal standard. He ended up with a system that placed a single race at the pinnacle, and then envisioned two symmetrical lines of departure away from this ideal toward greater and greater degeneration.

WE MAY NOW RETURN to the riddle of the name Caucasian, and to the significance of Blumenbach's addition of a fifth race, the Malay variety. Blumenbach chose to regard his own European variety as closest to the created ideal and then searched for the subset of Europeans with greatest perfection—the highest of the high, so to speak. As we have seen, he identified the people around Mount Caucasus as the closest embodiments of the original ideal and proceeded to name the entire European race for its finest representatives.

But Blumenbach now faced a dilemma. He had already affirmed the mental and moral equality of all peoples. He therefore could not use these conventional criteria of racist ranking to establish degrees of relative departure from the Caucasian ideal. Instead, and however subjective (and even risible) we view the criterion today, Blumenbach chose physical beauty as his guide to ranking. He simply affirmed that Europeans were most beautiful, with Caucasians as the most comely of all. This explains why Blumenbach, in the fist quote cited in this article, linked the maximal beauty of the Caucasians to the place of human origin. Blumenbach viewed all subsequent variation as departures from the originally created ideal—therefore, the most beautiful people must live closest to our primal home.

Blumenbach's descriptions are pervaded by his subjective sense of relative beauty, presented as though he were discussing an objective and quantifiable property, not subject to doubt or disagreement. He describes a Georgian female skull (found close to Mount Caucasus) as "really the most beautiful form of skull which . . . always of itself attracts every eye, however little observant." He then defends his European standard on aesthetic grounds: "In the first place, that stock displays . . . the most beautiful form of the skull, from which, as from a mean and primeval type, the others diverge by most easy gradations. . . . Besides, it is white in color, which we may fairly assume to have been the primitive color of mankind, since . . . it is very easy for that to degenerate into brown, but very much more difficult for dark to become white."

Blumenbach then presented all human variety on two lines of successive departure from this Caucasian ideal, ending in the two most degenerate (least attractive, not least morally unworthy or mentally obtuse) forms of humanity—Asians on one side, and Africans on the other. But Blumenbach also wanted to designate intermediary forms between ideal and most degenerate, especially since even gradation formed his primary argument for human unity. In his original four-race system, he could identify native Americans as intermediary between Europeans and Asians, but who would serve as the transitional form between Europeans and Africans?

The four-race system contained no appropriate group. But inventing a fifth racial category as an intermediary between Europeans and Africans would complete the new symmetrical geometry. Blumenbach therefore added the Malay race, not as a minor, factual refinement but as a device for reformulating an entire theory of human diversity. With this one stroke, he produced the geometric transformation from Linnaeus's unranked geographic model to the conventional hierarchy of implied worth that has fostered so much social grief ever since.

> I have allotted the first place to the Caucasian . . . which makes me esteem it the primeval one. This diverges in both directions into two, most remote and very different from each other; on the one side, namely, into the Ethiopian, and on the other into the Mongolian. The remaining two occupy the intermediate positions between that primeval one and these two extreme varieties; that is, the American between the Caucasian and Mongolian; the Malay between the same Caucasian and Ethiopian. [From Blumenbach's third edition.]

Scholars often think that academic ideas must remain at worst, harmless, and at best, mildly amusing or even instructive. But ideas do not reside in the ivory tower of our usual metaphor about academic irrelevance. We are, as Pascal said, a thinking reed, and ideas motivate human history. Where would Hitler have been without racism, Jefferson without liberty? Blumenbach lived as a cloistered professor all his life, but his ideas have reverberated in ways that he never could have anticipated, through our wars, our social upheavals, our sufferings, and our hopes.

I therefore end by returning once more to the extraordinary coincidences of 1776—as Jefferson wrote the Declaration of Independence while Blumenbach was publishing the first edition of his treatise in Latin. We should remember the words of the nineteenth-century British historian and moralist Lord Acton, on the power of ideas to propel history:

> It was from America that . . . ideas long locked in the breast of solitary thinkers, and hidden among Latin folios, burst forth like a conqueror upon the world they were destined to transform, under the title of the Rights of Man.

FOR FURTHER READING

Daughters of Africa. Margaret Busby, editor. Pantheon, 1992. A comprehensive anthology of prose and poetry written by women of African descent, from ancient Egyptian love songs to the work of contemporary Americans. The collection features the work of Phillis Wheatley, the first black to publish a book of poetry in the United States.

Color Blind

**Getting beyond race takes more than a program in the workplace.
An excerpt from a new book By Ellis Cose**

IN "THE ETHICS OF LIVING JIM CROW," AN AUTOBIO-
graphical essay published in *Uncle Tom's Children* in
1940, Richard Wright told of his first job at an eye-
glass lens-grinding company in Jackson, Mississippi.
He landed the job, in part, because the boss was impressed with his education, and Wright was promised
an opportunity to advance. "I had visions of working
my way up. Even Negroes have those visions," wrote
Wright. But even though he did his best to please, he
discovered, over time, that nobody was teaching him a
skill. His attempts to change that only provoked outrage.
Finally, a co-worker shook his fist in Wright's face and
advised him to stop making trouble: "This is a white
man's work around here, and you better watch your-
self."

Such sentiments obviously would not be openly
voiced in most companies today. The civil rights revolution has seen to that. Still, it seems that every so often
we get ugly reminders—of which the Texaco imbroglio
is the latest—that Jim Crow's spirit is not yet dead. In
1994, Denny's restaurant chain agreed—in a settlement
with the Justice Department—to put a civil rights monitor on its payroll and to cough up $45 million in dam-
ages, after a slew of complaints alleging discrimination
against customers and employees. The previous year
Shoney's, another restaurant chain, settled a suit for over
$100 million that alleged, among other things, that man-
agers were told to keep the number of black employees
down in certain neighborhoods.

People of color with training and experience are
"treated like s—t in too many places on the job," said
assistant labor secretary Bernard Anderson, whose responsibilities include the Office of Federal Contract Compliance Programs. Even within the labor department, said
Anderson, he had seen racial prejudice. When a black

colleague, a Rhodes scholar, appointed two other blacks
with impeccable credentials to positions, "the black lawyers were very empowered and encouraged by all of
this," recalled Anderson, but a number of the white lawyers . . . were just shaking in their boots." By and by, he
said, a "poison pen memorandum" found its way
around the department. The missive made insulting,
scatological comments, questioned the credentials of the
people who had been appointed, and declared that affirmative action had gone too far.

Resentment against minorities often surfaces in places
where "diversity" or affirmative action programs are in
place. And that resentment often breeds resistance that
results not merely in nasty comments but in outright
sabotage.

Some time ago, the black employees of a large, international corporation invited me to talk about a previous
book, *The Rage of a Privileged Class,* at a corporate-wide
event. In talking with my hosts, I quickly discovered
that they were not merely interested in my insights.
They wanted me to send a message to the management. They were frustrated because a corporate affirmative-action program, of which the management was
extremely proud, was not doing them any good. Mid-
level managers, it turned out, got diversity points for
hiring or promoting minorities, but the corporation
had defined minorities in such a way that everyone
who was not a U.S.-born white man qualified. In other
words, the managers got as much credit for transferring white men from Europe, Australia, and Canada
as they did for promoting African Americans. And that
is exactly what they were doing, according to the black
employees, who wanted me to let the management
know, in a nice and subtle way, that such behavior was
unacceptable.

Twelve Steps Toward Racial Harmony

AMERICANS HAVE LITTLE ALTERNATIVE BUT TO ACCEPT THE POSSIBILITY THAT RACE WILL CONTINUE TO divide us. Yet it is clear that society is more hospitable to minorities and more—racially—egalitarian than it was a few generations ago. There is every likelihood that it can become more so. Hence, we have to ask the question—if only as an experiment in thought: Do we have the vaguest idea how to create a society that is truly race neutral? The short answer, I suspect, is no. Otherwise we would be much further along the way than we are. Still, I believe we can get beyond such platitudes as "Let's just love one another" which is the verbal equivalent of throwing up our hands in noble resignation. Enumerating steps our society could take toward racial sanity is obviously not the same as putting America's racial goblins to rest. It is, however, a necessary prelude to moving the dialogue beyond the realm of reassuring yet empty platitudes. So what would some of those steps be?

1 WE MUST STOP EXPECTING TIME TO SOLVE THE PROBLEM FOR US: In "Guess Who's Coming to Dinner," there is a scene in which Sidney Poitier who plays a physician in his thirties in love with a young white woman) turns, in a fit of rage, to the actor playing his father. Only when the older generation is dead, Poitier declares, will prejudice wither away. The sobering realization is that Poitier is now older than his "father" was then, and the problem, obviously, remains.

Time doesn't heal all wounds; it certainly doesn't solve all problems. It is often merely an excuse for allowing them to fester. Our problems, including our racial problems, belong to us—not to our descendants.

2 WE MUST RECOGNIZE THAT RACE RELATIONS IS NOT A ZERO-SUM GAME: The presumption that America is a zero-sum society, that if one race advances another must regress, accounts, in large measure, for the often illogical reaction to programs that aim to help minorities. Such thinking even explains some of the hostility between members of so-called minority groups. *Can only one person of color rise within a given organization?* One hopes not. *Does an increase in Latino clout portend a decline in blacks' well-being?* It shouldn't.

Unfortunately, we have too often reveled in political rhetoric that puts across the opposite message; and have too often rewarded those who exploit our anxiety and insecurities—as opposed to those who demonstrate the willingness and ability to harness our faith in each other and in ourselves.

3 WE MUST REALIZE THAT ENDING HATE IS THE BEGINNING, NOT THE END, OF OUR MISSION: Occasionally, I turn on my television and am greeted by some celebrity exhorting me to stop the hate. I always wonder about the target audience for that particular broadside. I suspect that it is aimed mostly at people who don't hate anyone—perhaps as a reminder of our virtue. I certainly can't imagine a card-carrying member of the local Nazi group getting so fired up by the message that he turns to the television and exclaims, "Yes, you're right. I must immediately stop the hate."

Stopping the hate does little to bring people of different races or ethnic groups together. Certainly, it's better than stoking hate, but discrimination and stereotyping are not primarily the result of hatred. If we tell ourselves that the only problem is hate, we avoid facing the reality that it is mostly nice, nonhating people who perpetuate racial inequality.

4 WE MUST ACCEPT THE FACT THAT EQUALITY IS NOT A HALFWAY PROPOSITION: This century has seen huge changes in the status of black Americans. It has also seen the growth of largely segregated school systems, the development and maintenance of segregated neighborhoods, and the congealing of the assumption that blacks and whites belong to fundamentally different communities. The mistake was in the notion that social, economic, and political equality are not interrelated, that it was possible to go on living in largely segregated neighborhoods, socialize in largely segregated circles, and even attend segregated places of worship and yet have a workplace and a polity where race ceased to be a factor. As long as we cling to the notion that equality is fine in some spheres and not in others, we will be clinging to a lie.

5 WE MUST END AMERICAN APARTHEID: Americans have paid much homage to Martin Luther King's dream of a society where people would be judged only by the content of their character—even as they have yanked children out of schools when a delicate racial balance tipped, or planted themselves in neighborhoods determinedly monochromatic, or fought programs that would provide housing for poor blacks outside of the slums. There is something fundamentally incongruous in the idea of judging people by the content of their character and yet consigning so many Americans at birth to communities in which they are written off even before their character has been shaped.

6 WE MUST REPLACE A PRESUMPTION THAT MINORITIES WILL FAIL WITH AN EXPECTATION OF THEIR SUCCESS: When doing research with young drug dealers in California, anthropologist John Ogbu found himself both impressed and immensely saddened. "Those guys have a sense of the economy. They have talents that could be used on Wall Street," he remarked. "They have intelligence—but not the belief that they can succeed in the mainstream." Somewhere along the line, probably long before they became drug dealers, that belief had been wrenched out of them.

Creating an atmosphere in which people learn they cannot achieve is tantamount to creating failure. The various academic programs that do wonders with "at-risk" youths share a rock-hard belief in the ability of the young people in their care. These programs manage to create an atmosphere in which the "success syndrome" can thrive. Instead of focusing so much attention on whether people with less merit are getting various slots, we should be focusing on how to widen—and reward—the pool of meritorious people.

7 WE MUST STOP PLAYING THE BLAME GAME: Too often America's racial debate is sidetracked by a search for racial scapegoats. And more often than not, those scapegoats end up being the people on the other side of the debate. "It's your fault because you're a racist." "No, it's your fault because you expect something for nothing." "It's white skin privilege." "It's reverse racism." And on and on it goes. American culture, with its bellicose talk-show hosts and pugnacious politicians, rewards those who cast aspersions at the top of their lungs. And American law, with its concept of damages and reparations, encourages the practice of allocating blame. Although denying the past is dishonest and even sometimes maddening, obsessing about past wrongs is ultimately futile.

Certainly, loudmouths will always be among us and will continue to say obnoxious and foolish things, but it would be wonderful if more of those engaged in what passes for public discourse would recognize an obvious reality: It hardly matters who is responsible for things being screwed up; the only relevant question is, "How do we make them better?"

8 WE MUST DO A BETTER JOB AT LEVELING THE PLAYING FIELD: As long as roughly a third of black Americans sit on the bottom of the nation's economic pyramid and have little chance of moving up, the United States will have a serious racial problem on its hands. There is simply no way around that cold reality. It is pointless to say that the problem is class, not race, if race and class are tightly linked.

During the past several decades, Americans have witnessed an esoteric debate over whether society must provide equality of opportunity or somehow ensure equality of result. It is, however, something of a phony debate, for the two concepts are not altogether separate things. If America was, in fact, providing equality of opportunity, then we would have something closer to equality of racial result than we do at present. The problem is that equality of opportunity has generally been defined quite narrowly—such as simply letting blacks and whites take the same test, or apply for the same job.

Equality of opportunity is meaningless when inherited wealth is a large determinant of what schools one attends (and even whether one goes to school), what neighborhoods one can live in, and what influences and contacts one is exposed to. In *Black Wealth, White Wealth*, sociologists Melvin Oliver and Tom Shapiro pointed out that most blacks have virtually no wealth—even if they do earn a decent income. Whites with equal educational levels to blacks typically have five to ten times as much wealth, largely be-

cause whites are much more likely to inherit or receive gifts of substantial unearned assets. This disparity is a direct result of Jim Crow practices and discriminatory laws and policies.

America is not about to adopt any scheme to redistribute resources materially. What Americans must do, however, if we are at all serious about equality of opportunity, is to make it easier for those without substantial resources to have secure housing outside urban ghettos, to receive a high-quality education, and to have access to decent jobs.

9 WE MUST BECOME SERIOUS ABOUT FIGHTING DISCRIMINATION: In their rush to declare this society colorblind, some Americans have leaped to the conclusion that discrimination has largely disappeared. They explain away what little discrimination they believe exists as the fault of a few isolated individuals or the result of the oversensitivity of minorities.

Making discrimination a felony is probably not a solution, but more aggressive monitoring and prosecution—especially in housing and employment situations—would not be a bad start. Just as one cannot get beyond race by treating different races differently, one cannot get beyond discrimination by refusing to acknowledge it. One can get beyond discrimination only by fighting it vigorously wherever it is found.

10 WE MUST KEEP THE CONVERSATION GOING: Dialogue clearly is no cure-all for racial estrangement. Conversations, as opposed to confrontations, about race are inevitably aimed at a select few—those who make up the empathic elite. Yet, limited as the audience may be, the ongoing discourse is crucial. It gives those who are sincerely interested in examining their attitudes and behavior an opportunity to do so, and, in some instances, can even lead to change.

11 WE MUST SEIZE OPPORTUNITIES FOR INTERRACIAL COLLABORATION: Even those who have no interest in talking about the so-called *racial situation* can, through the process of working with (and having to depend on) people of other races, begin to see beyond skin color. Conversation, in short, has its limits. Only through doing things together—things that have nothing specifically to do with race—will people break down racial barriers. Facing common problems as community groups, as work colleagues, or as classmates can provide a focus and reduce awkwardness in a way that simple conversation cannot.

12 WE MUST STOP LOOKING FOR ONE SOLUTION TO ALL OUR RACIAL PROBLEMS: Meetings on racial justice often resemble nothing so much as a bazaar filled with peddlers offering the all-purpose answer. The reality is that the problem has no single or simple solution. If there is one answer, it lies in recognizing how complex the issue has become and in not using that complexity as an excuse for inaction. In short, if we are to achieve our country, we must attack the enemy on many fronts.

ELLIS COSE

I'm not sure what message the management ended up extracting from my speech, but I am sure that the frustrations those black employees felt are widespread—and that the cause lies less in so-called diversity programs than in the widespread tendency to judge minority group members more by color than by ability.

Some two decades ago, I received a brutal lesson in how galling such attitudes can be. At the time, I was a young (maybe twenty-one or twenty-two years old) columnist-reporter for the *Chicago Sun-Times*. Though I had only been in the business a few years, I was acquiring something of a regional reputation. I hoped to break into magazine writing by garnering a few freelance assignments from *Esquire* magazine, so I had made an appointment with one of its editors.

The editor with whom I met was a pleasant and rather gracious man, but what he had to say was sobering. He wasn't sure, he confided, how many black readers *Esquire* had, but was reasonably certain the number was not high. Since I had not inquired about his readership, the statement took me a bit by surprise. I had been a longtime reader of *Esquire,* and it had never previously occurred to me that I was not supposed to be, that it was not me whom *Esquire* had in mind as an audience—never mind as a contributor. I don't know whether the editor bothered to read my clippings, but then, the clips were somehow superfluous; the very fact that I had written them made them so. All the editor saw was a young black guy, and since *Esquire* was not in need of a young black guy, they were not in need of me. I left that office in a state of controlled fury—not just because the editor had rejected me as a writer, but because he had been so busy focusing on my race that he was incapable of seeing *me* or my work.

A nominal commitment to diversity does not necessarily guarantee an appreciably better outcome, as I came to see several years ago when I was approached by a newspaper publisher who was in the process of putting together his management team. He was interested, he said, in hiring some minority senior managers, so I gave him some names of people who might be likely candidates. Over the next several months, I watched as he put his team in place—a team, as it turned out, that was totally white. Only after he had largely assembled that group did he begin serious talks with some of the nonwhites I had recommended.

I don't doubt the man's sincerity. He did want to hire some minority managers, and eventually did so. But what was clear to me was that to him, minority recruitment meant the recruitment of people who couldn't be trusted with the organization's most important jobs. His

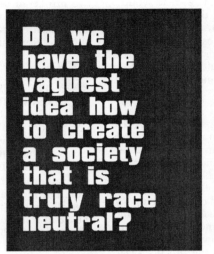

Do we have the vaguest idea how to create a society that is truly race neutral?

first priority was hiring people who could do the work—meaning whites—and only after that task was complete would he concern himself with the window dressing of diversity.

Over the years, I have learned that affirmative action in theory and affirmative action in practice are two different things. In the real world it is much more than simply opening up an organization to people who traditionally have been excluded; it is attempting, usually through some contrived measures, to make organizations do what they don't do naturally—and it goes down about as easily as castor oil. Shortly after I announced my resignation as editor of the editorial pages of the New York *Daily News,* I took one of my white staff members out to lunch. He told me he had enjoyed working with me and was sorry to see me go. He had cringed when he heard that I was coming, he confided, for he had feared that I would be just another affirmative action executive, presumably incapable of doing the job competently. He admitted that he had been pleasantly surprised.

I was pleased but also saddened by his confession—pleased that he felt comfortable enough to tell me how he truly felt and saddened that the very fact that a person of color got a high-ranking job would lead him (as it had led so many before him) to question that person's credentials. Yet, having occasionally been the target of affirmative-action recruiters, I am fully aware that (whatever they may say in public) they don't always pay as much attention to credentials as to color. Therefore, I understand clearly why even the ostensible beneficiaries of such recruitment tactics may find affirmative action, as practiced by major corporations, distasteful and even offensive. A decade and a half ago, for instance, I received a call from an associate of an executive search firm who, after verbally tap dancing for several minutes, essentially asked whether I wished to be considered for a job as a corporate director of equal opportunity. I was stunned, for the question made no sense. I was an expert neither on personnel nor on equal-employment law; I was, however, black, which seemed to be the most important qualification. I laughed and told him that I saw my career going in another direction. Still, I wondered just how serious the inquiry could be, since I seemed (to me, at least) so unsuited for the position. Since then, I have received other calls pushing jobs that have seemed every bit as outlandish.

At one point, a man called to discuss the presidency of a major foundation. I confessed I didn't understand why he was calling me, and he assured me that the client was extremely interested in having me apply. The man's earnestness intrigued me enough that I sent him a resume. I never heard from him again, which confirmed, in my mind at any rate, that his interest was anything but genuine. I imagined him sitting in his office with a long list of minority candidates, from whom he would collect resumes and promptly bury them in a file, merely so that his clients would be able to say they had considered minorities. Indeed, when the foundation head was finally named (he was a white man with a long professional association with the foundation trustees), it was clear to me that the supposed search had been a sham. After one takes a few such calls, one realizes that the purpose is often defensibility ("Yes, we took a hard look at fifteen minority candidates, but none quite fit the bill") and that the supposed high-level position is merely bait to attract the interest of people who don't really have a shot—but in whom everyone must pretend they are interested because an affirmative-action program is in place.

It's logical to argue for the replacement of such shameful practices with something better—for some form of meritocracy. Yet affirmative-action critics who extol the virtues of a meritocracy generally ignore the reality of how a real-world so-called meritocracy works. If qualified, capable, and talented minorities and women exist, they say, corporations will reward them because they will recognize that it is within their economic interest to do so. That may well be true. But it is also true that effective executives are trained, not born. They come about because companies make an investment in them, in their so-called human capital, and nurture their careers along—and if corporations only see the potential in white men, those are the people in whom the investments are likely to be made.

John Kotter, a Harvard Business School professor and author of *The General Managers*, discovered that effective executives generally benefited from what he called the "success syndrome." They were constantly provided with opportunities for growth: "They never stagnated for significant periods of time in jobs where there were few growth possibilities." The executives also, to be blunt about it, are often people of relatively modest intellectual endowment. They succeed largely because they are chosen for success.

> **Our problems, including our racial problems, belong to us—not to our descendants**

A true meritocracy would do a much better job of evaluating and choosing a broader variety of people. It would challenge the very way merit is generally imputed and, in giving people ample opportunity to develop and to prove themselves, it would create a truly level playing field.

Simply eliminating affirmative action would not bring such a true meritocracy about. Indeed, a large part of the reason affirmative action is so appealing to so many people is that a meritocracy that fully embraces people of color seems out of reach; and affirmative action is at least one method to get people to accept the fact that talent comes in more than one color.

Yet, by its very nature, affirmative action is polarizing. Wouldn't it be better, argue a growing number of Americans, to let it die in peace? A chorus of conservative critics even invoke the dream of Martin Luther King Jr. to make the case.

King would probably be more astonished than anyone to hear that conservatives now claim him as one of their own, that they have embraced his dream of a color-blind world and invoke it as proof of the immorality and undesirability of gender and racial preferences. But even if he had a bit of trouble accepting his status as a general in the war against affirmative action, he would appreciate the joke. And he would realize that it is the fate of the dead to be reborn as angels to the living. King no doubt would be pleased to have new friends in his fight for justice, but he would approach them with caution. After sharing his disappointment over past alliances with people whose commitment to change did not match his own, King would address his new associates bluntly. "All right," he might say, "I understand why you oppose affirmative action. But tell me: What is *your* plan? What is *your* plan to cast the slums of our cities on the junk heaps of history? What is *your* program to transform the dark yesterdays of segregated education into the bright tomorrows of high-quality, integrated education? What is *your* strategy to smash separatism, to destroy discrimination, to make justice roll down like water and righteousness flow like a mighty stream from every city hall and statehouse in this great and blessed nation?" He might then pause for a reply, his countenance making it unmistakably clear that he would accept neither silence nor sweet nothings as an answer.

THE END OF THE RAINBOW

The poverty of racial politics and the future of liberalism

BY MICHAEL LIND

IN THE CONCLUSION OF GOETHE'S EPIC *FAUST,* THE great magician who has made a pact with the devil hears the clinking of shovels. Faust, who is blind, believes he is listening to the sound of workers on a project he is promoting to reclaim land from the sea for the benefit of mankind. In fact, the shovels are in the hands of demons, who are digging Faust's own grave.

American liberalism faces a similar irony. For the past generation, the left has been identified with the strategy of what Jesse Jackson calls the Rainbow Coalition. Where the old left assigned the vanguard role in history to factory workers, the New Left assigns it to people of color. The assumption has been that policies such as affirmative action and racial redistricting would unite blacks, Hispanics, and Asian-Americans politically. Sympathetic whites would be permitted to join the coalition, but white concerns about reverse discrimination would be dismissed as racist. In time, many on the left assumed, "rainbow liberalism" would triumph purely as a result of demographic trends, as California, Texas, New York, and eventually the whole country acquired nonwhite majorities.

The strategy of rainbow liberalism has rested on two assumptions. The first is that conservatism would not appeal to nonwhite Americans. The second is that the very policies that promote the rainbow strategy—affirmative action and high immigration—would not produce tensions among the multiracial rainbow's constituent bands. If these assumptions are wrong, then rainbow liberalism is digging its own grave.

They are, and it is.

Already mainstream leaders in the GOP are rejecting white nativism. Some are even supporting affirmative action and immigration in the hope of appealing to socially or economically conservative blacks, Hispanics, or Asian-Americans. At the same time, affirmative action in higher education divides blacks and Hispanics from Asian-Americans, while high levels of immigration hurt black workers in some parts of the country. The rise of a multicultural right, though it may doom rainbow liberalism, provides an opening for a new liberalism that stresses social equality and national integration.

DOES RIGHT EQUAL WHITE?

In the past generation, conservatives have offered two incompatible responses to rainbow liberalism. One is a conservative-populist nativism, or white nationalism, whose spokesmen are Patrick Buchanan and Peter Brimelow. Reminiscent of the white supremacist populist of the Old South, this new nativism holds that nonwhite immigration is a racial and cultural threat to the country's diminishing white Euro-American "core." When combined with eugenics theory, as in the work of Charles Murray, this kind of white nationalism becomes even more sinister. For strategic reasons, liberals might hope that the nativist version prevails among conservatives. Already, nativist agitation (particularly in California) has arrested the drift of Hispanics toward the GOP and pushed many back into the Democratic Party. White racism is the perfect mortar for uniting the colors of the rainbow.

But the other conservative answer to the rainbow strategy has not been so conveniently stupid. Most mainstream Republicans have reacted to Buchananism with horror and have rejected white national populism. Contrary to the propaganda of the left, the members of the dominant business-class wing of the GOP are not more racist on average than elite white liberals. During his tenure as executive director of the Christian Coalition, Ralph Reed worked to reach out to conservative black, Hispanic, and Asian-American Christians. And Republicans count more prominent leaders who are partners in interracial marriages—Jeb

Reprinted with permission from *Mother Jones,* September/October 1997, pp. 39-43, 75. © 1997 by the Foundation for National Progress.

Bush, Phil Gramm, Clarence Thomas—than do the Democrats. This is not tokenism.

Even if it were consistently bigoted, the conservative white elite, unlike the white working class, would not compete with nonwhites for jobs or feel culturally threatened by blacks or Latin American or Asian immigrants. Indeed, members of the white professional elite may feel they have more in common with successful Asian-Americans, and perhaps affluent Hispanics and blacks as well, than with working-class whites. The country club Republicans, while they are sometimes both, are more classist than racist. They rail against "class war" while finding kind things to say about high immigration (which is good for business) and even affirmative action (which makes corporate America look more diverse to a diverse public).

The present danger liberals face is less a "fascist right" in America—our neo-Nazis hate the military and the police, and they have trouble taking over a ranch, much less a country—than a "Creole right" oligarchy that does not care what color your skin is, as long as you are wealthy. As the Latin American saying has it, "Money whitens." (For most white Americans, O. J. Simpson was just a rich celebrity.)

A "rainbow right" is possible, perhaps even likely. Black voters remain committed to the Democratic Party, despite Republican proselytizing. But Asian and Hispanic allegiances are in play. A majority of Asian-Americans voted for Bush in 1992. They could play a role in the Republican Party comparable to that of academically and economically successful Jews in the Democratic Party. In the 1992 elections, Hispanics gave the Democrats only about 60 percent of the vote. If close to half of American Hispanics sided against Democrats then, it is quite possible that a majority will follow white ethnic voters into the GOP in the future as they move up the socioeconomic scale. A moderately conservative white-Asian-Hispanic coalition, based in the growing South and West, could be a formidable opponent of the liberal white-Protestant-Jewish-black coalition, concentrated in the demographically declining Northeast.

This racially mixed conservative coalition might be reinforced by the large number of working-class whites who have been leaving states with high immigration, such as California, for the interior and the Rocky Mountain states. Such whites, who might have competed for jobs with Hispanic immigrants back in their home states, might become their political allies once they have moved to more or less lily-white states where white-Hispanic tensions are insignificant. What would hold this multiracial conservative coalition together? The answer is: (a) conservative social values (shared by many whites, East Asian immigrants, and Hispanics); (b) redistribution (the coalition's partisans in Congress would tax the Northeast and subsidize Republican defense contractors and agribusiness in the South and West); (c) a live-and-let-live states' rights compromise (for example, different affirmative action policies for the white-majority states and the nonwhite-majority states); and, last but not least, (d) a common hostility to the black urban poor, everybody's favorite scapegoat.

RACIALISM BREAKS UP THE RAINBOW

The assumption that right equals white, then, is no longer realistic. Equally flawed is the other premise of the rainbow liberal strategy—the belief that programs such as high immigration and affirmative action will unite rather than divide blacks, Hispanics, and Asian-Americans.

The high number of blacks who supported Proposition 187, California's anti-immigration referendum, should have sent a signal to liberal strategists. The tensions between blacks and Hispanic and Asian immigrants are deep. According to a recent Roger Poll, non-Hispanic blacks favor deep cuts in immigration by a ratio of 11-to-1 (even Hispanic Americans favored such cuts by 7-to-1). The continued immigration of poor workers (many of whom make up a significant percentage of the nearly 1 million *legal* immigrants we now have a year) may keep wages down and make union organizing more difficult. Three Harvard economists, George Borjas, Richard Freeman, and Lawrence Katz, have estimated that immigrant competition accounts for 44 to 60 percent of the drop in relative earnings high school dropouts suffered between 1979 and 1995. From the perspective of employers, of course, wages can never be too low. Little wonder, then, that the pro-immigration wing of the Republican Party, bolstered by the *Wall Street Journal's* editorial page, has beaten back the immigration restrictions favored by the nativist wing of the GOP.

Affirmative action, like immigration, divides rather than unites the rainbow. Ensuring the proportional representation of blacks and Hispanics in universities means discriminating against academically gifted Asian-Americans. The evolution of nonwhite-majority states such as California and Texas may not have the optimistic result rainbow liberals expect. As the percentage of whites diminishes, blacks and Hispanics and Asians will likely turn on one another, with representatives at each category demanding a "fair share" of political offices, jobs, and opportunities for higher education. Strict proportional representation, however, means overall racial numbers won't be a floor, but a *cap*. Blacks, who tend to be overrepresented in civil service jobs, would have *no more* than 12.5 percent of the positions in, say, the post office. Black representation in government jobs and politics would become directly threatened by the rainbow liberals' own policies. Indeed, in absolute numbers most of the beneficiaries of affirmative action (if it is not abolished) will soon be white women and immigrants from Latin America—not the black Americans for whom the program was intended in the first place. (By 1993, 74.9 percent of legal immigrants were eligible for affirmative action on the basis of race.)

Of course, in recent years the right has lost few chances to hammer a wedge between the bands of the rainbow, contrasting "hardworking" immigrants with the native black and white poor.

What's Your Favorite Statistic About Race?

These leading thinkers prove that questions of race rarely have simple—or numerical—answers.

C. ERIC LINCOLN, author of *Coming Through the Fire*
"By 2050, more than **half of the people** in the United States will be nonwhite. And the Tiger Woods syndrome is upon us."

GLENN C. LOURY, director of the Institute of Race and Social Division at Boston University.
"Between 1977 and 1994 the number of first professional degrees (law, business, and medical school, mainly) awarded to African-American women increased by 219 percent (from 776 to 2,477). That number grew by only 5.1 percent for African-American men (from 1,761 to 1,851)."

RON TAKAKI, professor of ethnic studies, University of California at Berkeley
"Bob Dole announced his support for **Proposition 209** in a speech at Little Saigon, in Orange County, Calif. There was a public perception that identified Asian-Americans with the eventually successful assault on affirmative action. But, according to the *Los Angeles Times*, **The Asian-American vote was 61 percent** against Prop. 209."

JOHN B. JUDIS, senior editor at the *New Republic*
"I live in Silver Spring, Md., a racially mixed, middle-class suburb of Washington, D.C., and my daughters go to public school there. They have always had black friends, but by the beginning of middle or high school, these friends had **departed for predominantly white private schools.** The reason, we learned, was that their parents feared that if they stayed in public schools, they would fall under the spell of other blacks who identified success in school with being white."

LINDA CHAVEZ, president, Center for Equal Opportunity
"According to a recent survey conducted by Lou Harris for the National Conference, 46 percent of Latinos and 42 percent of African-Americans agreed with the statement that Asians are **'unscrupulous, crafty, and devious in business,'** while only 27 percent of whites agreed; 68 percent of Asian-Americans and 49 percent of African-Americans agreed with the statement that Latinos, **'tend to have bigger families than they are able to support,'** as did 50 percent of whites; 33 percent of Latinos and 22 percent of Asian-Americans agreed with the statement that African-Americans **'even if given a chance, aren't capable of getting ahead,'** yet only 12 percent of whites agreed."

JAMES McBRIDE, author of *The Color of Water*
"**There are 60,000 black children** waiting to be adopted in the United States, while every week newspapers and magazines across the country are graced with ads by parents who are willing to pay huge bucks for a baby. Unspoken, of course, is their willingness to **pay for white babies,** which are apparently in short supply. As a black man raised by a white Jewish mother and black American father; I don't fault these folks for trying to obtain a baby who 'looks like them.' But I'm glad I'm not that baby."

TROY DUSTER, professor of sociology, University of California at Berkeley
"Cheryl Hopwood, a white female, sued the University of Texas Law School, claiming she had been the victim of racial discrimination because she was **not admitted even though she had higher test scores** than students of color who were admitted. The appellate court directed the lower court to consider damages to Hopwood, and she is seeking more than **$1** million from the state. In all these decades of racial exclusion, **no court in this nation has ever been directed to consider damages** for a single student of color."

PAUL BEGALA, advisor to President Clinton
"This year's incoming class at the University of Texas Law School—which once produced more African-American and Hispanic lawyers than nearly any other law school in the country—includes a **grand total of four African-Americans."**

RUY TEIXEIRA, director, Politics and Public Opinion Program, Economic Policy Institute
"In 1958, **44 percent of whites said they would move out** if a black person moved next door. In 1997, the figure is 1 percent. Yet the economic problems of blacks persist. This suggests that: (a) the problem is no longer racism or discrimination, but broader economic arrangements that intersect with race; or (b) racism has simply become covert."

JIM SLEEPER, author of *Liberal Racism*
"Almost all polling data reveal that **the closer black Americans get to middle-class life,** the more unhappy and untrusting toward whites they feel. Never mind that the indices of two-parent homes, education, mortality, and career mobility are improving among blacks; liberals still encourage thousands of diversity trainers and racial gatekeepers to create an industry for which **no good racial news can be real news.** Conservatives spent centuries telling blacks how different they were. Why have so many liberals replaced that historic racism with an elaborate thicket of treatments that prolong the disease?"

RUBÉN ORTIZ-TORRES, artist and photographer
"My favorite fact of the month is that **Che Guevara's car in Havana** was an emerald-green 1960 Chevy Impala with a V-8 Engine, automatic transmission, white upholstery, and an AM radio. Another interesting fact is that **the largest sombrero in the world** is the Sombrero Tower in a theme park called South of the Border next to North and South Carolina's border. The Sombrero Tower in 200 feet high and has an elevator that takes you to the top."

THE LEFT'S ACCIDENTAL SUICIDE

If a multicultural right threatens to kill rainbow liberalism, the left unwittingly may be acting as its own Dr. Kevorkian. We are so used to the routinized debate between the multicultural left and the unicultural right that we can hardly imagine a contest for the future of America between a multicultural right and a class-based, nationalist left. Throughout history, however, it has generally been the left that has favored more inclusive identities—class, nation, humanity—over the parochialisms of race, region, religion, and ethnicity. In the early 20th century, it should be recalled, the idea of the melting pot was progressive, if not radical. It has been conservatives and reactionaries who defended the parochial and the particular. Today, of course, it is the left that tends to insist on the permanence and inviolability of racial categories (misdescribed as "cultures") and to be hostile to the idea of a melting pot.

Liberals long before now should have seen that in many cases economics creates a community of interest between blacks and whites against immigration. The reason low-income whites have no prominent role in the left-liberal rainbow has to do with the evolution of the Democratic Party in the 1960s and the 1970s. During and after the civil rights revolution, black Americans found many allies among affluent whites (who did not compete with urban blacks for jobs and housing) and many of their political opponents among working-class whites (who often saw blacks as rivals). In taking over the Democratic Party, however, the civil rights coalition drove enough white Southerners and working-class Northern Catholics into the GOP to permit the Republicans to dominate first the presidency and now Congress.

Yet the New Deal coalition might have been kept intact while promoting the goals of the civil rights revolution. A white ethnic/white populist/black alliance against the bicoastal white overclass would not have been any more bizarre than the alliance of black Americans with wealthy white feminists against working-class white Catholics. A majority of liberal thinkers and activists, however, opted for rainbow liberalism. Instead of treating blacks as "ethnics" and "immigrants" who were owed an informal share in the spoils system, the liberal leadership has treated immigrant ethnic groups from Latin America and Asia, and even white women (whom it regards as members of a quasi-minority group), as "races," defined against a white power structure.

ONE NATION UNDER ELVIS

What is now needed is an alternative American liberalism; or liberal populism, that rejects the rainbow strategy in order to concentrate on the interests of working Americans from all backgrounds. Call it "one-nation liberalism." This would draw the lines differently. For example, affirmative action would be replaced by programs based on the horizontal line between classes, rather than the vertical lines between races.

One-nation liberals would not take it for granted that black Americans belong with immigrants from Latin America and Asia in a coalition opposed to native white Americans. The two largest groups of Americans living below the poverty level, in absolute numbers, are low-income whites and blacks. If immigration policy is considered as it should be—a form of labor policy—then the "liberal" approach ought to be to minimize the immigration of low-wage workers who might compete with the American working poor (including naturalized immigrants). A pro-labor immigration policy would not be xenophobic or racist; its logic would disfavor low-income white immigrants from postcommunist Europe.

If race is strategy, so is culture. To unite working-class and poor whites with working-class and poor blacks (at the expense, if necessary, of high levels of low-wage immigrants), a one-nation liberal coalition needs to be reinforced by a common identity. Such a superordinate community shared by whites and blacks, along with Americans of other backgrounds, cannot be defined by race (given the legacy of America's bipolar caste system); it might, just might, be provided by culture—the disproportionately black vernacular culture shared by American whites and blacks alike. That common national culture is Judeo-Christian, not Black Muslim; its holidays are Thanksgiving and Christmas and the Fourth of July, not Yul or Kwanza; its common institutions include sports and the military; its mythic homeland is not Europe or Africa, but North America; and it can find symbols in vernacular-culture heroes like Elvis Presley, the mixed-race, white/Cherokee prole who sang like a black man.

Many thinkers and artists on the left envisioned such an eclectic vernacular culture after the 1930s, when they rejected both European high culture and commercial kitsch in favor of the folk-influenced high art epitomized by Woody Guthrie, Aaron Copland, Jacob Lawrence, and Martha Graham. Today, Bruce Springsteen is one of the rare artists who recognizes the political as well as the artistic promise of this venerable and rich tradition.

Does one-nation liberalism slight the cultures of immigrants who arrived a week ago? Don't they represent the destiny of American culture? What about that fabled symbol of our supposed cosmopolitan future, the sushi burrito?

The radical transformation of American culture by the influx of new immigrants is unlikely. Historians have long recognized that later immigrant groups tend to assimilate to the founding cultures in an area. Americans of German and Irish descent today outnumber Americans of English and African descent. Nevertheless, the German and Irish elements of the common culture are minuscule by comparison. The same may occur with today's Asian and Latin American immigrants (though Mexican culture, because of Mexico's proximity, may prove more enduring and influential). Within a generation, outside of the most homogeneous ethnic enclaves, these immigrants—even the Mexican-Americans—will only speak English, and with

Table 1. *Comparison of US census classifications of race or colour, 1890–1990*[a]

1890	1900	1910	1920	1930	1940	1950	1960	1970[g]	1980[h]	1990[i]
White	White	White	White	White	White[e]	White[e]	White[f]	White	White	White
Black	Black	Black	Black	Negro	Negro	Negro	Negro	Negro or	Black or	Black or
Mulatto	Chinese	Mulatto	Mulatto	Mexican	Indian	American	American	Black	Negro	Negro
Quadroon	Japanese	Chinese	Chinese	Indian[d]	Chinese	Indian	Indian	Indian	Japanese	Indian
Octoroon	Indian[b]	Japanese	Japanese	Chinese	Japanese	Japanese	Japanese	(Amer.)	Chinese	(Amer.)
Chinese		Indian[b]	Indian[b]	Japanese	Filipino	Chinese	Chinese	Japanese	Filipino	Eskimo
Japanese		Other[c]	Other	Filipino	Hindu	Filipino	Filipino	Chinese	Korean	Aleut
Indian[b]				Hindu	Korean	Other	Hawaiian	Filipino	Vietnamese	Asian or
				Korean	Other		Part	Hawaiian	Indian	Pacific
				Other			Hawaiian	Korean	(Amer.)	Islander
							Aleut	Other	Asian Indian	(API)
							Eskimo		Hawaiian	Chinese
							Other, etc.[f]		Guamanian	Filipino
									Samoan	Hawaiian
									Eskimo	Korean
									Aleut	Vietnamese
									Other	Japanese
										Asian
										Indian
										Samoan
										Guamanian
										Other

Notes:
[a] The racial classifications are from the question on race or colour in each decennial population schedule. The source for Table 1 is US Bureau of the Census (1989).
[b] Separate enumerations of the Indian population on reservations were carried out in these years, in addition to the enumeration of Indians who lived among the 'general' population. The proportion of 'Indian blood' (whether 'full' or 'mixed blood') and type of mixture (with white or black) were also noted on the separate Indian schedules.
[c] The category, 'other,' included groups that varied in number and characteristics over time. The Census Bureau routinely instructed enumerators to assign these responses to one of the given classifications but sometimes retained a classification for 'other' (for example, Asian Indians in 1960).
[d] Beginning in 1930 there were no more separate schedules for enumerating Indians who live on reservations. Instead, a supplement was attached to the general population schedule in order to collect additional information on Indians who live on reservations.
[e] Mexicans were included in the white category, beginning in 1940.
[f] Enumerators were instructed to classify (by observation) Puerto Ricans, Mexicans, and other persons of Latin descent as 'white' when they were definitely not Negro, Indian, or some other race. Southern European and Near Eastern people were also to be considered 'white,' but Asian Indians were to be classified as 'other'.
[g] Respondents self-identified themselves on the race question but enumerators were instructed to change responses such as 'Chicano', 'La Raza', 'Mexican American', 'Moslem' or 'Brown' to 'White' and 'Brown (Negro)' to 'Negro' or 'Black'.
[h] In 1980, the lead-in to the question on race dropped any mention of race, Instead, the question read: 'Is this person —?'
[i] In 1990, the question on race read: 'What is —'s race?'

Source: "Racial Classifications in the US Census: 1890–1990," Sharon M. Lee, *Ethnic and Racial Studies*, January 1993, p. 78.

the loss of their native languages will go all but a few nonpolitical foreign traditions.

Among other things, this means that if conservatives appeal to Mexican-Americans by waving the U.S. flag and invoking Abraham Lincoln, while the left waves the red, white, and green and invokes Quetzalcoatl and Father Hidalgo, the right is likely to win. The left too often forgets that voluntary immigrants have come here—whether from Germany, Ireland, Mexico, or China—because they want to become Americans, to join a huge, diffuse nationality that, though far from cosmopolitan, is much more inclusive than most nations in the world. Liberals who generally favor personal choice have no business condemning, as "inauthentic," immigrants who choose to adopt America's mongrel culture as their own.

Some veterans of the left, having retreated from the political battlefield to campuses and editorial offices, may find all of this incomprehensible. A transracial populist liberalism, uniting non-elite whites and blacks, and encouraging the assimilation of immigrants to America's historic mulatto culture? Please—we'd rather wax rhapsodic about the dissolution of the nation-state thanks to the Internet, and ponder the significance of that sushi burrito.

It is easy to stick with the old rainbow strategy and hope that in time nonwhite majorities will bring about the repeatedly deferred revolution, just as it is easy to continue to treat inherited racial categories and alliances as facts of nature, rather than as constructs serving time-bound (and perhaps obsolete) strategies. Easy, but disastrous—for the rejection of strategy is itself a strategy for defeat.

Michael Lind is the author of The Next American Nation *(Free Press, 1995) and* Up From Conservatism *(Free Press, 1996).*

Part 1

American Ethnicities and the Politics of Inclusion

John A. Kromkowski

Table 1

National Index of Ethnic Variety: Self-Identification of Census Respondents

1990 Rank	Ancestry Group	Number	Percent	1990 Rank	Ancestry Group	Number	Percent
	Total population	248,709,873	100.0	40	Acadian/Cajun	668,271	0.3
1	German	57,947,374	23.3	41	Finnish	658,870	0.3
2	Irish	38,735,539	15.6	42	United States	643,561	0.3
3	English	32,651,788	13.1	43	Asian Indian	570,322	0.2
4	Afro American	23,777,098	9.6	44	Canadian	549,990	0.2
5	Italian	14,664,550	5.9	45	Croatian	544,270	0.2
6	American	12,395,999	5.0	46	Vietnamese	535,825	0.2
7	Mexican	11,586,983	4.7	47	Dominican	505,690	0.2
8	French	10,320,935	4.1	48	Salvadoran	499,153	0.2
9	Polish	9,366,106	3.8	49	European	466,718	0.2
10	American Indian	8,708,220	3.5	50	Jamaican	435,024	0.2
11	Dutch	6,227,089	2.5	51	Lebanese	394,180	0.2
12	Scotch-Irish	5,617,773	2.3	52	Belgian	380,498	0.2
13	Scottish	5,393,581	2.2	53	Romanian	365,544	0.1
14	Swedish	4,680,863	1.9	54	Spaniard	360,935	0.1
15	Norwegian	3,869,395	1.6	55	Colombian	351,717	0.1
16	Russian	2,952,987	1.2	56	Czechoslovakian	315,285	0.1
17	French Canadian	2,167,127	0.9	57	Armenian	308,096	0.1
18	Welsh	2,033,893	0.8	58	Pennsylvania German	305,841	0.1
19	Spanish	2,024,004	0.8	59	Haitian	289,521	0.1
20	Puerto Rican	1,955,323	0.8	60	Yugoslavian	257,994	0.1
21	Slovak	1,882,897	0.8	61	Hawaiian	256,081	0.1
22	White	1,799,711	0.7	62	African	245,845	0.1
23	Danish	1,634,669	0.7	63	Guatemalan	241,559	0.1
24	Hungarian	1,582,302	0.6	64	Iranian	235,521	0.1
25	Chinese	1,505,245	0.6	65	Ecuadorian	197,374	0.1
26	Filipino	1,450,512	0.6	66	Taiwanese	192,973	0.1
27	Czech	1,296,411	0.5	67	Nicaraguan	177,077	0.1
28	Portuguese	1,153,351	0.5	68	Peruvian	161,866	0.1
29	British	1,119,154	0.4	69	West Indies	159,167	0.1
30	Hispanic	1,113,259	0.4	70	Laotian	146,930	0.1
31	Greek	1,110,373	0.4	71	Cambodian	134,955	0.1
32	Swiss	1,045,495	0.4	72	Syrian	129,606	0.1
33	Japanese	1,004,645	0.4	73	Arab	127,364	0.1
34	Austrian	864,783	0.3	74	Slovene	124,437	0.1
35	Cuban	859,739	0.3	75	Serbian	116,795	0.0
36	Korean	836,987	0.3	76	Honduran	116,635	0.0
37	Lithuanian	811,865	0.3	77	Thai	112,117	0.0
38	Ukranian	740,803	0.3	78	Asian	107,172	0.0
39	Scandinavian	678,880	0.3	79	Latvian	100,331	0.0

1990 Rank	Ancestry Group	Number	Percent
80	Pakistani	99,974	0.0
81	Nigerian	91,688	0.0
82	Panamanian	88,649	0.0
83	Hmong	84,823	0.0
84	Turkish	83,850	0.0
85	Israeli	81,677	0.0
86	Guyanese	81,677	0.0
87	Egyptian	78,574	0.0
88	Slavic	76,931	0.0
89	Trinidad & Tobagonian	76,270	0.0
90	Northern European	65,993	0.0
91	Brazilian	65,785	0.0
92	Argentinean	63,176	0.0
93	Dutch West Indian	61,530	0.0
94	Chilean	61,465	0.0
95	Samoan	55,419	0.0
96	Eskimo	52,920	0.0
97	Australian	52,133	0.0
98	Costa Rican	51,771	0.0
99	Assyrian	51,765	0.0
100	Cape Verdean	50,772	0.0
101	Sicilian	50,389	0.0
102	Luxemburger	49,061	0.0
103	Palestinian	48,019	0.0
104	Basque	47,956	0.0
105	Albanian	47,710	0.0
106	Indonesian	43,969	0.0
107	Latin American	43,521	0.0
108	Western European	42,409	0.0
109	Icelander	40,529	0.0
110	Venezuelan	40,331	0.0
111	Maltese	39,600	0.0
112	Guamanian	39,237	0.0
113	British West Indian	37,819	0.0
114	Barbadian	35,455	0.0
115	Bolivian	33,738	0.0
116	Afghanistan	31,301	0.0
117	Ethiopian	30,581	0.0
118	Celtic	29,652	0.0
119	Bulgarian	29,595	0.0
120	Malaysian	27,800	0.0
121	Estonian	26,762	0.0
122	Prussian	25,469	0.0
123	Cantonese	25,020	0.0
124	Iraqi	23,212	0.0
125	Belizean	22,922	0.0
126	Bahamian	21,081	0.0
127	Jordanian	20,656	0.0
128	Macedonian	20,365	0.0
129	Ghanian	20,066	0.0
130	Moroccan	19,089	0.0
131	South African	17,992	0.0
132	Alsatian	16,465	0.0
133	Tongan	16,019	0.0
134	Aluet	15,816	0.0
135	Amerasian	15,523	0.0
136	Uruguayan	14,641	0.0
137	Sri Lankan	14,448	0.0
138	Eurasian	14,177	0.0
139	Flemish	14,157	0.0

1990 Rank	Ancestry Group	Number	Percent
140	North American	12,618	0.0
143	Grenadian	11,188	0.0
144	South American	10,867	0.0
145	Polynesian	10,854	0.0
146	Okinawan	10,554	0.0
147	Central American	10,310	0.0
148	German Russian	10,153	0.0
149	Liberian	8,797	0.0
150	Burmese	8,646	0.0
151	New Zealand	7,742	0.0
152	Soviet Union	7,729	0.0
153	Middle Eastern	7,656	0.0
154	US Virgin Islander	7,621	0.0
155	Basque, Spanish	7,620	0.0
156	Carpath Russian	7,602	0.0
157	Fijian	7,472	0.0
158	Antigua	7,364	0.0
159	Manx	6,317	0.0
160	Basque, French	6,001	0.0
161	Hong Kong	5,774	0.0
162	Vincent/Grenadine Islander	5,773	0.0
163	Tirol	5,748	0.0
164	Rom	5,693	0.0
165	Central European	5,693	0.0
166	Nova Scotian	5,489	0.0
167	Paraguyan	5,415	0.0
168	Newfoundland	5,412	0.0
169	Bermudan	4,941	0.0
170	Cypriot	4,897	0.0
171	Kenyan	4,639	0.0
172	Sierra Leon	4,627	0.0
173	Saxon	4,519	0.0
174	Saudi Arabian	4,486	0.0
175	Charnorro	4,427	0.0
176	Bavarian	4,348	0.0
177	Azorean	4,310	0.0
178	Belorussian	4,277	0.0
179	Eritrean	4,270	0.0
180	Yemeni	4,011	0.0
181	Northern Irish	4,009	0.0
182	Cornish	3,991	0.0
183	West German	3,885	0.0
184	Moravian	3,781	0.0
185	Ruthenian	3,776	0.0
186	Sudanese	3,623	0.0
187	Mongolian	3,507	0.0
188	St. Lucia	3,415	0.0
189	Micronesian	3,406	0.0
190	Algerian	3,215	0.0
191	Windish	3,189	0.0
192	Khmer	2,979	0.0
193	Kitts/Nevis Islander	2,811	0.0
194	Ugandan	2,681	0.0
195	Nepali	2,516	0.0
196	Singaporean	2,419	0.0
197	Cypriot, Greek	2,197	0.0

Source: 1990 CP-S-1-2, Detailed Ancestry Groups for States.

Table 2

Regional Indexes of Ethnic Variety for 1980 and 1990 Censuses

1990 Rank	Ancestry group	Number	Percent	1980 Rank	Ancestry group	Number	Percent
	NORTHEAST	50,809,229	100.0		NORTHEAST	49,135,283	100.0
1	German	9,928,722	19.5	1	Irish	9,753,664	19.9
2	Irish	9,420,118	18.5	2	German	9,359,415	19.0
3	Italian	7,503,740	14.8	3	English	8,174,976	16.6
4	English	5,873,052	11.6	4	Italian	6,929,876	14.1
5	Norwegian	3,869,395	7.6	5	Afro American	3,506,942	7.1
6	Afro American	3,658,088	7.2	6	French	3,377,762	6.9
7	Polish	3,499,502	6.9	7	Polish	3,342,944	6.8
8	French	2,637,321	5.2	8	Scottish	1,873,429	3.8
9	Welsh	2,033,893	4.0	9	Russian	1,333,813	2.7
10	Spanish	2,024,004	4.0	10	Dutch	1,133,936	2.3
11	Russian	1,292,472	2.5	11	Puerto Rican	1,057,461	2.2
12	Puerto Rican	1,289,858	2.5	12	Hungarian	700,947	1.4
13	American	1,275,211	2.5	13	Swedish	659,486	1.3
14	Scottish	1,088,462	2.1	14	Spanish	613,844	1.2
15	Dutch	1,020,383	2.0	15	American Indian	583,046	1.2
16	French Canadian	973,230	1.9	16	Portuguese	512,768	1.0
17	Scotch-Irish	772,250	1.5	17	Austrian	412,653	0.8
18	Slovak	759,264	1.5	18	Welsh	411,161	0.8
19	American Indian	754,051	1.5	19	Ukranian	402,054	0.8
20	Swedish	669,531	1.3	20	Slovak	388,964	0.8
21	Hungarian	564,216	1.1	21	Greek	388,120	0.8
22	Portuguese	563,801	1.1	22	French Canadian	363,347	0.7
23	Chinese	374,410	0.7	23	Lithuanian	350,308	0.7
24	Ukranian	374,282	0.7	24	Czech	336,994	0.7
25	Lithuanian	325,523	0.7	25	Norwegian	226,477	0.5

1990 Rank	Ancestry group	Number	Percent	1980 Rank	Ancestry group	Number	Percent
	MIDWEST	59,668,632	100.0		MIDWEST	58,865,970	100.0
1	German	22,477,450	37.7	1	German	20,244,888	34.4
2	Irish	9,643,261	16.2	2	English	11,538,184	19.6
3	English	7,293,707	12.2	3	Irish	10,572,753	18.0
4	Afro American	4,875,147	8.2	4	Afro American	3,506,942	6.0
5	Polish	3,468,832	5.8	5	French	3,488,677	5.9
6	French	2,640,874	4.4	6	Polish	3,153,476	5.4
7	Italian	2,429,651	4.1	7	Scottish	2,307,293	3.9
8	American	2,204,709	3.7	8	Dutch	2,235,006	3.8
9	Dutch	2,123,623	3.6	9	Italian	1,995,424	3.4
10	Norwegian	2,000,129	3.4	10	Norwegian	1,899,306	3.2
11	American Indian	1,907,001	3.2	11	Swedish	1,847,564	3.1
12	Swedish	1,858,855	3.1	12	American Indian	1,575,595	2.7
13	Scottish	1,135,343	1.9	13	Czech	931,233	1.6
14	Scotch-Irish	1,078,883	1.8	14	Mexican	705,349	1.2
15	Mexican	1,021,049	1.7	15	Hungarian	587,175	1.0
16	Czech	671,371	1.1	16	Danish	571,292	1.0
17	Slovak	648,461	1.1	17	Russian	474,573	0.8
18	Danish	555,346	0.9	18	Welsh	445,719	0.8
19	Hungarian	504,619	0.8	19	Swiss	381,596	0.6
20	Welsh	493,214	0.8	20	Finnish	304,319	0.5
21	Russian	473,588	0.8	21	Slovak	303,041	0.5
22	French Canadian	436,548	0.7	22	Greek	233,474	0.4
23	Swiss	378,239	0.6	23	Lithuanian	222,638	0.4
24	Finnish	310,855	0.5	24	Belgian	217,021	0.4
25	Greek	255,780	0.4	25	Austrian	211,265	0.4

Note: Data are based on a sample and subject to sampling variability. Since persons who reported multiple ancestries were included in more than one group, the sum of the persons reporting the ancestry is greater than the total; for example, a person reporting "English-French" was tabulated in both the "English" and "French" categories. Changes were made to the wording of the question, respondent instructions, coding procedures, and tabulation categories between the 1980 and 1990 censuses. Questions concerning comparability may be directed to the Ethnic and Hispanic Branch, Population Division, Bureau of the Census.

Source: 1990 CP-S-1-2, Detailed Ancestry Groups for States and PC80-S1-10, Ancestry of the Population by State: 1980.

Table 3

Regional Indexes of Ethnic Variety for 1980 and 1990 Censuses

1990 Rank	Ancestry group	Number	Percent	1980 Rank	Ancestry group	Number	Percent
	SOUTH	85,445,930	100.0		SOUTH	75,372,362	100.0
1	German	14,630,411	17.1	1	English	19,618,370	26.0
2	Irish	12,950,799	15.2	2	Irish	12,709,872	16.9
3	Afro American	12,936,066	15.1	3	Afro American	11,054,127	14.7
4	English	11,375,464	13.3	4	German	10,742,903	14.3
5	American	7,558,114	8.8	5	French	3,532,674	4.7
6	American Indian	4,086,342	4.8	6	Scottish	3,492,252	3.9
7	Mexican	3,774,379	4.4	7	American Indian	2,928,252	3.9
8	French	2,964,481	3.5	8	Mexican	2,663,868	3.5
9	Scotch-Irish	2,616,155	3.1	9	Dutch	1,651,125	2.2
10	Italian	2,473,371	2.9	10	Italian	1,555,340	2.1
11	Dutch	1,780,043	2.1	11	Polish	943,536	1.3
12	Scottish	1,768,494	2.1	12	Spanish	705,594	0.9
13	Polish	1,361,537	1.6	13	Swedish	511,426	0.7
14	White	946,103	1.1	14	Russian	441,287	0.6
15	Swedish	671,099	0.8	15	Cuban	373,695	0.5
16	Spanish	614,708	0.7	16	Welsh	360,272	0.5
17	Acadian/Cajun	609,427	0.7	17	Czech	348,110	0.5
18	Cuban	594,106	0.7	18	Norwegian	253,799	0.3
19	Russian	545,671	0.6	19	Hungarian	239,786	0.3
20	Welsh	545,082	0.5	20	Greek	167,926	0.2
21	British	440,352	0.5	21	Danish	147,029	0.2
22	French Canadian	423,497	0.5	22	Swiss	143,636	0.2
23	Norwegian	369,485	0.4	23	Austrian	140,666	0.2
24	Hispanic	347,411	0.4	24	Puerto Rican	120,394	0.2
25	United States	341,677	0.4	25	French Canadian	104,725	0.1

1990 Rank	Ancestry group	Number	Percent	1980 Rank	Ancestry group	Number	Percent
	WEST	52,786,082	100.0		WEST	43,172,490	100.0
1	German	10,910,791	20.7	1	English	10,266,505	23.8
2	English	8,109,565	15.4	2	German	8,876,940	20.6
3	Irish	6,721,361	12.7	3	Irish	7,129,413	16.5
4	Mexican	6,648,726	12.6	4	Mexican	4,261,286	9.9
5	Afro American	2,307,797	4.4	5	French	2,493,133	5.8
6	Italian	2,257,788	4.3	6	Scottish	2,375,842	5.5
7	French	2,078,259	3.9	7	Afro American	1,898,272	4.4
8	American Indian	1,960,826	3.7	8	Italian	1,703,052	3.9
9	Swedish	1,481,378	2.8	9	American Indian	1,628,926	3.8
10	Scottish	1,401,282	2.7	10	Swedish	1,326,916	3.1
11	American	1,357,965	2.6	11	Dutch	1,284,432	3.0
12	Dutch	1,303,040	2.5	12	Spanish	1,161,484	2.7
13	Norwegian	1,258,552	2.4	13	Norwegian	1,074,257	2.5
14	Scotch-Irish	1,150,485	2.2	14	Polish	788,081	1.8
15	Polish	1,036,235	2.0	15	Danish	657,792	1.5
16	Filipino	991,572	1.9	16	Japanese	607,630	1.4
17	Spanish	919,916	1.7	17	Filipino	540,680	1.3
18	Chinese	826,760	1.6	18	Russian	531,759	1.2
19	Danish	738,508	1.4	19	Chinese	487,530	1.1
20	Japanese	722,700	1.4	20	Welsh	447,446	1.0
21	Russian	641,256	1.2	21	Portuguese	419,844	1.0
22	Hispanic	555,029	1.1	22	Swiss	279,231	0.6
23	Welsh	548,974	1.0	23	Czech	276,119	0.6
24	White	501,934	1.0	24	Hungarian	248,994	0.6
25	Portuguese	468,812	0.9	25	Scandinavian	208,799	0.5

Source: 1990 CP-S-1-2, Detailed Ancestry Groups for States and PC 80-S1-10, Ancestry of the Population by State: 1980.

Table 4

Ancestry of the Population in the United States: 1990

Ancestry group	1990 Census		Ancestry group	1990 Census	
	Number	Percent		Number	Percent
Total population	248,709,873	100.0	Barbadian	35,455	0.0
EUROPEAN			Belizean	22,922	0.0
(excluding Hispanic groups)			Bermudan	4,941	0.0
Alsatian	16,465	0.0	British West Indies	37,819	0.0
Austrian	870,531	0.4	Dutch West Indies	61,530	0.0
Basque	47,956	0.0	Haitian	289,521	0.1
Belgian	394,655	0.2	Jamaican	435,024	0.2
British	1,119,154	0.4	Trinidad & Tobagoan	76,270	0.0
Cypriot	4,897	0.0	U.S. Virgin Islander	7,621	0.0
Celtic	29,652	0.0	West Indian	159,167	0.1
Danish	1,634,669	0.7	Other West Indian, n.e.c.	4,139	0.0
Dutch	6,227,089	2.5			
English	32,655,779	13.1	CENTRAL AND SOUTH		
Finnish	658,870	0.3	AMERICA		
French	10,320,935	4.1	(excluding Hispanic groups)		
German	57,985,595	23.3			
Greek	1,110,272	0.4	Brazilian	65,875	0.0
Icelander	40,529	0.0	Guyanese	81,665	0.0
Irish	38,739,548	15.6	Other Cen. & S. America,,	1,217	0.0
Italian	14,714,939	5.9	n.e.c.		
Luxemburger	49,061	0.0			
Maltese	39,600	0.0			
Manx	6,317	0.0	NORTH AFRICA AND SOUTH-		
Norwegian	3,869,395	1.6	WEST ASIA		
Portuguese	1,153,351	0.5			
Scandinavian	678,880	0.3	Algerian	3,215	0.0
Scotch-Irish	5,617,773	2.3	Arab	127,364	0.1
Scottish	5,393,581	2.2	Armenian	308,096	0.1
Swedish	4,680,863	1.9	Assyrian	51,765	0.0
Swiss	1,045,495	0.4	Egyptian	78,574	0.0
Welsh	2,033,893	0.8	Iranian	235,521	0.1
Albanian	47,710	0.0	Iraqi	23,212	0.0
Bulgarian	29,595	0.0	Israeli	81,677	0.0
Carpath Russian	7,602	0.0	Jordanian	20,656	0.0
Croatian	544,270	0.2	Lebanese	394,180	0.2
Czech	1,300,192	0.5	Middle Eastern	7,656	0.0
Czechoslovakian	315,285	0.1	Moroccan	19,089	0.0
Estonian	26,762	0.0	Palestinian	48,019	0.0
European	466,718	0.2	Saudi Arabian	4,486	0.0
German Russian	10,153	0.0	Syrian	129,606	0.1
Hungarian	1,582,302	0.6	Turkish	83,850	0.0
Latvian	100,331	0.0	Yemeni	4,011	0.0
Lithuanian	811,865	0.3	Other North African and South-	10,670	0.0
Macedonian	20,365	0.0	west Asian, n.e.c.		
Polish	9,366,106	3.8			
Rom	5,693	0.0			
Romanian	365,544	0.1	SUBSAHARAN AFRICA		
Russian	2,952,987	1.2			
Serbian	116,795	0.0	African	245,845	0.1
Slavic	76,931	0.0	Cape Verdean	50,772	0.0
Slovak	1,882,897	0.8	Ethiopian	34,851	0.0
Slovene	124,437	0.1	Ghanian	20,066	0.0
Soviet Union	7,729	0.0	Kenyan	4,639	0.0
Ukranian	740,803	0.3	Liberian	8,797	0.0
Yugoslavian	257,994	0.1	Nigerian	91,688	0.0
Other European, n.e.c.	259,585	0.1	Sierra Leon	4,627	0.0
			South African	17,992	0.0
WEST INDIAN			Sudanese	3,623	0.0
(excluding Hispanic groups)			Ugandan	2,681	0.0
Bahamian	21,081	0.0	African, n.e.c.	20,607	0.0

Ancestry group	1990 Census Number	Percent	Ancestry group	1990 Census Number	Percent
PACIFIC			French Canadian	2,167,127	0.9
			Pennsylvania German	305,841	0.1
Australian	52,133	0.0	United States	643,602	0.3
New Zealander	7,742	0.0	Other North American, n.e.c.	12,927	0.0
NORTH AMERICA			OTHER GROUPS OR UNCLASSIFIED		
Acadian	668,271	0.3			
American	12,396,057	5.0	Other groups, n.e.c.	63,562,346	25.6
Canadian	560,891	0.2	Unclassified or not reported	26,101,616	10.5
			n.e.c. represents "not elsewhere classified"		

Note: Data are based on a sample and are subject to sampling variability. Data for "Other Groups" include groups identified separately in the Race and Hispanic origin items. Since persons who reported multiple ancestries were included in more than one group, the sum of the persons reporting the ancestry group is greater than the total; for example, a person reporting "English-French" was tabulated in both the "English" and "French" categories.
Source: U.S. Department of Commerce, Bureau of the Census, Ethnic and Hispanic Branch, 1990 Census Special Tabulations.

Table 5

The Foreign-Born Population by Place of Birth for the United States: 1990

Place of Birth	1990 Census Number	Percent	Place of Birth	1990 Census Number	Percent
Foreign-born persons	21,631,601	100.0			
Europe	4,812,117	22.2	Asia	5,412,127	25.0
Austria	94,398	0.4			
Belgium	41,111	0.2	Afghanistan	28,988	0.1
Czechoslovakia	90,042	0.4	Burma	20,441	0.1
Denmark	37,657	0.2	Cambodia	119,581	0.6
Estonia	9,251	0.0	China	543,208	2.5
Finland	23,547	0.1	Hong Kong	152,263	0.7
France	162,934	0.8	India	463,132	2.1
Germany	1,163,004	5.4	Indonesia	50,388	0.2
Greece	189,267	0.9	Iran	216,963	1.0
Hungary	112,419	0.5	Iraq	45,936	0.2
Ireland	177,420	0.8	Israel	97,006	0.4
Italy	639,518	3.0	Japan	421,921	2.0
Latvia	26,380	0.1	Jordan	33,019	0.2
Lithuania	30,344	0.1	Korea	663,465	3.1
Netherlands	104,216	0.5	Laos	172,925	0.8
Norway	46,240	0.2	Lebanon	91,037	0.4
Poland	397,014	1.8	Malaysia	34,906	0.2
Portugal	218,525	1.0	Pakistan	93,663	0.4
Romania	92,627	0.4	Philippines	997,745	4.6
Spain	103,518	0.5	Saudi Arabia	17,312	0.1
Sweden	57,166	0.3	Syria	37,654	0.2
Switzerland	43,991	0.2	Taiwan	253,719	1.2
United Kingdom	764,627	3.5	Thailand	119,862	0.6
Yugoslavia	144,563	0.7	Turkey	65,244	0.3
Other Europe	42,338	0.2	Vietnam	556,311	2.6
			Other Asia	115,438	0.5
Soviet Union	336,889	1.6			

Place of Birth	1990 Census Number	Percent		Place of Birth	1990 Census Number	Percent
North America	8,524,594	39.4		Ecuador	147,867	0.7
				Guyana	122,554	0.6
Canada	870,850	4.0		Peru	152,315	0.7
Caribbean	1,986,835	9.2		Uruguay	21,628	0.1
Antigua-Barbuda	12,452	0.1		Venezuela	51,571	0.2
Bahamas	24,341	0.1		Other South America	20,853	0.1
Barbados	44,311	0.2				
Cuba	750,609	3.5				
Dominican Republic	356,971	1.7		Africa	400,691	1.9
Grenada	18,183	0.1				
Haiti	229,108	1.1		Cape Verde	14,821	0.1
Jamaica	343,458	1.6		Egypt	68,662	0.3
Trinidad/Tobago	119,221	0.6		Ethiopia	37,422	0.2
Other Caribbean	88,181	0.4		Ghana	21,714	0.1
Central America	5,650,374	26.1		Kenya	15,871	0.1
Belize	31,222	0.1		Morocco	21,529	0.1
Costa Rica	48,264	0.2		Nigeria	58,052	0.3
El Salvador	472,885	2.2		Senegal	2,369	0.0
Guatemala	232,977	1.1		South Africa	38,163	0.2
Honduras	114,603	0.5		Other Africa	122,088	0.6
Mexico	4,447,439	20.6				
Nicaragua	171,950	0.8		Oceania	122,137	0.6
Panama	124,695	0.6				
Other Central America	6,339	0.0		Australia	52,469	0.2
Other North America	16,535	0.1				
				Fiji	16,269	0.1
				New Zealand	18,039	0.1
South America	1,107,000	5.1		Tonga	11,040	0.1
				Western Samoa	12,638	0.1
Argentina	97,422	0.5		Other Oceania	11,682	0.1
Bolivia	33,637	0.2		Not reported	916,046	4.2
Brazil	94,023	0.4				
Chile	61,212	0.3				
Colombia	303,918	1.4				

Note: The foreign-born population includes 1,864,285 persons who were born abroad of American parents. Data for foreign-born persons by place of birth, citizenship and year of entry is planned for 1993. The former Soviet Union is now referred to as the following geopolitical entities: Armenia, Azerbaijan, Byelarus, Georgia, Kazakhstan, Kyrgyzstan, Moldova, Russia, Tajikistan, Turkmenistan, Ukraine, and Uzbekistan.
Source: U.S. Department of Commerce, Bureau of the Census, Ethnic and Hispanic Branch, 1990 Census Special Tabulations.

Second part of article follows.

Part 2

Not Quite So Welcome Anymore

As reflected in a TIME poll, the public mood over immigration is turning sour again

BRUCE W. NELAN

AFTER NEW YORK'S WORLD TRADE Center is rocked by a thundering explosion, police round up a string of Arab immigrants as suspects, including an Egyptian radical who was admitted to the U.S. by mistake. Off the shore of New York's Long Island, a rusty tramp steamer called the *Golden Venture* runs aground, disgorging nearly 300 frightened Chinese trying to enter the country illegally; 10 die. Newly elected President Bill Clinton, reneging on a campaign promise, denies entry to Haitian boat people, then is blindsided by hostile public reaction when his first two choices for Attorney General turn out to have hired illegal immigrants as household help. When Texas border patrols mount a round-the-clock blockade along 20 miles of the Rio Grande, hundreds of Mexicans, many of whom commute illegally to day jobs in El Paso, angrily block traffic on a bridge between the U.S. and Mexico, chanting, "We want to work."

The incessant drumbeat of episodes like these has Americans increasingly concerned that their country is under siege and, in the popular phraseology, "has lost control of its own borders." In a study published last June, Bard College economist Dimitri Papadimitriou concluded that new laws were needed to head off "a bitter struggle between these new immigrants and disadvantaged segments of the U.S. population for increasingly scarce low-skill, low-wage jobs."

These sentiments recall a judgment voiced in a New York *Times* editorial: "There is a limit to our powers of assimilation, and when it is exceeded the country suffers from something very

Which position is closer to your opinion?

	Sept. 1993	May 1985
Keep doors open to immigration	24%	27%
Strictly limit immigration	73%	67%

From a telephone poll of 1,108 adult Americans taken for TIME/CNN on Sept 8-9 by Yankelovic Partners Inc. Sampling error is ±3%.

like indigestion." That observation was not made recently, however, but in May 1880, when anti-immigrant sentiment was also on the rise. Then too there was no effective limit on the number of immigrants entering the U.S. The hard fact is that when times are good, few worry about how many newcomers arrive; when times are tough, as they are now, cries of opposition invariably rise.

Many Americans are confused about whether the continuous inflow of immigrants makes the country stronger or weaker. Economic studies abound claiming that immigration spurs new businesses and new taxpayers. With no less conviction, others contend that immigrants and their children evade taxes and overburden local welfare, health and education systems. To compound the confusion, many Americans believe—wrongly—that more foreigners enter the country illegally than do legally. As the doubts grow, so does the potential for back-

Are most immigrants coming into the U.S. legally or illegally?

	Poll Answers	Actual breakdown 1992
Legally	24%	76%
Illegally	64%	24%

lash. Polls show that almost two-thirds of Americans favor new laws to cut back on all immigrants and asylum seekers—legal as well as illegal. Though immigration is often regarded as a single issue, some distinctions are important:

• Legal immigrants. More than 1 million people are entering the U.S. legally every year. From 1983 through 1992, 8.7 million of these newcomers arrived—the highest number in any 10-year period since 1910. A record 1.8 million were granted permanent residence in 1991. Because present law stresses family unification, these arrivals can bring over their spouses, sons and daughters: some 3.5 million are now in line to come in. Once here, they can bring in *their* direct relatives. As a result, there exists no visible limit to the number of legal entries.

• Illegal immigrants. This is what makes Americans almost unanimously furious. No one knows the numbers, of course, but official estimates put the illegal—or "undocumented"—influx at more than 300,000 a year currently and almost 5 million over the past 10 years.

Where do you think the majority of recent immigrants came from?

	Poll Answers	Actual breakdown 1992
Latin America and Caribbean	53%	44%
Asia	27%	29%
Middle East	9%	4%
Eastern Europe	4%	4%
Africa	3%	3%
India	3%	4%

Toward which group of recent immigrants do you feel most favorably and least favorably?

	Most favorable	Least favorable
Latin America and Caribbean	22%	30%
Eastern Europe	20%	2%
Asia	18%	11%
Africa	6%	3%
Middle East	5%	26%
India	3%	2%
None	9%	10%

• Asylum seekers. Until a few years ago, applications were rare, totaling 200 in 1975. Suddenly, asylum is the plea of choice in the U.S. and around the world, often as a cover for economic migration. U.S. applications were up to 103,000 last year, and the backlog tops 300,000 cases. Under the present asylum rules, practically anyone who declares that he or she is fleeing political oppression has a good chance to enter the U.S. Chinese are almost always admitted, for example, if they claim that China's birth-control policies have limited the number of children they can have.

Right now, once aliens enter the U.S., it is almost impossible to deport

Would you favor changes in federal law to reduce the number of immigrants who enter the U.S. legally?

Favor	60%
Oppose	35%

Would you favor changes in federal law to reduce the number of immigrants who enter the U.S. illegally?

Favor	85%
Oppose	12%

them, even if they have no valid documents. Thousands of those who enter illegally request asylum only if they are caught. The review process can take 10 years or more, and applicants often simply disappear while it is under way. Asylum cases are piling up faster than they can be cleared, with the Immigration and Naturalization Service falling farther behind every year. At her confirmation hearings at the end of September, Doris Meissner, Clinton's nominee as commissioner of the INS, conceded, "The asylum system is broken, and we need to fix it."

With pressure rising to do something about immigration, Clinton felt he had to get out and lead—if for no other reason than to head off draconian legislative proposals already in the works. The President put forward measures last July to tighten screening of potential immigrants abroad, speed deportations of phony asylum seekers and add 600 officers to the border patrol. "We will not," he declared, "surrender our borders to those who wish to exploit our history of compassion and justice."

The Administration has not, however, joined the national majority that now says it favors cutting back on legal immigration. Nevada Senator Harry Reid, a rising Democratic star in the immigration wars, has introduced a bill that would establish both an annual limit of 300,000 newcomers, including "immediate relatives," and a national identification card.

These measures, along with others from the House of Representatives,

How important is it for the Federal Government to track down illegal aliens living in the U.S.?

	Sept. 1993	May 1985
Extremely important	39%	36%
Somewhat important	41%	42%
Not worth the cost	18%	21%

Do these statements apply to immigrants who moved to the U.S. in the past 10 to 15 years?

	Yes
Are hardworking	67%
Are productive citizens once they get their feet on the ground	65%
Take jobs from Americans	64%
Add to the crime problem	59%
Are basically good, honest people	58%

may come to life on Capitol Hill after the great debates on health care and the North American Free Trade Agreement are resolved. In fact, immigration questions already lurk beneath the surface of both these issues: should citizens carry a national medical identification card, and will the trade agreement lure more or fewer Mexicans north? Almost surely, Congress will try to reform immigration law again in 1994.

IMMIGRATION BACKLASH IS PARTICU-larly strong in New York, Florida, Texas and, most of all, California, which officials say contains more than half of all the illegal immigrants in the country. As the frequent bellwether of national changes, the state has already caught a low-grade fever from this issue. Governor Pete Wilson

The Numbers Game

Altogether, the foreign born had a higher per capita income than the native born ($15,033 vs. $14,367) in 1989, but their median family income was almost $4,000 less than that of the native born ($31,785 vs. $35,508).

% of population under 18 that is foreign-born

Los Angeles 21%
San Francisco 19%
Dade County (Miami) 18%
New York City 12%
Houston 10%
Chicago 7%
U.S. 3%

In 1976 there were 67 Spanish-speaking radio stations. Now there are 311, plus 3 Spanish–language TV networks and 350 Spanish-language newspapers.
Source: Market Segment Research, Inc.

Sources: Census Bureau, INS except where otherwise noted

32 MILLION PEOPLE IN THE U.S. (13%) SPEAK LANGUAGES OTHER THAN ENGLISH AT HOME.

Current Top 10 ancestry groups

		millions
1	German	58
2	Irish	39
3	English	33
4	African	24
5	Italian	15
6	Mexican	12
7	French	10
8	Polish	9
9	Native American	9
10	Dutch	6

IN 1940, 70% OF IMMIGRANTS CAME FROM EUROPE. IN 1992, 15% CAME FROM EUROPE, 37% FROM ASIA AND 44% FROM LATIN AMERICA AND THE CARIBBEAN.

JAPANESE AMERICANS marry non–Japanese Americans about 65% of the time, an out-marriage rate so high that since 1981 the number of babies born in the U.S. with one Japanese and one white parent has exceeded the number with two Japanese parents.

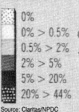

FOREIGN BORN AS A PERCENT OF TOTAL POPULATION

- 0%
- 0% > 0.5%
- 0.5% > 2%
- 2% > 5%
- 5% > 20%
- 20% > 44%

Source: Claritas/NPDC

Top 10 languages

		Number of speakers in millions
1	English only	198.6
2	Spanish	17.3
3	French	1.7
4	German	1.5
5	Italian	1.3
6	Chinese	1.2
7	Tagalog	.8
8	Polish	.7
9	Korean	.6
10	Vietnamese	.5

The unemployment rate for the foreign born was 7.8% in 1990, compared with 6.2% for the native born.

In 1990 the population was: Anglo 76%, Black 12%, Latino 9%, Asian 3%. By 2050 the breakdown is projected to be: Anglo 52%, Black 16%, Latino 22%, Asian 10%.

% who eat these ethnic foods at least once a week

Italian, other than pizza	39%
Mexican	21%
Chinese	18%
Cajun	5%
French	3%
Middle Eastern	3%
Indian	1%

Source: "Shopping for Health," Food Marketing Institute

Americans use 68% more spices today than a decade ago. The consumption of red pepper rose 105%, basil 190%.

Source: American Spice Trade Association

IN 1990 THERE WERE MORE EUROPEAN DESCENDANTS— including German, Irish, English, French, Dutch, Scots-Irish, Scottish, Swedish, Welsh and Danish, Portuguese, British and Swiss—living in California than in any other state. New York led in the number of Italians, Poles and Russians; Minnesota in Norwegians; Texas in Czechs; Pennsylvania in Slovaks; and Ohio in Hungarians.

Top 10 countries of origin for immigrants in fiscal year 1992

Mexico	22%
Vietnam	8.0%
Philippines	6.3%
Soviet Union	4.5%
Dom. Republic	4.3%
China	4.0%
India	3.8%
El Salvador	2.7%
Poland	2.6%
United Kingdom	2.1%

More than 100 languages are spoken in the school systems of New York City, Chicago, Los Angeles and Fairfax County, Va.

Source: Newcomers in American Schools, Rand

The foreign-born population in 1990 totaled a record 19.8 million (8%), surpassing previous highs of 14 million in 1930 and 1980.

Since 1901, 30% of the U.S. Nobel prize-winners have been immigrants.

88% of African-born residents had a high school education or higher in 1990, compared with 76% of Asian-born, 57% of Caribbean-born and 77% of native-born.

Seven out of 10 residents of Hialeah, Fla., are foreign-born. Other cities where more than half the population is foreign-born:
Miami, Fla. **60%**
Huntington Park, Calif. **59%**
Union City, N.J. **55%**
Monterey Park, Calif. **52%**
Miami Beach, Fla., Santa Ana, Calif. **51%** each

Top 5 non-Christian religions

		% of population
1	Jewish	1.8%
2	Muslim/Islamic*	.5%
3	Buddhist*	.4%
4	Hindu*	.2%
5	Bahai	.01%

Top 10 Christian religions

		% of population
1	Roman Catholic	26.2%
2	Baptist	19.4%
3	Protestant (no denomination supplied)	9.8%
4	Methodist	8.0%
5	Lutheran	5.2%
6	Christian (no denomination supplied)	4.8%
7	Presbyterian	2.8%
8	Pentecostal	1.8%
9	Episcopalian/Anglican	1.7%
10	Mormon/LDS	1.4%

*Adjustments for undercounts due to language problems

Source: One Nation Under God: Religion in Contemporary American Society by Barry A. Kasmin and Seymour P. Lachman. Based on a telephone survey of 113,000 randomly dialed American households

Once aliens enter the U.S., it is almost impossible to deport them, even if they have no valid documents. Thousands who enter illegally request asylum only if they are caught.

Do you favor these proposals?

	Yes	No
Charge a small fee to each individual who crosses the border between the U.S. and Mexico or Canada in order to pay for tighter security at those borders.	70%	26%
Spend more federal tax money to tighten security at the border between the U.S. and Mexico.	65%	32%
Make it more difficult for people from other countries who claim they are the victims of persecution in their own countries to enter the U.S.	61%	35%
Require all U.S. citizens to carry a national ID card.	50%	48%
Stop providing government health benefits and public education to immigrants and their children.	47%	48%
Build a fence along the entire border between the U.S. and Mexico.	29%	68%

Would you favor a constitutional amendment to prevent children born here from becoming U.S. citizens unless their parents were also U.S. citizens?

Favor	49%
Oppose	47%

How much does the presence of illegal aliens in this country concern you?

	Sept. 1993	May 1985
Great deal	48%	43%
Somewhat	40%	44%
Not at all	12%	12%

has won majority support for a proposed constitutional amendment that would prevent children born in the U.S. of illegal immigrants from automatically becoming citizens. Californians, more than most Americans, complain about special treatment for immigrants. TIME's poll indicates that 51% of Californians favor cutting off health benefits and public education to immigrants and their children, whereas nationally only 46% back such measures.

Because there is no national consensus, political leaders and activists stake out unpredictable and sometimes contradictory positions. Many liberals believe the doors should be open to all who seek new opportunities and hope to escape persecution. Other liberals argue that while open immigration policies are intrinsically good, they must be tempered to prevent newcomers from not only taking away American jobs but also competing with poor, ill-educated minorities already here.

Market-oriented conservatives still support immigration as a source of low-wage labor. But other conservatives call for immigration restrictions to halt the cultural transmogrification of American society. One of the most outspoken advocates for the latter is Daniel Stein, executive director of the Federation for American Immigration Reform, who favors a moratorium on all immigration, insisting that "nations do not have an unlimited capacity to absorb immigrants without irrevocably altering their own character"—an echo of a view enunciated more than a century ago.

But for all the hand wringing, American resistance falls far short of the hostility evident in Western Europe. Gangs of racist thugs in Britain engage in "Paki bashing." France has officially declared a target of "zero immigration." Germany insists it is "not a country of immigration," and neo-Nazis have taken the dictum literally enough to set fire to hostels for foreign workers and asylum seekers.

More than 100 million people around the world are currently displaced from their native land. Europe's xenophobia can only mean that more of them will want to come to the U.S. That is all the more reason for Americans to spend some time debating how many of them they are willing to take in.

—Reported by David Aikman/ Washington and David S. Jackson/San Francisco

More than 100 million people around the world are currently displaced from their native land. Europe's xenophobia can only mean that more of them will want to come to the U.S.

AE Article Review Form

We encourage you to photocopy and use this page as a tool to assess how the articles in **Annual Editions** expand on the information in your textbook. By reflecting on the articles you will gain enhanced text information. You can also access this useful form on a product's book support Web site at **http://www.dushkin.com/online/.**

NAME: _____ DATE: _____

_____

TITLE AND NUMBER OF ARTICLE:

_____

BRIEFLY STATE THE MAIN IDEA OF THIS ARTICLE:

_____

LIST THREE IMPORTANT FACTS THAT THE AUTHOR USES TO SUPPORT THE MAIN IDEA:

_____

WHAT INFORMATION OR IDEAS DISCUSSED IN THIS ARTICLE ARE ALSO DISCUSSED IN YOUR TEXTBOOK OR OTHER READINGS THAT YOU HAVE DONE? LIST THE TEXTBOOK CHAPTERS AND PAGE NUMBERS:

_____

LIST ANY EXAMPLES OF BIAS OR FAULTY REASONING THAT YOU FOUND IN THE ARTICLE:

_____

LIST ANY NEW TERMS/CONCEPTS THAT WERE DISCUSSED IN THE ARTICLE, AND WRITE A SHORT DEFINITION:

_____

ANNUAL EDITIONS revisions depend on two major opinion sources: one is our Advisory Board, listed in the front of this volume, which works with us in scanning the thousands of articles published in the public press each year; the other is you—the person actually using the book. Please help us and the users of the next edition by completing the prepaid article rating form on this page and returning it to us. Thank you for your help!

ANNUAL EDITIONS: Race and Ethnic Relations 00/01

ARTICLE RATING FORM

Here is an opportunity for you to have direct input into the next revision of this volume. We would like you to rate each of the 43 articles listed below, using the following scale:

1. Excellent: should definitely be retained
2. Above average: should probably be retained
3. Below average: should probably be deleted
4. Poor: should definitely be deleted

Your ratings will play a vital part in the next revision.
So please mail this prepaid form to us just as soon as you complete it.
Thanks for your help!

We Want Your Advice

RATING

ARTICLE

1. *Dred Scott v. Sandford*
2. Racial Restrictions in the Law of Citizenship
3. In a Judicial 'What If,' Indians Revisit a Case
4. *Brown et al. v. Board of Education of Topeka et al.*
5. Black America: The Rough Road to Racial Uplift
6. Black Progress: How Far We've Come—and How Far We Have to Go
7. Migrations to the Thirteen British North American Colonies, 1770–1775: New Estimates
8. The New Immigrants
9. U.S. Immigration
10. Newcomers and Established Residents
11. New Answers to an Old Question: Who Got Here First?
12. 12th Session of UN Working Group on Indigenous Peoples
13. A Deadly Mix
14. American Indians in the 1990s
15. Indians Hear a High-Tech Drumbeat
16. Specific Hispanics
17. Latin USA: How Young Hispanics Are Changing America, *and* Generacion Ñ and the Latino Century
18. Hardliners v. "Dialogueros": Cuban Exile Political Groups and United States–Cuba Policy
19. 10 Most Dramatic Events in African-American History
20. Black America
21. Shock Therapy: A Racist Murder Leads Texas Town to Probe Its Bedrock Prejudices
22. The Color of Justice

RATING

ARTICLE

23. Race, Politics and 2000: The Affirmative Action Battleground Shifts to the Heartland
24. Why Minority Recruiting Is Alive and Well in Texas
25. Misperceived Minorities: 'Good' and 'Bad' Stereotypes Saddle Hispanics and Asian Americans
26. The Challenge for U.S. Asians in the Year 2000
27. Trapped on a Pedestal
28. Who Are We?
29. Italian Americans as a Cognizable Racial Group
30. The Blind Spot of Multiculturalism: America's Invisible Literature
31. Mr. Dybek's Neighborhood: Toward a New Paradigm for Ethnic Literature
32. Unsealing Mississippi's Past
33. White Girl?
34. The Unbearable Whiteness of Being: They're Not Proud. They're Not Even Loud. A Race Rally of a Different Color
35. Balancing Act: A Police Chief Typifies Macedonia's Attempts at Ethnic Pluralism
36. Don't Expect This Conflict to End Anytime Soon
37. Belonging in the West
38. Ethnicity: An African Predicament
39. Ethnicity Is No Excuse for Espionage
40. The Geometer of Race
41. Color Blind
42. The End of the Rainbow
43. American Ethnicities and the Politics of Inclusion, *and* Not Quite So Welcome Anymore

(Continued on next page)

BUSINESS REPLY MAIL
FIRST-CLASS MAIL   PERMIT NO. 84   GUILFORD CT

POSTAGE WILL BE PAID BY ADDRESSEE

**Dushkin/McGraw-Hill
Sluice Dock
Guilford, CT 06437-9989**

ABOUT YOU

Name _____   Date _____

Are you a teacher? ☐   A student? ☐

Your school's name _____

Department _____

Address _____   City _____   State ____ Zip _____

School telephone # _____

YOUR COMMENTS ARE IMPORTANT TO US !

Please fill in the following information:

For which course did you use this book?
_____

Did you use a text with this *ANNUAL EDITION*? ☐ yes ☐ no
What was the title of the text?
_____

What are your general reactions to the *Annual Editions* concept?
_____

Have you read any particular articles recently that you think should be included in the next edition?
_____

Are there any articles you feel should be replaced in the next edition? Why?
_____

Are there any World Wide Web sites you feel should be included in the next edition? Please annotate.
_____

May we contact you for editorial input? ☐ yes ☐ no

May we quote your comments? ☐ yes ☐ no